GREENING SOCIAL WORK EDU

Edited by Susan Hillock

Despite urgent calls for global action, sustainable social work practice, and a solid "green" theoretical knowledge base, North American social work and helping professions have been slow to learn from community activists, acknowledge the international climate emergency, and act collectively to achieve climate justice.

Greening Social Work Education examines how social work educators can best incorporate sustainability content into social work curricula, integrate green teaching methods, and mobilize students and colleagues towards climate action, justice, and leadership. Drawing on Canadian content, this collection highlights Indigenous, eco-feminist, collective-action, and multi-interdisciplinary approaches to social work. The book provides a rationale for why the topic of greening is important for social work and the helping professions; discussion of current debates, tensions, and issues; useful ideas related to innovative interdisciplinary theoretical approaches, analyses, and constructs; and practical recommendations for teaching green social work education. In doing so, *Greening Social Work Education* strives to help social workers and educators gain the confidence and tools they need to transform their teaching and curricula.

SUSAN HILLOCK is a professor of social work at Trent University.

Greening Social Work Education

EDITED BY SUSAN HILLOCK

UNIVERSITY OF TORONTO PRESS
Toronto Buffalo London

© University of Toronto Press 2024
Toronto Buffalo London
utorontopress.com

ISBN 978-1-4875-5520-7 (cloth)   ISBN 978-1-4875-5523-8 (EPUB)
ISBN 978-1-4875-5522-1 (paper)   ISBN 978-1-4875-5524-5 (PDF)

Library and Archives Canada Cataloguing in Publication

Title: Greening social work education / edited by Susan Hillock.
Names: Hillock, Susan, 1963– editor.
Description: Includes bibliographical references.
Identifiers: Canadiana (print) 20230551939 | Canadiana (ebook)
    20230551971 | ISBN 9781487555207 (cloth) | ISBN 9781487555221
    (paper) | ISBN 9781487555245 (PDF) | ISBN 9781487555238 (EPUB)
Subjects: LCSH: Social work education – Environmental aspects.
Classification: LCC HV11.8.C3 G74 2024 | DDC 361.3071/071 – dc23

Cover design: Liz Harasymczuk
Cover image: iStock.com/AYDINOZON

We wish to acknowledge the land on which the University of Toronto
Press operates. This land is the traditional territory of the Wendat, the
Anishnaabeg, the Haudenosaunee, the Métis, and the Mississaugas of the
Credit First Nation.

This book has been published with the help of a grant from the Federation
for the Humanities and Social Sciences, through the Awards to Scholarly
Publications Program, using funds provided by the Social Sciences and
Humanities Research Council of Canada.

University of Toronto Press acknowledges the financial support of the
Government of Canada, the Canada Council for the Arts, and the Ontario Arts
Council, an agency of the Government of Ontario, for its publishing activities.

Canada Council   Conseil des Arts
for the Arts   du Canada

ONTARIO ARTS COUNCIL
CONSEIL DES ARTS DE L'ONTARIO
an Ontario government agency
un organisme du gouvernement de l'Ontario

Funded by the   Financé par le
Government   gouvernement
of Canada   du Canada

Contents

Preface

SUSAN HILLOCK

In the summer of 2019, I heard that the local Green Party needed a candidate for the upcoming Canadian federal election. I had been asked by various parties to run before – locally, provincially, and federally – but had never chosen to do so. I am not quite sure what the particular catalyst was that summer – my concerns about climate change, social injustice, and environmental racism, my sense of futility and despair about the limits of my own (and others') individual actions, my worry about my children's (and future grandchildren's) quality of life, extreme predictions that ran the gamut from, the oceans dying as early as 2035 to three-quarters of humanity being killed by 2075, my pessimism about the possibility of corporate and global change, or the fact that climate catastrophe, extreme weather events, and disaster migration were no longer harbingers from a distant future but happening currently – regardless, I decided that I would run. In the end, I dropped out of the race before the election because of corruption in the local party (a story for another day); however, that frustrating experience persuaded me that I needed to do something more meaningful in terms of my work to help save the planet.

Of course, I am not the only one who feels this way. Millions of people are concerned about the planet. Over the last twenty years, this concern has led to the burgeoning of a massive worldwide grass-roots Indigenous and student/youth–led mobilization to stop extreme extractivism, reliance on fossil fuels, social and economic inequality, and global ecocide, as well as to strengthen democracy and fight for civil rights. In addition, there has been an exponential growth of literature that discusses environmentalism and sustainability across many disciplines. In the social work literature, there have been several key articles and books about green social work, eco-social work, sustainable development, and the environment published over the last thirty years. This

scholarship has successfully been nudging the field in the green direction. As a result, it can no longer be said that a foundation for a green
theoretical and knowledge base in social work does not exist.

However, when I as a social work professor searched for resources to
help me *teach* about sustainability, climate change/action, and environmental racism and injustice, there was still little available to me in terms
of professional training and support, concrete information, or resources.
Given the proliferation of environmental and sustainability content and
information in the news, across social media, and on the Internet, one
might assume these curriculum gaps would have been filled by modern research and scholarship. Over the last few years some academic
disciplines, for example Indigenous and gender studies, education,
and environmental sciences, have made leaps and bounds in terms of
what to teach and *how* to teach this content. This has not been the case
across all disciplines, and particularly not in the helping professions.
Indeed, despite urgent calls for action and promising growth in sustainable social work practice in places like the United Kingdom, Australia,
and New Zealand, North American social work has been slow to mainstream these concepts into the curricula. Many educational gaps remain
in this area, especially in terms of teaching about the environment and
sustainability and preparing students in the helping professions for
future practice in this area. Correspondingly, I realized that what was
still missing in social work was a book that focused exclusively on *how*
to teach this content and offered practical ways to "green" social work
education.

In addition, recognizing that a multi/inter-disciplinary approach
is needed to tackle climate change and that social work benefits from
learning and working collectively with other academic disciplines (that
have already developed specific technological and pedagogical expertise in this area), I wanted to develop a book that highlighted diverse
perspectives from various academic disciplines. Thus, this multi-disci-
plinary book, informed by a social justice lens, Indigenous worldview,
and eco-feminist-socialist framework and featuring Canadian content
and context, aims to green social work education by bringing together
the voices, experiences, and expertise of leading Canadian scholars from
the social work field as well as experts from the disciplines of education
and professional learning; environmental science; gender and social justice; sociology; and social development, health and community, critical
animal, sustainability, cultural, and Canadian and Indigenous studies.
The book also provides a rationale about why this topic is important for
social work and the helping professions; discussion of current debates,
issues, and hot topics; and practical application and recommendations,

particularly for academics in the helping professions, who are responsible for training students to work with vulnerable populations that also tend to be the people most impacted by climate change.

Accordingly, this book examines how social work educators can best infuse sustainability content into social work curriculum, incorporate green teaching methods, and mobilize students and colleagues towards climate action/ justice/ leadership. Additionally, this collection strives to assist instructors to provide adequate and appropriate environmental/sustainability knowledge, training, and opportunities so that their students can reflect on their ethical and moral duties, responsibilities, behaviours, and attitudes about climate change/crises; explore complex local, provincial, national, and international policies and issues; reconceptualize social work's mandate, accreditation and ethical standards, vision, and theories; build skills particularly in terms of community – organizing, advocacy, activism, trauma, grief, and disaster preparation and intervention skills; and develop confidence, in order to feel more comfortable in helping others in their professional lives.

This topic and multi/inter-disciplinary approach are rich and untapped areas of scholarship, particularly within the helping professions, and this collection is the first of its kind in North America. The book is also aimed at professors and students who are interested in taking a leadership role in this area, more effectively supporting others, and improving curriculum and the quality of teaching of sustainability in social work education and the helping professions. Although not intended as a course textbook, this book, or chapters from it, may be of interest to those in various fields in higher education, and can certainly be used as required/recommended readings in a variety of college and university programs and across many generalist courses, or in stand-alone environmental courses.

A caveat: although I discuss the need to include content, skill development, and practice related to environmentalism/sustainability in field education, and while both Chapters 6 and 11 respectively present green recommendations for community practice and placements and provide excellent field and community-based case study examples, due to length constraints the book offers limited coverage of this topic. Most of the literature shows that this research is necessary and represents a large gap in training and scholarship across the helping professions. For future research, related questions that should be considered are: How do we ensure that sustainability/environmental content is covered in field practicum? How should field instructors teach/cover this content? How should students be supervised and evaluated for this content and learning? What field activities are best for students to try to learn this content? Hopefully, this book privides the impetus and resources for educators to further this research, develop ecological literacy for the classroom and field, and more effectively teach this content.

Finally, I want to take this opportunity to thank my two daughters, Ashley and Cassie, for their unconditional love and support. I also want to thank the University of Toronto Press, as well as all of the diligent contributors to this book.

GREENING SOCIAL WORK EDUCATION

Introduction

In many ways, I feel like I am coming late to this revolutionary party. Why? Like so many others, I really thought we still had many years left to resolve these environmental issues. At the same time, I was also trying to do my best as a responsible community member – recycling, reducing, and reusing – even though as a consumer I often felt power-less and confused about what I could best do to help the planet. I also wondered if these individual behaviours were enough to make a sig-nificant difference, when I knew that multinational corporations were the biggest polluters (Lysack, 2010; Riley, 2017). As a citizen, I had even joined grass-roots environmental movements and supported political parties that I thought could push forward a green agenda, but it has not always been clear whether these actions had the desired impact. Indeed, not until recently have I finally realized that the window to save the planet and humanity is closing fast. Like youth activist Greta Thunberg, in her passionate speech at the World Economic Forum in Davos, Switzerland, on 25 January 2019, I now recognize that this is an urgent global emergency, humanity's future is at stake, and, indeed, our "house is on fire" (Thunberg, 2019a, para. 1). Moreover, "we don't have to do anything to bring about this future. All we have to do is nothing" (Klein, 2014, p. 4).

This has motivated me to action as I believe that once people are aware, we then have an ethical and moral responsibility to do something about the climate crises. Montpelier (2019) agrees, acknowledging that "once you know, you can't let it go" (para. 1). I think this is particularly true for those of us who are from the generations that created the problems and who also may have the privilege, power, and voice to do something about them. Thunberg (2019b) underlines this point too, stating that "the bigger your carbon footprint – the bigger your moral duty. The bigger your platform – the bigger your responsibility" (para. 1).

Building a Green Social Work Education Knowledge Base

So, I made a personal and professional commitment to work towards creating the conditions necessary to ensure the planet's health for future generations. However, as stated in the preface, when I started to look for resources within social work on *how to teach* about sustainability and climate change/action, as well as environmental racism and injustice, there was little available to me in terms of professional training and support, practical information, or concrete recommendations. What I did find is that over the last thirty years social work scholars have been working hard to transform the social work profession by building new theories, concepts, and pedagogy about environmentalism and sustainability. Specifically, they have been developing new conceptual paradigms, as well as (re)discovering traditional Indigenous knowledges and approaches, to change how social workers think about and act upon their understandings of the natural and built worlds and their interconnected relationships with well-being, health, environmental justice, and sustainability (Bozalek & Pease, 2021; Coates, 2003; Coates & Gray, 2011; Coates et al., 2006; Dominelli, 2011, 2012, 2013, 2014, 2018; Gray & Coates, 2011, 2012; Zapf, 2009, 2010). It is important to note that Dominelli (2012) was the first to call this innovative work "green social work." See further below, and across the book, for a discussion of this growing scholarship.

As a result of this burgeoning research, it can no longer be said that a foundation for a green theoretical and knowledge base in social work does not exist. Despite this, a review of the literature also indicates that although there has been a push (that admittedly has waxed and waned) for social work to incorporate this essential knowledge base into social work education, with renewed calls for action over the last few years (Moth & Morton, 2009), not enough has been accomplished, particularly in North America, to mainstream this content. This not only highlights the need for collections like this one, that aim to centre a green social work knowledge base, but also the need to help social work educators build confidence to start applying this knowledge directly in their work.

Although progress has been slow, I am optimistic that a philosophical seed change is starting to occur in our profession and that we have begun to successfully move our field in the green direction. This is evident in the development of international environmental coalitions and groups, as well as the evolution of social work professional standards and ethical codes. For instance, an international social work coalition that focuses on "environmental sustainability" and is called the Global Agenda for Social Work and Social Development has been developed (Krings et al., 2020, p. 276), and a Global Alliance for a Deep Ecological Social Work (Zapf, 2009, p. 102) has been formed. In terms of social work practice, an "ecological credo" for social work has been published (Coates, 2003, pp. 104–105), and a practice model called the "Green Social Work Wheel of Knowledge for Action" (Dominelli, 2012, p. 27) has been created. In addition, "codes of ethics in countries such as India, Chile, and El Salvador" now clearly link "environmentalism and social work practice" (Dominelli, 2012, p. 27), and the United States has added language in its 2015 social work education accreditation standards that explicitly connects environmental justice with competency. And the Canadian Association of Social Work Education – Association canadienne pour la formation en travail social (CASWE-ACFTS) has, along with its 2017 commitment to support Indigenous self-determination, sovereignty, and implementation as laid out in the Truth and Reconciliation Commission of Canada's (TRC) (2015) *Calls to Action*, finally added a new environmental accreditation standard (CASWE-ACFTS, 2021a).

The Protest and Apology Decades

Simultaneously, over the last twenty to thirty years, we have seen a ratcheting up of the global environmental movement, social media coverage, and increasing numbers of intersectional social justice protests and marches such as the Women's March on Washington (Hillock, 2017). This is also evident in the Me Too (https://metoomvmt.org, #MeToo), Time's Up (https://www.timesupnow.com, #Time'sUp), Idle No More (https://idlenomore.ca, #IdleNoMore), Occupy (http://occupywallst.org, #Occupy), Standing Rock (https://americanindian.si.edu/nk360/plains-treaties/dapl, #StandingRock), and Black Lives Matter (https://blacklivesmatter.com, #BlackLivesMatter) protests and movements. Indeed, 2010–20 has been called the decade of protests (Harbage & Bloch, 2019). One could also fairly call the last twenty years the apology decades (Wattie, 2009); however, as anti-racist/colonialist, feminist, socialist, and Indigenous groups and climate activists rightly point out, apologies (and empty rhetoric) – without meaningful action, funding, regulation, and enforcement – are not enough to solve social injustice and the climate crisis. In response, there has been a massive grass-roots Indigenous and student/youth–led mobilization to stop extreme extractivism, reliance on fossil fuels, overconsumption, social and economic inequality, and global ecocide, as well as efforts made to strengthen democracy and fight for civil rights. As a result, "there

are over one million organizations involved in environmental efforts"
(Hawken, 2006, 2007, as cited in Gray & Coates, 2011, p. 240).

Failure to Mainstream: Social Work Inaction

This rigorous anti-racist and anti-colonialist environmental activism,
highlighted by global protests and massive mobilization, stands in stark
contrast to the social work profession's relative inaction. The important
question is, why has the social work profession been slow to mainstream this knowledge and support environmental justice/activism?

Growth of Neo-liberalism

I believe that some of the reasons for this inaction can be found in the
corresponding growth over the last few decades of neo-liberalism,
including privatization, deregulation, and the general lack of enforcement of climate agreements (Ramsay & Boddy, 2017), as well as the
strong conservative pushback on and denial of the seriousness of the
current climate crises that have occurred alongside overwhelming scientific evidence related to climate change and global activism (Nesmith
& Smyth, 2015). Along with social work's historic tendency to avoid
major disruptions of dominant narratives (Hillock, 2011; Unger, 2002),
I believe that this push-pull tension has limited/stalled the social work
profession from fully integrating these new ideas and content into curricula and incorporating them into mainstream social work education.

"Doing" Green Social Work

Despite the urgency and the fact that a green social work theoretical
knowledge base now exists, Besthorn (2014) suggests that what is also
still missing is the actual know-how, the "doing dimension" (p. 204) of
environmental social work. Since the early 2000s, there has certainly
been progress made in this area, for example the green social work
literature coming out of Europe, Australia, and New Zealand. Exemplars include Dominelli's (2012) *Green Social Work*, which makes the
case that social workers have a duty to care for the planet as well as
all of its flora and fauna; her practice model already mentioned above
(2012); and her 2018 *Routledge Handbook of Green Social Work*, which
includes a greening social work education section that highlights
what can been done to transform social work. Other international
exemplars (as will be discussed in Chapters 9, 10, and 11 of this volume) include European students learning about disaster response and

prevention (Cuadra and Eydal, 2018), Aotearoa/New Zealand students engaging in Māori-based sustainable field work (Ellis et al., 2018), and green teaching approaches for social work being developed in Australia (Nipperess and Boddy, 2018). In addition, new approaches to feminist post-humanism and new materialism have emerged (Bozalek & Pease, 2021). According to Bozalek and Pease (2021), these perspectives "alert us to the necessity to trouble binaries between nature and culture, human and non-human, the material and the discursive" (p. xxi). In addition, in terms of social work education specifically, Dominelli (2012, 2018), Gray et al. (2013), Holbrook et al. (2019), Jones (2008), and Peeters (2012) have begun the process of building a pedagogical foundation related to practical recommendations on how to green social work education.

However, despite these advances, many gaps are still evident. In particular, concrete recommendations are scarce in terms of best teaching and social work practices about the environment and sustainability, integrating interdisciplinary perspectives, preparing students in the helping professions for future practice in this area, and mobilizing students, colleagues, and community members to climate justice/action (Jones, 2008; Peeters, 2012; Ungar, 2002). Furthermore, broad philosophical questions remain, including how to best teach social action and civil disobedience, make large-scale social change, mobilize enough critical mass to make a difference, and motivate people to act in time (Hillock, 2011, 2021). As well, given social work's history of maintaining the status quo (ibid.), we still do not know what it will take to get the social work profession to wake up, join the climate conversation, mobilize for social change, and act as leaders in the battle to save humanity and the planet.

In the end, my argument is that no matter what the individual practitioner's preference, paradigm, or lens, social workers will have no choice but to act – to deal with climate change, migration, and ecological disasters – as these will soon affect every aspect of our lives. If survival is our goal (and I presume it is), then whatever our political or theoretical stripe, it is imperative that we incorporate a green perspective. Consequently, I realized that what was needed in Canadian social work education was a resource like this book, that not only focused on practical ways to "green" social work education but also endeavoured to help educators build confidence in making necessary paradigm shifts to green their work.

To start meeting these goals and filling these scholarship gaps, this introduction explores the following themes: why this topic is important for social work; what social work and the helping professions need to understand and know about the climate crisis, key issues, and relevant science to effectively teach this information; what we can learn from other academic disciplines that have more expertise and experience teaching in this area; how we can continue to build the knowledge base by centring Indigenous approaches, developing and critically examining innovative new theoretical constructs and theories (i.e., the need for a revolution in thought, attitudes, and behaviour) such as green social work/eco-social work, eco-feminism, and eco-socialism, and creating new teaching methods, materials, and resources; what the barriers are to mobilization, change, and collective action; what practical recommendations would be useful for social work educators to green their teaching and curricula; and the importance of finding and teaching hope to better motivate and mobilize people towards social change.

Why Is Climate Education Important for Social Work?

In this book, I make the case that, although other academic disciplines such as education, environmental sciences, and feminist and Indigenous studies have been writing on, debating about, and researching this topic for years, and the social work profession is ethically bound to do what it can to protect the environment, pursue social justice, and dismantle inequality (Canadian Association of Social Workers [CASW], 2005), social work and the helping professions have been slow to learn from these experts, incorporate current climate change knowledge and content into our curriculum, and collectively act together stop climate change, ensure social justice, and intervene in the international climate emergency. As a first step, I take a historical look at the origins of our profession to argue that greening social work education is essential, not only for social work to remain relevant, but also for it to stay true to its original mandate and mission. I also explore what I think every social worker needs to know about the climate crisis. In addition, I explain why climate education/literacy is important for social work and why we need to join, and more to the point, take a leadership role in local and global environmental movements.

History: Returning to Our Roots

From the early beginnings of the social work profession in Britain, charity workers – nascent social workers – from various Christian agencies and organizations had, as their original mandate and mission, a drive to help the most vulnerable – children, women, immigrants, and the working poor – in terms of what would now be described as public health and safety issues, in workplaces, factories, and communities: stopping child labour and exploitation; identifying the need for sanitary and hygienic conditions in factories and communities, including clean water and air; worker safety; employment and safety regulation; and alleviating poverty, housing, and food insecurity (Hillock et al., 2021).These charity workers – mostly upper-class white Christian women – were in many ways the forerunners of modern social workers but also our first public health workers and community organizers/developers.

Similarly, from the 1890s, the Settlement House movement is another example of our profession's community and eco-minded origins. For example, Jane Addams and Ellen Gates Starr, founders of Hull House (1889), were part of building the Settlement House Movement in the United States (Hillock & Mulé, 2016). Their American activism appears to have been heavily influenced by Addams's 1887 visit to London's Toynbee Hall, where she witnessed its innovative community efforts to improve the working/living conditions of impoverished groups and immigrants (Addams, 1912; Reinders, 1982). As a result, in contrast to Mary Richmond's early emphasis on individual and family pathology (Besthorn, 2014; Richmond, 1922), Addams developed the belief that "the environment, not the individual, was the locus of change efforts" (1912, p. 201). As such, settlement houses are classic examples of eco-friendly practices including efforts such as urban planning, garden development, food/housing security, and public health, as well as sorting garbage, reusing, and recycling (Besthorn, 2014; Fogel et al., 2016). So, in my estimation, as I have said in previous work, not only is Addams the foremother of community development and queer theory in social work (Hillock & Mulé, 2016), she can also be considered a trailblazer in terms of nascent North American environmental social work.

In Canada, early social workers, also influenced by the British tradition, including the infamous Charlotte Whitton (1943), were concerned about the poor and their working/housing conditions, emphasized the need for income security, and recognized the interplay of social forces, intervention, and community-centred social themes (Hillock et al., 2021; Whitton, 1943), including the development and protection of public green spaces/parks. In addition, early reformers posited moral imperatives for reducing the risks and increasing supports for immigrants and migrants settling in a new country, often within precarious urban settings (Hillock et al., 2021).

Similar to current calls for more progressive frameworks to deal with the ecological crisis, early libertarian and feminist ideologists, along with socialist ideologies such as Fabian socialism, the Co-operative Commonwealth Association, and Marxist-Leninisn, also promoted a range of leftist social interventions from social care to social action to revolution (Hillock et al., 2021). The depression era also had Canadian social workers and community activists continuing their fight against poverty, including successfully pressuring governments to implement universal programs. Despite these community-based efforts, in the 1940s to 1950s social work, in its quest for professional status, for the most part moved to more individually focused approaches, such as the use of the medical model and reliance on quasi-psychological theories.

By the 1960s and 1970s, as the middle class grew and leisure opportunities expanded, interest in recreation and nature (i.e., hiking, day trips, and camping) grew, and as a result environmental concerns about deforestation, pollution, overconsumption, and the use of fossil fuels began to be voiced (Besthorn, 1997; Zapf, 2009). Influenced by the budding civil rights movement, social work once again became more deeply involved in community organizing, planning, and development à la Saul Alinsky (1969, 1971), began to grapple with feminist/ structural analysis (e.g., Helen Levine, 1976; Maurice Moreau, 1979), and adopted systems theory as our predominant assessment and intervention tool (i.e., the person-in-environment [PIE] model) (Germain & Gitterman, 1980; Pincus & Minahan, 1973). In terms of education, the progressive elements of the profession also leaned heavily on Paulo Freire's (1970) transformational learning perspectives. Therefore, although interest has ebbed and flowed over time, since the beginnings of the profession and up to the mid-1970s, we have had a fairly continuous (although sometimes tenuous) historic connection with and interest in community development and urban human-built and physical environments.

What came next in the late 1970s and early 1980s was the birth of the conditions for the later growth of neo-liberalism and political-economic globalization, which as I argued earlier seems to have distracted much of social work from its original intent/mission. Indeed, as the neo-liberal paradigm became more dominant, our focus again shifted away from the root causes of human suffering to a more conventional view that "seeks to comfort victims of social problems, rather than a critical approach that seeks fundamental social change or transformation" (Mullaly, 2006, p.145). Thus, for decades the social work profession has demonstrated a contradictory mixed bag, in terms of carrying forward its original mission and mandate in its community development work and helping marginalized populations while also emphasizing individual pathology and medical diagnosis.

Undoubtably, the 1980s and 1990s expanded the focus on identity politics, human rights, and social justice, including the exploration and expansion of queer, critical race, post-colonial, Indigenous, postmodern, structural, and intersectional feminist and Black theories within social work (Briskin, 1992; Brotman & Pollack, 1997; Collins, 1991; hooks, 1989, 1991, 1993; Jagose, 1996; R. Mullaly, 1993, 1997). However, the Earth and its natural environment, including flora and fauna, as a domain of assessment and intervention continued to be mostly ignored. If and when attention was paid to the environment, the focus tended to be solely on humans and their social environments, from an anthropocentric lens (Bozalek & Pease, 2021; Molyneux, 2010). Even the more progressive theories of the time, such as queer theory, anti-racism, intersectional feminism, and structural social work can be critiqued for failing to view the natural, physical, and built environments as integral parts of social work practice and education (hooks, 1993; Närhi & Matthies, 2018).

Significantly, the 1980s and 1990s were also very difficult for service users and the social work profession alike as neo-liberalism and globalization swept the political-economic world, led by the United States, United Kingdom, and Canada, which resulted in massive social-service spending cuts, an emphasis on austerity measures (although one could fairly ask: austerity for whom?), and progressively increased gaps globally between the rich and poor (Hillock et al., 2021). According to Klein (2014), "the three policy pillars of this new era are familiar to us all: privatization of the public sphere; deregulation of the corporate sector; and lower corporate taxation, paid for with cuts to public spending" (p. 19). These forces simultaneously set the global conditions for the current ecological crisis that we are facing.

Social Work and the Environment: Emergent Climate Literacy Themes

As noted earlier, the late 1980s and 1990s witnessed the beginning of a body of robust international social work scholarship related to the environment (Faruque & Ahmmed, 2013; Negi & Furman, 2010). Borrowing much from other disciplines regarding communities, societies, and geographies (see Besthorn, 1997, 2014; Bozalek and Pease, 2021; Dominelli, 2018l and Gray et al., 2013 for more information on this nascent work), what emerged, especially out of Europe, the United Kingdom, Australia, and New Zealand, were foundational works in terms of understanding how social work might begin to incorporate sustainability and the environment into its mission, curriculum, and practice (Bozalek & Pease, 2021; Dominelli, 2012, 2018; Gray et al., 2013; Faruque & Ahmmed, 2013). Early social work authors who tackled these integration challenges include Soine (1987), Berger and

Kelly (1993), Hoff and Pollack (1993), Hoff and McNutt (1994), and Besthorn (1997).

Out of this emergent literature, three dominant constructs eventually evolved: environmental justice and deep ecology (Besthorn, 2014); ecological social work (Ungar, 2002) or eco-social work (Jones, 2018; Lysack, 2011); and eco/green social work (Dominelli, 2018; Gray et al., 2013; Holbrook et al., 2019; Jones, 2018; Lysack, 2011). Based upon Indigenous, eco-feminist, socialist/Marxist, and interdisciplinary perspectives, these approaches speak to the need for humans to recognize and also value the fact that all living beings and non-living elements are interdependent and connected. The latter two constructs additionally challenge modernist assumptions that support current and historic systems of stratified inequality of oppression such as capitalism, patriarchy, colonialism, and racism (i.e., "man's" superiority, control, and ownership over all other beings and things) (Bell, 2020; Coates, 2003; Nicholson, 2021). This focus on sustainability, highlighting Indigenous and eco-feminist/socialist values (Sugirthta & Little Flower, 2015), also prioritizes notions of "degrowth, collectivism, ecological justice and global citizenship" (Boetto, 2017, p. 276). (See Chapters 8–11 of this volume for a more nuanced discussion of these terms and their meanings for social work education.)

Meanwhile, in North America, with many Canadian social work scholars taking the lead, the last twenty years have seen exponential growth in the publication of articles, resources, and books featuring sustainable development, environmental racism, eco-feminism/socialism, and Indigenous approaches, as well as nature and animal therapies. Examples include Coates's (2003), Zapf's (2009), Gray, Coates, and Hetherington's (2013), and Fogel, Barkdull, and Weber's (2016) pivotal books that urge social workers to incorporate environmental awareness and justice issues into their everyday living and practice.

Greening Social Work Education: Developing a New Model

This volume explores the above themes and, as stated above, seeks to aid in the development of a comprehensive green model of social work education. Based on the existing knowledge and literature, it is clear that a green model must be global in scope; recognize the impact of climate change; centre Indigeneity; emphasize the importance of interdependent relationships; critique modernity and capitalist inequality, imperialism, and stratified inequality; celebrate interdisciplinarity; and highlight the need for both social and environmental justice (Teixeira & Krings, 2015). For the purposes of this book, the term "green social work" (à la Dominelli, 2012, 2013, 2018), as an overarching term, is used to describe the paradigm shifts required to develop and apply this new model.

Accordingly, Part 1 of this book centres Indigeneity and examines key concepts from an interdisciplinary lens, Part 2 presents environmental content necessary for social work education, and Part 3 examines multiple approaches to "greening" social work curricula, teaching methods, and educational process/content. Furthermore, this collection recognizes the tensions and debates about how this content should be applied. Indeed, scholars are divided about whether ecological literacy should be simply added to existing social work curricula as an extra layer (Boetto et al., 2014), used to transform/expand the person-in-environment model (Ramsay and Boddy, 2017), or be incorporated into all aspects of social work programs, including policies, decision-making, funding, curriculum, and field (Powers et al., 2019).

Science and the Climate Crisis: What Every Social Worker Needs to Know

To develop ecological literacy and effectively teach this content, it is essential that social work and the helping professions understand the climate crisis, key issues, and the relevant science. If we accept this argument, and agree that this is necessary teaching content, we need to first understand what the scientific facts are. To begin, I want to make clear that I am not an expert on climate science. However, based on the current literature and research, I suggest the following items as important starting places to assist readers in exploring the knowledge base, conceptual analysis, materials, and content relevant to their discipline to help them start greening their teaching and curricula.

Facts Please, Just the Facts

Accordingly, what are the environmental facts that social work educators need to know? Since the Industrial Revolution, humans have been "pumping fossil fuels into the air" and have "triggered cascading problems" including global warming, extinction events, and biodiversity loss (Borenstein & Larson, 2021, para. 7). Indeed, scientists have been warning us for decades that if we are unable to keep global temperatures below 1.5 degrees centigrade, global warming and climate catastrophe will occur – increased droughts, famine, flooding, forest fires, human and natural disasters, air, water, and soil pollution, more extreme weather events like hurricanes, monsoons, and tornadoes, depletion of the ocean's fishery, death of the coral reefs, toxic algae blooms, melting ice caps and glaciers, species extinction and collapse of the food chain, as well as massive global climate migration as people flee damaged areas (Achstatter, 2014; Intergovernmental Panel on Climate Change, 2018; McGrath, 2019).

As a result of these greenhouse gas effects, continuing overconsumption, overpopulation, deforestation, pollution, and destruction/extinction of flora and fauna and their habitats (what Leakey calls the "Sixth Extinction") (1996, as cited in Kahn, 2003, para. 4), there is a "high likelihood of human civilisation coming to an end by 2050" (Cockburn, 2019, p. 1). Even the World Bank, known for its ultra-conservative views, has warned that we are "on track for a 4°C warmer world (by century's end) and marked by extreme heat waves, declining global food stocks, loss of ecosystems and biodiversity, and life-threatening sea level rise" (as cited in Klein, 2014, p. 13). If that happens, scientists state that "warming of 4°C is incompatible with an organized global community" and "would be devastating to the majority of ecosystems" (Cockburn, 2019, p. 6). To avoid this fate, humanity must cut "emissions of carbon dioxide by 45% by 2030" (McGrath, 2019, para. 3).

To accomplish this goal, a concerted effort – from all countries, governments, corporations, and peoples of the world – is required. Unfortunately, many authors suggest that the political and economic will required to make these necessary changes just does not exist, and so instead they call for a huge groundswell of grass-roots mobilization and activism to force the hands of politicians (Alston, 2015; Klein, 2014). Motivated by successful climate change litigation across the globe, activists are now choosing to bypass ineffective governments, "increasingly turning to the courts to try to compel change" (Arsenault, 2021, para. 11) and therefore putting intense legal pressure on those same governments. Sadly, even with these efforts, and if we somehow manage to meet the above targets, it may already be too late to avoid the worst impacts of climate crises, as many argue that the window to change the most devastating outcomes is closing or has already closed (Arsenault, 2021; McGrath, 2019).

At this point, I will leave further discussion of scientific details in the capable hands of this book's expert contributors, who are better positioned from their various disciplines to present and analyse the most salient information and make recommendations about how best to teach this content. However, two useful teaching tools are an excellent starting place: a BBC video called *What Is Climate Change? A Really Simple Guide* (BBC, 2021), and former US vice president Al Gore's (2006) documentary *An Inconvenient Truth*, in which he "declared the environmental crisis to be a 'planetary emergency'" (as cited in Zapf, 2009, p. 16).

The Environmental Movement

John Tyndall is often credited with being the first scientist, in 1859, who studied "global warming" – "how gases absorb radiant heat" (Suzuki, 2020, para. 2). However, it was a female scientist, Eunice Foote, who actually identified and studied the "greenhouse effect" years before him, in 1856 releasing a paper called "Circumstances Affecting the Heat of the Sun's Rays" at the American Association for the Advancement of Science's annual meeting (para. 2). The first use of the word "ecology" dates back to 1866, when Ernst Haeckel studied the "interdependencies among organisms in the natural world" (Haeckel, as cited in Klemmer & McNamara, 2020, p. 2), but the term did not become popularized until the early 1960s. Alongside early climate change warnings and the birth of civil rights movements, Rachel Carson's (1962) classic book *Silent Spring* is credited with starting the mass environmental movement and galvanizing people to care about the impact of humans on the environment and pressure governments to protect nature and wildlife habitat.

This public interest culminated in the creation, in April 1970, of an annual global Earth Day (https://www.earthday.org/history) that continues to this day. Also, several environmental organizations either became more prominent during this era, such as the long-standing Ducks Unlimited and Sierra Club, or were founded, including the anti-nuclear Canadian organization Greenpeace (Klein, 2014) and various US organizations like the Natural Resources Defence Council, Friends of the Earth, and League of Conservation Voters (Earth Island, 2022). In Canada, as described in Chapter 2, several significant pieces of legislation were introduced, including the Clean Air Act (1971), Canada Water Act (1972), and Environmental Contaminants Act (1976), and in 1971 a federal department responsible for the environment was created (MacDowell, 2012).

The 1980s and 1990s saw the environmental justice movement continue to build and grow. In 1980, the term "sustainable development" first entered the world's lexicon when it was used in a document titled *World Conservation Strategy* produced by the International Union of Conservation of Nature and Natural Resources (Gray et al., 2013). Then, in 1987, the World Commission on Environment and Development published a now famous report integrating "environmental, economic, and social strategies into development work" (Gray et al., p. 65), titled *Our Common Future* (or the Brundtland Report). In 1988, the United Nations'

16 Susan Hillock

Intergovernmental Panel on Climate Change (IPCC) (https://www.ipcc.ch) was created to track and record climate change effects and research possible solutions. Additionally, the differential and unjust impact of intersecting forces of environmental degradation, poverty, and racism was finally recognized and resulted in the term "environmental racism" being coined by Bullard, who defined it as "the process whereby black and other disenfranchised minority communities bear a disproportionate share of the effects of environmental pollution" (1990, as cited in Dominelli, 2012, p. 97).

By the mid-1990s, the international community was becoming more alarmed; several global conferences were organized, including the Rio Earth Summit in 1992 (Gray et al., 2013), and major climate action agreements were created that committed countries to measures such as limiting or reducing greenhouse gases, regulation, and enforcement. Key agreements have followed, among them the Kyoto Protocols (1997; https://unfccc.int/kyoto_protocol) and the Paris Agreement (2015; https://unfccc.int/process-and-meetings/the-paris-agreement/the-paris-agreement). More recently, in 2021, the United Nations' Climate Change Conference (COP26) met again, this time in Glascow, Scotland. Although these groups keep meeting and global agreements have been signed by multiple countries, including Canada, there has been limited action/enforcement. As a result, as outlined previously, the current situation is dire; emissions are still on the rise and the window of opportunity to save the planet is closing, as corporations, in a desperate bid for increased profit margins, turn to more extreme extraction options such as the Alberta tar sands oil projects and natural gas fracking, further poisoning our land, water, and air. Megaprojects like these also result in Indigenous (and racialized) peoples around the world losing the land, animals, plants, and ecology that are part of their spiritual, cultural, and cosmic existence.

Why Should Social Work Care?

One might think that social work and environmentalism would be a natural fit, as a major part of our work includes an ethic of care (Tronto, 1993), human rights and social justice approaches, community organization/development, a moral and ethical mandate to help marginalized and vulnerable populations, and a dominant assessment paradigm that rests on a person-in-environment approach (although it has been used in a far more limited way than could be done, mostly focusing on human and social aspects) (Coates, 2003; Germain & Gitterman, 1980; Zapf, 2009). If we truly support these concepts – serving vulnerable populations, dismantling oppression, and intervening to promote social justice for all, which I see as essential parts of our professional identity – then saving the planet must become a priority and *is* indeed our mission going forward.

Intersectionality

I argue, then, that we are ethically and morally obligated to help those who are most affected by climate crises and environmental racism, those who because of systemic structural inequality (e.g., sexism, classism, and racism) are more likely to experience pollution, unemployment/underemployment, extraction work, residences near factories, poverty, unsafe water and air, refugee status, and food and housing insecurity. These vulnerable groups, already under stress, also have the least amount of resources to avoid damage and recover from extreme weather events and human-made and natural disasters (Hetherington & Boddy, 2013). This intersectional analysis is important, as climate change has a differential impact on various groups and therefore affects people's capacity to "bounce back" and be resilient. Those who are poor, racialized, Indigenous, disabled, female, very young or old, and from the Global South are more likely to be at risk and face harsher and longer-lasting climate change conditions and outcomes, including displacement, poverty, trauma, illness/injury, and so on, than dominant groups (Bywaters et al., 2009; Dominelli, 2018). In fact, over one hundred million people around the world are currently displaced due to disasters, wars, and extreme weather events, with many more expected to become climate refugees in the years to come (see Chapter 7 of this volume for more information on this topic).

Disasters

Research has shown that extreme weather events as well as natural and human-made disasters are increasing in frequency and severity (Lysack, 2010). For example, in Canada "the costs of natural disasters from extreme weather are rising rapidly, averaging $1.9 billion annually, up about $400 million from a decade ago" (Arsenault, 2021, para. 2). Even without specialized disaster training, social workers are already on the ground doing emergency care and relief after these catastrophic events (e.g., mobilizing community responses, meeting immediate needs, providing shelter, food, and water, etc.) (Kemp & Palinkas, 2015). Moreover, according to Dass-Brailsford (2010), those in the helping professions can play a vital role in climate disasters/emergencies, not only in terms of disaster relief but also to help communities to prepare, complete community risk assessments, avoid environmental degradation, and build resilience.

Gender Analysis

As mentioned previously, not only was it a woman, Eunice Foote, who first "studied the greenhouse effect" (Suzuki, 2020, para. 2), but eco-feminists have long contended that exploitation, control, and "mastery" of nature for the purposes of the economy and profit-making (i.e., structural forces of patriarchy, racism, colonialism, and capitalism) go hand-in-hand with the exploitation and domination of women and racialized peoples (Isla, 2019; Noble, 2021; Waldron, 2018). According to Isla (2019), an eco-feminist lens is critical as it problematizes the nature of white and "male domination of women and nature" (p. 19). Eco-feminists have also been at the forefront in pointing out the similarities between violence against women and vulnerable peoples as colonial objects to be used, exploited, and sold for the dominant group's enjoyment, consumption, and labour, and violence towards the planet, animals, and habitats for similar reasons and purposes. Prominent eco-feminist Silvia Federici describes this as "the systematic subjugation and appropriation of women, nature, bodies, and labour" (as cited in Isla, 2019, p. 20).

   Because of systemic inequality, women (and children) are the most vulnerable to environmental degradation and climate crises as they make the least money, have the least assets, are blocked from education resulting in literacy and numeracy issues, often do not have the right to say no to unwanted sex, early marriage, and pregnancy, lack affordable and accessible contraception and thus bear the burden of most child-rearing and home care, and globally have limited economic and political power, voice, and representation. Examples include women "being more likely than men to need to visit [the] ER for asthma and respiratory related conditions during wildfires"; experiencing reproductive issues, as "extreme weather events are associated with greater risks of low birth weight and preterm births"; and being excluded from the climate conversation, as "women make up only 19% of people interviewed, featured or quoted in climate-related news coverage" (Sierra Club, 2020b, para. 3). Accordingly, environmental social work must work towards achieving gender, class, and race equality and consider these as "a crucial nexus at which climate resilience must be built" (Sierra Club, 2020a, para. 3).

   Thus, to be effective, green social work must also – ipso facto – be feminist. This includes a recognition of women's traditional caretaking/

food provision roles and close relationships with those who are most vulnerable, including the flora, fauna, and planet (Isla, 2019; Mellor, 1997). This ethics of care perspective (Tronto, 1993) is essential to valorizing women's roles and relationship to/with/for other beings and Mother Earth and also strongly connects with Indigenous views and values related to interdependence with nature and stewardship of the land (Bozalek & Pease, 2021; Green, 2018).

In addition, as I explain further in Chapter 12 of this collection, I believe that green social work must also be structural (B. Mullaly, 2006) and socialist (Wallace, 2018). That is, alongside supporting and promoting anti-oppressive feminist values, beliefs, and approaches such as intersectional analyses; reproductive, property, voting, literacy, and numeracy rights; and women's (and those who are othered's) ways of knowing (Klemmer & McNamara, 2020; Wallace, 2018; Wilkin & Hillock, 2014), green social work must also work towards dismantling the structural forces that harm humans (and non-humans). Again, also central to this world view are Indigenous understandings of stewardship, wholism, interdependence, and connectedness in terms of our relationships with each other, nature, and the Earth (Isla, 2019; Skwiot, 2008; Waldron, 2018; Williams et al., 2018).

What Social Work Can Learn from Other Disciplines

Not only does social work need to quickly develop an interest in finding solutions to climate crises and building better relationships with other humans and the planet (and its flora and fauna), but it must also recognize that to be effective, this work has to be done in concert with other academic disciplines, as well as community activists and social justice groups, initiatives, and movements. According to Närhi and Matthies (2018), in order to be successful we must continue to unite a host of "different disciplines and societal actors to look for a holistic model of sustainable development that would distance itself from the present model committed to economic growth" (p. 496). A multi/inter-disciplinary approach is recommended as it fosters reciprocal relationships/ partnerships and community/democracy building (Clark et al., 2011; Vincent & Focht, 2011). Once we recognize that a multi/inter-disciplinary approach is needed to tackle climate change and that social work benefits from learning and working collectively with community members and other academic disciplines, the need for a book like this one, that highlights social work education in concert with diverse academic perspectives, becomes evident.

Because social work education is still in the initial stages of trying to mainstream environmental/sustainability content and develop its ecological literacy, I recommend that, rather than reinventing the wheel, it is time to break down the traditional silos that exist between academic disciplines (and between the ivory tower and communities), that also keep us isolated from each other and limit the collaborative research and outcomes we could achieve (Besthorn, 2014; Semerjan, Zurayk, & El-Fadel, 2004). Indeed, social work can benefit a great deal from partnering with, and learning from, our academic colleagues and community activists who have more expertise and experience with teaching/ applying this content and integrating this material into their work/ curricula.

For example, some academic disciplines, such as Indigenous and gender studies, education, and environmental sciences, have made huge progress, and developed specific technological and pedagogical expertise, in terms of *what* to teach and *how* to teach this content (Vincent & Focht, 2011). Accordingly, Part 1 of this book features interdisciplinary approaches to climate literacy that can be adopted/adapted within social work. In addition, a myriad of international journals from various academic disciplines have been launched that can be useful for social work application, including *Nature Climate Change* (https:// www.nature.com/nclimate); *Global Environmental Change* (https:// www.journals.elsevier.com/global-environmental-change); *Environment International* (https://www.journals.elsevier.com/environment -international); *Ecology and Society* (https://www.ecologyandsociety.org); *Journal of Environmental Psychology* (https://www.journals.elsevier .com/journal-of-environmental-psychology); *Environmental Politics* (https://www.tandfonline.com/loi/fenp20); *Environmental Ethics* (https://www.pdcnet.org/enviroethics); and *Environmental Research* (https://www.journals.elsevier.com/environmental-research). In terms of education, there are also several journals of interest, including the *Canadian Journal of Environmental Education* (https://cjee.lakeheadu .ca); *International Electronic Journal of Environmental Education* (https:// dergipark.org.tr/en/pub/iejeegreen); *Environmental Education Research* (https://www.tandfonline.com/loi/ceer20); *International Journal of Sustainability in Higher Education* (https://www.emerald.com/insight /publication/issn/1467-6370); and *Green Teacher* (https://greenteacher .com).

However, recognizing the need to borrow and adapt from other disciplines does not mean that social work itself has nothing of value to contribute, that we are passive recipients, empty vessels, as it were. Just as social workers might ask themselves, "What do we know about science, pollution, or responding to disasters?," scientists would be well advised to ask themselves what they know about community networking, organizing, and mobilization; dealing with mental health, wellness, grief, or anxiety; risk reduction; and building individual and community resilience. Who then is better positioned to carry out these tasks, and provide leadership in these particular areas, other than those of us already trained to do so and serving these very same vulnerable communities?

Lack of Social Work Leadership

All of this raises the question, as pointed out earlier, of where exactly social work is in all of this. More pointedly, as Zapf (2009) speculates, "does social work have any relevance as humankind faces these serious challenges" (p. 17)? Although North American social work has, as I have said, an established history of using the person-in-environment approach (albeit from an anthropocentric lens), can begin to adopt sustainable social work practice knowledge and examples from the United Kingdom, Australia, and New Zealand, and "might be expected to play a leadership role in the planning stages of any new environmental state … we have generally been silent on the serious threats to human well-being and continued existence" (Zapf, 2009, pp. 17–18). Furthermore, even though there has recently been backlash aimed at science, intellectualism, and progressive values and ideals (e.g., ex-US president Donald Trump and his supporters, climate change deniers, and COVID anti-vaxers/maskers), I argue that part of the remedy is for social work to take an active leadership role in transforming and reconceptualizing its knowledge and theoretical base, and by doing so return to its original mission to help those who are most vulnerable, through centring Indigeneity, developing ecological literacy, greening social work education, and becoming environmental activists/warriors.

Accordingly, although I strongly recommend that we can (and should) learn as much as we can from colleagues from other disciplines and community activists who have taken the lead in this area, instead of being left out of the conversation (which seems to be where the profession sits now), social work needs to do a better job of identifying and highlighting the specific expertise and skills it can bring to the table. Examples include community knowledge, networking, and organizing, group work, communication skills, consciousness raising, social justice/ action, risk assessment, disaster preparedness and intervention training, and trauma, anxiety, and grief work to effectively prepare students to assist individuals and communities in terms of climate migration, environmental racism, and ecological disaster (Dass-Brailsford, 2010; Dominelli, 2018; Fogel et al., 2016; Gray et al., 2013; Klein, 2014; Linklater, 2014; Schmitz et al., 2012). As well, social work can bring to the table various alternative grass-roots models that feature the democratic co-production of knowledge, research, and solutions from the "ground up," such as feminist, Indigenous, and participatory action research and methods; community engagement, organization, and mobilization tools; and advocacy strategies and skills (Anderson-Nathe et al., 2013; Gamble and Weil, 2010; Healy, 2000; Skwiot, 2008).

Carving Out Spaces of Innocence: Barriers to Change

One of the most perplexing questions that we need to resolve is: now that so many of us know the scientific facts, why is most of humanity still not acting to make necessary change? Indeed, the same can be said for decades of research, statistics, knowledge building, and activism about structural inequality, and yet we still have not accomplished a great deal in terms of dismantling racism, capitalism, and patriarchy. Clearly, what the Trump (i.e., facts/fiction debacles) and COVID 19 era (with its anti-maskers and vaccine resistors) have demonstrated is that scientific facts and truth are often not enough for people to believe the science or change their behaviours. What else needs to be done to move people to action? And specifically, in terms of social work education and the helping professions, what are the barriers to mobilization, change, and collective action?

Denial and Innocence

Interestingly, Murdock (2021) implicates the structural forces of colonialism, racism, and whiteness when she addresses the problematic issue of denial, including "the number of times well-meaning white people ask about what *we* are supposed to do to combat planetary climate change" (para. 1), and ponders why they seem so shocked that we are in this situation. Speaking truth to power, she argues that white people actually "know what to do, they just don't want to do it" (para. 2) and that "white people and people proximate to whiteness are [more] deeply invested in appearing both innocent and responsible than actually doing this work" (para. 5). She makes the case that this "feigned innocence" signifies an attempt, on behalf of dominant peoples, to "carve out a space of innocence – a hiding place beneath, within, or close to whiteness that might protect them" from taking full responsibility and experiencing consequences for their actions (para. 3). In contrast, she makes the case that colonized peoples are not afforded this luxury, as

> these histories live in the minds, hearts, bodies, and spirits of the global populations who have borne the brunt and lived the apocalypses that white supremacist colonization, imperialism, and capitalism have created and continue to create. (para. 3)

Waiting for a Superhero

Over the last few years, it has been interesting to witness the cultural phenomenon of the proliferation of fantasy, apocalyptic, horror, and superhero books, video/online games, television shows, and movies. These formats tend to have two major themes: first, there is an impending doom-and-gloom feeling that the world is coming to an end (a pretty reasonable fear given the times), and second, we (the victims) are passively waiting for someone else to save us. The basic plot tends to revolve around some evil being, outside of regular good humanity (read that as white, heterosexual, Western, and able-bodied), that is about to destroy the planet, and we, the people, confused and blameless, are powerless to stop it. The plot then requires that a superhero (read that as a white, masculine, Western being) rescue us at the very last minute, when all else seems about to fail, by violently killing all of the bad guys. The notions that might makes right and the man with the most artillery and biggest guns wins are predominant. Who cares if the he(ro) kills a bunch of innocent people/animals or if his machines of war destroy the environment and affect villagers and landscapes for years to come? No price is too high to pay (with the sole exception of his ever having to give up his own entitlement and supremacy), if it means beating the bad guys. Unfortunately, as eco-feminists have contended for decades (and as has been mentioned previously), these tropes of masculine violence, control and mastery over others and nature, and the language of war are born from (and perpetuate) the same capitalist, classist, racist, and patriarchal ethos that has put humanity and the planet in this dire situation in the first place.

Interestingly, these movies, books, and games are also the exact personification of the denial of culpability, the failure to act, and the creation of spaces for white innocence that Murdock (2021) mentions. This conceptual theme lets us, as audience and as entertainment consumers, metaphorically and cathartically off the hook in terms of personal and corporate morality, responsibility, and action, if (1) we do not see *ourselves* as the cause of this disaster and (2) we just have to wait for *someone else* to fix it. Murdock rightly points out the futility of waiting for rich white men to save us and solve all of our problems, when essentially they are the root of why we are in the current position.

Ironically, and despite evidence to the contrary, we still wait to be rescued anyway. After all, many of us have been programmed, in terms of Judeo-Christian (and other) religious and resurrection themes, to wait for the great (white) saviour to rise from the ashes like the proverbial phoenix, to wash us clean from our sins and save us. Similar to Murdock's work, Klein's (2014) problematizes what she calls the potential "billionaire saviors" (p. 252), including the likes of Bill Gates, Jeff Bezos, Elon Musk, and Richard Branson. Demonstrating that "the emperor has no clothes," Klein eviscerates this rich saviour myth by summarizing and analysing the ineffectiveness, risk, and danger of their various miracle schemes (that are continually touted by the elite, corporations, and global capital), outlining their limitations, and highlighting these billionaires' inept and often unkept promises. Moreover, Kahn (2003) warns that those of us "who stand with the global oppressed should then be especially dubious, if not in outright objection, of ... policies that are formed by those who live in great opulence and ease but which are always directed at those surrounded by despair" (para. 2).

Green Capitalism: An Oxymoron

One of the many solutions that is presented, often by these same billionaires, is that entrepreneurship, indeed capitalism, the fossil fuel industry itself, and massive investment in the private for-profit sector will somehow manage, through technological innovation, to solve the climate crisis. Some of the proposals include switching to green hydrogen as a primary fuel source, decreasing carbon emissions through cap-and-trade schemes, carbon sequestering and taxes, "fertilizing the oceans with iron" (Klein, 2014, p. 257), and seeding the skies with "particles" to control global warming and extreme weather (p. 258). The major problem with these proposals is that not only are they likely to be dangerous and have unanticipated outcomes, they also continue to rely on the old-fashioned strategy of finding new sources of (finite) resources to secure and maintain certain dominant groups' lifestyles and activities, rather than slowing down, reducing our overall global energy use, decreasing overconsumption/overpopulation, and preventing continuing environmental degradation.

In addition, big business is smart. Although green capitalism is being marketed as a possible solution, its actual goal is to continue to make more money through what has been called "greenwashing," by branding companies and their activities and products as "green" as a way to increase profits (Klein, 2014, p. 206). Examples include large "environmental" corporations that are heavily invested in fossil fuels, the propagation of recycling myths (i.e., labelling something as recyclable or organic to increase profits), downshifting corporate responsibility to consumers and pretending to recycle when much of North American waste is offloaded to the Global South (Marketplace, 2021; Rabson, 2019), doubling down on pipelines and fossil fuels, and investing in profitable re-insurance disaster businesses (Dominelli, 2018; Klein, 2014). Add to this a lack of effective regulation and enforcement of climate agreements, corruption at many government levels, and the fact that multinational companies control much of the global agenda, resources, and capital, and one soon finds that waiting for green capitalism to save the day becomes the equivalent of asking the fox to guard the chicken coop.

Lack of Relevant Professional Standards

As mentioned earlier, you would think that green social work would be a natural fit with environmentalism, especially in terms of serving marginalized, poor, and immigrant/refugee populations. However, historically, our various codes and standards of professional accreditation and conduct have not included anything specific about the natural or built environments as domains of assessment and intervention. In fact, in terms of the push-pull mentioned above, the power of the dominant neo-liberal paradigm has been reflected in our Canadian Code of Ethics (CASW, 2005), which can be seen as diminishing our ethical responsibility to protect the environment. In a revealing turn of phrase from the older code of ethics (CASW, 1997), we moved from "[social workers] shall advocate change in the best interest of the client, and for the overall benefit of society, the environment and the global community" (p. 1) to the 2005 statement that we "promote social development and environmental management in the interests of all people" (CASW, 2005, p. 5). Anthropocentric to the extreme, this makes no mention of protecting or serving other interests such as flora, fauna, or the planet itself, nor is there any recognition of our interdependent/interconnected relationships with nature.

Historically, there have also been no Canadian accreditation standards in this area, which has resulted in a lack of direction for schools of social work to change their processes or curricula, and without relevant standards or rules there has been no way of enforcing the topic's inclusion. However, as I noted previously, and this is perhaps indicative of a global seed change in terms of social work's ecological literacy, there has been a significant update to the Canadian national standards, as the CASWE-ACFTS (2021a) has finally added an environmental standard, titled *Environmental Sustainability and Ecological Practice*, which states:

Social work students shall have opportunities to …

a)   understand the need to create ecologically sustainable communities, economies and natural and built environments, in which all life forms and eco-systems can survive and thrive;

b)   identify and challenge environmental injustice and racism, i.e. the inequitable burdens borne by those who are socially and economically marginalised in relation to environmental degradation and hazards;

c)   advance environmental sustainability across individual, organizational and professional contexts;

d)   and, embrace the role of social workers in advocacy for public policies and social practices that will ensure ecological health and environmental sustainability at local, regional, national and global levels. (p. 16)

Of particular note is that, even though these changes occurred in 2021, the committee members who worked on them candidly admit, in their briefing notes, that they had not even thought of including the environment as an issue of concern in their initial drafts. In fact, they did not do so until a social work member gave them feedback about this oversight (CASWE-ACFTS, 2021b, pp. 12–13). To me, this means that, although the accreditation changes are certainly an improvement, green social work still has a long way to go before being mainstreamed in Canada.

Lack of Application Know-How

Of course, now that a standard exists, how (and how quickly) will it be translated into the curricula, processes, and teaching in Canadian schools of social work? Hopefully, now that a new accreditation standard exists, schools of social work will be obligated to, at minimum, discuss the new standard, attempt to apply it, and demonstrate how they have integrated it across their programs. However, even though, as I have noted, sound scholarship has been developed that provides a green theoretical, conceptual, and knowledge base to teach this content and transform curricula and there is a growing body of literature concerning application to social work education, there remains limited theoretical and/or applied literature, research, exemplars, experiential exercises, and scholarship available on *how* to best teach it (or practice it) (Besthorn, 2014; Jones, 2008; Peeters, 2012). These are the gaps that this book is intended to fill.

Lack of Interest and Support

Even when standards exist, there is congruency with our code of ethics, and pressure (gentle or not) is applied to implement new standards of education and practice, there may still not be support from universities, departments, colleagues, and students. For instance, just because our profession has decided that something is important to teach does not mean that schools of social work and our colleagues will actually teach the content (or teach it well). Over time, I have learned that not all colleagues or students welcome topics that challenge dominant spaces and narratives (Hillock, 2021). An example that immediately comes to comes to mind is teaching about racism, heterosexism, capitalism, and patriarchy. Although these subjects are very important, and affect all of our lives, colleagues seem reluctant to trouble the waters by teaching progressive approaches that challenge the status quo (Hillock, 2021). And given the continuing historic resistance of the profession – to fully move towards more progressive approaches (e.g., the preponderance of cognitive behavioural treatment [CBT] and psychoanalytical clinical models vs. anti-oppressive practice (AOP) approaches in schools of social work), delays in implementing the TRC's educational recommendations (2015), and minimal change in moving the profession (and students) to unionism and activism – despite what feminist, queer, anti-racist/colonialist, and structural scholars have contributed in critical and intersectional analysis over the last thirty years – one could rightly ask, "How motivated as a profession are we, really, to make change and disrupt dominant narratives?"

Of course, this resistance may also be related to the fact that the social work profession, particularly in Canada, is overwhelmingly dominated by white and middle-class social workers, who are clearly implicated in perpetuating and maintaining their privilege and who benefit the most from maintaining the status quo, including environmental racism. In addition, academia is far from being immune from the pervasive influence of global capital and neo-liberalism. In fact, "it's virtually impossible to do public interest work in any scale – in academia or journalism or activism – without taking money of questionable origin, whether the origin is the state, corporations, or private philanthropy" (Klein, 2014, p. 198).

Moreover, although many students are concerned about the environ-ment and would like to see more content and skill development in their social work education (Jones, 2008; Jung, 2016; Muldoon, 2006; Peeters, 2012), some students are also resistant to this content. Ironically, in a social media and Internet age where we have unprecedented access and exposure to environmental and social justice information/educa-tion, some students have what I would describe as an intense discom-fort with any discussion or content remotely related to real talk about environmental racism, the possibility of the world ending, and what our ethical and moral responsibilities are, as global citizens and educa-tors, to serve the people most affected by climate crises. For example, one time in class a white female student came to me crying and asked me to never mention climate change again because she found it too "upsetting." When I respectfully declined, she then asked me to give the class a trigger warning each time before I spoke about it so that she could leave the classroom. Like the proverbial ostrich, sticking our heads in the sand (and proclaiming innocence) is not going to make climate change go away or help prepare future social workers to work with vulnerable peoples.

Workload Issues

Additionally, there are, of course, all of the reasons why it is hard to implement any new substantive content within social work programs – too little time, too many topics of importance, difficulty finding room in overpacked and overextended curricula, too much departmental and university service, high teaching loads, lack of funding generally for resources, for course buy-outs, and for curriculum development, and absence of role models. Other barriers include a lack of knowledge, education, and training on this topic as well as colleagues who may not see this topic as part of their scope of practice or their areas of exper-tise. Furthermore, I cannot overlook the gendered nature of our profes-sion. Although women produce lower overall emissions and thus have a lower carbon footprint than men, and we are often at the forefront of resistance movements (perhaps because we have so much more to lose) and environmental protection, for example, Indigenous women's traditional roles as water carriers, finders, and protectors (Isla, 2019; Williams et al., 2018), we are already overtaxed with too much profes-sional and personal responsibility in terms of caring for everyone else. So I am sympathetic to the gendered reality that we, the ones who are most exhausted, must not only continue to look after everyone else but now, as an additional burden, are being asked as a profession to help save the planet. An important lesson here, then, is that we cannot, and indeed must not, do this alone.

Mission Possible: Teaching Hope

Although the COVID 19 pandemic has been terrible, resulting in millions of deaths and literally stopping the world in its economic tracks, I think it would be helpful for us to consider this experience as nature's early warning system of an impending global climate catastrophe that is affecting everyone on the planet. We ignore what we have learned from the COVID pandemic at our own peril. Thus, we have serious and urgent choices to make. We can either use all our time, energy, and resources trying to return to and maintain the status quo (which is not working for the majority of people, flora, and fauna on the planet), or humanity can pull together – its money, resources, science, and goodwill – to make a massive effort to try to save the planet. After all, as popular social media memes make clear, there is no Planet B. Social work too has a radical choice to make: do we support a new social work ethic that is founded on interdependence, minimalism, collectivism, and peace in order to make the drastic changes required now to save humanity and the planet, or do we continue to support a status quo that is predicated on individualism, violence, capitalism, and stratified inequality until the planet is destroyed and humanity is extinguished?

Moreover, given the naysayers and climate change deniers, frightening statistics, and real-life complex issues, the critical question is, how do we persuade people to be hopeful, to find the motivation to act, and to develop the personal and political will to change what needs to change at all levels? To borrow a turn of phrase from the Green Party of Canada platform (2019), how do we move from feeling overwhelmed to achieving the seeming impossible?

To this end, I argue that to be effective in teaching this content it is essential that we teach about hope. Recognizing that the topic of climate change can be overwhelming and may trigger anxiety, inertia, depression, and panic, Kelsey, in her book *Hope Matters* (2019), concurs, proclaiming that "doom and gloom won't help us solve the climate crisis" (Pereira, 2020, para. 1). Meaningful change is not possible if we stay stuck in grief, anxiety, or despair. Indeed, Kelsey notes that maintaining hope is essential to mobilize activism, is a "powerful political act," and "sustains us to keep fighting for social and ecological justice" (para. 1). Consequently, although this book is intended to offer helpful suggestions, it is also meant to be inspirational. By providing specific examples of hope across the book – that can be shared with family, friends, colleagues, and students – its ultimate goal is to motivate readers to increase their ecological literacy, build confidence to green their teaching, and become ecological warriors/activists.

How Can Social Work Education Best Contribute?

In the end, the critical question is: what can we all do, in the short and long term, to save the planet, its flora and fauna, and humanity? Furthermore, in terms of this book's purpose, how can social work education best contribute to these efforts? There is still room for optimism; if we act now, we may have time to mitigate some of the most severe impacts of climate change. In this vein, the IPCC has recommended potential solutions, including

> adaptation initiatives drawn from the knowledge of Aboriginal populations; a move toward renewable energy resources; fossil fuel divestment; mitigation measures for all transportation modes; infrastructure and urban redevelopment investments; industry improvements (reduce, reuse, recycle); and lifestyle, behavioural, and cultural changes. One of the most highlighted solutions was the need for a shift in the broader social consciousness. (2014, as cited in Cumby, 2013, p. 12)

For me, this last recommendation is central in order for us to resolve the moral and ethical dilemmas that we face regarding environmental racism, inequality, and humanity's survival, and speaks to the pivotal role of education as a critical (re)socialization tool and process that can help humanity shift its consciousness and move forward towards sustainability. Indeed, one of the fundamental purposes of this book is to explore how we can introduce, learn, and teach a green – collectivist, democratic, egalitarian, and politically activist – lifestyle and philosophy as a starting place to mobilize communities, students, and colleagues to climate action and social justice.

Accordingly, I believe that social work education can play an important role in successfully negotiating emerging cultural, ecological, economic, political, and social sustainability challenges, building individual and community resilience, ensuring social and environmental justice, strengthening democracy, and preparing future social work practitioners to act as leaders to meet these new realities. Therefore, I argue that how social work educators can most help is by returning to our original professional mission to do what we have been trained to do best: support/serve vulnerable populations, challenge thinking and paradigms, transform minds, and mobilize colleagues, communities, and students to social action/justice.

To summarize this book's major themes, I believe that carrying forward helpful values and traditions from our social work origins; challenging neo-liberalism, capitalism, globalization, patriarchy, and human-first perspectives; centring Indigenous, feminist/socialist, and green knowledges, analyses, and methods; mobilizing for social change; celebrating multi/inter-disciplinarity; supporting social justice and environmental movements; and participating in climate activism must be actively encouraged in order for us to successfully green social work education. This book explores these interconnected themes across its three main sections, entitled "Centring Indigenous Approaches and Celebrating Multi/Inter-disciplinarity," "Key Environmental Issues: What Every Social Worker Should Know," and "Greening Social Work Education: Practical Application."

REFERENCES

Achstatter, L. C. (2014). Climate change: Threats to social welfare and social justice requiring social work intervention. *21st Century Social Justice, 1*(1), 1–22.

Addams, J. (1912). *Twenty years at Hull House*. Macmillan.

Alinsky, S. (1969). *Reveille for radicals*. Vintage.

Alinsky, S. (1971). *Rules for radicals*. Vintage.

Alston, M. (2015). Social work, climate change and global cooperation. *International Social Work, 58*, 355–363. https://doi.org/10.1177/0020872814556824

Anderson-Nathe, B., Gringeri, C., & Wahab, S. (2013). Nurturing "critical hope" in teaching feminist social work research. *Journal of Social Work Education, 49*(2), 277–291. https://doi.org/10.1080/10437797.2013.768477

Arsenault, Chris. (2021, June 29). *$1. 9 billion a year to address natural disasters in Canada among 4 takeaways from federal climate report*. CBC News. https://www.cbc.ca/news/science/canada-climate-change-insurance-infrastructure-lawsuits-1.6082920

BBC. (2021, October 13). *What is climate change?: A really simple guide video*. https://www.bbc.com/news/science-environment-24021772

Bell, L. (2020). *Exploring social work: An anthropological perspective*. Policy.

Berger, R. M., & Kelly, J. J. (1993). Social work in the ecological crisis. *Social Work, 38*(5), 521–526. https://doi.org/10.1093/sw/38.5.521

Besthorn, F. H. (1997). *Reconceptualizing social work's person-in-environment perspective: Explorations in radical environmental thought* [Doctoral dissertation]. University of Kansas. UMI Microform 981157.

Besthorn, F. H. (2014). Eco-psychology, meet eco-system work: What you might not know – A brief overview and reflective comment. *Egopsychology*, 6(4), 199–206. https://doi.org/10.1089/eco.2014.0024

Boetto, H., Moorhead, B., & Bell, K. (2014). Broadening the "environment" in social work: Impacts of a study abroad program. *Critical Social Work*, 15(1), 1–17. https://doi.org/10.22329/csw.v15i1.5902

Borenstein, S., & Larson, C. (2021, June 10). *UN: Climate and extinction crises must be tackled together.* CTV News. https://www.ctvnews.ca/climate -and-environment/un-climate-and-extinction-crises-must-be-tackled -together-1.5464975

Bozalek, V., & Pease, B. (2021). *Post-anthropocentric social work: Critical posthuman and new materialist perspectives.* Routledge.

Briskin, L. (1992). Socialist feminism. In M. Patricia Connelly and P. Armstrong (Eds.), *Feminism in action* (pp. 263–293). Canadian Scholars.

Brotman, S., & Pollack, S. (1997). The problem of merging postmodernism with feminist social work. *Canadian Social Work Review*, 14(1), 9–22.

Bywaters, P., McLeod, E., & Napier, L. (2009). *Social work and global health inequalities: Practice and policy developments.* Policy.

Carson, R. (1962). *Silent Spring.* Mariner Books.

CASW (Canadian Association of Social Workers). (1997). *Code of ethics.* https://www.casw-acts.ca/files/attachements/code_of_ethics_-_printable _poster.pdf

CASW. (2005). *Code of ethics.* https://www.casw-acts.ca/en/Code-of-Ethics %20and%20Scope%20of%20Practice

CASWE-ACFTS (Canadian Association of Social Work Education – Association canadienne pour la formation en travail social). (2021a). *Accreditation standards.* https://caswe-acfts.ca/wp-content/uploads/2021/04/EPAS -2021.pdf

CASWE-ACFTS. (2021b). *Briefing notes.* https://caswe-acfts.ca/wp-content /uploads/2021/04/Briefing-Note-5.pdf

Clark, S. G., Steen-Adams, M. M., Pfirman, S., & Wallace, R. L. (2011). Professional development of interdisciplinary environmental scholars. *Journal of Environmental Studies and Science*, 1(2), 99–113. https://doi.org/10.1007/s13412-011-0018-z

Coates, J. (2003). *Ecology and social work: Toward a new paradigm.* Fernwood.

Coates, J., & Gray, M. (2011). The environment and social work: An overview and introduction. *International Journal of Social Welfare*, 21(3), 230–238. https://doi.org/10.1111/j.1468-2397.2011.00851.x

Coates, J., Gray, M., & Hetherington, T. (2006). An "eco-spiritual" perspective: Finally a place for Indigenous approaches. *British Journal of Social Work*, 36(3), 381–399. https://doi.org/10.1093/bjsw/bcl005

Cockburn, H. (2019, June 5). "High likelihood of human civilisation ending" by 2050, report finds. *The Independent*. https://www.independent.co.uk

/climate-change/news/climate-change-global-warming-end-human
-civilisation-research-a8943531.html

Collins, P. H. (1991). *Black feminist thought*. Routledge.

Cuadra, C. B., & Eydal, G. B. (2018). Towards a curriculum in disaster risk reduction from a green social work perspective. In L. Dominelli (Ed.), *The Routledge Handbook of Green Social Work* (pp. 522–534). Routledge.

Cumby, T. (2013). *Climate change and social work: Our roles and barriers to action* [Unpublished master's thesis]. Trent University.

Dass-Brailsford, P. (2010). *Crisis and disaster counselling: Lessons learned from Hurricane Katrina and other disasters*. Sage.

Dominelli, L. (2011). Climate change: Social workers' roles and contributions to policy debates and interventions. *International Journal of Social Welfare, 20*, 430–438. https://doi.org/10.1111/j.1468-2397.2011.00795.x

Dominelli, L. (2012). *Green social work: From environmental crises to environmental justice*. Polity.

Dominelli, L. (2013). Environmental justice at the heart of social work practice: Greening the profession. *International Journal of Social Welfare, 22*, 431–439. https://doi.org/10.1111/ijsw.12024

Dominelli, L. (2014). Promoting environmental justice through green social work practice: A key challenge for practitioners and educators. *International Social Work, 57*(4), 338–345. https://doi.org/10.1177/0020872814524968

Dominelli, L. (2018). *The Routledge handbook of green social work*. Routledge. https://ebookcentral.proquest.com/lib/umontreal-ebooks/detail.action?docID=5331755

Earth Island. (2022). https://www.earthisland.org/index.php/david-brower

Ellis, L. M., Napan, K., and O'Donoghue, K. (2018). Greening social work education in Aotearoa/New Zealand. In L. Dominelli (Ed.), *The Routledge handbook of green social work* (pp. 535–546). Routledge.

Faruque, C. J., & Ahmmed, F. (2013). Development of social work education and practice in an era of international collaboration and cooperation. *Journal of International Social Issues, 2*(1), 61–70.

Fogel, S. J., Barkdull, C., & Weber, B. A. (2016). *Environmental justice: An issue for social work education and practice*. Routledge.

Freire, P. (1970). *Pedagogy of the oppressed*. Penguin.

Gamble, D., & Weil, M. (2010). *Community practice skills: Local to global perspectives*. Columbia University Press. Retrieved July 23, 2021, from http://www.jstor.org/stable/10.7312/gamb11002

Germain, C., & Gitterman, A. (1980). *The life model of social work practice*. Columbia University Press.

Gray, M., & Coates, J. (2011). The environment and social work: An overview and introduction. *International Journal of Social Welfare, 21*(3), 230–238. https://doi.org/10.1111/j.1468-2397.2011.00852.x

Gray, M., & Coates, J. (2012). Environmental ethics for social work: Social work's responsibility to the non-human world. *International Journal of Social Welfare, 21*, 239–247. https://doi.org/10.1111/j.1468-2397.2011.00852.x

Gray, M., Coates, J., & Hetherington, T. (2013). *Environmental social work.* Routledge.

Green, S. (2018). Aboriginal people and caring within a colonised society. In B. Pease, A. Vreugdenhil, & S. Stanford (Eds.), *Critical ethics of care in social work: Transforming the politics and practices of caring* (pp. 139–147). Routledge.

Green Party of Canada. (2019). *Mission possible.* https://www.greenparty.ca /sites/default/files/mission_possible_letter_en.pdf

Harbage, C., & Bloch, H. (2019, December 31). *The 2010s: A decade of protests around the world.* National Public Radio. https://www.npr.org/sections /pictureshow/2019/12/31/790256816/the-2010s-a-decade-of-protests -around-the-world

Healy, K. (2000). *Social work practices: Contemporary perspectives on change.* Sage.

Hetherington, T., & Boddy, J. (2013). Eco-social work with marginalized populations: Time for action on climate change. In M. Gray, J. Coates, & T. Hetherington (Eds.), *Environmental social work* (pp. 46–61). Routledge.

Hillock, S. (2011). *Conceptualizing oppression: Resistance narratives for social work* [Unpublished doctoral dissertation]. Memorial University of Newfoundland.

Hillock, S. (2017). *Trent University women's march on Washington* [Video]. Youtube. https://www.youtube.com/watch?v=zAEwSweYzl0&feature=youtu.be

Hillock, S. (2021). Teaching from the margins: No good deed goes unpunished. In R. Csiernik & S. Hillock (Eds.), *Teaching social work: Reflections on pedagogy and practice* (pp. 248–264). University of Toronto Press.

Hillock, S., Kimberley, D., Hardy Cox, D., & Csiernik, R. (2021). Revisiting the first hundred years of social work education in Canada: Now what? [Manuscript submitted for publication]. Department of Social Work, Trent University.

Hillock, S., & Mulé, N. J. (2016). *Queering social work education.* UBC Press.

Hoff, M., & McNutt, J. (Eds.), (1994). *The global environmental crisis. Implications for social welfare and social work.* Ashgate.

Hoff, M., & Pollack, R. (1993). Social dimensions of the environmental crisis: Challenges for social work. *Social Work, 38*(2), 204–211. https://doi.org /10.1093/sw/38.2.204

Holbrook, A. M., Akbar, G., & Eastwood, J. (2019). Meeting the challenge of human-induced climate change: Reshaping social work education. *Social Work Education, 38*(8), 955–967. https://doi.org/10.1080/02615479.2019 .1597040

hooks, b. (1989). *Talking back: Thinking feminist, thinking black.* South End.

hooks, b. (1991). Theory as liberatory practice. *Yale Journal of Law and Feminism, 4*(1), 1–12. https://heinonline.org/HOL/P?h=hein.journals/yjfem4&i=7

hooks, b. (1993). bell hooks speaking about Paulo Freire – The man and his work. In P. McLaren and P. Leonard (Eds.), *Paulo Freire: A critical encounter* (pp. 146–154). Routledge.

Intergovernmental Panel on Climate Change. (2018). *Global warming of 1.5 degrees.* https://www.ipcc.ch/sr15/

Isla, A. (2019). *Climate chaos: Ecofeminism and the land question.* Inanna/Education Inc.

Jagose, A. (1996). *Queer theory: An introduction.* New York University Press.

Jones, P. (2008). *Expanding the ecological consciousness of social work students: Education for sustainable practice.* Retrieved from http://ro.ecu.edu.au/cgi/viewcontent.cgi?article=1026&context=ceducom

Jones, P. (2018). Greening social work education: Transforming the curriculum in pursuit of eco–social justice. In L. Dominelli (Ed.), *Handbook of green social work* (pp. 558–568). Routledge.

Jung, C. B. (2016). *Social work students' attitudes toward the natural environment* [Master's thesis]. Arizona State University.

Kahn, R. (2003). Paulo Freire and eco-justice: Updating pedagogy of the oppressed for the age of ecological calamity. *Freire Online Journal.* https://www.academia.edu/167231/Paulo_Freire_and_Eco_Justice_Updating_Pedagogy_of_the_Oppressed_for_the_Age_of_Ecological_Calamity

Kemp, S. P., & Palinkas, L. A. (2015). Strengthening the social response to the human impacts of environmental change. *American Academy of Social Work and Social Welfare, 5,* 1–32.

Klein, N. (2014). *This changes everything.* Vintage Canada.

Klemmer, C. L., & McNamara, K. A. (2020). Deep ecology and ecofeminism: Social work to address global environmental crisis. *Journal of Women and Social Work, 35*(4), 503–515. https://doi.org/10.1177/0886109919894650

Krings, A., Victor, B. G., Mathias, J., and Perron, B. E. (2020). Environmental social work in the disciplinary literature, 1991–2015. *International Social Work, 63*(3), 275–290. https://doi.org/10.1177/0020872818788397

Levine, H. (1976). Feminist counselling: A look at new possibilities. In *Canadian Association of Social Workers: Au-delà de '76 and beyond* (pp. 12–15). CASW.

Linklater, R. (2014). *Decolonizing trauma work: Indigenous stories and strategies.* Fernwood.

Lysack, M. (2010). Environmental decline and climate change: Fostering social and environmental justice on a warming planet. In R. Furman and N. Negi (Eds.), *Transnational social work* (p. 52–75). Columbia University Press.

MacDowell, L. S. (2012). The environmental movement and public policy. In *An environmental history of Canada* (pp. 243–267). UBC Press.

Marketplace. (2021). *Tracking your plastic: Exposing recycling myths* [Video]. Youtube. https://www.youtube.com/watch?v=c8aVYb-a7Uw

McGrath, M. (2019, July 24). *Climate change: 12 years to save the planet? Make that 18 months.* BBC News. https://www.bbc.com/news/science-environment-48964736

Mellor, M. (1997). *Feminism & ecology.* New York University Press.

Molyneux, R. (2010). The practical realities of eco-social work: A review of the literature. *Critical Social Work, 11*(2), 61–69. https://doi.org/10.22329/csw.v11i2.5824

Montpelier, R. (2019, July 25). *The climate crisis: This is not something you can just like on Facebook.* Below 2°C. https://below2c.org/2019/07/the-climate-crisis-this-is-not-something-you-can-just-like-on-facebook/

Moreau, M. (1979). A structural approach to social work practice. *Canadian Journal of Social Work Education, 5*(1), 78–94.

Moth, R., & Morton, D. (2009). *Social work and climate change: A call to action.* Retrieved from https://socialworkfuture.org/social-work-and-climate-change-a-call-to-action-rich-moth-a-dan-morton/

Muldoon, A. (2006). Environmental efforts: The next challenge for social work. *Critical Social Work, 7*(2). https://doi.org/10.22329/csw.v7i2.5729

Mullaly, B. (2006). *The new structural social work: Ideology, theory, practice.* Oxford University Press.

Mullaly, R. (1993). *Structural social work ideology, theory, and practice.* Oxford University Press.

Mullaly, R. (1997). *Structural social work ideology, theory, and practice* (2nd ed.). Oxford University Press.

Murdock, E. (2021, April 29). *On telling the truth unflinchingly: Climate catastrophe and colonialism.* Atmos. https://atmos.earth/climate-crisis-colonization-environmental-justice/

Närhi, K, & Matthies, A.-L. (2018). The eco-social approach in social work as a framework for structural social work. *International Social Work, 61*(4), 490–502. https://doi.org/10.1177/0020872816644663

Negi, N. J., & Furman, R. (2010). *Transnational social work practice.* Columbia University Press.

Nesmith, A., & Smyth, N. (2015) Environmental justice and social work education: Social workers' professional perspectives. *Social Work Education, 34*(5), 484–501. https://doi.org/10.1080/02615479.2015.1063600

Nicholson, A. (2021). *Eco-social work in Australia.* PodBean. https://newworldviews.podbean.com/e/a-european-perspective-on-ecosocial-work-education-and-training/

Nipperess, S., and Boddy, J. (2018). Greening Australian social work practice and education. In L. Dominelli (Ed.), *The Routledge handbook of green social work* (pp. 547–557). Routledge.

Noble, C. (2021). Eco-feminism to feminist materialism: Implications for anthropocene feminist social work. In V. Bozalek & B. Pease (Eds.),

Post-anthropocentric social work: Critical posthuman and new materialist perspectives (pp. 95–107). Routledge.

Peeters, J. (2012). The place of social work in sustainable development: Towards eco-social practice. *International Journal of Social Welfare, 21*(3), 287–298. https://doi.org/10.1111/j.1468-2397.2011.00856.x

Pereira, J. (2020, September 25). In her new book Hope Matters, Elin Kelsey argues doom and gloom won't help us solve the climate crisis. *Globe and Mail.* https://www.theglobeandmail.com/arts/books/article-doom-and-gloom-wont-help-us-solve-the-climate-crisis-elin-kelsey/

Pincus, A., & Minahan, A. (1973). *Social work practice: Model and method.* Peacock.

Powers, M., Schmitz, C., & Beckwith Moritz, M. (2019). Preparing social workers for eco-social work practice and community building. *Journal of Community Practice, 27*(3–4), 446–459. https://doi.org/10.1080/10705422.2019.1657217

Rabson, M. (2019). *Canada violated international law by dumping garbage in the Philippines: Lawyers.* Global News. https://globalnews.ca/news/5179164/canada-philippines-garbage-law/).

Ramsay, S., & Boddy, J. (2017). Environmental social work: A concept analysis. *British Journal of Social Work, 47*(1), 68–86. https://doi.org/10.1093/bjsw/bcw078

Reinders, R. C. (1982). Toynbee Hall and the American settlement movement. *Social Service Review, 56*(1), 39–54. https://doi.org/10.1086/643979

Richmond, M. (1922). *What is social case work?* Arno.

Riley, Tess. (2017, July 10). Just one hundred companies responsible for 71% of global emissions, study says. *The Guardian.* https://www.theguardian.com/sustainable-business/2017/jul/10/100-fossil-fuel-companies-investors-responsible-71-global-emissions-cdp-study-climate-change

Schmitz, C. L., Matyók T., Sloan, L. M., & James, C. (2012). The relationship between social work and environmental sustainability: Implications for interdisciplinary practice. *International Journal of Social Welfare, 21*(3), 278–286. https://doi.org/10.1111/j.1468-2397.2011.00855.x

Semerjan, L., Zurayk, R., & El-Fadel, M. (2004). Interdisciplinary approach to environmental education. *Journal of Professional Issues in Engineering Education and Practice, 130*(3), 173–181. https://doi.org/10.1061/(ASCE)1052-3928(2004)130:3(173)

Sierra Club. (2020a, March 2). *How research on gender will help us craft climate justice policy.* https://www.sierraclub.org/articles/2020/03/how-research-gender-will-help-us-craft-climate-justice-policy

Sierra Club. (2020b, March 2). *Landmark report highlights critical need for gender-based climate policies in US.* https://www.sierraclub.org/press-releases/2020/03/landmark-report-highlights-critical-need-for-gender-based-climate-policies-us

Skwiot, R. (2008, Fall). *Green dream: Environmental justice is emerging from the shadows*. Social Impact. https://openscholarship.wustl.edu/cgi/viewcontent.cgi?article=1020&context=socialimpact

Soine, L. (1987). Expanding the environment in social work: The case for including environmental hazards content. *Journal of Social Work Education*, 23(2), 40–46. https://doi.org/10.1080/10437797.1987.10801460

Sugirtha, J. T., & Little Flower, F. X. L. (2015). Global warming, climate change and the need for green social work. *Indian Journal of Applied Research*, 5(12), 102–104.

Suzuki, D. (2020, March 5). *The woman who discovered global warming – in 1856!* David Suzuki Foundation. https://davidsuzuki.org/story/the-woman-who-discovered-global-warming-in-1856/

Teixeira, S., & Krings, A. (2015) Sustainable social work: An environmental justice framework for social work education. *Social Work Education*, 34(5), 513–527. https://doi.org/10.1080/02615479.2015.1063601

Thunberg, Greta. (2019a, January 25). "Our house is on fire": Greta Thunberg, 16, urges leaders to act on climate. *The Guardian*. https://www.theguardian.com/environment/2019/jan/25/our-house-is-on-fire-greta-thunberg16-urges-leaders-to-act-on-climate

Thunberg, Greta. (2019b, May 30). *Treat our climate crisis like our house is on fire – Because it is*. HuffPost. https://www.huffingtonpost.co.uk/entry/greta-thunberg-climate-change_uk_5ceea942e4b07666546f76d3

Tronto, J. C. (1993). *Moral boundaries: A political argument for an ethic of care*. Routledge.

Truth and Reconciliation Commission of Canada. (2015). *Calls to action*. https://www2.gov.bc.ca/assets/gov/british-columbians-our-governments/indigenous-people/aboriginal-peoples-documents/calls_to_action_english2.pdf

Ungar, M. (2002). A deeper, more social ecological social work practice. *Social Service Review*, 76(3), 480–497. https://doi.org/10.1086/341185

Vincent, S., & Focht, W. (2011). Interdisciplinary environmental education: Elements of field identity and curriculum design. *Journal of Environmental Studies and Science*, 1(1), 14–35.

Waldron, I. R. G. (2018). *There's something in the water: Environmental racism In Indigenous and Black communities*. Fernwood.

Wallace, V. (2018). *Red-green revolution: The politics and technology of eco-socialism*. Political Animal Press.

Wattie, C. (2009). Sorry! The decade's best public apology. *Globe and Mail*. https://www.theglobeandmail.com/news/national/sorry-the-decades-best-public-apology/article4296845/

Whitton, C. (1943). Report on Canadian social security. *Social Service Review*. 17(4), 500.

Wilkin, L., & Hillock, S. (2014). Enhancing MSW students' efficacy in working with trauma, violence, and oppression: An integrated feminist-trauma framework for social work education. *Feminist Teacher, 24*(3), 184–206. https://doi.org/10.5406/femteacher.24.3.0184

Williams, L., Fletcher, A., Hanson, C., Neapole, J., & Pollack, M. (2018). *Women and climate change impacts and action in Canada.* SSHRC-CURA.

Zapf, M. K. (2009). *Social work and the environment: Understanding people and place.* Canadian Scholars.

Zapf, M. K. (2010). Social work and the environment: Understanding people and place. *Critical Social Work, 11*(3), 30–46. https://doi.org/10.1080/0312407X.2010.500654

PART ONE

Centring Indigenous Approaches and Celebrating Multi/Inter-disciplinarity

SUSAN HILLOCK

Centring Indigenous Approaches

In weaving these interconnected themes across this book, I think there is no better way to start this volume than with centring Indigenous worldviews – particularly in terms of land, sense of place, treaty rights, traditional knowledges, and sovereignty, or as Zapf (2009) might put it, seeing people "in, with, and as" place (p. 39) – as a means of preparing people to transform their thinking about the environment. Accordingly, Chapter 1, "Indigenous Sovereignty Is Climate Action: Centring Indigenous Lands and Jurisdiction in Social Work Education towards Climate Justice," by Elizabeth Carlson-Manathara and Chris Hiller, explores the international clarion call that proclaims that "Indigenous sovereignty is climate action." Many scholars, climate activists, and land defenders, both Indigenous and settler, have joined this cry, asserting that Indigenous sovereignty – the enactment of Indigenous peoples' jurisdictions, authorities, and relations to their lands – is our best hope for survival.

And yet, the authors note that even as social work education begins to more seriously integrate content and analysis related to climate crises, Indigenous sovereignty as a priority continues to be overlooked. In this chapter, they examine this silence, analysing how settler-colonial assumptions and erasures play out in environmental social work in general and in social work education and climate action in particular. Centring the work of Indigenous scholars within social work, throughout Canada, and across a range of disciplines, the authors maintain that "green" social work must be anchored in education that explores what it means – for differently positioned Indigenous and non-Indigenous peoples – to resist settler colonialism and *live in* Indigenous sovereignty. They make the case that Indigenous sovereignty must be foregrounded, as it is essential to helping social work students understand, honour, and concretely support Indigenous peoples' struggles to protect and assert jurisdiction over their lands – for the ultimate good of the planet.

Celebrating Multi/Inter-disciplinarity

It is critical to continue the search for new and innovative ways to think about and critically analyse key environmental issues and debates, as is recognizing that a multi/inter-disciplinary approach is needed to tackle climate change (Besthorn, 2014; Närhi & Matthies, 2018; Semerjan et al., 2004). The next three chapters in this collection explore how social work and the helping professions can benefit from learning and working collectively with other academic disciplines and community activists (many of whom have already developed specific technological and pedagogical expertise in this area).

Thus, I am proud to present three chapters from my colleagues at Trent University, which the Green Metric World University Rankings has ranked among the top one hundred of the "most sustainable university campuses" (para. 1) and third in Canada (Trent University, 2020). This organization "measures participating universities' commitment in developing environmentally friendly infrastructure … based on performance across six categories: education and research, setting and infrastructure, energy and climate change, waste, water, and transportation" (para. 3). My colleagues come from the School of Environmental Sciences, Indigenous Environmental Studies and Sciences (IESS) Program, as well as the Faculty of Education, and have done a great deal of innovative work, particularly in terms of creating green content, centring Indigeneity, transforming curricula, and building leadership networks.

In Chapter 2, "Nature for Whom? Justice in Environmental Education," Stephen Hill, Stephanie Rutherford, and James Wilkes trace the history of the pedagogy of environmental science and studies, focusing on the recent turn to environmental justice and its potential relevance to social work education. They begin by examining environmental teaching in the 1970s and 1980s. The primary focus at that time was on finding and documenting evidence to substantiate that the environmental crisis was occurring. Later on, the 1990s saw great cooperation between various disciplines, for example, business and engineering, which provided fertile ground for interdisciplinary creativity and intervention. However, during this same era, material conditions of stratified inequality as well as intersectional awareness and analysis of the differential impacts of climate change were often ignored – and in some cases, reproduced in this work. It was not until the early 2000s, with the expansion of grass-roots environmental movements, that the ecological problems of marginalized people and communities were seriously considered. In terms of this chapter, this juncture – which involves foregrounding the intersections of racial, class, and gender justice – is suggested as a place where social work and environmental studies can work together to assist learners to better understand the roots of and potential solutions to environmental harm. The authors conclude by inviting social work educators to work collaboratively with environmental scientists, to develop the necessary tools to bring these insights into teaching.

In Chapter 3, Paul Elliott presents "The Challenges of Reorienting Pre-service Teacher Education for Sustainability," making the case that higher education has a pivotal role to play in helping society respond to the urgent need to transform for a sustainable future. Professional disciplines, such as social work and education, should prioritize preparing graduates to make an immediate contribution. While individual departments can make significant headway in this work, collaborative efforts across institutions can yield even greater dividends. This chapter documents the aims, efforts, and successes of a Canada-wide initiative to strengthen and develop the preparation of teacher candidates for careers likely to be dominated by sustainability issues. Specifically, he outlines a Trent university–led provincial and national initiative that resulted not only in significant curriculum change in education standards related to environmental content in schools and teacher-education programs, but also in the development of several other innovative educational projects/products that have the potential to serve as an environmental model for other disciplines in higher education, including social work and other helping professions.

In recognition of the value of learning from other academic disciplines and continuing the multi/inter-disciplinary theme of this book, Chapter 4, "An Invitation to the Learning Garden: Green Lessons from a School of Education," by Kelly Young and Karleen Pendleton Jiménez, outlines practical initiatives they have undertaken to foster environmental leadership in higher education in a rural university in Ontario. They began to introduce environmental perspectives in 2006 when the education faculty at Trent University as a group decided to change their mission statement to include eco-social justice perspectives, because including "eco" was an important signal that all are interconnected to each other and the Earth. Since that bold declaration, they continue to infuse sustainability content into the education curriculum by incorporating green teaching methods and mobilizing students and colleagues towards climate action/justice/leadership. Drawing on their knowledge and experience, they present concrete applications and recommendations about how to best teach about sustainability within higher education as well as suggesting options for social work educa-tion. They also draw from an interdisciplinary framework (i.e., envi-ronmental, social justice, and Indigenous education) to infuse environ-mental education across their higher education program in a way that engages pre-service teachers in innovative teaching methods, develops community partnerships, and fosters environmental leadership across all levels of curriculum (kindergarten to graduate level). Ultimately, they describe innovative programs they have developed, a mandatory environmental-Indigenous course they created, and how they infused other courses with an environmental focus.

REFERENCES

Besthorn, F. H. (2014). Eco psychology, meet ecosystem work: What you might not know – A brief overview and reflective comment. *Egopsychology*, *6*(4), 199–206. https://doi.org/10.1089/eco.2014.0024

Närhi, K., & Matthies, A-L. (2018). The ecosocial approach in social work as a framework for structural social work. *International Social Work*, *61*(4), 490–502. https://doi.org/10.1177/0020872816644663

Semerjan, L., Zurayk, R., & El-Fadel, M. (2004). Interdisciplinary approach to environmental education. *Journal of Professional Issues in Engineering Education and Practice*, *130*(3), 173–181.

Trent University. (2020, December 10). *Trent university ranked third most sustainable university in Canada*. https://www.trentu.ca/news/story/28743

Zapf, M. K. (2009). *Social work and the environment: Understanding people and place*. Canadian Scholars.

1 Indigenous Sovereignty Is Climate Action: Centring Indigenous Lands and Jurisdiction in Social Work Education Towards Climate Justice

ELIZABETH CARLSON-MANATHARA AND CHRIS HILLER

"Indigenous sovereignty is climate action" is a galvanizing cry that is chanted and inscribed on signs at round dances and protests unfolding across Turtle Island and around the globe. This anthem finds an echo in the words of a growing number of scholars, climate activists, and land defenders, Indigenous and settler. These voices collectively assert that Indigenous sovereignty – the enactment of Indigenous peoples' jurisdictions and relations to their lands – is humanity's best hope for ensuring the planet's survival.

As we write, Indigenous peoples everywhere are defending their lands and sovereignties, often being jailed and labelled as terrorists by the Canadian state as a result of peacefully reoccupying their lands. Wet'suwet'en land defenders have been resisting the invasion of their lands by Coastal GasLink's pipeline for years (Unist'ot'en Camp, 2017), while the corporation's efforts are being supported by the British Columbia government and courts, resulting in the arrest of land defenders and their allies (Martens, 2019; Zussman, 2020). Meanwhile, the Secwepemc-led Tiny House Warriors erect small houses along the proposed Trans Mountain pipeline route to reassert their authority and prevent the Trans Mountain pipeline from crossing Secwepemc Territory, where it threatens wildlife and sacred waters and does violence to communities (Tiny House Warriors, 2020). At the same time, since 2002 the Anishinaabeg of Grassy Narrows have continued their long-standing blockade against clear-cut logging on their territory (Aiken, 2020; Da Silva, 2010); in Minnesota, Indigenous land defenders are also blocking Line 3 of Enbridge's pipeline expansion that brings tar sands oil from Alberta to Wisconsin and risks oil spills that threaten water, wetlands, and Anishinaabe ancestral lands (Arvin, 2021).

In the face of these unfolding actions, Indigenous social work scholars and students are asking: Where is social work practice when Indigenous people are defending their lands? This question arose during a 3 March 2021 teach-in entitled "Lighting the Fire: Social Work and Indigenous Land and Water Sovereignty" (Allan et al., 2021) and supported by the Canadian Association for Social Work Education – Association canadienne pour la formation en travail social (CASWE-ACFTS). As settler (non-Indigenous) social work educators who seek to hold up this question in our own work and accountabilities, we were moved and inspired to see it taken up in such a powerful way in a social work education context. We valued what was shared during the teach-in about the roles of Indigenous peoples as caretakers of the land. We also took to heart in a renewed way the challenges offered to settler peoples, and specifically to social workers: to understand what it means to live within spaces of Indigenous sovereignty, to stand with land and water defenders, to centre Indigenous community relations in our practice, to support Treaty fulfillment, and to actively oppose colonizing power relations.

Despite the multitude of actions by Indigenous peoples in the past and present to defend their lands in the face of climate change, and despite the leadership of Indigenous social work scholars and students in highlighting the importance of social work's response to these struggles, Indigenous sovereignty as a concept continues to be confined to the margins of climate action conversations. In this chapter, we interrogate this sidelining effect, considering the ways in which settler colonial assumptions and erasures play out in environmental social work in general and in social work education about climate action in particular. Centring the work of Indigenous scholars within social work and across a range of disciplines, we argue that social work curricula aimed at responding to the climate emergency must be anchored in explorations of what it means – for differently positioned Indigenous and non-Indigenous peoples – to resist settler colonialism and *live in* Indigenous sovereignty. This education is essential for social work, as students and instructors alike need to understand, honour, and concretely support Indigenous peoples' struggles to protect and assert jurisdiction over their lands for the ultimate good of the planet – aims that do not fit easily with current environmental social work frameworks.

Tracing Settler Colonial Relations within Environmental Social Work Education

Among environmentally oriented social work practice frameworks, efforts to address the emerging climate crisis seem to align most often with environmental *justice* perspectives, which have been identified by national and international social work bodies as a critical focus for social work teaching and practice (CASWE, 2021; Council on Social Work Education, 2015; International Federation of Social Workers, 2020; Teixeira & Krings, 2015). These practice frameworks push social work as a discipline "to think through 'the connections between social work, sustainability, human rights, and social justice'" (Hawkins, as cited in Kemp, 2011, p. 1201). As Kemp powerfully notes: "This is not an academic issue. The human impacts of environmental challenges fall most heavily on those to whom social workers are most accountable. While social work drags its feet, its constituents face increasingly devastating environmental realities" (p. 1205). Within environmental justice frameworks, the climate crisis itself is understood in part as an exacerbation of existing social inequities born of globalized industrial capitalism (Tischler, 2011). Thus, environmental justice education in social work tends to foreground the differential human impact of climate change and teach strategies for bringing about a more equitable distribution of environmental benefits and hazards (Teixeira & Krings, 2015).

Moreover, advocates of environmental justice education in social work see social workers as already "primed to be strong partners in environmental movements" (Teixeira & Krings, 2015, p. 515), especially when the human right to a safe environment is at stake. Hearkening back to the Settlement House era, when community workers focused centrally on threats and injustices in the physical environment (Kemp, 2011, p. 1204), these theorists argue that social work "not only has the skills and tools to address environmental problems, but, as a discipline, our theories and perspectives make us uniquely qualified to work at the intersection of social and environmental justice" (Teixeira & Krings, 2015, pp. 515, 524). Social workers are also viewed as uniquely equipped to play central roles in addressing the climate crisis through raising public consciousness and mobilizing individual and community action (Dominelli, 2011; Holbrook et al., 2019; Kemp, 2011). What is needed, argue these theorists, is a fundamental paradigm shift in social work education: where social work students are encouraged to "perceive environmental justice as an issue within the profession's purview" (Teixeira & Krings, 2015, p. 524) and where they are taught to "use our existing skill sets and models of intervention to simultaneously address environmental degradation" (p. 517) through multilevel environmental interventions.

And yet this argument for using social work's current perspectives and approaches to address the climate crisis fails to recognize the settler colonial logics and assumptions within mainstream social work practice in general and environmental social work in particular. As we have summarized elsewhere (Hiller & Carlson, 2018), Indigenous scholars point out that social work as a discipline remains slow to interrogate its complicity in settler colonialism as an ongoing structure of dispossession. Social workers have reinforced this dispossession by surveilling and pathologizing Indigenous peoples and families (Clarke & Yellow Bird, 2021; Weaver, 2000), promoting agendas of assimilation by administering Indian welfare (Shewell, 2001, 2004), participating in the genocidal project of forcibly removing and transferring Indigenous children to residential schools (Blackstock, 2009; R. Sinclair, 2007), and orchestrating the Sixties Scoop (R. Sinclair, 2004). Ongoing practices of child welfare and Indigenous child removal in particular serve as a "necessary precursor to land and resource acquisition" (R. Sinclair, 2016, p. 9) on the part of the Canadian state (Baskin, 2011; Blackstock, 2007, 2009; R. Sinclair, 2007; Waterfall, 2006).

We have also argued elsewhere (Hiller & Carlson, 2018) that environmentally oriented forms of social work practice are not immune to settler colonial erasures. While eco-social work's aims of bringing about "mutually enriching and sustainable human/Earth relationships" (Coates, as cited in Kemp, 2011, p. 1202) seem to align well with Indigenous realities and struggles, for example, these frameworks generally "fail to make Indigenous presence and ongoing colonization, particularly in the Americas, foundational to their analysis" (Lawrence & Dua, 2005, p. 127); nor do they address Indigenous peoples' land defence struggles in any concerted way (Hiller & Carlson, 2018). Similarly, while eco-spiritual approaches embrace "the fundamental interdependence of living and physical systems, and the value of [I]ndigenous ecological knowledges" (Kemp, 2011, p. 1201), they generally fail to address the power relations that subordinate Indigenous identities, denigrate Indigenous cultures, and render Indigenous lands open to extraction, pillage, and devastating forms of development (Hiller & Carlson, 2018; Jeffery, 2014, 2015).

Environmental justice social work effects similar erasures through its tendency to lump Indigenous peoples together with other racialized or economically marginalized communities situated on lands that are "often the site of risky fossil fuel extraction and waste disposal" (Holbrook et al., 2019, p. 959). This conflation conceals the settler colonial logics and agenda behind this particular dispersal of environmental impacts; it also sidelines Indigenous rights and relations to land, not to mention questions of Treaties, histories of settlement and dispossession, and nation-to-nation relationships. Together, these moves lead educators to overlook the United Nations Declaration on the Rights of Indigenous Peoples (United Nations, 2007) as a critical orienting frame for global environmental justice social work (Teixeira & Krings, 2015).

When Indigenous peoples do receive specific mention in this scholarship – and even in Dominelli's (2012) *Green Social Work*, which includes
an explicit Indigenous rights framework and highlights case studies of
Indigenous land defence movements – Indigenous communities often
appear as romanticized *victims* of environmental injustice, and as the
primary *recipients* of environmental social work interventions aimed at
assisting them in "mitigating risk and building resilience in their communities" (Dominelli, 2011, p. 235; see Hiller & Carlson, 2018, p. 56). Particularly
in relation to the climate crisis, environmental justice scholarship tends
to exhort social work educators to teach students how to "recognize
strengths" of Indigenous communities, to "harness their potential for
action and empowerment," and to mobilize campaigns to shift political
and economic conditions that "may not be easily addressed by fragmented,
politically disenfranchised communities" (Teixeira & Krings, 2015,
pp. 517, 521). Ironically, social work's preoccupation with advocating
technological solutions to climate change based on Western science at
times devolves into practice aimed at assisting Indigenous peoples in
finding alternatives to their *own* unsustainable practices rather than
standing with Indigenous peoples in tackling the central drivers of climate change itself (Dominelli, 2011, p. 435).

Indeed, as we have argued elsewhere (Hiller & Carlson, 2018),
absent from mainstream theories of environmental social work is
"critical and sustained attention to two foundational realities: the
pervasive imperative of settler colonialism to clear, claim, settle, and
assert jurisdiction, control, and sovereignty over Indigenous lands,
and Indigenous peoples' enduring and multifaceted resistance to that
imperative" (p. 60). Further, little attention is paid to questions of
Indigenous sovereignty and leadership, and what these might mean
for environmental justice practice at every level, but especially for
warding off a climate apocalypse. But what is the impact of these
erasures within environmental social work, especially given the escalating climate crisis? Before we can address this question, we must
take a moment to explore Indigenous conceptions of sovereignty and
relations to land.

Disrupting Settler Colonialism and Holding Up Indigenous Sovereignty and Resistance as Keys to Responding to the Climate Crisis

Over millennia, Indigenous peoples have continued to maintain and
assert their sovereignties – their relationships with and inherent jurisdiction upon their lands. Rather than being based on concepts of state

power and dominion that are undergirded by European cultural values (Alfred, 2005), Indigenous conceptions of sovereignty emphasize their source in the Creator and in relationships with lands (Chiefs of Ontario, n.d.; L. B. Simpson, 2015). Leanne Betasamosake Simpson (2015), a Mishig Nishnaabeg scholar, understands from her Nishnaabeg Elders that the core of Indigenous sovereignty is "relationships with each other and with plant and animal nations, with our lands and waters and with the spiritual world" (p. 18). Haudenosaunee scholar Patricia Monture-Angus (1999) sees sovereignty as a right to live out one's responsibilities in relationship with a territory. In other words, "Indigenous scholars, leaders, and Knowledge Keepers speak of sovereignty as living the powerful, complex, practiced, and sustaining relationships with specific lands that nurture them physically, relationally, culturally, spiritually, and as distinct peoples" (Hiller & Carlson, 2018, p. 50). This close and sacred connection is based on the love Indigenous peoples feel from the Earth as a mother, revealed in "the food, the medicines ... and most importantly, in the teachings, natural laws, and connection she brings us" (Nii Gaani Aki Inini, 2016, para. 12). Cajete (1994) emphasizes that Indigenous identities derive from enduring relationships with the natural community of particular lands, rather than of land in the abstract, with Indigenous peoples finding life and education in their distinctive contexts: "the desert, a mountain valley, or along a seashore" (p. 113). These relationships are reflected in Indigenous laws, and from them flow rights and responsibilities, constituting identities, ontologies, and sovereignties (Poelina, 2020, as cited in Ross, Bennett, & Menyweather, 2021; Chiefs of Ontario, n.d.).

Many Canadians who have been taught to believe in the assumed sovereignty of the Crown and Canadian state may wonder which of the lands occupied by Canada are sovereign Indigenous lands. The Crown's claim to sovereignty in Canada is supported by the doctrine of discovery, which has as its foundation a series of papal bulls from the 1400s that have "been used for centuries to expropriate indigenous lands and facilitate their transfer to colonizing or dominating nations" (United Nations, 2012, para. 1). These papal bulls urge colonizers to "discover" and claim any lands that are not inhabited by Christians, becoming the basis of European claims to lands in the Americas (Manuel & Derrickson, 2015, p. 108). However, this narrative of assumed Canadian sovereignty has been disputed successfully in Canadian courts. For example, Manuel and Derrickson (2015) state that the *Delgamuukw* decision of 1997 confirmed Aboriginal title as a "collective right to the land ... that could not be extinguished without our consent" (p. 116). Importantly, after concerted petitions by Indigenous peoples over many years, Pope

Francis officially repudiated the doctrine of discovery in March 2023 (Chappell, 2023). It remains to be seen what impact this repudiation will have, if any, on Canadian law when the mindset of Canadian sovereignty so permeates Canadian society and structures.

On Treaty lands, the written Crown versions of Treaties are another source of confusion for many settlers. These documents would have us believe that Indigenous nations ceded Treaty lands to the Crown for settlement, with the exception of small reserves. Indigenous Treaty perspectives offer a contrasting view: "The land was to be shared with the newcomers but that did not mean a loss of ownership" (Office of the Treaty Commissioner, 2007, p. 18; see also Alook et al., 2023). The leadership of the Robinson Huron Treaty of 1850 First Nations write, "At minimum, we clearly stated and had written into our Treaty that we shall always have reserved jurisdictions over our full territory" (Robinson Huron Waawiindaa-maagewin, 2020, para. 15). If we refuse to legitimate the colonizing doctrine of discovery, and if we believe Indigenous Treaty perspectives, then we must maintain literally that all lands occupied by the Canadian state are indeed Indigenous lands and spaces of Indigenous sovereignty. This reality has profound implications for how settlers live with and care for these lands (Carlson-Manathara with Rowe, 2021).

Settler Colonialism as a Structure of Erasure and
Environmental Destruction

While the doctrine of discovery may have launched Europe into its colonization of the Americas, this initial process of land dispossession was only the beginning of settler colonialism in Canada, which continues to sustain itself as a structure "by making Indigenous land into property" (Tuck et al., 2014, p. 7); this process happens through a web of legal and bureaucratic mechanisms, backed by police and military force, that actively target Indigenous relationships with land (Coulthard & Simpson, 2016; Hiller & Carlson, 2018; LaRocque, 2010; Manuel & Derrickson, 2015; L. B. Simpson, 2013; Tuck et al., 2014; Whyte, 2019). L. B. Simpson (2013) describes this cumulative process of dispossession:

> Over the past two hundred years, without our permission and without our consent, we have been systematically removed and dispossessed from most of our territory. We have watched as our homeland has been cleared, subdivided, and sold to settlers from Toronto. We have watched our

waterfronts disappear behind monster cottages ... our most sacred places have been made into provincial parks for tourists, with concrete buildings over our teaching rocks. (p. 51)

Kānaka Maoli scholar Michael Spencer and his colleagues (2020) explicitly link settler colonialism to extractive capitalist systems that commodify land, including plants, animals, and other elements of the natural world, "allowing for their removal for the profit and benefit of settler colonial powers while simultaneously and intentionally depriving Indigenous bodies access to safe and healthy environments" (p. 8). Further, "environmental damage to the land/animals (through resource extraction, animal extinction, land clearance, and pollution) [is inherently] intertwined with socio-cultural genocide of the Indigenous peoples of the land" (Korteweg & Oakley, as cited in Tuck et al., 2014, p. 6). Such processes sever relationships "between humans and the soil, between plants and animals, between minerals and our bones" (Davis & Todd, 2017, p. 770).

Despite decades of wilful denial, in 2022 the UN's Intergovernmental Panel on Climate Change (IPCC) finally acknowledged the historical and ongoing roles of colonialism in climate change (IPCC, 2022). At the same time, habits of settler denial and erasure continue to plague much scholarship and activism around the climate crisis and associated environmental movements, obscuring the significant role of settler colonialism in weaving the web of environmental destruction (Davis & Todd, 2017; Whyte, 2018a). Similarly, Canadian social workers and social work educators are beginning to recognize the dynamics, processes, and structures of settler colonialism, and yet struggle to link this analysis to the environmental sphere (Bell et al., 2019; Hiller & Carlson, 2018). To challenge this erasure, Indigenous Knowledge Keepers and environmental scholars argue that colonialism and colonial land relations should be understood as central initiators and drivers of the current climate crisis (Alook et al., 2023; Cameron et al., 2021; Davis & Todd, 2017; Whyte, 2019; Yanchapaxi et al., 2022). This insight leads Bell et al. (2019) to conclude: global environmental climate changes cannot adequately be addressed "without simultaneously dismantling one of the foundations on which they were built: colonialism" (p. 284); thus, climate justice efforts must be explicitly anti-colonial (Whyte, 2019).

Indigenous Sovereignty as Core to Addressing the Climate Crisis

Indigenous sovereignty is a corrective to both the climate crisis and to settler colonialism, in which the crisis is rooted (Alook et al., 2023;

Davis & Todd, 2017). Further, settler environmental activist Naomi Klein (2015) indicates that "a great many Canadians are discovering that First Nations land rights and title – if robustly defended – represent the most powerful barrier" (p. xi) to environmental destruction and extractivism. Indeed, while governments enable rapacious developers to wreak havoc on the earth and its inhabitants, "Indigenous movements and their allies are asserting their rights and sovereignties to protect land, water, and people for future generations" (Noisecat, 2017, paras. 3, 4). Indigenous Treaty and land rights, which are recognized by decisions of the Supreme Court of Canada and by the United Nations through its Declaration on the Rights of Indigenous Peoples, along with Indigenous-led social movements, put pressure on the Canadian government to respect Indigenous lands and sovereignty. We saw this writ large in the intensification of solidarity after the arrest of Wet'suwet'en land defenders in early 2020. In fact, Cree environmental activist Thomas-Muller (2014) contended that "there had not been a major environmental victory won in Canada in the last thirty years without First Nations at the helm asserting their Aboriginal rights and title" (p. 249). He recounts that the Aboriginal and Treaty rights enshrined in Section 35 of the Canadian Constitution have "been validated by more than 170 Supreme Court victories" (p. 251), as well as by the Treaties. Even seasoned non-Indigenous climate change activists are seeing the ineffectiveness of working within the current corporate oligarchy for change, and are advocating for a dual climate justice and Indigenous rights focus and for organizing through Indigenous-led movements (Coats, 2014) that centre decolonization and challenge the "legitimacy of the nation-state structure itself" (Davis & Todd, 2017, p. 774).

Along with being effective political strategies for addressing climate change, decolonization and Indigenous sovereignty centre Indigenous knowledges that have the potential to shift settler values, thoughts, and ways of being – away from those based on extractivism and greed towards those based on life and relationship (Cameron et al., 2021; Carlson-Manathara with Rowe, 2021; L. B. Simpson, as cited in Klein, 2013). Respecting Indigenous self-governance, Indigenous law, and Indigenous sovereignty positions settlers to "reimagine not only human relationships, but also what it means to be human" (Sâkihitowin Awâsis, 2014, p. 260); it entails learning to live in a reciprocal kin relationship of care with human and non-human communities that include the land, water, and animals (Davis & Todd, 2017; Sâkihitowin Awâsis, 2014; M. Sinclair, 2020).

Centring Indigenous Sovereignty and Settler Colonialism within Environmental Social Work Education: Insights from Indigenous Social Work Educators

But what does this mean for our efforts to address climate change in the classroom? Once again, Indigenous social work educators are leading the way. They are joining with Indigenous scholars across disciplines in putting forward specifically Indigenous conceptions of environmental justice – ones that target imperialism, extractive capitalism, and settler colonialism as the main drivers of environmental injustice and degradation (Alook et al., 2023; McGregor et al., 2020; Spencer et al., 2020; Whyte, 2018b). These educators also seek to disrupt the ways in which mainstream practices of environmental education reinforce a settler land ethic and "justify settler occupation of stolen land, or encourage the replacement of Indigenous peoples and relations to land with settlers and relations of property" (Tuck et al., 2014, p. 8). Anishinaabe-kwe social work scholar Kathy Absolon (2019), for example, describes colonizing assumptions and educational practices that justify and support extractive processes as "disconnecting all peoples from their sense of responsibility to the land, water, and sources of life" (p. 24); thus, decolonizing in social work practice and education "ignites a connection between social work, environmental racism, land dispossession, and oppressive social policies" (p. 25).

Indigenous social work educators and their allies also argue that the narrative of the climate crisis that social work students need to be taught is one that takes settler colonialism seriously as a fundamental cause: "The forced climate change of colonization is the foundation on which both the US and Canadian industrial societies were built, to the benefit of their settlers and settler descendants, and to the detriment of the planet" (Bell et al., 2019, p. 284). They point out that "many of the worst expected outcomes of a changing climate – species extinction, forced migration, hunger, disease, lack of clean water, rapidly shifting environmental changes – are all conditions that European invaders, settlers, and their descendants forced upon North American people and continue to do so" (p. 283). What is more, Billiot et al. (2019) see climate change as *furthering* the settler colonial agenda of erasure, by subjecting Indigenous peoples to environmental toxins and other devastating changes brought on by unlimited resource extraction (p. 300).

Indigenous social work educators also challenge mainstream environmental social work frameworks that refer to the "physical environment" in abstract and reductive ways; instead, they envision human relationships with the natural world in which "each partner in this relationship is living and has inherent value" (Spencer et al., 2020, p. 14) and thus "the elements of the Earth are entities of value, not objects" (p. 16). Rather than focusing solely on the human dimensions of environmental justice, Indigenous social work educators also draw on Indigenous knowledges to expand the circle of justice to include "justice for species outside of our own and for the Earth itself" (p. 14); they uphold human thriving while also respecting and investing in the interdependent relationships of life.

While seeming to align here with eco-social and eco-spiritual social work perspectives, Indigenous social work educators and their allies also refuse to depoliticize these knowledges or to distance them from their settler colonial context (Bell et al., 2019; Hiller & Carlson, 2018); instead, they describe traditional environmental knowledge as that which Indigenous communities glean from being rooted over millennia in reciprocal relationships with the land and beings of a particular place, but also from surviving the onslaught of settler colonial violence, specifically aimed at *stamping out* those very relationships (Bell et al., 2019). For example, Shanondora Billiot and her colleagues (2019) interweave Indigenous knowledges within pedagogies that "engage students in critical place-based learning about the inextricably linked experiences of colonial violence, settler occupation, and environmental injustice" (p. 307). Echoing Tuck et al. (2014), they call for narrative and experiential pedagogies that "restory" the "history of the land as Indigenous" (p. 3), and that highlight Indigenous epistemologies as well as the ongoing lived realities of real Indigenous peoples. "Environmental justice," in the view of these educators, "can only take place with Indigenous peoples and epistemologies at the center" (p. 17). As well, Indigenous social work educators model how to work with and learn from local Indigenous communities in creating environmental justice programs that centre Indigenous knowledge and that "highlight how this way of knowing cultivates a path to revitalization and community resilience" (Spencer et al., 2020, p. 4). Again, while community resilience is a prime focus of other environmental social work frameworks, particularly in relation to the climate crisis (Dominelli, 2011; Holbrook et al., 2019; Kemp & Palinkas, 2015), Indigenous scholars and their allies disrupt the concept's preoccupation with "adaptation to environmental change" (see also Tierney, 2015) by keeping Indigenous survivance and resistance to settler colonialism at its core. As Billiot and her colleagues (2019) note, involving social work students in these engagements with Indigenous communities "empowers Indigenous students to decolonize and heal from legacies of western educational and colonial processes related to land exploitation"; it also "allows non-Indigenous students to learn about the damage of these legacies and assists them in identifying ways to disrupt ongoing land occupation and exploitation" (p. 304).

Finally, Dennis and Bell (2020) call on non-Indigenous social workers to recognize and hold up the incredible environmental leadership of Indigenous peoples and of Indigenous women in particular. Indigenous women are often at the forefront of land defence movements; like the Nishnaabeg Water Walkers, these women "have taken on the responsibility of protecting the Earth's resources as a sacred duty for millennia" (p. 1; see also L. B. Simpson, 2017), often putting their bodies on the line during environmental crises and risking criminalization (Dennis & Bell, 2020; McGregor, 2013). Dennis and Bell call for environmental justice social work to include both individual and institutional forms of support for these critical land defenders.

Centring the Leadership and Resistance of Indigenous Peoples in Social Work Education for Climate Action

In 2017, Indigenous Knowledge Keepers from around the globe met with environmental leaders at the Turtle Lodge of Sagkeeng First Nation in ceremony and dialogue for the Onjisay Aki International Climate Summit (Cameron et al., 2021; Turtle Lodge, 2021). The Knowledge Keepers conveyed the importance of addressing colonialism and its associated values and behaviours if climate change is to be addressed, and of "decolonization as a multifaceted climate solution" (Cameron et al., 2021, p. 42). The calls to action that arose from this gathering emphasized the importance of: education based in the traditional and ancestral knowledge of Indigenous Elders and Knowledge Keepers; Indigenous sovereignty as a means of ensuring environmental stewardship; relationships with the Earth, Indigenous communities, and with one another; and the Indigenous-led transformation of humans and the planet (Turtle Lodge, 2021).

Where is social work in this? Questions raised by Allan et al. (2021) during the Lighting the Fire teach-in are emblematic of the gulf between social work and the priorities of many Indigenous peoples and communities. This gulf is taken up compellingly by Yellow Bird and Gray (2008), who assert that rather than the types of social workers typically graduated by mainstream accredited social work programs, Indigenous communities are seeking "highly motivated social workers to serve their communities' drive for self-determination, empowerment, and complete return of their lands and other resources illegally stolen by colonial societies" (p. 59). These communities also seek social workers who possess a "complete belief in the sovereignty of Indigenous Peoples and an ability to successfully assert it on their behalf" (p. 60). An anti-colonial social work practice that resists colonialism, supports Indigenous resurgence, and regenerates relationships to land, then, is what is needed (Bell et al., 2019; Corntassel, 2012; Dennis & Bell, 2020; Hart et al., 2017). The *2021 Educational Policies and Accreditation Standards for Canadian Social Work Education* (CASWE, 2021) supports this approach with core learning objectives, including "Colonialism and Social Work," "Indigenous Peoples and Communities," and "Environmental Sustainability and Ecological Practice."

To interrupt settler colonial practices while also centring Indigenous sovereignty, environmental justice education within social work must root out social work discourses and practices that serve to justify settler occupation of stolen land (Tuck et al., 2014). This pedagogy must also challenge settler colonial assumptions about who sets the terms, frameworks, and agenda of environmental practice (La Paperson, 2014; L. R. Simpson, 2004; Smith & Sterritt, 2010; Weaver, 2000), working instead to consistently "uphold the incredible Indigenous survivance and profound leadership of Indigenous peoples in the face of centuries of encroachment and environmental devastation" (Hiller & Carlson, 2018, p. 62). For students and educators alike, this form of environmental education requires a willingness to learn from, engage with, and beholden ourselves to the calls from Indigenous scholars and Knowledge Keepers. It entails living in accordance with the laws of the peoples on whose lands we abide (Borrows, 2005; Johnson, 2007; Poelina, 2020); it also involves recognizing Treaty relationships as entailing a responsibility to learn how to live in these territories, including how to know, care for, and relate to their waters, lands, and animals (Johnson, 2007, p. 21). In the end, perhaps the most powerful and effective practices that environmentally minded social workers, social work educators, and social work students can employ in addressing climate change are those that support Indigenous land rights, Treaty rights, and sovereignty, as well as Indigenous-led movements. As Indigenous Climate Action (2021) powerfully asserts, "colonialism caused climate change. Indigenous rights are the solution" (p. 5).

Acknowledgment

Some arguments in this article are condensed from the following publication and are used with permission: Hiller, C., & Carlson, E. (2018), These are Indigenous lands: Foregrounding settler colonialism and Indigenous sovereignty as primary contexts for Canadian environmental social work, *Canadian Social Work Review, 35*(1), 45–70.

REFERENCES

Absolon, K. (2019). Decolonizing education and educators' decolonizing. *Intersectionalities: A Global Journal of Social Work Analysis, Research, Polity, and Practice, 7*(1), 9–28.

Aiken, M. (2020, August 22). *Grassy members remain vigilant about logging.* Treefrog. https://treefrogcreative.ca/grassy-members-remain-vigilant-about-logging-2/

Alfred, T. (2005). Sovereignty. In J. Barker (Ed.), *Sovereignty matters: Locations of contestation and possibility in Indigenous struggles for self-determination* (pp. 33–50). University of Nebraska Press.

Allan, B. Z., Gabriel, W., Martin, C., Batak, M., & Thibodeau, A. (2021, March 3). Lighting the fire: Social work and Indigenous land and water sovereignty. Canadian Association for Social Work Education [unrecorded virtual presentation].

Alook, A., Eaton, E., Gray-Donald, D., Laforest, J., Lameman, C., & Tucker, B. (2023). *The end of this world: Climate justice in so-called Canada.* Between the Lines.

Arvin, J. (2021, March 25). *The Indigenous-led fight to stop the Line 3 oil pipeline expansion in Minnesota, explained.* Vox. https://www.vox.com/22333724/oil-pipeline-expansion-protest-minnesota-biden-climate-change

Baskin, C. (2011). *Strong helpers' teachings: The value of Indigenous knowledges in the helping professors.* Canadian Scholars.

Bell, F. M., Dennis, M. K., & Krings, A. (2019). Collective survival strategies and anti-colonial practice in ecosocial work. *Journal of Community Practice, 27*(3–4), 279–295. https://doi.org/10.1080/10705422.2019.1652947

Billiot, S., Beltran, R., Brown, D., Mitchell, F. M., & Fernandez, A. (2019). Indigenous perspectives for strengthening social responses to global environmental changes: A response to the social work grand challenge on environmental change. *Journal of Community Practice, 27*(3–4), 296–316. https://doi.org/10.1080/10705422.2019.1658677

Blackstock, C. (2007). Residential schools: Did they really close or just morph into child welfare? *Indigenous Law Journal, 6*(1), 71–78.

Blackstock, C. (2009). The occasional evil of angels: Learning from the experiences of Aboriginal people in social work. *First People's Child and Family Review, 4*(1), 28–37. https://doi.org/10.7202/1071292ar

Borrows, L. (2005). Indigenous legal traditions in Canada. *Washington University Journal of Law & Policy, 19,* 167–223. https://openscholarship.wustl.edu/law_journal_law_policy/vol19/iss1/13/

Cajete, G. (1994). *Look to the mountains: An ecology of Indigenous education.* Kivaki.

Cameron, L., Courchene, D., Ijaz, S., & Mauro, I. (2021). "A change of heart": Indigenous perspectives from the Onjisay Aki Summit on climate change. *Climate Change, 164*(43) 1–21. https://doi.org/10.1007/s10584-021-03000-8

Canadian Association for Social Work Education (CASWE). (2021). *Educational policies and accreditation standards for Canadian social work education.* https://caswe-acfts.ca/wp-content/uploads/2021/04/EPAS-2021.pdf

Carlson-Manathara, E., with Rowe, G. (2021). *Living in Indigenous sovereignty.* Fernwood.

Chappell, B. (2023, March 30). The Vatican repudiates "Doctrine of Discovery," which was used to justify colonialism. National Public Radio (NPR). https://www.npr.org/2023/03/30/1167056438/vatican-doctrine-of-discovery-colonialism-indigenous

Chiefs of Ontario. (n.d.). *Understanding First Nation sovereignty.* http://chiefs-of-ontario.org/faq

Clarke, K., & Yellow Bird, M. (2021). *Decolonizing pathways towards integrative healing in social work.* Routledge.

Coats, E. (2014). What does it mean to be a movement? A proposal for a coherent, powerful, Indigenous-led movement. In T. Black, S. D'Arcy, T. Weiss, & J. K. Russell (Eds.), *A line in the tar sands: Struggles for environmental justice* (pp. 267–278). Between the Lines.

Corntassel, J. (2012). Re-envisioning resurgence: Indigenous pathways to decolonization and sustainable self-determination. *Decolonization: Indigeneity, Education & Society, 1*(1), 81–101.

Coulthard, G., & Simpson, L. B. (2016). Grounded normativity/Place-based solidarity. *American Quarterly, 68*(2), 249–255. https://doi.org/10.1353/aq.2016.0038

Council on Social Work Education. (2015). *Educational policy and accreditation standards.* https://www.cswe.org/getattachment/Accreditation/Standards-and-Policies/2015-EPAS/2015EPASandGlossary.pdf.aspx

Da Silva, J. (2010). Grassy Narrows: Advocate for Mother Earth and its inhabitants. In L. Davis (Ed.), *Alliances: Re/Envisioning Indigenous–non-Indigenous relationships* (pp. 69–76). University of Toronto Press.

Davis, H., & Todd, Z. (2017). On the importance of a date, or decolonizing the Anthropocene. *ACME: An International Journal for Critical Geographies, 16*(4), 761–780. https://www.acme-journal.org/index.php/acme/article/view/1539

Dennis, M. K., & Bell, F. L. (2020). Indigenous women, water protectors, and reciprocal responsibility. *Social Work, 65*(4), 378–386. https://doi.org/10.1093/sw/swaa033

Dominelli, L. (2011). Climate change: Social workers' roles and contributions to policy debates and interventions. *International Journal of Social Welfare, 20*(4), 430–438. https://doi.org/10.1111/j.1468-2397.2011.00795.x

Dominelli, L. (2012). Green social work: From environmental crises to environmental justice. *British Journal of Social Work, 42*(8), 1636–1637. http://doi.org/10.1093/bjsw/bcs183

Hart, M. A., Straka, S., & Rowe, G. (2017). Working across contexts: Practice considerations of doing Indigenist/anti-colonial research. *Qualitative Inquiry, 23*(5), 332–342. https://doi.org/10.1177/1077800416659084

Hiller, C., & Carlson, E. (2018). These are Indigenous lands: Foregrounding settler colonialism and Indigenous sovereignty as primary contexts for Canadian environmental social work. *Canadian Social Work Review, 35*(1), 45–70. https://doi.org/10.7202/1051102ar

Holbrook, A. M., Akbar, G., & Eastwood, J. (2019). Meeting the challenge of human-induced climate change: Reshaping social work education. *Social Work Education, 38*(8), 955–967. https://doi.org/10.1080/02615479.2019.1597040

Indigenous Climate Action. (2021, March). *Decolonizing climate policy in Canada: Report from phase one.* Indigenous Climate Action.

Intergovernmental Panel on Climate Change (IPCC). (2022). *Climate Change 2022: Impacts, adaptation, and vulnerability.* Contribution of Working Group II to Sixth Assessment Report of the IPCC. Cambridge University Press.

International Federation of Social Workers. (2020, August). *Global standards for social work education and training.* https://www.ifsw.org/global-standards-for-social-work-education-and-training/#4corecurricula

Jeffery, D. (2014). Environmentalism in social work: What shall we teach? *Journal of Women and Social Work, 29*(4), 492–498. https://doi.org/10.1177/0886109914533697

Jeffery, D. (2015). Green encounters and Indigenous subjectivity: A cautionary tale. In J. Caitlin, D. Jeffrey, & K. Smith (Eds.), *Unravelling encounters: Ethics, knowledge and resistance under neoliberalism* (pp. 71–93). Wilfrid Laurier Press.

Johnson, H. (2007). *Two families: Treaties and government.* Purish.

Kemp, S. P. (2011). Recentring environment in social work practice: Necessity, opportunity, challenge. *British Journal of Social Work, 41*(6), 1198–1210. https://doi.org/10.1093/bjsw/bcr119

Kemp, S. P., & Palinkas, L. A. (2015). *Strengthening the social response to the human impacts of environmental change.* American Academy of Social Work and Social Welfare. https://grandchallengesforsocialwork.org/wp-content/uploads/2015/12/WP5-with-cover.pdf

Klein, N. (2015). Foreword. In A. Manuel & R. Derrickson, *Unsettling Canada: A national wake-up call.* Between the Lines.

La Paperson. (2014). A ghetto land pedagogy: An antidote for settler environmentalism. *Environmental Education Research, 20*(1), 115–130. http://doi.org/10.1080/13504622.2013.865115

LaRocque, E. (2010). *When the other is me: Native resistance discourse, 1850–1990.* University of Manitoba Press.

Lawrence, B., & Dua, E. (2005). Decolonizing antiracism. *Social Justice, 3*(4), 120–143. http://web.ebscohost.com.libproxy.wlu.ca/ehost/pdfviewer/pdfviewer?sid=462aa2b8-a6a1-4ddd-94c4-a2db58ed84a2%40sessionmgr11&vid=4&hid=21

Manuel, A., & Derrickson, R. M. (2015). *Unsettling Canada: A national wake-up call*. Between the Lines.

Martens, K. (2019, January 8). *14 arrested as RCMP enforce injunction on Wet'suwet'en territory*. APTN. https://www.aptnnews.ca/national-news/14-arrested-as-rcmp-enforce-injunction-on-wetsuweten-territory/

McGregor, D., Whitaker, S., and Sritharan, M. (2020). Indigenous environmental justice and sustainability. *Current Opinion in Environmental Sustainability*, *43*, 35–40. https://doi.org/10.1016/j.cosust.2020.01.007

McGregor, S. (2013). Indigenous women, water justice and zaagidowin (love). *Canadian Woman Studies*, *31*(2–3), 71–78.

Monture-Angus, P. (1999). *Journeying forward: Dreaming First Nations' independence*. Fernwood.

Nii Gaani Aki Inini. (2016, August 2). *Making an alliance with the earth* [Keynote presentation]. Communication & Culture in a Sustainable World Conference, Winnipeg, Manitoba. http://www.turtlelodge.org/2016/08/nii-gaani-aki-inini-keynote-making-an-alliance-with-the-earth-august-2-2016-at-communication-culture-in-a-sustainable-world-conference-2016/

Noisecat, J. B. (2017, January 19). In the fight for climate justice, Indigenous people set the path – and lead the way. *The Guardian*. https://www.theguardian.com/commentisfree/2017/jan/19/fight-climate-justice-indigenous-people-lead-the-way

Office of the Treaty Commissioner. (2007). *Treaty implementation: Fulfilling the covenant* [Report]. http://www.otc.ca/public/uploads/resource_photo/55757_TreatyWeb.pdf

Poelina, A. (2020). Foreword. In D. Ross, M. Brueckner, M. Palmer, & W. Eaglehawk (Eds.), *Eco-activism and social work: New directions in leadership and group work* (pp. iix–xii). Routledge.

Robinson Huron Waawiindaamaagewin. (2020, September 9). *The Anishinaabek of the 1850 Robinson Huron Treaty Waawiindaamaagewin Declaration*. http://rhw1850Treaty.com/wp-content/uploads/2020/09/RHTC-DECLARATION-FINAL-VERSION-1.pdf

Ross, D., Bennett, B., & Menyweather, N. (2021). Towards a critical post-humanist social work: Trans-species ethics of ecological justice, nonviolence and love. In V. Bolazek & B. Pease (Eds.), *Post-anthropocentric social work: Critical posthuman and new materialist perspectives* (pp. 175–186). Rouledge.

Sâkihitowin Awâsis. (2014). Pipelines and resistance across Turtle Island. In T. Black, S. D'Arcy, T. Weiss, & J. K. Russell (Eds.), *A line in the tar sands: Struggles for environmental justice* (pp. 253–266). Between the Lines.

Shewell, H. (2001). What makes the Indian tick? The influences of social sciences on Canada's Indian policy, 1947–1964. *Social History*, *34*, 133–167.

Shewell, H. (2004). *"Enough to keep them alive": Indian social welfare in Canada, 1873–1965*. University of Toronto Press.

Simpson, L. B. (2013). Liberated peoples, liberated lands. In S. Heinrichs (Ed.), *Buffalo shout, salmon cry: Conversations on creation, land justice, and life together* (pp. 50–57). Herald.

Simpson, L. B. (2015). The place where we all live and work together: A gendered analysis of "sovereignty." In S. Nohelani Teves, A. Smith, & M. H. Raheja (Eds.), *Native studies keywords* (pp. 18–24). University of Arizona Press.

Simpson, L. B. (2017). *As we have always done: Indigenous freedom through radical resistance*. University of Minnesota Press.

Simpson, L. R. (2004). Strategies for the recovery and maintenance of Indigenous knowledge. *American Indian Quarterly, 28*(3/4), 373–384. https://doi.org /10.1353/aiq.2004.0107

Sinclair, M. (2020, December 17). Indigenous leadership is crucial to protecting the planet. *Maclean's*. https://www.macleans.ca/opinion/indigenous -leadership-is-crucial-to-protecting-the-planet/

Sinclair, R. (2004). Aboriginal social work education in Canada: Decolonizing pedagogy for the seventh generation. *First Peoples Child and Family Review, 1*(1), 49–61. https://doi.org/10.7202/1069584ar

Sinclair, R. (2007). Identity lost and found: Lessons from the sixties scoop. *First Peoples Child & Family Review, 3*(1), 65–82. https://doi.org/10.7202/1069527ar

Sinclair, R. (2016). The Indigenous child removal system in Canada: An examination of legal decision-making and racial bias. *First Peoples Child & Family Review 11*(2), 8–18. https://doi.org/10.7202/1082333ar

Smith, M., & Sterritt, A. (2010). Towards a shared vision: Lessons from collaboration between First Nations and environmental organizations to protect the Great Bear Rainforest and coastal First Nations. In L. Davis (Ed.), *Re/Envisioning relationships: Indigenous–non-Indigenous alliances and coalitions for social and environmental justice* (pp. 131–148). University of Toronto Press.

Spencer, M. S., Fentress, T., Touch, A., & Hernandez, J. (2020). Environmental justice, Indigenous knowledge systems, and Native Hawaiians and other Pacific Islanders. *Human Biology, 92*(1), 45–57. https://doi.org/10.13100 /humanbiology.92.1.06

Teixeira, S., & Krings, A. (2015). Sustainable social work: An environmental justice framework for social work education. *Social Work Education, 34*(5), 513–527. https://doi.org/10.1080/02615479.2015.1063601

Thomas-Muller, C. (2014). The rise of the Native rights-based strategic framework: Our last best hope to save our water, air, and earth. In T. Black, S. D'Arcy, T. Weiss, & J. K. Russell (Eds.), *A line in the tar sands: Struggles for environmental justice* (pp. 240–252). Between the Lines.

Tierney, K. (2015). Resilience and the neoliberal project: Discourses, critiques, practices – and Katrina. *American Behavioral Scientist, 59*(10), 1327–1342. https://doi.org/10.1177/0002764215591187

Tiny House Warriors. (2020, October 16). *Joint statement by Secwepemc * Gidimt'en land defenders*. http://www.tinyhousewarriors.com/2020/10 /joint-statement-by-secwepemc-gidimten-land-defenders/

Tischler, A. E. (2011). Climate change and social work: steps to an eco-social work practice [Master's thesis]. Smith College. Smith Scholar Works. https://scholarworks.smith.edu/theses/1023

Tuck, E., McKenzie, M., & McCoy, K. (2014). Land education: Indigenous, post-colonial, and decolonizing perspectives on place and environmental education research. *Environmental Education Research, 20*(1), 1–23. http:// doi.org/10.1080/13504622.2013.877708

Turtle Lodge. (2021). *Onjisay Aki international climate calls to action*. http:// onjisay-aki.org/onjisay-aki-international-climate-calls-action

Unist'ot'en Camp. (2017). *Timeline of the campaign: A timeline*. https:// unistoten.camp/timeline/timeline-of-the-campaign/

United Nations. (2007). *United Nations Declaration on the Rights of Indigenous Peoples*. https://www.un.org/development/desa/indigenouspeoples /wp-content/uploads/sites/19/2018/11/UNDRIP_E_web.pdf

United Nations. (2012, May 8). *"Doctrine of Discovery," used for centuries to justify seizure of Indigenous land, subjugate peoples, must be repudiated by United Nations, permanent forum told*. https://www.un.org/press /en/2012/hr5088.doc.htm#:~:text=The%20Doctrine%20of%20 Discovery%20had,mechanism%2C%20under%20United%20Nations %20auspices

Waterfall, B. (2006). Native peoples and child welfare practices: Implicating social work education. In A. Westhues (Eds.), *Canadian social policy: Issues and perspectives* (4th ed., pp. 223–244).Wilfred Laurier University Press.

Weaver, H. N. (2000). Activism and American Indian issues: Opportunities and roles for social workers. *Journal of Progressive Human Services, 11*(1), 3–22. https://doi.org/10.1300/J059v11n01_02

Whyte, K. P. (2018a). Indigenous science (fiction) for the Anthropocene: Ancestral dystopias and fantasies of climate change crises. *Environment and Planning E: Nature and Space, 1*(1–2), 224–242. https://doi.org/10.1177 /2514848618777621

Whyte, K. P. (2018b). Reflections on the purpose of Indigenous environmental education. In E. A. McKinley & L. T. Smith (Eds.), *Handbook of Indigenous education* (pp. 1–21). Springer. https://doi.org/10.1007/978-981-10-1839-8_66-3

Whyte, K. P. (2018c, April 3). White allies, let's be honest about decolonization. *Yes!* https://www.yesmagazine.org/issue/decolonize/2018/04/03/white -allies-lets-be-honest-about-decolonization

Whyte, K. P. (2019). Way beyond the lifeboat: An Indigenous allegory of climate justice. In K. Bhavnani, J. Foran, P. A. Kuiran, & D. Munshi (Eds.), *Climate futures: Reimagining global climate justice* (pp. 11–20). Zed.

Whyte, K. P. (2019). The Dakota Access Pipeline, environmental injustice, and US settler colonialism. In C. Miller & J. Crane (Eds.), *The nature of hope: Grassroots organizing, environmental justice, and political change* (pp. 320–337). University of Colorado Press.

Yanchapaxi, M. F., Liboiron, M., Crocker, K., Smiles, D., & Tuck, E. (2022). Finding a good starting place: An interview with scholars in the CLEAR Lab. *Curriculum Inquiry, 52*(2), 162–170. https://doi.org/10.1080/03626784.2022.2052637

Yellow Bird, M., & Gray, M. (2008). Indigenous people and the language of social work. In M. Gray, J. Coates, & M. Yellow Bird (Eds.), *Indigenous social work around the world: Towards culturally relevant education and practice* (pp. 59–70). Ashgate.

Zussman, R. (2020, January 29). *Horgan concedes Trans Mountain pipeline will go ahead while repeating support for Coastal GasLink.* Global News. https://globalnews.ca/news/6480102/horgan-trans-mountain-go-ahead/

2 Nature for Whom? Justice in Environmental Education

STEPHEN HILL, STEPHANIE RUTHERFORD,
AND JAMES WILKES

As we work to heal the earth, the earth heals us.
>   – Joanna Macy (as cited in Kimmerer, 2013, p. 340)

This chapter traces the modern history of environmental studies and sciences education in Canada, focusing on the recent turn to environmental justice and its relevance to social work education. We treat environmental education as an evolving body of knowledge and practice, one that is growing beyond Western (Eurocentric) perspectives to include engagement with multiple knowledge systems and communities of practice. We begin by exploring environmental teaching in the 1970s and 1980s, which was primarily concerned with providing evidence of the ecological crisis through Western science. While this approach supplied crucial support to a burgeoning environmental movement, it often sidestepped – and in some cases reproduced – the way inequality and power are embedded in ecological politics. The 1990s offered opportunities for greater interdisciplinary interventions, in which connections between the environment and professional disciplines, such as business and engineering, were strengthened. But it was not until the environmental justice movement made progress in academia in the 2000s that the ecological effects on marginalized peoples and communities were foregrounded. The amplification of racial and economic justice concerns in environmental teaching offers learners a complex understanding of the roots and potential solutions to environmental harm. It is here where social work and environmental studies overlap. We end the chapter with an invitation for social work educators to help us develop tools to bring these insights into teaching.

The Birth of the Modern Environmental Movement

Public concern about the environment has ebbed and flowed through several waves, with a first wave from 1965 to 1975, a second wave from 1987 to 1992, a third from 2005 to 2008, and a fourth from 2015 to the present (O'Connor, 2014; Paehlke, 1992). Environmental concerns have often been framed by the science of ecology, an integrated study of species, habitats, and their relationships. For example, in the early 1960s Rachel Carson (1962) powerfully rang the alarm about the impacts of industrial chemicals on our natural world. In addition, Farley Mowat (1963) beautifully showed us how wolves were not an evil threat to humans but rather an intricate part of ecological systems. Both writers' work represented a shifting idea about humanity's relationship with the environment: that we are no different from other species in terms of ecological science. In the late 1960s, ecologists such as Paul Erhlich (1968) and Barry Commoner (1971) were writing about the perilous fate of humanity due to population growth, overconsumption, industrial pollution, and nuclear weapons. Indeed, systems approaches rooted in ecology became central to the mathematical models used in *The Limits to Growth* (Meadows et al., 1972), a study by MIT scientists that used computer modelling to project the environmental impacts of unchecked population growth, industrial pollution, and resource depletion. Growing understanding that the Earth's resources are limited were captured in Fuller's (1969) notion of 'Spaceship Earth,' the idea that humans travel together on this tiny planet and share a collective responsibility for its future. The image of the Earthrise from the Apollo 8 space mission in 1968 is an iconic environmental photo and powerful visual image showing the ecological limits of Spaceship Earth. Astronaut William Anders, who took the Earthrise photo, said, "from our tiny capsule, it seemed as if the whole Earth was smaller even than the space the three of us inhabited ... We set out to explore the moon and instead discovered the Earth" (Anders, 2018, para 15).

Modern environmental thinking was also shaped by urban citizens' increased access to nature. Growing affluence from the unprecedented era of economic expansion in the decades following the Second World War afforded more middle-class Canadians the opportunity to pursue outdoor leisure activities such as canoeing, camping, and cottaging. This increased exposure to the natural world is thought to have increased environmental values and concern (Dunlap and Heffernan, 1975; Jackson, 1986).

The 1960s set the stage for a social movement focused on the environment as manifested in the first Earth Day celebration in April 1970

(Rome, 2010). Throughout the 1970s, local and regional ecological change created concern about human impacts on the environment. Headlines about the "Death of Lake Erie" (Edmonds, 1965; Read, 1996) led to large-scale scientific studies like those in the Experimental Lakes Area of northern Ontario, which showed how phosphorous was changing aquatic ecosystems (Schindler, 1974). Western science was also central in shaping our understanding of ozone-depleting substances (Parson, 2003) and acid rain (Likens & Bormann, 1974). Federal and provincial governments in Canada introduced new policies and legislation related to clean air and water in the 1970s. Federally, the Department of the Environment was created in 1971 to implement the new Clean Air Act (1971), Canada Water Act (1972), and Environmental Contaminants Act (1976) (MacDowell, 2012). Provinces established comparable departments and implemented similar legislation, but there still was a lack of a national strategy, owing to the ambiguous division of constitutional powers over the environment. These new policies and departments were important for institutionalizing environmental issues in the machinery of government. However, the natural and physical sciences, rather than the social sciences and humanities, were the main framework for shaping government responses to environmental problems (Dunlap & Mertig, 1991); and these new environmental departments and policies, although important, did not structurally alter conventional pathways of development and consumption in Western countries (MacDowell, 2012).

While much public attention focused on a scientific and ecological understanding of the environment, there was also some political and social thinking about underlying causes such as population growth (Ehrlich, 1968), unfettered technological development (Toffler, 1970), and the human domination of nature (Leiss, 2023). Environmentalists during this era often critiqued conventional economic development and proposed alternative development pathways, including design with nature (McHarg, 1969), soft energy paths (Lovins, 1979), and zero population growth (Normandin & Valles, 2015). For example, in 1972 Bob Paehlke and Jim White launched the *Alternatives Journal* at Ontario's Trent University, with an activist mandate of translating academic research to create tangible community action (Alternatives Journal, n.d.). The journal's underlying message was that solutions to environmental problems are complex, requiring expertise from a diversity of disciplines as well as communication and interaction with the public. Indeed, "anyone who proposes to cure the environmental crisis undertakes to change the course of history" (Commoner, 1971, p. ix). Environmental studies and sciences were becoming more adept at treating the symptoms of environmental issues, much like our modern approach to health care. However, as we argue later, if we do not address the root causes of the environmental crisis, namely the patterns of human development and our relationship with nature, the symptoms will continue. Environmental educators have come to understand that how we think about and relate to the environment is key to identifying the causes of environmental issues.

The Origins of University Environmental Education

Canadian universities expanded quickly in the 1960s and 1970s to meet the educational needs of baby boomers born in the mid-twentieth century (Grayson, 2018; Owram, 1997). Interdisciplinary approaches to post-secondary education became increasingly popular during this time (Klein, 1990), and newer universities promoted interdisciplinary programs to distinguish themselves from more established schools (Salter & Hearn, 1997). Environmental studies is inherently interdisciplinary (as discussed further below) and appealed to students during the first environmental wave in the 1970s, which led to the recruitment of new environmentally oriented faculty members with training in traditional disciplines across the natural and physical sciences, economics, history, and political science. For example, Trent, Waterloo, York, Simon Fraser, Victoria, and Calgary – all newly established universities – created dedicated environmental programs during this era. Newer universities were seemingly more willing to bend disciplinary boundaries than established schools and took the lead in creating interdisciplinary departments focused on the environment. New tenure track hires mostly came from traditional disciplines but had a research focus on the environment. At Trent, the Environmental and Resource Studies (ERS) program was highly interdisciplinary. The 1975–76 Trent University calendar describes it this way:

> The program is offered through the *co-operation of ten university departments* ... Students in the Program are required to take Environmental and Resource Science 100 and it is recommended in addition that they also take Geography 101, a one-hundred series Biology course, and at least one of Economics 100, Politics 100 or Statistics 100. (Trent University, 1975, p. 37, emphasis added)

Even though environmental studies seeks to be interdisciplinary, a fair assessment would suggest that the natural and physical sciences dominated environmental curriculum in the 1970s, 1980s, and 1990s. To illustrate, when it began in the mid-1970s, Trent's ERS program offered a bachelor of science and bachelor of arts degree; nonetheless, a scientific examination of the environment was a core feature of the curriculum. The required first-year environmental course focused on the "scientific bases of environmental problems" (Trent University, 1975, p. 38), including air and water pollution, resource consumption, waste disposal, and energy. One of the authors of this chapter (Hill) has coordinated the first-year environmental course at Trent since 2003 and can attest that most introductory environmental textbooks continue to be framed as though environmental studies is primarily a matter of understanding the scientific basis of environmental problems.

It bears noting that faculty hired in the 1960s and 1970s were predominantly men, often trained at universities in the United Kingdom or United States, who brought with them their disciplinary traditions, biases, and cultural backgrounds. From our observations, many environmental faculty members had experience camping, canoeing, and cottaging in the (so-called) Canadian wilderness. It should not come as a surprise that post-secondary environmental education grew out of the dominant epistemologies constructing environmental knowledge in the 1960s to 1980s, namely through the normative lenses and identities of the usually white, straight, male faculty who were tasked with researching and teaching environmental studies and sciences. Environmental faculty members had backgrounds in traditional Eurocentric disciplines such as chemistry, physics, biology, geography, politics, and economics, with their environmental values shaped by their interaction with the broader environmental movement. They were also often keen on nature-based and outdoor recreation, and thus the environmental curriculum regularly included field trips and outdoor education. Given the background of new faculty at the time, it is also not surprising that environmental pollution and resource management courses were largely disconnected from struggles for economic, gender, and racial justice. If social justice was mentioned at all, it was sometimes framed in terms of international development and global poverty. Even then, the environmental movement was mostly led by conventional scientists and experts (e.g., Commoner, 1971) rather than rooted in the lived experience of those experiencing poverty or racial injustices (largely because those lived experiences were uncommon among the faculty). An exception to this was the emerging recognition of connections between resource development and the injustices affecting Indigenous people in Canada such as (among many examples) the social and environmental assessment of the Mackenzie Valley Pipeline (Berger, 1977), efforts to protect the rights of the James Bay Cree during the major hydroelectric developments in the 1970s through the 1990s (Diamond, 1985; Hornig, 1999), and the ongoing case of mercury contamination from pulp and paper production in Asubpeeschoseewagong Netum Anishinabek (Grassy Narrows First Nation) in northern Ontario (Erikson, 1995; Vecsey, 1987). However, it would be longer still before ways of being and knowing in environmental education were expanded to include Indigenous ontologies and epistemologies about our responsibilities as human beings to the environment.

Environmental education has also been at the forefront of expanding how the non-human world and other species are considered. Going back to Aldo Leopold's land ethic (1949) or John Livingston's *Fallacy of Wildlife Conservation* (1981), environmental studies has led the call for including other species in our ethical frameworks and rejecting the idea that nature and humans are separate. For example, Livingston (1981) writes about his intimate connection to the non-human world during his childhood in Toronto: "Plans were revealed for the construction of a storm sewer through 'my' ravine. Shock, dismay, and all the rest of it were mine early. The ten-year old mind is not subtle: how can I warn the frogs and toads and newts? Can I get them out of there, take them away somewhere?" (p. 101). He writes, "For some of us, the experience of non-human Nature is the most vivid recollection of young childhood. Not the cognitive, but the affective experience" (p. 119). This rejection of the separation between nature and humans is central to much environmental studies and has recently found traction in social work (for example, see Bozalek & Pease, 2020).

Global Environmentalism

In the 1980s and 1990s, environmental issues evolved to focus directly on global risks such as biodiversity loss (Heywood & Watson, 1995), long-lived toxic chemicals (e.g., Safe, 1994), ozone depletion, acid rain, and climate change (Houghton, 1996). These issues required cooperation among nations and across borders. Indeed, international groups of experts and scientists drove much of the agenda related to global environmental risks. For instance, the scientific understanding and assessment of ozone depletion was coordinated by the United Nations Environment Program (UNEP) and the International Council of Scientific Unions (ICSU) and led to the 1985 Vienna Convention for ozone, the framework for the Montreal Protocol (Morrisette, 1989; Parson, 2003). On climate change, the World Climate Conference of 1979 was the start of a series of international scientific workshops held in Villach, Austria, and was organized by the World Meteorological Organization, the ICSU, and UNEP. The level of activism by the scientists at the Villach meetings and after led to the *intergovernmental* structure of the Intergovernmental Panel on Climate Change (IPCC), namely the creation of an expert scientific body that included government review of scientific findings (Agrawala, 1998). A purpose of having governments review the expert assessments of climate change was to limit scientific activism in advancing the environmental agenda.

Sustainable Development

The concept of sustainable development – "development that meets the needs of the present without compromising the ability of future generations to meet their own needs" (World Commission on Environment and Development [WCED], 1987, p. 7) – stemmed from the WCED's three years of hearings and research in the mid-1980s, which sought to reconcile concerns over environmental degradation on the one hand, and global poverty and injustice on the other. Sustainable development supplied the conceptual foundation for international negotiations that led to the watershed 1992 Earth Summit in Rio de Janeiro, where Agenda 21, the Biodiversity Convention, and the United Nations Framework Convention on Climate Change were signed (United Nations, n.d.). From the standpoint of environmental education, sustainable development was central to the second environmental wave and was woven quickly into teaching. For instance, the report of the World Commission on Environment and Development, *Our Common Future* (WCED, 1987), was the textbook for undergraduate courses taken by chapter authors Hill in 1988 and Wilkes in 1998. At Trent University, *Our Common Future* was also the inspiration for the development of an interdisciplinary course on bioregionalism that asked students to "think globally, and act locally" (Avery, 2003). The bioregionalism course also embedded the practices of community-based research into the environmental curriculum (Strand, 2000).

Corporate Sustainability, Eco-efficiency, and Environmental Professionalism

Mainstream environmentalism was also influenced by neoliberal thinking in the 1980s and 1990s. Prior to the Earth Summit in Rio, Maurice Strong, a Canadian businessperson and secretary-general to the Earth Summit, asked Swiss industrialist Stephane Schmidheiny to formulate the view of business towards sustainable development (Stigson & Rendlen, 2005). The World Business Council for Sustainable

Development (WBCSD) was formed and put forward the notion that sustainable development was about "eco-efficiency," which was defined as technological innovations that reduced environmental costs and economic costs (Schmidheiny, 1992, p. xii). Competitive advantage became a chief motivation underlying corporate approaches to sustainable development and the environment. Concepts such as industrial ecology (Ayres & Ayres, 2002), clean production (Chavez, 2015), design for the environment (Chen, 2001), and triple-bottom-line thinking (Elkington, 1998) soon followed. Because of the diminished political appetite for governments to enact environmental regulations (Winfield & Jenish, 1998), voluntary environmental programs grew in importance and corporations sought to self-regulate their activities and environmental impacts. At the time, voluntary environmental management programs such as ISO 14000, Pollution Prevention Pays at 3M (Reed, 2002), and Responsible Care in the chemical industry (King & Lenox, 2000) were a focus of much environmental activity. The reliance on volunteerism and the significant role of business in shaping environmental policy led to the apparent powerlessness of governments to exert regulatory authority over environmental issues (e.g., Clapp, 2005; Macdonald, 2007).

The concept of eco-efficiency soon became important to environmental education because business, engineering, and law schools began to incorporate environmental and sustainability issues in their curriculum. Business schools developed curriculum about how the natural environment had implications for corporate strategy, operations management, accounting, and management systems (Gladwin et al., 1995). Engineering and law schools developed courses and programs in environmental engineering and law. The Sustainable Enterprise Academy at York University is one example, where business executives were introduced to ideas of sustainability (Wheeler et al., 2005). These new programs drove a great deal of environmental activity and led to the emergence of quasi-professional standards and expectations for environmental education. For instance, ECO (Environmental Careers Organization) Canada was founded in 1992 to manage and examine the skills and human resource needs in the environmental sector and has developed professional certification programs and accreditation of educational programs (https://eco.ca). We also observed, in the late 1990s and 2000s, an increasing number of certifications for specialized topics such as environmental auditing, life cycle assessment, land classification, site assessment, and greenhouse gas accounting, each of which highlighted the skills and expectations of environmental professionals working in industry. However, during this era the connections between environmentalism and the helping professions, such as nursing, medicine, and social work, while present (for example, calls for greater involvement of social work in environmental issues include Besthorn, 2012; Hoff & Polack, 1993; Hoff & McNutt, 1994; and Peeters, 2012), were less obvious. Environmental collaboration and interdisciplinary curriculum geared to the helping professions were much less common than in engineering and business.

Transitioning to Environmental Justice in Environmental Studies and Sciences

The birth of the concept of environmental justice is often tied to the 1991 First National People of Color Environmental Leadership Summit held in Washington, D.C., at which hundreds of racialized delegates gathered to articulate the principles of a new environmental movement. Of course, it was not new; activists in racialized communities, especially women of colour, had been working on these issues for decades. What *was* new was the insistence that the mainstream environmental movement – characterized as it was (and often still is) by white and middle-class preoccupations with '"wilderness"' – pay attention to the environmental struggles of people of colour in often poor, urban communities. As Dana Alston noted in her report on the conference for *Race, Poverty & the Environment*, "for people of color, the environment is woven into an overall framework and understanding of social, racial and economic justice" (1991/1992, p. 1). The refusal to imagine nature as separate from where people 'work, live, and play' remains the hallmark of the environmental justice movement.

The impact of the environmental justice movement continues to be profound, reshaping our understanding of the ways that colonialism, racism, sexism, and classism are intimately tied to environmental harm. The concept of environmental racism elaborates this intersectional connection, showing how racialized communities are disproportionately exposed to environmental harms while simultaneously being less likely to have access to green space and pollution-free air, or to environmental decision-making authorities in both the United States (Bullard, 1993) and Canada (Gosine & Teelucksingh, 2008). Several scholar-activists began to explore the ways in which environmental racism was a fundamental part of daily life for many racialized communities, tied to systems of racial capitalism, patriarchy, and settler colonialism (see, e.g., Agyeman et al., 2003; Agyeman et al., 2009; Pellow, 2002). There was also an important vein of environmental justice work that traced the specificity of environmental racism in Canada in terms of how it disproportionately affects Indigenous communities (Dhillon & Young, 2010; Mascarenhas, 2007; Westra, 2008; Wiebe, 2017).

Some of this work also centres Indigenous ontologies and epistemologies as a pathway to environmental justice that rejects the logics of settler-colonial capitalism. For example, McGregor, Whitaker, and Sritharan (2020) emphasize the ways in which Indigenous approaches to environmental justice begin from fundamentally different conceptions of the relationships and responsibilities between humans and more-than-humans, as well as notions of justice that have not been reflected in Western understandings of environmental issues. Indeed, the authors note that Indigenous peoples have often experienced the solutions put forward to environmental issues like climate change – for instance, carbon trading and conservation that involves forcing people off traditional lands – as "false solutions" that rehearse the same structures and logics of colonialism that caused the crisis in the first place (p. 36; see also Rising Tide North America and Carbon Watch, 2014). These more expansive notions of justice "offer a diagnosis and path forward that answers the call for the 'transformative change' needed to alter global society's current trajectory" (McGregor et al., 2020, p. 36).

Climate Justice Movements

It took a long while for these ideas to take root in academic environmental studies and sciences pedagogies, in part because the faculty remained (remains) overwhelmingly white, male, and middle class. It was not until the 2010s that the (inter)discipline began to truly heed critiques that it had failed to pay attention to marginalized voices and communities. The existential threat presented by climate change also dramatically changed the terrain. Specifically, the youth climate justice movement unapologetically insisted on amplifying the voices of those racialized and poor communities who would feel the burden of climate change both first and hardest, yet were the least economically equipped to adapt to its threats (Klein, 2014). Racialized youth activists, tired of being ignored by the mainstream environmental movement, academics, and policymakers alike, crafted new modes of understanding the inequalities produced at the intersection among settler colonialism, racial capitalism, patriarchy, and climate emergency. Moreover, the voices of Indigenous environmental, eco-feminist, and climate justice activists and scholars have been crucial to this conversation (see, for example, Gaard, 2015; Indigenous Environmental Network, n.d.; Isla, 2019; Klein, 2014; McGregor, 2009; Sengupta, 2020).

Expanding Environmental Education

The youth climate justice movement's radical re-imagining of green politics also shaped how environmental studies and sciences are taught. In the Trent School of the Environment, our students pushed us on our race, gender, and class privilege, pointing to the ways in which our construction of the studies and sciences curriculum erased their lived experience. This was an important wake-up call for us, both as educators and as members of the environmental movement. And it has reshaped what and how we teach. Environmental justice is now a core element in many of our environmental studies courses. For instance, environmental ethics, a third-year course open to all majors, offers a unit on the ways in which the environmental justice critique has reshaped our understanding of environmental problems and our ethical responses to them. Students explore how environmental justice research and organizing offer a counterpoint to the 'Spaceship Earth' narrative explored above, noting that we do not all inhabit the earth equally, nor are we subject to the same environmental risks. This course emphasizes, in the words of Jim Tarter (2002), that "some live more downstream than others" (p. 213), something that has become more acutely obvious with the impacts of the COVID-19 pandemic, which has exposed these very same global social and economic inequalities of marginalized peoples and countries. Further, one of this chapter's authors (Rutherford) designed and teaches a course in transnational environmental justice, which puts race, class, gender, and nation at the centre of teaching about global environmental issues. Exploring topics from coercive conservation to climate justice and the claiming of ecological space, this course arose precisely out of student demand for education that reflects the ways that power works in the production of environmental harm. The course has offered a generative space to critique the world as it is and begins to imagine how it could be otherwise. At the graduate level, we have also been teaching for the past decade in the sustainability studies master's program, led by our colleague Asaf Zohar, which promotes collaboration and community-based research about the environment, social justice, Indigenous thought, and organizational leadership.

Centering Indigeneity

An important element in teaching about environmental justice has been the relationship formed between Indigenous studies and environmental studies through the establishment of the Indigenous Environmental Studies and Sciences (IESS) program at Trent University, the first of its kind in North America. With a focus on multiple knowledge systems at its core, IESS offered its first courses as part of a diploma-granting program in 2000 and since 2009 as part of a degree-granting program, under the leadership of Dan Roronhiakewen Longboat, Chris Furgal, and more recently Barbara Wall. The program provides students opportunities to engage with Indigenous cultural understandings and perspectives of Elders, Knowledge Holders, and IESS practitioners. Prior to IESS, environmental studies and sciences were predicated on a Eurocentric (Western) way of seeing the world. By recognizing and privileging the authority and plurality of Indigenous knowledges of the environment, the program offers students a multiplicity of tools to identify and discern the root causes of today's environmental issues. This emerging discipline of IESS is further outlined by Evering and Longboat (2013) and Whyte (2018a). In accord with environmental justice, IESS continues to challenge students to question the dominant paradigms and metaphysics of Western and Eurocentric environmentalism, by addressing ideological, colonial, national, patriarchal, and capitalist assumptions of knowledge production, nation-state building, and even the environmental conservation movement itself. Indeed, human values and thinking are continually changing, and we must address the underlying thinking and behaviour that caused the problems we see today. By moving beyond a single way of seeing the world, IESS is a continually emerging body of knowledge that provides students with a sense of purpose and hope, to become the change makers of today and the innovators of tomorrow.

This reshaping has not been without its own tensions; as Danielle Purifoy has pointed out in an article in *Inside Higher Ed*, this transformation of environmental pedagogy has often been less than robust, instead "replicat[ing] white-centered brands of environmentalism" under the banner of diversity and inclusion (2018, para 14). Thus, this chapter is not meant as a pat on the back for a job well done; instead, we recognize that much work remains to uproot colonialism, sexism, racism, and classism, in the classroom and in the field. But the transition to justice in environmental studies and sciences has momentum and has fundamentally altered the (inter)discipline in ways that make it more attuned to power, not only in environmental issues, but across academia.

Implications for Social Work Education

In terms of this book's themes, how might this history and these stories of including justice in environmental studies and sciences teaching apply to the helping professions and social work education? David

Firang (2020) and our editor Susan Hillock provide some insight. Echoing what Hillock explains in this book's introduction, Firang (2020) notes that despite the 2018 call by the Canadian Association for Social Work Education – Association Canadienne Pour La Formation En Travail Social for educators to emphasize environmental along with social and economic justice, the response was muted until the most recent educational policy framework (CASWE-ACFTS, 2021). Dominelli (2012) also explains that although social work commonly uses the person-in-environment framework for assessment and intervention, it often fails to consider the natural, physical, and built environments. (See the introduction for more detail on the CASWE's evolution on this matter.)

This general lack of action continues to happen, even though attention to all forms of injustice is implicit in how social work educators understand the principles of their work. As explained in the *CASWE Code of Ethics and Scope of Practice* (2005), the discipline "responds to needs of individuals, families, groups, and communities and addresses barriers and injustices in organizations and society." This approach can clearly accommodate, and indeed may demand, attention to the way that intersecting systems of power – including environmental injustice – work synergistically to produce harm. Like Firang and Hillock, we contend that not including questions of environmental injustice in a broader analysis of power, and specifically ones regarding the forms of oppression racialized communities face, means that understanding the challenges can only ever be partial. This is particularly the case as the climate crisis accelerates and we witness, in real time, its racialized, gendered, and classed impacts (Gardiner, 2020; Levy & Patz, 2015). Given these facts, we invite social work educators to transition towards environmental justice in their own pedagogical practice.

Recommendations

In our work as environmental educators, we have found a range of approaches, resources, and materials that are immensely helpful in communicating to our students the connections between race, gender, class, and environmental harm. We often begin with the specific, rooting our conversations in place-based studies of environmental inequality. For instance, we focus on case studies like Asubpeeschoseewagong Netum Anishinabek (Grassy Narrows First Nation) in which students can see how environmental racism, through both mercury poisoning and logging, has led to intergenerational harm in this Indigenous community. Another clear case study is offered by ENRICH (https://www.enrichproject.org/), the community-based project that mapped the ways in which Black and Indigenous communities experience environmental racism in Nova Scotia (Waldron, 2018). Neither of these cases can easily be understood without paying attention to the imbrication of settler colonialism, racism, sexism, classism, and environmental marginalization. In our experience, a case study approach allows students to dig deep into the specificities of site examples and to understand how these sites are reflective of broader forms of oppression in the dominant society.

We also centre the scholarship and activism of racialized, feminist, queer, and Indigenous writers who have been at the forefront of environmental justice movements. The writings of Carolyn Finney (2014), Winona LaDuke (1999), Deborah McGregor (2009), Leanne Betasamosake Simpson (2002, 2017), Rachel Stein (2004), Julie Sze (2020), Ingrid Waldron (2018), and Kyle Whyte (2018a, 2018b) have been particularly important guides for us in understanding how environmental harm is rooted in, and sustained through, other forms of oppression and how dismantling it requires taking on multiple forms of liberation.

Finally, we emphasize resistance to environmental inequality. Racialized communities have not been passive victims of environmental harm; they have actively organized against these systems of marginalization and apocalypse. By emphasizing their work, we highlight not just the ways in which communities fight back against oppressive structures, but also how these efforts offer a radical re-imagining of human-environment relationships that we need in this time of environmental crisis.

Conclusion

We do not pretend to know the best path forward for social work educators and the helping professions, but make the modest suggestion that Indigenous environmental approaches offer useful guidance (Cajete, 2000; Iwama et al., 2009; Simpson, 2002). For instance, one of this chapter's authors (Wilkes) teaches IESS courses both at Trent University and within the context of Indigenous community-based social work at FNTI (First Nations Technical Institute) in Tyendinaga Mohawk Territory. Employing an IESS approach of the five Rs – relationship, respect, responsibility, reciprocity, and restoration (Evering & Longboat, 2013) – Indigenous social work students (and allies) are encouraged to (re)consider the symbiosis of environmental repair and Indigenous cultural revitalization as an essential aspect of social work education. Engaging multiple ways of knowing and understanding, we may also look to the plurality of wisdom traditions for insight. According to Zen master Thich Nhat Hanh, "when we're in ill health, we sometimes lose ourselves. We have to return to our mother, the Earth, to be healed again" (2013, p. 36). Beyond the human-social dimensions of trauma, grief, addiction, and suicide, social work practitioners are becoming re-attuned to the healing power of engaging with the Earth, as well as recognizing the spiritual importance of people in-with-as place (Zapf, 2009). Through environmental restoration and land-centred healing, Indigenous social workers are leading the way and reconnecting with the foundational ecological support systems at the core of their communities and nations. All human beings have a role in this socio-ecological work; together, we can uphold our responsibilities to help restore the planet and humankind.

Acknowledgment

The authors thank Roronhiakewen (Dan Longboat) and Brigitte Evering for helpful comments and suggestions on earlier drafts of this chapter.

REFERENCES

Agrawala, S. (1998). Context and early origins of the Intergovernmental Panel on Climate Change. *Climatic Change, 39*(4), 605–620. https://doi.org/10.1023/A:1005315532386

Agyeman, J., Bullard, R., & Evans, B. (Eds.). (2003). *Just sustainabilities: Development in an unequal world*. MIT Press.

Agyeman, J., Cole, P., Haluza-DeLay, R., & O'Riley, P. (Eds.). (2009). *Speaking for ourselves: Environmental justice in Canada*. UBC Press.

Alston, D. (1991/1992). Transforming a movement. *Race, Poverty & the Environment, 2*(3/4), 1, 28–29.

Alternatives Journal. (n.d.). *The Alternatives Journal story*. Retrieved June 11, 2021, from https://www.alternativesjournal.ca/about-aj/the-alternatives-journal-story/

Anders, W. (2018, December 24). *50 years after "Earthrise," a Christmas Eve message from its photographer*. Retrieved March 4, 2021, from https://www.space.com/42848-earthrise-photo-apollo-8-legacy-bill-anders.html Space.com

Avery, H. M. (2003). *"Seeing through serpent and eagle eyes": Enacting community in service-learning experiences* [Unpublished doctoral dissertation]. University of Toronto.

Ayres, R. U., & Ayres, L. (Eds.). (2002). *A handbook of industrial ecology*. Edward Elgar.

Berger, T. R. (1977). *Northern frontier, northern homeland: The report of the Mackenzie Valley Pipeline Inquiry*. Government of Canada.

Besthorn, F. H. (2012). Deep ecology's contributions to social work: A ten-year retrospective. *International Journal of Social Welfare, 21*(3), 248–259. https://doi.org/10.1111/j.1468-2397.2011.00850.x

Bozalek, V., & Pease, B. (Eds.). (2020). *Post-anthropocentric social work: Critical posthuman and new materialist perspectives*. Routledge.

Bullard, R. (1993). The threat of environmental racism. *Natural Resources & the Environment, 7*(3), 23–26, 55–56.

Cajete, G. (2000). *Native science: Natural laws of interdependence*. Clear Light.

Canadian Association of Social Workers. (2005). *CASW code of ethics and scope of practice*. https://www.casw-acts.ca/en/Code-of-Ethics%20and%20Scope%20of%20Practice

Canadian Association for Social Work Education (2021). *Educational policies and accreditation standards for Canadian social work education*. Retrieved June 10, 2021, from https://caswe-acfts.ca/wp-content/uploads/2021/04/EPAS-2021.pdf

Carson, R. (1962). *Silent spring*. Houghton Mifflin.

Chavez, F. (2015). From cleaner production to sustainable development: The role of academia. *Journal of Cleaner Production, 96*, 30–43. https://doi.org/10.1016/j.jclepro.2014.01.099

Chen, C. (2001). Design for the environment: A quality-based model for green product development. *Management Science, 47*(2), 250–263. https://doi.org/10.1287/mnsc.47.2.250.9841

Clapp, J. (2005). Global environmental governance for corporate responsibility and accountability. *Global Environmental Politics, 5*(3), 23–34. https://doi.org/10.1162/1526380054794916

Commoner, B. (1971). *The closing circle: Nature, man and technology*. Alfred A. Knopf.

Dhillon, C., & Young, M. G. (2010). Environmental racism and First Nations: A call for socially just public policy development. *Canadian Journal of Humanities and Social Sciences, 1*(1), 23–37.

Diamond, B. (1985). Aboriginal rights: The James Bay experience. In M. Boldt & J. A. Long (Eds.), *The Quest for justice: Aboriginal peoples and Aboriginal rights* (pp. 265–285). University of Toronto Press.

Dominelli, L. (2012). *Green social work: From environmental crisis to environmental justice*. Polity.

Dunlap, R. E., & Heffernan, R. B. (1975). Outdoor recreation and environmental concern: An empirical examination. *Rural Sociology, 40*(1), 18.

Dunlap, R. E., & Mertig, A. G. (1991). The evolution of the US environmental movement from 1970 to 1990: An overview. *Society & Natural Resources, 4*(3), 209–218. https://doi.org/10.1080/08941929109380755

Edmonds, A. (1965, November 1). Death of a Great Lake. *Maclean's*, 28–29, 42–46.

Ehrlich, P. R. (1968). *The population bomb*. Random House.

Elkington, J. (1998). *Cannibals with forks: The triple bottom line of 21st century business*. New Society.

Erikson, K. (1995). *A new species of trouble: The human experience of modern disasters*. W.W. Norton & Co.

Evering, B., & Longboat, D. R. (2013). An introduction to Indigenous environmental studies: From principles into action. In A. Kulnieks, D. R. Longboat, & K. Young (Eds.), *Contemporary studies in environmental and Indigenous pedagogies: A curricula of stories and place* (pp. 241–258). Sense.

Finney, C. (2014). *Black faces, white spaces: Reimagining the relationship of African Americans to the great outdoors*. University of North Carolina Press.

Firang, D. (2020). Joining the call to incorporate sustainability into the Canadian social work profession. *Canadian Social Work Review, 37*(2), 27–50. https://doi.org/10.7202/1075110ar

Fuller, R. B. (1969). *Operating manual for spaceship earth*. Lars Müller.

Gaard, G. (2015). Ecofeminism and climate change. *Women's Studies International Forum, 49*, 20–33. https://doi.org/10.1016/j.wsif.2015.02.004

Gardiner, B. (2020). Unequal impact: the deep links between racism and climate change. *Yale Environment 360*. https://e360.yale.edu/features/unequal-impact-the-deep-links-between-inequality-and-climate-change

Gladwin, T. N., Kennelly, J. J., & Krause, T. S. (1995). Shifting paradigms for sustainable development: Implications for management theory and research. *Academy of Management Review, 20*(4), 874–907. https://doi.org/10.5465/amr.1995.9512280024

Gosine, A., & Teelucksingh, C. (2008). *Environmental justice and racism in Canada: An introduction*. Emond.

Grayson, J. P. (2018). The "first generation" in historical perspective: Canadian students in the 1960s. *Journal of Historical Sociology, 31*(4), 512–525. https://doi.org/10.1111/johs.12203

Heywood, V. H., & Watson, R. T. (1995). *Global biodiversity assessment*. Cambridge University Press.

Hoff, M. D., & McNutt, J. G. (1994). *The global environmental crisis: Implications for social welfare and social work*. Avebury

Hoff, M. D., & Polack, R. J. (1993). Social dimensions of the environmental crisis: Challenges for social work. *Social Work, 38*(2), 204–211. https://doi.org/10.1093/sw/38.2.204

Hornig, J. F. (Ed.). (1999). *Social and environmental impacts of the James Bay hydroelectric project*. McGill-Queen's University Press.

Houghton, E. (1996). *Climate change 1995: The science of climate change: Contribution of working group I to the second assessment report of the Intergovernmental Panel on Climate Change* (Vol. 2). Cambridge University Press.

Indigenous Environmental Network. (n.d.). https://www.ienearth.org/

Isla, A. (Ed.). (2019). *Climate chaos: Ecofeminism and the land question*. Inanna /Education Inc.

Iwama, M., Marshall, M., Marshall, A., & Bartlett, C. (2009). Two-eyed seeing and the language of healing in community-based research. *Canadian Journal of Native Education*, 32(2), 3–23. https://doi.org/10.14288/cjne.v32i2.196493

Jackson, E. L. (1986). Outdoor recreation participation and attitudes to the environment. *Leisure Studies*, 5(1), 1–23. https://doi.org/10.1080 /02614368600390011

Kimmerer, R. W. (2013). *Braiding sweetgrass: Indigenous wisdom, scientific knowledge and the teachings of plants*. Milkweed.

King, A. A., & Lenox, M. J. (2000). Industry self-regulation without sanctions: The chemical industry's responsible care program. *Academy of Management Journal*, 43(4), 698–716. https://doi.org/10.5465/1556362

Klein, J. T. (1990). *Interdisciplinarity: History, theory, and practice*. Wayne State University Press.

Klein, N. (2014). *This changes everything: Capitalism versus the climate*. Simon & Schuster.

LaDuke, W. (1999). *All our relations: Native struggles for life and land*. South End.

Leiss, W. (2023). The domination of nature. New ed. McGill-Queen's Press.

Leopold, A. (1949). *A sand county almanac*. Oxford University Press.

Levy, Barry S., & Patz, J. A. (2015). Climate change, human rights, and social justice. *Annals of Global Health*, 81(3), 310–322. https://doi.org/10.1016 /j.aogh.2015.08.008. Medline:26615065

Likens, G. E., & Bormann, F. H. (1974). Linkages between terrestrial and aquatic ecosystems. *BioScience*, 24(8), 447–456.

Livingston, J. A. (1981). *The fallacy of wildlife conservation*. McClelland & Stewart.

Lovins, A. B. (1979). *Soft energy paths: Toward a durable peace*. Harper Colophon.

Macdonald, D. (2007). *Business and environmental politics in Canada*. University of Toronto Press. https://doi.org/10.3138/9781442603257

MacDowell, L. S. (2012). The environmental movement and public policy. In *An environmental history of Canada* (243–267). UBC Press.

Macy, J. (2007). *World as lover, world as self: Courage for global justice and ecological renewal*. Parallax.

Mascarenhas, M. (2007). Where the waters divide: First Nations, tainted water and environmental justice in Canada. *Local Environment*, 12(6), 565–577. https://doi.org/10.1080/13549830701657265

McGregor, D. (2009). Honouring our relations: An Anishinaabe perspective on environmental justice. In J. Agyeman, P. Cole, R. Haluza-DeLay, & P. Riley (Eds.), *Speaking for ourselves: Environmental justice in Canada* (27–41). UBC Press.

McGregor, D., Whitaker, S., & Sritharan, M. (2020). Indigenous environmental justice and sustainability. *Current Opinion in Environmental Sustainability*, *43*, 35–40. https://doi.org/10.1016/j.cosust.2020.01.007

McHarg, I. L. (1969). *Design with nature*. Natural History Press.

Meadows, D. H., Meadows, D. L., Randers, J., & Behrens III, W. W. (1972). *The limits to growth: A report for the Club of Rome's project on the predicament of mankind*. Universe Books.

Morrisette, P. M. (1989). The evolution of policy responses to stratospheric ozone depletion. *Natural Resources Journal*, *29*, 793–820.

Mowat, F. (1963). *Never cry wolf*. McClelland & Stewart.

Nhat Hanh, T. (2013). *Peace of mind: Becoming fully present*. Parallax.

Normandin, S., & Valles, S. A. (2015). How a network of conservationists and population control activists created the contemporary US anti-immigration movement. *Endeavour*, *39*(2), 95–105. https://doi.org/10.1016/j.endeavour.2015.05.001. Medline:26026333

O'Connor, R. (2014). *The first green wave: Pollution Probe and the origins of environmental activism in Ontario*. UBC Press.

Owram, D. (1997). *Born at the right time: A history of the baby-boom generation*. University of Toronto Press.

Paehlke, R. (1992). Eco-history: Two waves in the evolution of environmentalism. *Alternatives*, *19*(1),18–23.

Parson, E. A. (2003). *Protecting the ozone layer: Science and strategy*. Oxford University Press.

Peeters, J. (2012). The place of social work in sustainable development: Towards ecosocial practice. *International Journal of Social Welfare*, *21*(3), 287–298. https://doi.org/10.1111/j.1468-2397.2011.00856.x

Pellow, D. N. 2002. *Garbage wars: The struggle for environmental justice in Chicago*. MIT Press.

Purifoy, D. (2018). *On the stubborn whiteness of environmentalism*. Inside Higher Ed. https://www.insidehighered.com/advice/2018/06/22/how-environmentalism-academe-today-excludes-people-color-opinion

Read, J. (1996). "Let us heed the voice of youth": Laundry detergents, phosphates and the emergence of the environmental movement in Ontario. *Journal of the Canadian Historical Association/Revue de la Société historique du Canada*, *7*(1), 227–250. https://doi.org/10.7202/031109ar

Reed, K. E. (2002). Everyone takes the field: How 3M encourages employee involvement in promoting sustainable development. *Corporate Environmental Strategy*, *9*(4), 383–389. https://doi.org/10.1016/S1066-7938(02)00109-4

Rising Tide North America and Carbon Watch. (2014). *Hoodwinked in the hothouse: False solutions to climate change* (2nd ed). https://risingtidenorthamerica.org/wp-content/uploads/2014/11/FS-BOOKLETT_FINAL.pdf

Rome, A. (2010). The genius of Earth Day. *Environmental History, 15*(2), 194–205.

Safe, S. H. (1994). Polychlorinated biphenyls (PCBs): Environmental impact, biochemical and toxic responses, and implications for risk assessment. *Critical Reviews in Toxicology, 24*(2), 87–149. https://doi .org/10.3109/10408449409049308. Medline:8037844

Salter, L., & Hearn, A. (1997). Interdisciplinarity. In *Outside the lines: Issues in interdisciplinary research* (26). McGill-Queen's University Press.

Schindler, D. W. (1974). Eutrophication and recovery in experimental lakes: Implications for lake management. *Science, 184*(4139), 897–899. https:// doi.org/10.1126/science.184.4139.897. Medline:17782381

Schmidheiny, S., & Timberlake, L. (1992). *Changing course: A global business perspective on development and the environment*. MIT Press.

Sengupta, S. (2020, June 3). Black environmentalists talk about climate and anti-racism. *New York Times*. https://www.nytimes.com/2020/06/03 /climate/black-environmentalists-talk-about-climate-and-anti-racism.html

Simpson, L. (2002). Indigenous environmental education for cultural survival. *Canadian Journal of Environmental Education, 7*(1), 13–25.

Simpson, L. B. (2017). *As we have always done: Indigenous freedom through radical resistance*. University of Minnesota Press.

Stein, R. (Ed.). (2004). *New perspectives on environmental justice: Gender, sexuality, and activism*. Rutgers University Press.

Stigson, B., & Rendlen, B. (2005). Drivers of business behaviour in the realm of sustainable development: The role and influence of the WBCSD, a global business network. In F. Wijen, K. Zoeteman, & J. Pieters (Eds.), *A handbook of globalizationtion and environmental policy: National government interventions in a global arena* (pp. 313–332). Edward Elgar.

Strand, K. J. (2000). Community-based research as pedagogy. *Michigan Journal of Community Service Learning, 7*(1), 85–96.

Sze, J. (2020). *Environmental justice in a moment of danger*. University of California Press.

Tarter, J. (2002). Some live more downstream than others: Cancer, gender and environmental justice. In J. Adamson, M. M. Evans, & R. Stein (Eds.), *The environmental justice reader: Politics, poetics, and pedagogy* (pp. 213–28). University of Arizona Press.

Toffler, A. (1970). *Future shock*. Random House.

Trent University. (1975). ERS 100. In *Trent University 1975–76 Academic Calendar*. http://digitalcollections.trentu.ca/objects/tula-5280

United Nations. (n.d.). United Nations Conference on Environment and Development, Rio de Janeiro, Brazil, June 3–14, 1992. https://www .un.org/en/conferences/environment/rio1992

Vecsey, C. (1987). Grassy Narrows reserve: Mercury pollution, social disruption, and natural resources: a question of autonomy. *American Indian Quarterly, 11*(4), 287–314.

Waldron, I. R. G. (2018) *There's something in the water: Environmental racism in Indigenous and Black communities*. Fernwood.

Waldron, I. R. G. (2019). African Nova Scotians on the front lines: Narratives of resistance in the fight against environmental racism. In M. Mascarenhas (Ed.), *Lessons in environmental justice: From civil rights to Black Lives and Idle No More* (pp. 250–268). Sage.

Westra, L. (2008). *Environmental justice and the rights of Indigenous peoples: International and domestic legal perspectives*. Earthscan.

Wheeler, D., Zohar, A., & Hart, S. (2005). Educating senior executives in a novel strategic paradigm: Early experiences of the Sustainable Enterprise Academy. *Business Strategy and the Environment, 14*(3), 172–185. https://doi.org/10.1002/bse.448

Whyte, K. (2018a). Critical investigations of resilience: A brief introduction to Indigenous environmental studies & sciences. *American Academy of Arts & Sciences, 147*(2), 136–147. https://doi.org/10.1162/DAED_a_00497

Whyte, K. (2018b). Settler colonialism, ecology and environmental injustice. *Environment & Society, 9*(1), 125–144. https://doi.org/10.3167/ares.2018.090109

Wiebe, S. (2017). *Everyday exposure: Indigenous mobilization and environmental justice in Canada's Chemical Valley*. UBC Press.

Winfield, M. S., & Jenish, G. (1998). Ontario's environment and the "Common Sense Revolution." *Studies in Political Economy, 57*(1), 129–147.

World Commission on Environment and Development. (1987). *Our Common Future*. Oxford University Press.

Zapf, M. K. (2009). *Social work and the environment: Understanding people and place*. Canadian Scholars.

3 The Challenges of Reorienting Pre-service Teacher Education for Sustainability

PAUL ELLIOTT

Our planet is threatened by the climate crisis and other anthropogenic factors such as biodiversity and habitat loss, soil erosion, and various forms of toxic pollution. Together, or even individually, these represent potentially existential threats not only to our species, but to all life on Earth. At the immediate and local level, people in many communities struggle to thrive because they live in food deserts, suffer from poor air quality or contaminated drinking water, and lack access to green spaces. These issues, both local and global, raise concerns for all sectors of society, including education and social work.

What role should the education system play in addressing sustainability, and what parallels are there with social work? Concerns that the education system is making environmental problems worse by prioritizing the preparation of young people for an economic paradigm that is unsustainable, and is framing success in terms of economic wealth and consumption, have been voiced for a long time. Notably, David Orr (1991), asking "What is education for?," asserts that "all education is environmental education" in that all teaching sends implicit messages about our relationship with the planet (p. 54). Orr (2005) suggested that education requires radical realignment to promote a sustainable future where the concept of "success" will have a different meaning.

In this chapter, I argue that through their work with students, post-secondary educators should play a pivotal role in helping society respond to the urgent need to transform our relationship with the planet to ensure a sustainable future. Teaching and social work are two endeavours where professionals can choose to work with service users to help them identify ways they can enhance personal well-being and that of the planet, by advocating for their communities, embracing sustainable behaviours, and contributing to society's restorative actions. Indeed, I believe that professional disciplines, such as social work and education, need to prioritize preparing their graduates to make an immediate contribution to this work.

If we agree on these objectives, how then can social work programs (as well as other helping professions) successfully establish sustainability as a central pillar of their work? To accomplish this goal, it may be useful to consider the parallel and ongoing challenges faced by teacher educators striving to realign their programs to properly address sustainability issues. Examining the strategies they have employed to try and meet these challenges, and reviewing the successes to date, may provide insights for those aiming to transform social work programs. That is not to say that all is rosy in the world of teacher education: while some progress has been made, there is still much to be done.

There are some clear parallels between initial teacher education and post-secondary social work programs. Both of the professions for which these programs prepare students can be considered person-focused caring professions; they both have professional codes of conduct, work with vulnerable populations, and are accredited by bodies external to the academy. One key difference, however, is that virtually all student teachers have experienced schooling from the perspective of a student, usually twelve years or more of primary and secondary schooling, whereas some student social workers may not have experienced their profession's work from the perspective of service user. So, whereas almost all student teachers begin their program with a well-established, evidence-based set of preconceptions about and experiences with the teaching profession, this may not be the case for a social work student.

At the same time, the preconceptions that people bring to initial teacher education programs, such as ideas about what constitutes effective pedagogy or the role of assessment and evaluation, can pose a challenge because, while these programs should be one of the most powerful avenues for stimulating change in the practices of schooling, there is a constant struggle to persuade students to relinquish some of their strongly held preconceptions. A major factor that the sectors have in common, though, is that both involve complex undertakings with centralized organizational structures that inevitably have the potential to be a source of inertia, frustrating those working in the field trying to advocate for and instigate change. This hurdle will have implications for faculty whether they are educating potential teachers or social workers. For instance, bringing about change in kindergarten to grade 12 (K–12) schooling can be a slow and frustrating process; the reasons for this, based upon my personal experience, will be explored later. Some of these reasons also apply to teacher education programs themselves, but despite this, pre-service teacher education represents one of the best avenues for bringing about changes in schooling. Pre-service teachers can be seen as "'Trojan horses' smuggling new ideas and alternative frameworks into established school systems" to challenge and disrupt the status quo, with ideas that tumble out when they take up placements, or later when they obtain their first employment (DiGiuseppe et al., 2019, p.132). The same analogy may be valid for work with social work students.

Infusing Environmental and Sustainability Education

Efforts to infuse environmental and sustainability education (ESE) content in pre-service teacher education in Canada have, until recently, mostly been undertaken only by dedicated individuals, often working in isolation within their faculty of education. A number of surveys have shown that while some progress has been made in incorporating ESE in programs across Canada, it has been at a slow pace, is patchy in its reach, and is dependent on the presence of committed individual faculty members (Lin, 2002; Sims & Falkenberg, 2013; Swayze et al., 2012; Towler, 1980). Since 2013, the situation has gradually begun to change, initially with faculty from several institutions in Ontario beginning to collaborate by sharing ideas and successful strategies and working to exert pressure for change within and beyond their faculties. This collaboration has now spread across the country. The work represents a systems approach to changing teacher education, one first pioneered in Queensland, Australia (Evans et al., 2016) and requiring "transformational leadership" (Bass & Steidlmeier, 1999, p. 184). This approach recognizes that for lasting change to occur in a professional discipline, it is necessary to engage multiple players, with different responsibilities and interests, not just those within academia. In the Canadian context, this includes engaging with the provincial ministries of education (for example, the Ontario Ministry of Education, https://www.ontario.ca/page/ministry-education) and accrediting bodies, such as the Ontario College of Teachers (OCT; http://www.oct.ca). These organizations determine, respectively, what should be taught in schools, how new teachers should be prepared, and what skills they should acquire.

Setting the Scene

When I first started working in pre-service teacher education in Ontario, in 2007, I took steps to include ESE topics in my own teaching, but it was apparent that there was no coordinated effort to ensure that our bachelor of education program addressed the topic. This experience was typical of the situation in most faculties and schools of education at that time, with just a few, often isolated, individuals working to address a pressing need as best they could. This began to change in 2009 when Ontario's Ministry of Education published a framework document on environmental education, *Acting Today, Shaping Tomorrow* (2009). Among other things, the framework requires all teachers in every grade (K–12) and of every curriculum subject to include environmental education in their teaching and calls on pre-service teacher education to prepare new teachers for this role. The publication of the framework provided an opportunity to move ESE up the agenda, if only a little. While I was chairing a small departmental working group seeking ways to ramp up the representation of ESE in the B.Ed. program, it became clear that our options were limited. Other, admittedly very important, topics already dominated a program that is intense in nature, constrained by challenging timetabling logistics, and compounded by the scheduling of practica. Making a case for change was also hobbled by the requirement that the program meet the criteria of the accrediting body, the OCT. Its current accreditation criteria almost totally ignore ESE: the term "environmental education" is used only once (OCT, 2017, p. 9) and the term "sustainability education" (or similar wording) not at all in their forty-four-page *Accreditation Resource Guide*. While the guide contains extensive reference to teacher candidates' need to understand how to promote student well-being, there is no mention of the recognized benefits of outdoor learning or anything about ensuring the planet's well-being. A similar section relates to the needs of Indigenous students but nowhere mentions the importance of land-based learning or treaty implications in Indigenous education. Clearly, a revision of the accreditation criteria is desirable and may soon appear, but in the meantime we had to press ahead without being able to argue that accreditation requires a good grounding in ESE.

A breakthrough moment came when we realized there was nothing to prevent us from offering an extracurricular opportunity for our teacher candidates. This would sidestep the problems of an overcrowded timetable and the need to make a case based upon OCT accreditation requirements. Unfortunately, it was not a perfect solution since it would not allow us to reach all of our students, because involvement would have to be optional. Coming on top of an already intense program, we knew uptake would be limited, with participation made more difficult for students with family or employment commitments. However, it would at least offer something for those who already recognized that

ESE should be part of their role as teachers. Indeed, it quickly became apparent that, for some of our student teachers, the wish to engage in ESE work was a driving motivation in their desire to become educators, to the extent that some arranged childcare or rearranged work commitments so that they could take part.

The extracurricular opportunity we developed, the eco-mentor program (Bell et al., 2013), comprises a series of workshops offered in a collaboration between the School of Education and Professional Learning and nearby Camp Kawartha (http://www.campkawartha.ca), an award-winning outdoor education centre. To bypass the constraints of the timetable, the workshops are held on five Saturday mornings, spread through the academic year. Participants can gain a certificate by attending the workshops and then demonstrating how they have mobilized their knowledge during one or more of their practical placements. The certificate is an "unofficial" one, which means in creating the program we avoided the need to steer a proposal through the university's committee process, enabling us to move swiftly. Jacob Rodenburg, executive director of Camp Kawartha, and I give our time freely, and the minor costs incurred are met by small grants. The program ran for the first time in 2010–11. Since then, 10 to 20 per cent of our teacher candidates complete the program each year, around three hundred in total so far. In 2012, we made a presentation on the eco-mentor program to other teacher educators in Ontario: it was a lightbulb moment for several of them, resulting in a number of other universities in the province developing similar solutions to our common problem and, ultimately, leading to a collaborative effort to promote ESE in teacher education.

Individual faculty members working in teacher education across Canada have been able to promote ESE using a variety of tactics, mostly by working at the margins of their programs to provide opportunities, some similar to the eco-mentor program but also themed day-conferences and alternative setting placements with ESE-related host organizations (DiGiuseppe et al., 2019; Kool et al., 2021; Sims, Inwood, Elliott et al. 2021). Some colleagues have been able to establish ESE-related elective courses and, occasionally, to lobby successfully for new ESE-related core courses to be taken by all teacher candidates, as is the case at my university. Such victories have had the cumulative effect of boosting the representation of ESE in teacher education, but they have relied heavily on grass-roots leadership from faculty with the time and dedication to make the case for their inclusion, characterized as "emergent environmental leaders" and "champions of change" by Taylor (2012, p. 817). While there has been a national call for more attention to be paid to ESE in teacher education (Swayze et al., 2012), as well as some provincial calls, these messages have often been drowned out by other requirements. Some calls for reforms in teacher education, such as those for a focus on numeracy and literacy work, attention to early years preparation, and various aspects of equity, seem to have been heard by a broader and more receptive audience among university faculty. The fact that the ultimate success of each of these reforms is dependent upon our crafting a sustainable way to exist on the planet is often overlooked or goes unrecognized – despite the fact that a sustainable future is the only one in which people can be healthy, happy, and fulfilled, and that many equity issues, such as access to healthy food, have a strong environmental aspect to them (UNESCO, 2017).

A one-day provincial roundtable, hosted by the Ontario Institute for Studies in Education (OISE) in 2013, brought like-minded faculty together to discuss the limited response in faculties of education to the Ministry of Education's environmental education framework, and to seek ways to address the shortfall. A small group of four colleagues (myself, Hilary Inwood, Doug Karrow, and Maurice DiGiuseppe) emerged from this meeting resolved to work together to try to address the problems by sharing ideas, conducting research, and persuading others of the need for change. It was this original decision to collaborate that has enabled the significant developments that have since occurred. Neo-liberal political agendas have encouraged academic institutions to regard each other, to some extent, as rivals competing for the same of students and funding (Palmer, 2014). As result, institutions have often worked independently to develop their programs and ensure they have distinctive features, but the need for a transition to sustainable education and practices is so urgent and existential in nature that there is no room for such institutional competition, but rather a need for collaboration. Collaboration not only enables the sharing of ideas and strategies, but can also create a critical mass of voices calling for reforms: no doubt social work programs can benefit from the same approach.

Following the successful provincial roundtable of 2013, our small team developed ambitious plans for a national roundtable on ESE in teacher education (ESE-TE). This three-day event was held at Trent University in June 2016 and attended by over seventy interested parties from eight provinces. The event gave participants an opportunity to report on initiatives to address ESE-TE, but also included various sessions to discuss how programming could be enhanced. Key outcomes of the meeting were the production of the *Otonabee Declaration* and a

National Action Plan (see Karrow & DiGiuseppe, 2019). The Otonabee Declaration concluded with this statement:

> We urge leaders in Canadian faculties of education, ministries of education, boards of education, and bodies that regulate the teaching profession to make Environmental and Sustainability Education a mandatory component of initial teacher education. (p. 16)

The ESE-TE National Action Plan identified four priorities: (1) to establish a national organization to support environmental and sustainability education in pre-service teacher education (ESE-PTE – since amended to "ESE-TE" so that the scope can be widened to include in-service teacher education) in Canada; (2) to assess the state of ESE-PTE in Canada; (3) to develop supports for ESE-PTE in Canada; and (4) to advocate for the crucial importance of ESE-PTE in Canada. Work to address each of these priorities is ongoing, but the plan has already yielded significant results, each of which will now be discussed.

PRIORITY: ESTABLISH A NEW NATIONAL ORGANIZATION

The team investigated various options for setting up a national organization to promote ESE-TE. We realized that charitable status was desirable because it enables an organization to seek funding from a wider variety of sources than would otherwise be possible, because some funding opportunities are accessible only to charities. Unfortunately, there are formidable legal and logistical hurdles to overcome and significant costs to setting up a new charitable body, and the time taken to do so would have interrupted our momentum. Eventually, it was agreed that we should approach an existing charitable organization with the suggestion of forming an offshoot body, rather than going to the expense and bureaucracy of setting up a new organization. Various candidates were considered as possible hosts before we identified the Canadian Network for Environmental Education and Communication (EECOM; http://eecom.org) as the best fit. EECOM is Canada's only national, bilingual, and charitable network that works to promote environmental learning. The EECOM board of directors was approached and agreed to collaborate, enabling the formation of the ESE-TE standing committee in 2017. The standing committee recruited like-minded representatives from across Canada, with most provinces now represented, from British Columbia in the west to Nova Scotia in the east. We have yet to succeed in recruiting representation from the territories, but note that teacher education in the north is provided under the auspices of institutions in the south. Most members of the committee are from faculties and schools of education, but some represent other organizations that are actively involved in teacher education, such as Learning for a Sustainable Future (LSF; http://www.lsf-lst.ca). The EECOM board has a representative on the standing committee, and ESE-TE has reciprocal representation on the main board of EECOM.

PRIORITY: ASSESSING THE STATE OF ESE-TE IN CANADA

In 2019–20, several members of the ESE-TE standing committee, together with a number of other interested faculty members from across Canada, worked to devise and conduct a nationwide survey of ESE programming in faculties of education. The group also recruited United States–based Emily Lin because she had experience carrying out a similar survey in Canada, at the end of the last century, as part of her doctoral research (Lin, 2002). Lin summarized her findings thus: "Environmental education remains at the fringe of most pre-service teacher training programs and the prospect of significant environmental education program implementation appears dim" (p. 212). Our aim was to produce a detailed, up-to-date overview of the present state of practice, something that had not been attempted since Lin's survey two decades earlier. Members of faculty involved in teacher education that were identified as having an interest in ESE were invited to complete the survey. An initial report on the findings of the new survey was published in March 2021 (Kool et al. 2021). The results show that a majority of respondents believe that ESE should be accorded a higher priority in their programs, with fewer than half of those programs currently including core components addressing the topic and only just over half offering relevant elective courses. Reasons identified for the under-representation of ESE in their programs included its interdisciplinary nature – which is at odds with the traditional "silo" approach to the curriculum – and lack of support from senior administrators, colleagues, and professional bodies. Many stated that the failure of their provincial K-12 curriculum to address sustainability properly was adversely influencing the content of their pre-service programs. Many suggested that if their provincial K-12 curricula were clearer in prioritizing ESE, it would pressure their faculties to do the same. Having this up-to-date analysis of the state of practice provides a clearer understanding of where the challenges are that still need to be addressed if we are to achieve the aims of the standing committee. The data also helps to strengthen arguments and assist with the identification of the potentially most profitable avenues to pursue in the quest for better representation of ESE in TE.

PRIORITY: DEVELOPING SUPPORTS

To help support colleagues across Canada in their ESE-TE work, the first priority was to establish a digital hub where ideas, resources, and curricula could be shared. This hub (http://www.eseinfacultiesofed.ca) became active in 2017 and has grown to share developments in research, case studies demonstrating innovative practice, as well as syllabi and videos created for an ESE-TE YouTube channel (Environmental Learning in Faculties of Education). The hub makes resources freely available and broadcasts information about events such as conferences and webinars. ESE-TE members have also collaborated to publish a book: *Environmental and Sustainability Education in Teacher Education: Canadian Perspectives* that features work presented at the National Roundtable held at Trent University (Karrow & DiGiuseppe, 2019). They have also collaborated on the production of numerous other book chapters and academic papers, including guest editing a special volume of the Canadian Journal of Environmental Education in 2020 (https://cjee.lakeheadu .ca/issue/view/89/showToc) exclusively concerned with teacher education; and the provision of a series of webinars. Three research symposia have been held in association with the EECOM annual conference, the first in 2018 at Cranbrook, British Columbia, the second held remotely in 2021, and the third in Toronto in 2023. At these symposia, teacher educators have taken the opportunity to share their research and programmatic and pedagogical developments. A national, extra-curricular E-course for teacher candidates was piloted in 2021–22. Participants attended monthly synchronous sessions hosted by experts from across Canada and also completed asynchronous work that included readings and tasks. The E-course provided opportunities for teacher candidates in those institutions where ESE is still not well established and gave them access to the expertise of leaders in ESE-TE. As education is provincially organized, this E-course is believed to be the first of its kind in that it enables teacher candidates from across the country to interact with each other and share ideas.

PRIORITY: ADVOCATING FOR THE CRITICAL
IMPORTANCE OF ESE-TE IN CANADA

Another priority identified by the standing committee was to lobby deans of education to ensure that ESE features in their institutions' programs. The issue was raised with the Association of Canadian Deans of Education (ACDE), who subsequently invited several members of faculty from Ontario and Quebec to address them on the topic at meeting, held in Montreal in October 2018. It helped that the chair role of ACDE was about to pass to the dean at Trent University, Dr. Cathy

Bruce, someone sympathetic to our cause, and also that one of our team members became an acting dean at this time. An outcome of the meeting was the ACDE's commitment to produce an accord on Education for Sustainability. The accord joins five existing accords (https://csse-scee .ca/acde/publications-2/) that guide and influence practice across institutions throughout Canada. This was major achievement for the ESE-TE team in terms of starting to achieve system change. The Accord on Education for a Sustainable Future was finally released in April 2022 (MacDonald, Barwell, Airini et al., 2022).

Indigenous Education and ESE in Teacher Education

Throughout this work, we have recognized the close relationship between ESE and Indigenous education. My colleague, Nicole Bell, puts it succinctly: "You cannot do Indigenous education without environmental education, and you should not do environmental education without Indigenous education" (N. Bell, personal communication, 2016). The ACDE accord on Indigenous Education (2010) and the work of the Truth and Reconciliation Commission of Canada and its *Calls to Action* (2015) helped to make Indigenous education a focus of reforms within teacher education. Prior to this, in many ways, Indigenous education content in teacher education was as disparate (Memon, 2011) as ESE and as dependent on a few committed individuals to ensure that it had some presence. However, the new emphasis on Indigenous education in teacher education has also presented some opportunities to promote ESE because of the close links between the two. When the Ontario government decreed that all B.Ed. programs should move from one-year to two–year duration, beginning in 2016, it obliged faculties to review their programming. The move from one to two years allowed for a greater breadth and depth of content. At Trent University, several members of faculty advocated for more prominence for both ESE and Indigenous education in the revised program. The result of this advocacy was a new core course that addresses both of these topics (Elliott et al., 2018). This alignment of ESE and Indigenous education is particularly appropriate for a number of reasons, especially because it lends itself to "two-eyed seeing," the benefits of which are explored by McKeon (2012, p. 133). Two-eyed involves simultaneously viewing an issue through the lenses of both Western science and Indigenous teachings. There are synergistic benefits to addressing the two disciplines in tandem, for instance, the land-based learning that is central to Indigenous education also works well for ESE, as can the exploration of Traditional

Ecological Knowledge. Indigenous ways of knowing, with concepts such as respect, relationship, reciprocity, and responsibility (Bell et al., 2013), certain Indigenous philosophies and world views, such as the belief that everything is interconnected, and teachings such as the Iroquois principle of "Seven Generations" (Lyons, 1980) can all help to challenge Western, anthropocentric world views. Add to this the fact that many of the issues facing Indigenous communities in Canada are environmental in nature, such as access to safe drinking water, damage to traditional territories caused by extractive industries, and food security, and it becomes apparent that Indigenous education has to address ESE (Elliott et al., 2018).

The Future

The national ESE-TE survey results (Kool et al., 2021) show that there is still much to be done to ensure that all pre-service teachers are adequately prepared for their work in ESE. It is not simply a question of getting them ready to address sustainability as an "add-on" to the curriculum, but helping them to appreciate that it can, and should, inform and underpin their whole approach to teaching. A vital part of such an aim is helping them to appreciate that this should be done in tandem with adoption of content and pedagogy that recognizes and respects the necessity to bring Indigenous perspectives and philosophies into mainstream schooling. Developments in pre-service teacher education alone will struggle to truly achieve this transformation in schooling; a systems-based change is required so that the accreditation regime helps to drive change and the school system supports and embraces those changes. More broadly, the post-secondary sector in general can do more to embrace the ethos of sustainability (Leal Filho et al., 2020). Ensuring that all undergraduates receive courses relating to sustainability, adopting sustainable procurement practices, divesting from fossil fuels, and funding research into sustainability-focused pedagogy are all ways in which the sector can contribute. The whole raison d'être of all schooling needs to be reevaluated so that it becomes part of the sustainability solution rather than part of the problem. Fixing the problems in pre-service teacher education can only be the first step. Next steps for ESE-TE need to include efforts to influence ministries of education and accrediting bodies, persuading them to ask themselves Orr's question about the purpose of education and to reach the conclusion that a sustainable future is the only desirable option and one that they have a duty to promote more effectively.

Conclusion

The extensive progress made by ESE-TE since 2017 can serve as a model for other disciplines in professional post-secondary institutions, including social work and other helping professions. Tactics that should be equally productive in social work include the following:

1. collaboration between colleagues across the sector, enabling sharing of ideas, promotion of new research initiatives, and building the strength in numbers that helps to make the case for institutional change;
2. putting traditional institutional and personal professional rivalries aside to help demonstrate to third parties how earnestly change is sought;
3. harnessing students' desire and enthusiasm to learn how their profession can contribute to sustainability issues;
4. identifying relevant opportunities to couple sustainability issues with Indigenous interests and leadership to benefit from a synergistic effect; and
5. leveraging relationships with existing organizations.

These approaches could yield benefits for social work programs, and a compelling case can be made for adopting a two-eyed seeing approach in the realignment of social work programs to address sustainability issues. Involvement in ESE-TE work has motivated individuals who previously felt like voices in the wilderness to press on with the good work they are already doing and to continue to advocate for reforms in their own institutions. Incidentally, it has also generated a team of friends who benefit from the motivation that friendship provides and who celebrate each person's small victories in their shared mission. Working in isolation to try to bring about changes in programming and philosophy within a professional program can be a lonely and dispiriting business, but by reaching out across institutions to others with common interests, it is possible to envision and build a hopeful future.

REFERENCES

Bass, B. M., and Steidlmeier, P. (1999). Ethics, character, and authentic transformational leadership behavior. *Leadership Quarterly*, 10(2), 181–217. http://doi.org/10.1016/S1048-9843(99)00016-8

Bell, N., Elliott, P., Rodenburg, J., & Young, K. (2013). Eco-mentorship: A pre-service outdoor experiential teacher education initiative at Trent University. *Pathways: The Ontario Journal of Outdoor Education, 25*(3), 14–17.

DiGiuseppe, M., Elliott, P., Ibrahim Khan, S., Rhodes, S., Scott, J., & Steele, A. (2019). Rising to the challenge: Promoting environmental education in three Ontario faculties of education. In D. Karrow & M. DiGiuseppe (Eds.), *Environmental and sustainability education in teacher education: Canadian perspectives* (pp. 131–159). Springer.

Elliott, P., Bell, N., & Harding, B. (2018). Indigenous environmental inquiry. *Green Teacher, 116*, 25–28.

Evans, N., Ferreira, J., Davis, J., & Stevenson, R. (2016). Embedding EfS in teacher education through a multi-level systems approach: lessons from Queensland. *Australian Journal of Environmental Education, 32*(1), 65–79, https://doi.org/10.1017/aee.2015.47

Karrow, D., & DiGiuseppe, M. (2019). *Environmental and sustainability education in teacher education: Canadian perspectives.* Springer.

Kool, R., Karrow, D. D., & DiGiuseppe, M. (2021). *Environmental and sustainability education in Canadian faculties of education, 2017–2018: A research report for the EECOM standing committee on Environmental and Sustainability Education in Teacher Education.* http://www.eseinfacultiesofed.ca/research-pages/policy-reports.html

Leal Filho, W., Eustachio, J. H. P. P., Caldana, A. C. F., Will, M., Lange Salvia, A., Rampasso, I. S., Anholon, R., Platje, J., & Kovaleva, M. (2020). Sustainability leadership in higher education institutions: An overview of challenges. *Sustainability, 12*(9), 3761. https://doi.org/10.3390/su12093761

Lin, E. (2002). Trends of environmental education in Canadian pre-service teacher education programs from 1976 to 1996. *Canadian Journal of Environmental Education, 7*(1), 199–215. https://cjee.lakeheadu.ca/article/view/283

Lyons, O. (1980). An Iroquois perspective. In C. Vecsey & R. W. Venables (Eds.), *American Indian environments: Ecological issues in Native American history* (pp. 171–174). Syracuse University Press.

MacDonald, R., Barwell, R., Airini, Bell, N., Cheechoo, K.-L., Cormier, M., Dyment, J., Elliott, P., Falkenberg, T., Howard, P., Montgomery, K., Schmidt, E., St. Clair, R., & Tupper, J. (2022). *Accord on education for a sustainable future.* Association of Canadian Deans of Education.

McKeon, M. (2012). Two-eyed seeing into environmental education: Revealing its "natural" readiness to Indigenize. *Canadian Journal of Environmental Education, 17*, 131–147. https://cjee.lakeheadu.ca/article/view/1071

Memon, N. (2011). Diverse perspectives in teacher education. In L. Thomas (Ed.), *What is Canadian about teacher education in Canada? Multiple perspectives on Canadian teacher education in the twenty-first century* (pp. 357–378).

Canadian Association for Teacher Educators. https://cate-acfe.ca/wp
-content/uploads/2020/07/What-is-Canadian-about-Teacher-Education-in
-Canada-1.pdf

Ontario College of Teachers. (2017). *Accreditation resource guide.* https://www
.oct.ca//media/PDF/Accreditation%20Resource%20Guide/Accreditation
_Resource_Guide_EN_WEB.pdf

Ontario Ministry of Education. (2009). *Acting today, shaping tomorrow.* Queen's
Printer. http://www.edu.gov.on.ca/eng/teachers/enviroed/Shape
Tomorrow.pdf

Orr, D. (1991). What is education for? Six myths about the foundations of
modern education, and six new principles to replace them. *The Learning
Revolution, 27,* 52–55. https://www.context.org/iclib/ic27/orr/

Orr, D. (2005). Recollection. In M. K. Stone and Z. Barlow (Eds.), *Ecological
literacy: Educating our children for a sustainable world* (pp. 96–106). Sierra Book
Clubs.

Palmer, N. (2014). The modern university and its transaction with students.
In M. Thornton (Ed.), *Through a glass darkly: The social sciences look at the
neoliberal university* (pp. 121–140). Australian National University Press.
www.jstor.org/stable/j.ctt13wwvss.14

Sims, L., & Falkenberg, T. (2013). Developing competences for education for
sustainable development: A case studies of Canadian faculties of education.
International Journal of Higher Education, 2(4), 1–14. https://doi.org/10.5430
/ijhe.v2n4p1

Sims, L., Inwood, H., Elliott, P., & Gerofsky, S. (2021). Innovative praxis for
environmental learning in Canadian faculties of education. *Australian
Journal of Environmental Education, 37*(3), 240–253. https://doi.org/10.1017
/aee.2021.2

Swayze, N., Creech, H., Buckler, C., & Alfaro, J. (2012) *Education for sustainable
development in Canadian faculties of education.* Council of the Ministers of
Education, Canada. https://www.cmec.ca/9/Publication.html?year
=2012

Taylor, A. C. (2012). Champions of change: Emergent environmental leaders. In
D. R. Gallagher (Ed.), *Environmental leadership: A reference handbook* (pp. 2–17).
Sage. https://us.sagepub.com/en-us/nam/environmental-leadership
/book234216

Towler, J. O. (1980). A survey of Canadian pre-service training in environmental
education. *Journal of Environmental Education, 12*(2), 11–16. https://doi.org
/10.1080/00958964.1981.10801893

Truth and Reconciliation Commission of Canada. (2015). *Calls to action.*
https://nctr.ca/records/reports/#trc-reports

UNESCO. (2017). *UNESCO moving forward the 2030 agenda for sustainable
develop*ment. https://unesdoc.unesco.org/ark:/48223/pf0000247785

4 An Invitation to the Learning Garden: Green Lessons from a School of Education

KELLY YOUNG AND
KARLEEN PENDLETON JIMÉNEZ

Land and Learning at the School of Education

We write these words "on the treaty and traditional territory of the Mississauga Anishnaabeg. We offer our gratitude to the First Nations for their care for, and teachings about, our earth and our relations. May we honour those teachings" ("Land acknowledgement," 2019, p. 3). The land is our first teacher (Bell, 2020; Cajete, 1994). To understand the pedagogy of a classroom, it is important to learn about the land where it rests (Haig-Brown & Hodson, 2009). Trent University is located on beautiful land. The land is lush, green lawns and hillsides during the spring, bright reds and oranges during the fall, and curvy, fluffy snow during the winter. There are rabbits, squirrels, hedgehogs, and robins outside our office windows. We hear the clatter of bird song and watch visiting dogs of faculty and students sneak fruit from crab apple trees. Evergreens surround our buildings, and we take our students outside and teach in the quad, in the nearby forest, at the Environmental Centre, or down beside the Otonabee River, where the students slip their toes into the water as we learn about the standards of professional practice (https://www.oct.ca/public/professional-standards/standards-of-practice).

In order to understand the successful infusion of eco-justice, as part of the curriculum of the School of Education, the land is vital. Surrounded by the stunning landscape at Trent, we follow an eco-justice framework in education that influences the pedagogy and research of the university across disciplines. Our understanding of eco-justice comes from the work of the late Chet Bowers (2004), who defines it as employing the following actions:

> (1) eliminating the causes of eco-racism, (2) ending the North's exploitation and cultural colonization of the South (Third World cultures),

(3) revitalizing the commons in order to achieve a healthier balance between market and non-market aspects of community life, (4) ensuring that the prospects of future generations are not diminished by the hubris and ideology that drives the globalization of the West's industrial culture, (5) reducing the threat to what Vandana Shiva refers to as "earth democracy" – that is, the right of natural systems to reproduce themselves rather than to have their existence contingent upon the demands of humans; ecojustice provides the larger moral and conceptual framework for understanding how to achieve the goals of social justice. (para. 1)

Thus, the themes that permeate our courses include, but are not limited to, sustainability, eco-racism, community relationships, globalization, anti-colonization, and social justice, which Bowers indicates are important aspects for educational reform. Trent's mission statement compels us to "foster sustainability, in its environmental, social and economic dimensions, on our campuses and in all aspects of our work" (Trent University, 2021, para. 2). This message influences those who want to teach here, research here, learn here, and live here. Academic departments and professional schools are all part of the landscape at Trent University. As a pre-service teacher education program, we engage in a range of pedagogical practices that draw upon an eco-justice theoretical framework. It is our hope that our approach to greening higher education may serve as a helpful model for our colleagues in the helping professions, and particularly in our cognate discipline of social work. There are many similarities between education and social work; both are caring professions and help vulnerable people. Our practice in teacher training also involves both classroom and field experience in the same way that social work programs do.

In this chapter, we discuss the significance of environmental immersion and relationships in sustaining an effective eco-justice identity in professional programs. As background, we provide a historical overview of environmental education in Ontario as well as our faculty hiring practices, policy statements, curricular approaches, and niche alternative placement opportunities. We also present concrete applications for teaching about sustainability within higher education. Ultimately, we outline how the School of Education adopted an eco-justice framework through relationships among land and institution, among colleagues, and among community.

Environmental Leadership in Higher Education:
A Historical Perspective

In the 1990s, environmental education across the province of Ontario was reduced through the Mike Harris government's curriculum revision. The curriculum revision diminished the depth of environmental issues in the curriculum through its outcome-based focus and infusion of standardized testing (Gidney, 1999). At the same time, there was a global rise in awareness of the environmental crisis, evidenced in the fact that the years 2005 to 2014 were labelled the United Nations Decade of Education for Sustainable Development (UNDESD). According to the United Nations Educational, Scientific, and Cultural Organization UNESCO:

> The overall goal of the UN Decade of Education for Sustainable Development (DESD) was to integrate the principles, values and practices of sustainable development into all aspects of education and learning. This educational effort encouraged changes in behaviour that created a more sustainable future in terms of environmental integrity, economic viability and a just society for present and future generations. (2021, para. 2)

In addition, during this same period there was a call for renewal of the original "Haudenosaunee Address to the Western World" that was first presented at a non-governmental organization's conference titled "Discrimination Against the Indigenous Populations of the Americas" at the United Nations in 1977 in Geneva. The address was subsequently published in a collection titled *Basic Call to Consciousness* (Akwesasne Notes, 2005) with contributions from, among others, John Mohawk and Chief Oren Lyon. This call entailed, among other things, respecting the environment for future generations by listening to Indigenous Knowledge Keepers and restoring the Earth. In addition, Al Gore's film *An Inconvenient Truth* (Guggenheim, 2006) rose in popularity in the mainstream media.

During this same decade, the School of Education's bachelor of education program was launched at Trent University in 2003 with a social justice focus. At the inception of the program, we did not have an environmental or Indigenous knowledge(s) course offering, nor did our mission statement contain the prefix "eco-" or the terms "ecology" or "environment." However, a few courses had environmental issues embedded in the curriculum, such as science (which was required to address surface-level environmental subject matter in the kindergarten to grade 12 Ontario curriculum of the day) and English (which included an eco-justice approach that addressed how language can act as a barrier between humans and nature).

Developing an Environmental Focus

In terms of identity, we write as two faculty members who both teach in the School of Education at Trent University. Kelly Young is a cis woman settler of European descent who has been an educator in K–12 for over twenty-five years and whose research interests include the infusion of environmental perspectives and Indigenous epistemologies in preservice education, language and literacy, and curriculum theorizing. Karleen Pendleton Jiménez is a butch/trans, white/Mexican lesbian who has been a community educator for over twenty-five years whose research interests include queerness, gender diversity, Latinx identity, and arts-based inquiry. Our professional program leads students to an Ontario teacher certification and a graduate degree in education. At the outset of the program, in 2003, I (Kelly) brought an environmentally focused approach to pedagogy and research, through an emphasis on inquiry into the ways in which language can be a barrier to human relationships with the natural world (Bowers, 2002). As the 2000s progressed, my colleagues and I attempted to infuse both environmental and Indigenous knowledges throughout the program (Longboat et al., 2013; Young, 2007, 2009). At this time, when I sat at the table at the School of Education, my environmental approach to teacher education was mostly met with uninterest. Human development was the predominating theme of the day, and it was difficult to conceive of how environmental education could be an integral part of human development or other teaching subjects, apart from science.

I (Karleen) arrived at Trent University in 2005 with a focus on social justice (i.e., queer pedagogy and critical race theory) to teach the course "Sociocultural Perspectives on Human Development and Learning." My work had been primarily devoted to anti-homophobia and Latinx identity, and it was initially difficult for me to understand how eco-justice education fit into learning about people. However, I had just finished my doctorate, during which my supervisor (Dr. Celia Haig-Brown) had taught me that Indigenous and environmental education should be central to all types of curricula. Through my conversations and friendship with Kelly, in which she advocated for the infusion of environmental studies across the program, I was able to build upon my previous learning and develop the confidence to include eco-justice in our human development course (required for all teacher education students). In it, I started asking students to situate themselves through their relationship with the landscape, and I also included environmental learning as a major topic of the course. While this move was initially challenged by other instructors, a few discussions about eco-oriented course content on syllabi helped to bring others on board. By the end of 2007, Kelly and I had received a grant from our university's Academic Innovation Fund (AIF), to host our first "Eco-Social-Justice Alternative Settings Placement" for pre-service teachers. This placement provided our students with an opportunity to engage for a sustained period in a dialogue about the intersection of environment and human development. Students participated in a seventy-five-hour placement with invited researchers and pedagogues in both fields. We also brought together readings that integrated human development/learning and ecology (Bowers, 2002; Bronfenbrenner, 1979). To promote systemic influence, we realized that we needed to hire more faculty who had the environment on their radar.

Hiring with an Eco-Justice Sensibility

Now, when we invite applicants to apply to be part of our faculty, we want them to understand that environmental learning is one of our core values. As such, our job advertisements provide an overview of our program within the Trent University context, indicating that

> Trent is situated on the banks of the Otonabee River in Peterborough, Ontario, Canada, and is surrounded by natural beauty. Trent is known for its radical and innovative undergraduate and graduate programs. The School of Education has undergraduate, post-graduate, and graduate programs that are well-known for their high quality and rigor including emphasis in literacies, issues of environmental and social justice, infusion of educational technologies, Indigenous studies, and discipline-specific excellence. Coursework offered in the programs incorporates theory and research that encourages our students to think creatively and critically about their professional practices with attention to meeting individual learners' needs, valuing diversity and multiple modes of learning, and enacting effective practices that demonstrate subject excellence and a strong commitment to social and ecological justice, leading to responsible action. (School of Education, sample job ad)

While we do hire professors with expertise to cover a diversity of subjects, we want them to know that eco-justice perspectives are highly valued and integral to our programming. By placing this language in our job advertisements, we also make a commitment to valuing the environmental knowledge that potential candidates might bring. Through this process, we have hired several tenure-stream scholars who focus on environmental pedagogies in their teaching and research. For example, we hired Dr. Paul Elliott, a scholar in "insect ecology, bat conservation, biodiversity education, scientific literacy and the influence of the environment in which science is taught" (Elliott, n.d., para. 8), to help infuse our curriculum with environmental perspectives. We also hired

Dr. Nicole Bell, a scholar in "Indigenous culture-based education, infusion of Indigenous knowledge into public schooling and teacher education, decolonization and healing, and Indigenous research theory and methodology" (Bell, n.d., para. 1). Finally, we hired Dr. Blair Niblett, a scholar who is drawn to "education [for its] potential to develop global citizens who can co-create a more socially and ecologically just world" (Niblett, n.d., para. 1).

We believe that our ability to attract multiple faculty members with an interest in environmental education made it possible for us to successfully infuse eco-justice education across our program. We needed the numbers and the relationships to give each other confidence, momentum, and power to tip the balance in favour of environmental learning across our school. With these faculty members in place, and others persuaded by their energy and commitment to join them, our eco-justice education framework focus began to acquire critical mass.

Mission Statement and Conceptual Framework

In 2005, our program doubled in size, and we began to review our program goals and curricula. Conversations about social justice expanding to include eco-justice were part of the day-to-day discourse among faculty. We changed our mission statement to include eco-social justice perspectives. Furthermore, including "eco-" is an important signal that we are all interconnected to each other and the Earth. Our mission statement was updated to include ecological justice.

We also revised our conceptual framework principles to better reflect our commitment to environmental and social justice. For example, we added "teaching and learning that promotes inclusivity is based on a commitment to equity, diversity and environmental sustainability; and respect and appreciation for Indigenous Knowledges, perspectives and pedagogies is central to teaching and learning" (https://www.trentu.ca/education/conceptual-framework, p. 2). These changes were significant as they were a solid indication of our commitment to a program that infuses ecological and Indigenous perspectives. What follows is a discussion of our current ecologically focused curricula and programs.

Ecologically Focused Curricula

ECO-MENTORSHIP PROGRAM
In 2011–12, the Eco-Mentorship Certificate program was introduced by Dr. Paul Elliott through a partnership with Camp Kawartha. The model is cross-curricular, as it brings together Indigenous, scientific,

technological, eco-justice, and place-based outdoor education in an interdisciplinary environmental curriculum. Through four three-hour workshops, a cohort of pre-service teacher candidates engage in environmentally focused activities (e.g., workshops and curriculum planning and development) for environmental leadership development. The program was developed with the following themes: "Drawing on Nearby Nature" (engaging students in hands-on activities in the landscape at the Environmental Centre at Trent University), "Removing Barriers to Environmental Education" (local experts share how to access funding for outdoor excursions and resources to help promote environmental education, and an eco-justice framework is introduced), "Inspiring Hope" (encouraging children to embrace nature through a physical exploration of school grounds), and "Environmental Education Across the Curriculum" (exploring an integrated approach to environmental education across K–12 subject courses). These themes are aimed at integrating local and global forms of knowledge about, in, and for the environment (Bell et al., 2013).

Selected examples of activities in the eco-mentor program include a capstone project and an evaluation of an environmentally sustainable education framework. The capstone project engages pre-service teachers in an eco-mentorship action project where they implement an activity into their practice teaching placement and report on their engagement. This project can be in the form of developing a lesson plan infused with environmental themes, organizing an extracurricular activity such as an eco-club, or developing a classroom resource related to environmental learning. Teacher candidates are also provided an environmental sustainability framework for community collaboration and asked to "evaluate and comment" on it. A "Pathway to Stewardship and Kinship" document with a simple chart of "principles" coupled with "stewardship opportunities" (Elliott, Dueck, & Rodenburg, 2020, p. 93) was met with enthusiasm from students. In addition, "the links to community-based resources further reassure them that there are people in the wider community well-placed to assist them in this work" (pp. 94–95). Finally, some teacher candidates had the opportunity to join with local teachers in implementing the framework and will be encouraged to use the document to help guide their planning in practica.

LEARNING GARDEN ALTERNATIVE PLACEMENT

In 2012, I (Kelly) developed a partnership between GreenUP/Ecology Park and the School of Education at Trent. Together, we created a seventy-five-hour Learning Garden Alternative Placement. Ten of the hours involve workshops that include a traditional teaching from a local

Elder, a tour of the teaching/learning space and curriculum at Ecology Park, a lesson in eco-justice literacy in terms of the ways in which language can be a barrier to human relationships with the natural world, and a review and critique of Ontario's environmental education policy.

In 2009, the Ontario Ministry of Education developed a policy document titled *Acting Today, Shaping Tomorrow: A Policy Framework for Environmental Education in Ontario Schools*:

> Through extensive research and consultation with education stakeholders, this framework promotes an integrated approach to environmental education, encourages targeted approaches to professional development, emphasizes community involvement, and provides models for guiding implementation and reviewing progress. (2009, p. 7)

However, the policy document failed to include Indigenous knowledge in its conceptualization and recommendations (Young, 2009). We use this text with our students as a tool to develop critical thinking about environmental education and to illuminate the ways in which a solely scientific inquiry model is neither inclusive nor holistic.

Another example of *The Learning Garden* curricular practice involves a lesson in eco-justice literacy that highlights the abstract nature of language through comparisons such as "drain" versus "stream" and asks learners to identify associations of these words. "Drain" is abstract and stems from a mechanistic root metaphor – students often associate it with the product Draino that is used to unclog a drain (as not being part of the environment) – whereas "stream" is more ecological, usually associated with nature. Both lead to the natural environment, but abstract language has a way of interfering with our relationship and associations with nature. Other examples include "trees" versus "lumber" or "forest" versus "timber." Associations are often made that nature is a commodity when language such as "lumber" and "timber" are used, while learners' associations of trees and forests are frequently environmental and conservationist in kind (Bowers, 2002; Martusewicz et al., 2015). Ultimately, in this program, pre-service teachers engage in environmental education and make connections to curriculum through language arts, math, science and social studies, physical and health education, and the arts (Young, 2021).

LEARNING FROM THE LAND AND INDIGENOUS PEOPLE
Another popular opportunity for our teacher candidates to explore environmental education is the Learning from the Land and Indigenous People placement developed by Dr. Nicole Bell, an associate professor

with the School of Education. On the Trent School of Education website (Bell, 2021), she describes the placement as follows:

> [Nicole] is Anishinaabe – Bear Clan from Kitigan Zibi First Nation and is the founder of an Anishinaabe culture-based school for Indigenous children and youth. Collaboratively with Nicole, Teacher Candidates experience land-based activities in Burleigh Falls and Lovesick Lake to personally develop a connection to the environment and an awareness of the Anishinaabe culture. This alternative placement provides Teacher Candidates with the knowledge, motivation, and skills to facilitate the transmission of an environmental consciousness to their future students. Additionally, the placement assists Teacher Candidates in establishing inclusive learning spaces that meet the cultural needs of Indigenous students and the cross-cultural learning needs of non-Indigenous students. These objectives assist Teacher Candidates in implementing *The First Nation, Métis, and Inuit Education Policy Framework*, and the *Acting Today, Shaping Tomorrow: Environmental Education in Ontario Schools Policy Framework*. (2007, para. 1)

In Dr. Bell's teaching, environmental education and Indigenous knowledge are inseparable. As an Indigenous scholar and educator, she sees environmental education as central to her teaching of Indigenous culture. In her article "Land as Teacher: Using Learnings from the Land and Indigenous People to Shape Tomorrow's Teachers" (2020), she explains her rationale for developing this alternative settings placement, beginning in 2007:

> Since the worldview of Indigenous peoples is connected to the environment, and since there is a global/universal need for all students to learn about the state of the planet, I felt a land-based program would serve the dual purpose of learning about Indigenous people while instilling an ecological consciousness in teacher candidates, and ultimately their future students. (para. 9)

Bell describes her approach to environmental education within this placement in terms of three main concepts – respect, responsibility, and relationship:

> Respecting the land requires re-spect, looking again, at all that the natural world provides; seeing ourselves as inextricably linked, and thus in relationship, with the natural world; engaging with the natural world in reciprocal and balanced ways; and acting with responsibility, or response-ability, to ensure respect, relationship, and reciprocity. (para. 20)

In response, teacher candidates have expressed their appreciation for their learning within the placement. One placement student described an aspect of their environmental learning as follows: "the image of Earth as mother has further deepened my respect and love for the Earth" (Bell, 2020, para. 14). We can only hope that this respect and love for the Earth might translate to a lifelong commitment to teaching about eco-justice education in Ontario classrooms.

INFUSING ENVIRONMENTAL EDUCATION INTO
THE TWO-YEAR B.ED. PROGRAM

Finally, in 2015, in response to a Ministry of Education requirement, our program changed from a one-year to a two-year Bachelor of Education program format. During this time, we introduced a mandatory course for all students in Indigenous environmental studies (IES) that

> examines current issues and theories of Indigenous education, environmental and eco-justice pedagogies, and cultural and linguistic diversity as they pertain to the learning environment for K–12 classrooms. Students examine and critically assess these issues and theories as they develop personal philosophies related to their own teaching and learning. (Trent University, 2021–2022, p. 169)

The course provides readings/videos/websites and discussion on environmental and Indigenous education perspectives. In addition, three assignments are required to challenge students to analyse and apply their learning: completion of a background report on a course text, a presentation, and creation of a resource pack to support lesson planning and delivery, with links to Ontario curricular expectations.

Environmental Infusion – Challenges and Changes for 2021 and Beyond

As we look back over the last fifteen years in the School of Education, we can see how our environmentally focused hiring enables us to offer both niche programming and the capacity to infuse eco-justice education throughout the department. We encourage faculty with a social justice or educational subject methods background to continue to bring eco-justice to the forefront of their teaching. While many faculty members are committed to environmental infusion, with such a large group of part-time instructors required to deliver our professional program it is challenging to encourage *all* faculty to engage in this important practice; we continually reach out and offer support in this area through expansive notices on bulletin boards, pedagogical resources on the School of Education website, discussion at committee meetings, and a collaborative review of accreditation materials. We have also now built a reputation that has had an impact on student recruitment. Indeed, prospective students point to our environmentally focused programs as part of the reason that they might choose to study in our Bachelor of Education professional program. In addition, we have plans to further develop our own teaching space, outside of our building, with a focus on the connections between the environment and Indigenous knowledge. Through the years, the School of Education has fostered ecological habits of mind as a taken-for-granted approach to teaching and research.

We offer our practices at the School of Education as one model for fostering environmental leadership in higher education. There are others: for examples of incorporating gardens within social work, see Bailey et al., 2018; Mailhot, 2015; and Cluff, 2020; and for further examples from education, see Lochner et al., 2021; Williams & Dixon, 2013; Gaylie, 2012; and Williams & Brown, 2012. We believe that our faculty's fundamental commitment to linking social justice approaches with eco-justice approaches was key to infusing environmental content across the program; it is the recognition that humans are always in relationship with the land. Perhaps such an epistemological move in social work programs could offer a similar shift towards more immersive environmental practices, in hiring, policy, and curricular offerings? We concur with the idea of renaming the field of social work as eco- or green social work, as recommended by key social work authors (Dominelli, 2012, 2018; Gray et al., 2013;). Finally, we recommend that our social work colleagues initiate environmentally focused curricular mapping to reveal the environmental gaps and strengths in their programs. We also offer those colleagues our unfinished wish list – both of what we already have and what we dream of: environmental courses; environmentally infused courses on a variety of subjects, certificates, alternative placements (see Chapter 11 of this book for interesting exemplars), special events, protests, inspiring speakers, forest walks, podcasts, TikToks, tipis (with Indigenous supervision), canoeing, and blogs … a list of curricular planning limited only by our imaginations.

REFERENCES

Akwesasne Notes. (2005). *The basic call to consciousness*. Native Voices.
Bailey, S., Hendrick, A., & Palmer, M. (2018). Eco-social work in action: A place for community gardens. *Australian Social Work, 71*(1), 98–110. https://doi.org /10.1080/0312407X.2017.1384032

Bell, N. (2020, March 5). *Land as teacher: Using learnings from the land and Indigenous people to shape tomorrow's teachers*. EdCan Network. https://www.edcan.ca/articles/land-as-teacher/

Bell, N. (2021). *Learning from the land and Indigenous people*. Trent School of Education. https://www.trentu.ca/education/alternative-settings-placement/learning-land-and-indigenous-people

Bell, N. (n.d.). *Nicole Bell*. Trent School of Education. https://www.trentu.ca/education/faculty-research/full-time-faculty/nicole-bell

Bell, N., Elliott, P., Rodenburg, J., & Young, K. (2013). Eco-mentorship: A pre-service outdoor experiential teacher education initiative at Trent University. *Pathways: The Journal of Outdoor Education, 25*(3), 14–17.

Bowers, C. A. (2002). Toward an eco-justice pedagogy. *Environmental Education Research, 8*(1), 21–34. https://doi.org/10.1080/13504620120109628

Bowers, C. A. (2004). *Eco-justice dictionary*. https://cabowers.net/dicterm/CAdict010.php

Bronfenbrenner, U. (1979). *The ecology of human development: Experiments by nature and design*. Harvard University Press.

Cajete, G. (1994). Indigenous education and its role in individual transformation. In *Look to the mountain: An ecology of Indigenous education* (pp. 209–229). Kivaki.

Cluff, W. (2020). Community gardens. *Journal of Advanced Generalist Social Work Practice*, 75–82. https://springfield.edu/sites/default/files/inline-files/SC_Graduate_Social_Work_Journal_2020_Article10.pdf

Dominelli, L. (2018). *The Routledge handbook of green social work*. Routledge.

Dominelli, L. (2012). *Green social work: From environmental crises to environmental justice*. Polity.

Elliott, P. (n.d.). *Paul Elliott*. Trent School of Education. https://www.trentu.ca/education/faculty-research/professor-emeritus/paul-elliott

Elliott, P., Dueck, C., & Rodenburg, J. (2020). Activating teacher candidates in community-wide environmental education: The Pathway to Stewardship and Kinship Project. *Canadian Journal of Environmental Education, 23*(1), 85–101.

Gaylie, V. (2012). The learning garden: Ecology, teaching, and transforming. Peter Lang.

Gidney, R. D. (1999). *From hope to Harris: The reshaping of Ontario schools*. University of Toronto Press.

Gray, M., Coates, J., & Hetherington, T. (2013). *Environmental social work*. Routledge.

Guggenheim, D. (Director). (2006). *An Inconvenient Truth* [Film]. Paramount.

Haig-Brown, C., & Hodson, J. (2009). Starting with the land: Toward Indigenous thought in Canadian education. In P. A. Woods & G. J. Woods (Eds.), *Alternative education for the 21st century: Philosophies, approaches, visions* (pp. 167–187). Palgrave Macmillan. https://doi.org/10.1057/9780230618367_10

Land acknowledgement. (2019). In *Trent University Michi Saagiig protocol guidebook* (p. 3). https://www.trentu.ca/fphl/sites/trentu.ca.fphl/files/documents/TrentU_MichiSaagiigGuidebook_Web.pdf

Lochner, J., Rieckmann, M., & Robischon, M. (2021). (Un)expected learning outcomes of virtual school garden exchanges in the field of education for sustainable development. *Sustainability (Basel, Switzerland), 13*(10), 5758. MDPI AG. https://doi.org/10.3390/su13105758

Longboat, D., Kulnieks, A., & Young, K. (2013). Beyond dualism: Toward a transdisciplinary Indigenous environmental studies model of environmental education curricula. In A. Kulnieks, D. Longboat, & K. Young (Eds.), *Contemporary studies in environmental and Indigenous pedagogies: A curricula of stories and place* (pp. 9–18). Brill/Sense. (Previously published in *The EcoJustice Review*, 2009, https://web.archive.org/web/20100919120531/http://ecojusticeeducation.org/index.php?option=com_content&task=view&id=67&Itemid=44)

Mailhot, J. (2015). *Green social work & community gardens: A case study of the North Central Community Gardens* [Master's thesis]. University of Nordland, Norway. https://nordopen.nord.no/nord-xmlui/bitstream/handle/11250/2385188/Mailhot.pdf?sequence=1&isAllowed=y

Martusewicz, R. A., Edmundson, J., & Lupinacci, J. (2015). *EcoJustice education: Toward diverse, democratic, and sustainable communities* (2nd ed.). Routledge.

Niblett, B. (n.d.). *Blair Niblett*. Trent School of Education. https://www.trentu.ca/education/faculty-research/full-time-faculty/blair-niblett

Ontario Ministry of Education. (2007). *Ontario First Nation, Metis, and Inuit education policy framework*. https://www.ontario.ca/page/ontario-first-nation-metis-and-inuit-education-policy-framework-2007

Ontario Ministry of Education. (2009). *Acting today, shaping tomorrow: A policy framework for environmental education in Ontario*. https://www.ontario.ca/page/policy-environmental-education-schools.

School of Education, Trent University. (2020). *Annual report 2019–2020*. https://www.trentu.ca/education/programs

School of Education, Trent University. (2021). *Bachelor of education program*. https://www.trentu.ca/futurestudents/degree/bachelor-education?target=undergraduate

Trent University. (2021) *Vision/mission statement*. https://www.trentu.ca/about/vision-mission#:~:text=We%20offer%20an%20enriched%20learning,individuals%20and%20as%20global%20citizens

Trent University. (2021–2022). *Trent University undergraduate calendar 2021–2022*. https://www.trentu.ca/registrar/sites/trentu.ca.registrar/files/documents/TrentCalendar2021FINAL_online.pdf

United Nations Educational, Scientific, and Cultural Organization (UNESCO). (2021). *United Nations Decade of Education for Sustainable Development*

(UNDESD) 2005–2014. https://en.unesco.org/themes/education-sustainable
-development/what-is-esd/un-decade-of-esd

Williams, D. R., & Brown, J. (2012). *Learning gardens and sustainability education: Bringing life to schools and schools to life.* Routledge.

Williams, D. R., & Dixon, P. (2013). Impact of garden-based learning on academic outcomes in schools: Synthesis of research between 1990 and 2010. *Review of Educational Research, 83*(2), 211–235. https://doi.org/10.3102/0034654313475824

Young, K. (2007). Environmental educational leadership and its origins. In W. T. Smale & K. Young (Eds.), *Approaches to educational leadership and practice* (pp. 220–236). Brush Education.

Young, K. (2009). Reconceptualizing elementary language arts curriculum: An eco-justice approach. In L. Iannacci & P. Whitty (Eds.), *Early childhood curricula: Reconceptualist perspectives* (pp. 299–325). Brush Education.

Young, K. (2021). Developing ecological literacy as a habit of mind in teacher education through ecojustice progressive curricula. In A. Dentith, D. Flinders, J. Lupinacci, & J. Thom (Eds.), *Ecological perspectives on curriculum and the work of C. A. Bowers* (pp. 148–167). Routledge.

PART TWO

Key Environmental Issues: What Every Social Worker Should Know

SUSAN HILLOCK

This next section explores specific topic areas that provide the knowl-edge base and content foundation for social work educators to teach this subject, while continuing to build a green social work knowledge base. The next four chapters present key environmental issues about what is at stake for humanity and the planet: clean water, soil, and air; food/housing security; and equality, peace, and non-violence for all liv-ing things.

To start, Chapter 5, "Social Ecology, Hierarchy, and Social Action: Opportunities for Eco-social Work Education," by Robert A. Case, explores a "grass-roots-up" view of the intersections between commu-nity resilience, environmental justice, and sustainability. Viewing these through the lens of social ecology (e.g., Bookchin, 1982), Case critically examines what those intersections suggest for greening social work and social work education. To accomplish this, he presents a case study about Wellington County, Ontario, where local activists have been battling the multinational corporation Nestlé Waters for more than a decade over access to groundwater for for-profit bottling. This conflict over groundwater has raised questions about local participation in water governance, the institutions used to protect public goods against privatization, and colonization and Indigenous land rights, particu-larly with Nestlé's 2015 expansion into the Haldimand Tract of the Six Nations of the Grand River.

Case demonstrates how community-based environmental activism not only can address specific, often local, environmental harms but also, in the process, can help build and renew community, mobilize resis-tance to neo-liberal globalization, build momentum around global and climate justice, and create just and sustainable alternatives for the pur-suit of social justice. By the same token, he explains how community-based environmental activism presents great opportunities for social work and social work education to engage directly with matters of the natural environment, and through that engagement create, define, and begin asserting a new paradigm for our profession (Coates, 2003). In doing so, Case reveals the potential of social work to contribute to climate justice/action and highlights concrete opportunities for bringing the conceptual frameworks, theoretical tensions, and strategies and dynamics of environmental activism into social work theory and practice through case study explorations, practicum placements, and other pedagogical approaches.

Reflective of the popular protest slogan "You can't drink gas and you can't eat money," Chapter 6, "Nutritional Social Work: An Avenue for Teaching in Social Work Education about Sustainability and the Climate Emergency" by Arielle Dylan, Jenni Cammaert, and Lea Tufford, elaborates on the important issues of food (in)security, (over) production/consumption, and climate change/crises. They explain that the term "nutritional social work" has recently been introduced into the social work lexicon but has yet to enjoy a place in social work curricula. Nutritional social work encompasses not only issues of food security and insecurity, and various dimensions of human health, but also broader considerations connected with sustainability and climate change. They propose that nutritional social work highlight and promulgate those practices most conducive to highest nutritional yields that are consistent with earth-friendly, people-friendly, non-factory-farming approaches. In this chapter, the authors explain how including content, anaylsis, and teaching about nutrition can help "green" social work. Accordingly, they suggest multiple ways to incorporate this innovative material into social work curricula and classrooms, recommend the exploration and development of multi/inter-disciplinary approaches as well as participatory action community-based research, and advocate for the creation of nutrition-forward field placement opportunities. Moreover, they make the case that integrating nutritional social work can help mobilize students, colleagues, universities, and communities to more seriously consider sustainability and tackle the climate emergency in practical and transformative ways.

In Chapter 7, "The War-Climate Nexus: Educating Future Social Workers about the Global Adversities Related to War, Climate Change, and Environmental Degradation," author Bree Akesson explains that on a global scale, the first two decades of the twenty-first century were characterized by an overwhelming number of social challenges related to ills such as poverty, war, political instability, and climate change. These ills have been linked to climate change – considered by many the most consequential global threat of the century – as scarcity of water, food, and livelihoods caused by climate change encourages desperate populations to challenge their governments, thereby increasing the risk of inter- and intra-state conflicts. Amplified natural disasters related to climate change continue to displace vulnerable populations at an unprecedented rate: nearly eighty million people have been forced to leave their homes. Combined, these pressing and overlapping forms of adversity greatly affect the well-being of individuals, families, and communities around the world. In order to address these critical issues, Akesson insists that we must teach the next generation of social workers to understand and tackle these realities at micro-, mezzo-, and macro-levels. This chapter also provides social work educators with the context, approaches, and tools to help students learn about the relationship between climate change and war, with a specific focus on the bio-psycho-social implications of loss of home as a result of disaster.

The final chapter in this section, Chapter 8, "Finding a Place for Animals in Green Social Work Education and Practice" by Jasmine Tiffany Ferreira, Atsuko Matsuoka, and John Sorenson, focuses on animal welfare as a key environmental issue for social work. To help build a stronger theoretical basis for green social work education and practice to challenge structural inequality and promote social justice and decolonization, this chapter examines ways of going beyond anthropocentrism by introducing a critical animal studies lens. To accomplish this, the authors explore how animals are, and are not, considered in green social work education and practice.

They also explain how critical animal studies incorporates political economy and eco-feminist approaches, using concepts such as transspecies social justice and speciesism that expand our understanding of the non-human world. For instance, they note that discussions of impacts of "natural" disasters on sustainable farming and food security in green social work often overlook animals, even when they discuss industrial agribusiness. Yet these systems contribute significantly to climate change, biodiversity loss, structural inequality, and colonization affecting human and non-human animals alike. The authors' analyses reveal how continued exploitation, subjugation, and violence towards non-human animals is interconnected with other forms of oppression and violence that also affect humans. Ultimately, these hierarchal categorizations of non-human animals as pets, wild, farm, or products are rooted in anthropocentric concepts, consumption, and profit; significantly, these hierarchies interact with power relations among humans. To assist social work to pursue ecological justice for all living beings, this chapter also presents timely theoretical insights for green social work education and practice. By understanding inclusion and exclusion of animals in green social work, we can challenge socially constructed concepts of nature and environmental issues, and work towards dismantling oppressive systems rather than sustaining them.

REFERENCES

Bookchin, M. (1982). *The ecology of freedom*. AK Press.
Coates, J. (2003). *Ecology and social work: Toward a new paradigm*. Fernwood.

5 Social Ecology, Hierarchy, and Social Action: Opportunities for Eco-social Work Education

ROBERT A. CASE

Building on the work of pioneers like Lena Dominelli (2012), John Coates (2003), Fred Besthorn (2000, 2012), and Nancy Mary (2008), social work scholars have made tremendous progress in the past decade in trying to bring matters of the natural environment into the mainstream of social work research, theory, and literature. Despite this growing acceptance of the need for social work and social workers to join the struggle against climate change and its consequences, significant challenges remain for integrating matters of the natural environment into professional practice.

A number of authors have pointed out that with a justice-seeking imperative and practice traditions in policy advocacy, coalition building, and community organization, social work represents a set of analytical perspectives and skills that could be of great value in community-based efforts to protect the environment and build momentum around climate action (e.g., Hetherington & Boddy, 2013; Peeters, 2012; Schmitz et al., 2012). By the same token, community-based environmental activism presents great opportunities for social work and social work education to engage directly with environmental issues, and through that engagement to create, define, and begin asserting a new paradigm for our profession (Coates, 2003) that closes the well-documented divide that lingers still, in our profession, between the social and natural environments.

In this chapter, I draw on my experiences from participation in and research on community-based water activism in my own community of Guelph, Ontario, to illustrate the interconnectedness of social and environmental issues. Through this case example, I also aim to highlight the correspondence of grass-roots environmental activism with the values and goals of social work, and to begin contemplating the implications for social work education. Throughout, in an effort to avoid reinforcing a conceptualization of "the environment" and "nature" as something from which humanity can be separated, I use the phrase "non-human environment" to refer to what is often referred to as the "natural environment." By "environmentalism" or "environmental activism," I mean social action that includes the protection or improvement of some aspect of the non-human environment as an explicit aim, even if the ultimate goal is the promotion of social well-being or simply the preservation of human existence on a changing planet. I have also elected to use phrases like "environmentally minded scholars" to refer to the many different approaches to integrating matters related to the natural environment into social work theory and practice. While the differentiations that some scholars make between "eco-social," "green," "environmental" social work, as well as other terms, are significant and useful (see, for example, Kemp, 2011), distinguishing among them is not necessary for my purposes in this chapter.

Social Work and the Non-human Environment

Whether or not social work should be involved, as a profession, in environmentalism and environmental protection has been all but resolved in the literature. With a focus on serving the most marginalized and those most in need, social workers are already involved in one way or another, as environmental degradation and climate change advance, disrupting livelihoods, dislocating communities, undermining self-sufficiency, and destroying lifestyles in their wake (e.g., Dominelli, 2012; Muldoon, 2006; Naranjo, 2020; Nyahunda, 2021; Peeters, 2012; Ramsay & Boddy, 2017). A growing body of social work literature draws our attention, also, to the intersections of environmental issues with the issues of equity and social justice around which social work increasingly defines itself (e.g., Boetto, 2019; Gray & Coates, 2015; Matthies & Närhi, 2016). Within the literature is a growing recognition that the most marginalized populations – the communities that social work is most concerned with – are also the most vulnerable to climate change, environmental accidents, and ecological crisis (Dominelli, 2013; Gray & Coates, 2012; Miller et al., 2012). Countless examples show that economically marginalized communities and communities of Black people, Indigenous people, and peoples of colour are disproportionately affected by the pollution and environmental destruction so often associated with industrial and commercial development (e.g., Banzhaf et al., 2019; Benz, 2019; Bullard, 1990; Fletcher, 2003; Ilyniak, 2014; Mascarenhas, 2012; Nyahunda, 2021; Shokane, 2016). As anti-oppressive social workers align themselves with equity and social justice against a status quo built on hierarchies of domination, matters of environmental justice can no longer be disentangled from the individual or family-level issues for which social workers may have been involved in the first place. So widely accepted are the intersections between social work and the environment that attention to matters of the non-human environment is beginning to appear regularly in social work scholarship, curriculum, and statements of professional ethics (Krings et al., 2020; Ramsay & Boddy, 2017).

Despite the growing recognition of a need to bring social work into communion with environmental issues and movements, the means of doing so remain elusive. Research has found that social work students (at least in the United States) are no more environmentally aware than the general population (Shaw, 2013), and that even among environmentally minded social work students and practitioners, considerable uncertainty remains about exactly how to go about bringing environmental issues into practice settings (Crawford et al., 2015; McKinnon, 2013; Nesmith & Smyth, 2015; Rambaree, 2020). As Ramsay and Boddy (2017) point out, numerous social work authors note that social work has also been relatively absent from "public environmental discourse" (p. 69).

A number of specific practice domains have been identified where the non-human environment plays a clear role in social work practice. Clinical social workers, for instance, are recognizing and finding creative ways take advantage of the therapeutic effects of time spent in forests and wilderness (e.g., Berger & Tiry, 2012; Heinsch, 2012; Norton and Watt, 2014; Hansen et al. 2017; Sidenius et al., 2017; Varning Poulsen et al., 2021). In direct practice with refugees and other immigrants, as well as disaster relief and rehabilitation work, environmental crisis is increasingly apparent as a significant variable in the life stories and well-being of those affected. Community social workers have long recognized the opportunities that participation in environmental projects like community gardens, tree-planting campaigns, and climate activism represents for the building of social ties, social support, and community – often across generations and ethno-cultural differences (e.g., Bailey et al., 2018; Boetto, 2017; Ross et al., 2019). My work in this vein suggests that underlying locally rooted "environmental" activism are objectives to which community social workers can relate: self-reliance, grass-roots democratic participation, and the building of resilience at the community level (Case, 2017). Yet the key to integrating the environment with the core functions of social work remains elusive. As Crawford et al. (2015) put it, based on their research on field education, an environmentally oriented social work remains "more conceptual than actual" (p. 595).

In much of the social work literature regarding the environment, calls are made to move beyond the separation that exists in social work between the social environment and non-human nature (Bozalek & Pease, 2021). As Boetto (2017) lays out very clearly, what is needed for social work to fully engage with the environment and with environmentalism goes beyond a paradigm shift that changes our understanding about the relationship of humanity to the natural world within social work. What is required in addition is an understanding of the ways in which oppression and environmental degradation are tied together and sustained by the same underlying institutions of power (including state-based social work itself), and a plan of action for challenging, changing, and displacing those institutions.

Water Activism in Guelph and Wellington County, Ontario

Guelph and Wellington County, in south-western Ontario, Canada, may seem an unlikely context for grass-roots concern about water. For the most part, residents of the county, like much of southern Canada, can turn on their taps every day and access a seemingly endless supply of safe, clean water at minimal cost. Yet residents of Guelph and pockets of Wellington County are organized and active around a number of threats they perceive to their water supply. The specific factors underlying local water concerns are as varied as the individuals and communities involved, but a major lightening rod that has galvanized community activism in Wellington County has been the local bottling operations of Nestlé Waters. In 2000, Nestlé Waters purchased the Aberfoyle Springs bottling company and its facilities in Aberfoyle, in the southern end of the county, and established its national headquarters there, along with Canada's largest water bottling plant (Jaffee & Case, 2018). The purchase included two wells in Wellington County: one at the Aberfoyle site, for which Nestlé acquired a permit from the provincial government to take up to 3.6 million litres of groundwater per day for bottling, and another well twenty-five kilometres to the east near Hillsburgh, for which Nestlé acquired a permit to take up to 1.1 million litres of groundwater per day, which it trucks to Aberfoyle for bottling.

At first, Nestlé's arrival in Wellington County went largely unnoticed and uncontested, but once people noticed and started raising questions about it, action to oppose Nestlé's bottling operations grew rapidly. In late 2006, with the discovery that Nestlé Waters would be submitting an application the following spring to renew its permit to take water, people in the community recognized an opportunity to voice some opposition. In early 2007, a small group of friends and activists got together and formed the Wellington Water Watchers (WWW) to lead that opposition (Case & Connor, 2023). By May 2007, as a result of WWW's work to organize the community through community events, direct face-to-face organizing, and media advocacy, the City of Guelph was abuzz with discussion, media headlines, and various actions related to the controversial water-mining operation just south of the city.

Despite continued effort and successive waves of activism, WWW and related networks have not been successful in ending corporate water bottling in Ontario. On 31 March 2021, Nestlé Waters sold its North American holdings to One Rock Capital Partners investment group, but water pumping and bottling continues uninterrupted in Wellington County under the new ownership, as it does in other parts of the province by other corporations (Armstrong, 2021). The activism of WWW and associated networks, nonetheless, has brought local, national, and international attention to this Canadian front in the global fight against predatory corporate water-taking.

Over the past fifteen years, organizing and activism surrounding water issues in Wellington County has continued to grow in momentum and sophistication, and new relationships are being forged as a result. Through WWW and affiliated groups, residents of Wellington County have had significant influence on municipal politics in Guelph and in townships in Wellington County and some influence on provincial rules pertaining to groundwater protection. Since 2017, for instance, grass-roots activism has led successive provincial governments to impose stronger scientific monitoring requirements and higher levies on water bottlers (Government of Ontario, 2020) and give municipal governments the power to reject permits to take water for bottling in their jurisdiction, as activists had long demanded (Environmental Registry of Ontario, 2021). Where municipal governments previously had limited ability to influence provincial permitting decisions, municipalities in Ontario can now say no to water bottling. More significant for this current analysis, however, are the ways in which involvement in water activism reveals the interconnections between social, economic, and political dynamics in concrete terms and in defiance of social/environmental (or human/nature) dualism – the false separation of humanity from nature (Bookchin, 1990) – with which social work struggles.

On the surface, the contestation of water bottling in Wellington County seems more reformist in its goals and tactics than radical or transformative. Many of the concerns raised are explicitly environmental in nature,

like the risks of water-taking to local ecology, the plastic waste associated with water bottling, and the climate impacts of plastics manu-
facturing and transportation of water bottles across great distances.
The tactics deployed focus primarily, at least at an instrumental level,
on bringing about progressive policy change (and resisting regressive
change) within the established structures and processes of the nation
state. A consistent target of action has been the environment ministries of successive provincial governments. Letter-writing campaigns,
petitions, and rallies have – with some success – put pressure on local
elected officials and provincial legislators. Public comment on permit
applications and proposed regulation changes, participation on provincial committees, and delegations to town council, provincial ministry
offices, and legislative committees also reflect engagement with formal
political processes. Consistent with important critiques of mainstream
environmental organizations in North America (Curnow & Helferty,
2018; Gibson-Wood & Wakefield, 2013), most of the visible participants
and leaders have, until very recently, been white and middle class.

When asked what drives their activism, however, water activists in
Wellington County's networks of water activism reveal a different narrative. Underlying the environmental concerns on the surface of the
campaigns is a popular consensus that puts the assurance of long-term
universal access to water ahead of profit-making (Case, 2016). "Water is
for life, not profit!," Wellington County water activists assert, in solidarity with land and water protectors elsewhere (WWW, 2018).

Water Bottling and Hierarchies of Domination

In many places around the globe, the commodification and privatization of water highlights conflicts between profit-making and local community needs, leading to community-based actions to resist the incur-
sion of foreign-based, for-profit interests into local water supply. The
struggles over water in Bolivia in the early 2000s are an iconic example
(Spronk & Webber, 2007). Massive street protests against the privatization of municipal water services in Cochabamba and El Alto, beginning
in 2000, forced the Bolivian government to cancel contracts given to
transnational water companies, and rolled into waves of protests that
led to the resignation of President Carlos Mesa in 2005. While less dra-
matic than in Bolivia, similar battles are being fought in communities in
every corner of the globe (Barlow, 2007, pp. 102–124).

Over the past three decades, bottled water has emerged and has
established itself as a new paradigm of for-profit water delivery
in many places, often beneath the radar of the mass protest (and

academic analysis) that privatization of public water services has received (Greene, 2018). In numerous contexts, nonetheless, though "highly contingent" upon the availability of safe water from other sources (Hawkins et al., 2015, p. 109), the extraction of groundwater for bottling has attracted considerable community opposition, particularly where for-profit, transnational corporations are involved. The water-bottling industry profits directly from "markets" where public water-delivery systems or private wells are unreliable or non-existent, and acts to sustain a sense of water scarcity, most directly by exploiting limited groundwater supplies and indirectly by accentuating and exploiting fears of water scarcity or unreliability as a rationale for purchasing their product (Hawkins et al., 2015). In some contexts, like Flint, Michigan, in the midst of its water crisis, continued water-taking from nearby aquifers for bottling and export to far-away markets, in combination with local profiteering in a context where many residents resorted to bottled water even for bathing, added another layer to the activism already happening around water issues (Pauli, 2019, p. 250). In other contexts, like in Pueblo, Mexico, and right here in Ontario, Canada, incursions of water bottlers into water-stressed Indigenous territories has sparked outrage and vociferous assertion of autonomy, self-determination, and Indigenous principles of water stewardship, against the colonizing impacts of water depletion, water insecurity, and water commodification. In Pueblo, Mexico, Indigenous communities, acting together as "Pueblos Unidos," occupied a Danone water bottling plant for months, beginning on World Water Day (22 March) 2021, until they were forcibly dispersed by the National Guard (Tricks, 2021). In some places, like Plachimada, Kerala, McCloud, California, Standwood, Michigan, and Centre Wellington, Ontario (in my case example), community protest has been strong enough to halt or prevent the expansion of water-taking operations of companies such as Coca Cola, Pepsi, and Nestlé Waters.

In Ontario, while governments, the corporation, and some water experts tend to reduce the impacts of water-taking for bottling to a volumetric assessment of water scarcity, local water activists point to the economic and political factors – to human-made institutions like privatization and colonization – that create scarcity and inequitable access (Jaffee & Case, 2018). The conflict over groundwater in Wellington County, as elsewhere around the world, has raised questions about the institutions presumed to protect public goods against privatization, about local participation in water governance (or the lack thereof), and about the arbitrariness, in ecological terms, of political institutions and jurisdictions that govern us. It has pitted community values against the profit logic, grass-roots democracy against the state, and commons against commodity (Case, 2016).

The conflict over groundwater in Wellington County has also created the ethical and strategic necessity for local water activists to confront, in practical terms, questions of colonization, Indigenous rights, and race-based inequities in access to water. Some among WWW's leadership, partners, and supporters have long recognized, as Hiller and Carlson (2018) argue (see also Hiller and Carslon-Manathara's Chapter 1 in this volume), that environmentalism in the North American context must start with a critical understanding of settler colonialism, how it contributes to ecological destruction, and how the efforts of even progressively minded environmentalists can serve to uphold its underlying presumptions, structures, and practices. Nonetheless, operating from and immersed within a settler-colonial viewpoint, and focused on the immediate, instrumental goal of ending water-taking for corporate profiteering, anti-bottling campaign activities have often treated Indigenous land rights as a secondary concern if acknowledged at all.

In 2015, Nestlé Waters Canada moved to expand its bottling operations in Wellington County by purchasing a third well, known as the "Middlebrook Well," just outside the town of Elora and well within the boundaries of the Haldimand Tract, a strip of land along the Grand River that was relinquished to the Haudenosaunee Six Nations by the colonial government through the Haldimand Treaty of 1784 (Six Nations Council, 2008). Water-bottling operations in Wellington County had always involved territories and waters over which the Haudenosaunee, Anishinaabeg, and other Indigenous peoples claim territorial and treaty rights. With Nestlé's move into the Haldimand Tract, however, WWW and its networks were brought into direct confrontation with this fact and with the glaring juxtaposition of water abundance enjoyed by non-Indigenous water activists against the severe water insecurity on the nearby Six Nations reserve (Shimo, 2018). In the process, they were faced with demands and provided with concrete opportunities to deepen WWW's engagement with Haudenosaunee community leaders and grass-roots water protectors on a common cause.

Whether and how far actions being taken based on these emerging relationships have actually moved WWW and its networks closer to the ethical form of environmentalism called for by Hiller and Carlson (2018, as well as in their Chapter 1 in this volume) would require considerable critical investigation to assess. The inclusion of consent of Indigenous communities as one of four demands of WWW's 2017–19 "Say No to Nestlé" campaign (WWW, n.d.), collaboration with Haudenosaunee youth and leaders in actions opposing corporate water-taking (e.g.,

Robinson, 2019), and the 2021 "Nestlé Troubled Waters" international campaign's demand that Nestlé Waters's Wellington County holdings be relinquished to the Six Nations (Advertiser Staff, 2020), suggest at least some progress in this direction. Regardless, the case example of water activism illustrates the absurdity of treating water issues as separate from the social environment, and suggests engagement in social action as a potential pathway for confronting, problematizing, and then finding ways to overcoming this separation through concrete action. More broadly, this case example reinforces the notion that at the heart of the problems of environmental degradation, environmental injustice, and climate change, are human-made institutions of hierarchy and domination, capitalism and colonialism in particular.

Social Ecology and the Emergence of Hierarchy

Social ecology is a theoretical framework that is based on the belief that "environmental" problems originate with the ways in which domination has been structured into the social institutions of hegemonic Western societies, and spread through the world through colonization, patriarchy, and the pursuit of capital accumulation (Bookchin, 2005). Resolving environmental problems, from this point of view, means identifying, challenging, and changing or replacing the institutions and practices that maintain hierarchies of domination. The synergy between social ecology and anti-oppressive social work, at this level, is self-evident.

While dominance hierarchies are observable in non-human animal communities, social ecologists point out that the *idea* of domination and subordination, and its propagation through the establishment of hierarchical cultural, economic, and political institutions, is uniquely human and far from an evolutionary or historical inevitability. In human society, history demonstrates, hierarchical order and domination is neither innate nor universal, but rather evolved over centuries in certain contexts (Graeber & Wengrow, 2021). Over time, in some human communities, differentiation and reciprocity gradually gave way to "a hierarchical sensibility that ranked people as superior or inferior by a given standard, and then used that ranking to justify the domination of the latter by the former" (Biehl, 1999, p. 76). Eventually, from these fledgling "epistemologies of rule," social institutions of hierarchy and dominance began to emerge, accelerating concentrations of power and the assimilation, subordination, or displacement of contravening ideologies and practices based in egalitarianism and cooperation (Bookchin, 2005, p. 159).

As inequality and domination took root in the institutions governing some societies, the idea of dominating nature also emerged, along with an accelerated ability to exploit it for short-term gain and to marginalize all that stands in the way. As hierarchy and domination mutated into institutions of patriarchy, class, white supremacy, private property, and the nation state, with a consequent acceleration of displacement of communities from the land through war, industrialization, and colonization, the seeds were planted for conceiving of and advancing a conceptualization of humanity as not only separate from non-human nature but superior to it (Bookchin, 2006). In the pre-Enlightenment period in western Europe, the scientific revolution provided methods through which to observe nature as an external entity, ostensibly unmediated by human subjectivity, and in combination with the "predominant cultural force" of Christianity at the time, entrenched a Baconian concept of human mastery over nature within the foundations of modernity (Leiss, 1994; White, 1967). The idea of human domination over nature (and the ability to efficiently exercise that domination), in other words, is tied to the separation of humanity from non-human nature, which itself is derived and inseparable from the emergence of institutions fostering domination of humans by humans. As eco-feminists point out, for instance, domination of nature has been advanced by the subordination of women and the consequent displacement, devaluation, and appropriation of life-affirming knowledges, priorities, and practices of women – developed within roles like caregivers and food-and-water providers – that reinforce and keep visible the interconnections between human community and the non-human environment (Shiva & Mies, 2014; see also Isla, 2019, and Gobby, 2020).

Advocating for a "transformative approach to eco-social work," Boetto (2017) asserts that a "fundamental reorientation" is needed away from anthropocentric perceptions of the world "towards views that reflect a holistic interdependent view of humans as part of the natural world" (p. 49). Indigenous scholarship, in a similar vein, reminds us of the existence and durability of paradigms in which a distinction between humanity and nature makes no sense in the first place (e.g., Baskin, 2016; Little Bear, 2000; McAdam, 2019). The Haudenosaunee creation story, for instance, and the social, cultural, and political institutions built upon it, Kayanesenh Paul Williams explains, place "human beings squarely in the midst of the natural world in which they form an integral part, and in which each part has been given responsibilities" (2018, p. 34). While we should take seriously the critique of a tendency among some non-Indigenous environmentalists to co-opt Indigenous ecological knowledge "in ways that reify their privilege" (Hiller &

Carlson, 2018, p. 53, citing Simpson, 2004), the possibilities that Indigenous worldviews suggest for reorienting social work towards a post-anthropocentric (Bozalek & Pease, 2021) integration of human well-being with the non-human environment are gaining well-deserved attention in environmentally oriented social work scholarship.

Transforming Social Work: The Potentialities of Social Action

As already argued, the domination of nature, while enabled by the separation of humanity from non-human nature, did not begin there. Rather, as the case example of water activism in Wellington County illustrates, the domination of non-human nature is rooted in the hierarchical thinking built into social institutions that dominate people. As Boetto (2017) asserts, explicitly drawing on eco-feminism, in order for social work to participate effectively in the realization of a just and sustainable future for life on Earth, it is "essential" that the profession "eliminate not only the domination of nature, but also the hierarchical feature of many human relationships" (p. 53). A fundamental challenge confounding this effort within social work is what Boetto identifies as the profession's "most central paradox: its inherent modernist roots that contradict the philosophical base of practice" (p. 48). Rooted in co-dependence with capitalism, patriarchy, and the state – and in Canada with settler colonialism in particular (Fortier & Wong, 2019) – the social work profession is itself an institution of hierarchical society that, while simultaneously seeking social justice and the liberation of peoples from oppression, serves to facilitate the assimilation or adaptation of excluded groups to a hierarchical status quo and/or to manage the fallout when this adaptation is resisted or rejected, or simply fails. Overcoming this paradox, Boetto (2017) observes, will require considerable activism within the profession.

In proposing a "transformative eco-social model" for social work, Boetto (2017) consolidates work of earlier scholars and makes considerable progress in articulating a framework for shifting social work towards reconciling its philosophical foundation with principles of critical progressive practice. Within the model, Boetto recognizes the role of social action in protecting the environment and facilitating economic and political change. To this analysis, I offer the observation that stepping beyond the traditional bounds of social work, into community-based eco-social action, can also generate direct experiences that challenge the fallacy of the human-nature divide, reveal the human-made institutions that limit progress towards a just and sustainable planet, and create incentives and opportunities for communities to engage in imagining, articulating, and experimenting with new ways of relating to one another. The community-based effort to oppose corporate water bottling in Wellington County, Ontario, is not free from the trappings of Eurocentric modernism and hierarchical thinking. In many ways, despite progress being made in this regard, the priorities and assumptions underlying it are still at odds with those of Indigenous peoples in the area, as is often the case with non-Indigenous environmental action (Smith & Sterritt, 2010). Nonetheless, what is revealed in the case example is the way in which community-based environmental activism brings into view the operations of capitalism, the state, patriarchy, and colonialism, and the potential that lies within the contradictions these forces generate for reconstituting relationships and building momentum towards establishing alternative paradigms and defending those that already exist.

Hierarchy, the Environment, and Social Work Education

The most obvious domain in which matters of the non-human environment might be integrated into social work practice – to make this integration more actual than conceptual (Crawford et al., 2015) – is in the community sector. As already noted and as elaborated elsewhere, underlying so-called environmental conflict at the community level are priorities and objectives that are directly aligned with those of community social work praxis, as well as a clear need for the kinds of knowledge, skills, and analytical frameworks community social work has to offer. How matters of the non-human environment might be integrated into front-line practice in reactive domains such as child protection and hospital social work – and the degree to which they should be – is a question for further investigation. Ultimately, for social work to more fully engage with environmentalism and matters of the environment, social workers need to be prepared to work outside the current confines of the profession, on social-environmental impact assessment, in environmental non-governmental organizations and social movement organizations, and with grass-roots groups and community-based organizations.

Understood as a grass-roots response to the operations of hierarchy and domination, what the foregoing discussion suggests for the greening of social work education is that eco-social activism, even if it remains marginal as a field of practice for most social workers, provides a rich pedagogical context from which to analyse the operations of power and resistance that are at the heart of critical and anti-oppressive social work. As a step towards closing the divide that persists in social work between the social and non-human elements of the environment, schools of social work should be encouraged to develop practicum placements in environmental organizations and initiatives. More generally, social work faculty should be encouraged not only to look to examples of grass-roots eco-social activism to illustrate methods in community praxis, but to integrate them throughout the curriculum as case studies in the structure and philosophies of power that underlie poverty, oppression, and the destruction of the non-human environment alike. In addition to developing case studies that illustrate the clinical benefits and community practice dimensions of engagement with the non-human environment, environmentally oriented social work scholars can support this integration by developing case studies of eco-social activism that focus on the social, economic, and political dimension underlying so-called environmental causes and actions.

Latent within community-based activism, as the case example of water activism in Wellington County illustrates, is considerable potential for uncovering and disrupting institutions of domination at the root of both social and environmental issues. Realizing this potential without reproducing dominant hierarchical relations and moving environmentalism beyond narrow reformist confines will require radical vision, critical understandings of capitalism, patriarchy, and oppression, skills in community organization, an understanding of the intersectional potentialities of social movement mobilization, and expertise in the development and preservation of counter-institutions based in grass-roots democracy, equity, and mutual aid. In this regard, the environmental movement has a great deal to gain from the analytical perspectives and practice traditions at what have been viewed as the radical edges of social work, such as the work of eco-feminists (Isla, 2019), as they simultaneously offer concrete and complex opportunities for social work educators and students to develop, through experience and praxis, theoretical and practical interventions aimed at unleashing the transformational potential latent within such contexts.

Conclusion

Critical engagement with grass-roots eco-social activism not only provides rich opportunities for the development, practice, and application of community social work ideas and approaches, but brings into practical sight the human/nature dualism that limits social work's engagement with matters of the non-human environment in the first place. As illustrated in the case example of Wellington County's grass-roots campaigns against corporate water-taking for bottling, involvement in eco-social activism reveals the contradictions of capitalism, colonization, and other forms of domination that underlie so-called environmental conflicts, illustrates the complex ways in which hierarchical thinking is reproduced in responses to it, and uncovers potential pathways towards transforming relationships between people and communities and between humans and the rest of nature. In this sense, eco-social activism offers an additional lens and concrete case examples through which to deepen analysis and critical education on the operations of hierarchy and domination for social work students of all kinds.

Important questions remain about how and if the social work profession can overcome the contradictions of its modernist, state-based roots, and find ways to integrate non-human nature throughout professional practice without reproducing hegemonic, hierarchical social relations. Bringing humanity back into harmony with non-human nature will take more than intensified grass-roots efforts to protect natural spaces and remediate ecological harm. As social ecologists and environmentally oriented social work scholars point out, "the ways human beings deal with each other as social beings is crucial to addressing the ecological crisis" (Bookchin, 2006, p. 20). What is required now, if we aspire to the realization of social justice, environmental sustainability, and continued existence on this planet, is the dissolution of hierarchical organization, and the reinforcement of paradigms and social institutions that resist it and/or the creation of new ones. Social work has a crucial role to play in the effort to move forward towards a just and sustainable future whether from within the profession or from the margins.

REFERENCES

Advertiser Staff. (2020, October 21). Group "demands" Nestle Waters sell/ gift assets to municipalities, Six Nations. *Wellington Advertiser*. https:// www.wellingtonadvertiser.com/wellington-water-watchers-demands -nestle-waters-sell-gift-assets-to-municipalities-six-nations/

Armstrong, K. (2021, April 2). Nestle Waters sale finalized and a day later Ontario lifts moratorium on permits. *Guelph Today*. https://www .guelphtoday.com/local-news/nestle-waters-sale-finalized-and-a-day -later-ontario-lifts-moratorium-on-permits-3597877

Bailey, S., Hendrick, A., & Palmer, M. (2018). Eco-social work in action: A place for community gardens. *Australian Social Work, 71*(1), 98–110. https:// doi.org/10.1080/0312407X.2017.1384032

Banzhaf, S., Ma, L., & Timmins, C. (2019). Environmental justice: The economics of race, place, and pollution. *Journal of Economic Perspectives, 33*(1), 185–208. https://doi.org/10.1257/jep.33.1.185

Barlow, M. (2007). *Our water commons: Toward a new freshwater narrative*. The Commons.

Baskin, C. (2016). *Strong helpers' teachings: The value of Indigenous knowledges in the helping professions*. Canadian Scholars.

Benz, T. A. (2019). Toxic cities: Neoliberalism and environmental racism in Flint and Detroit Michigan. *Critical Sociology, 45*(1), 49–62. https://doi.org/10.1177/0896920517708339

Berger, R., & Tiry, M. (2012). The enchanting forest and the healing sand – Nature therapy with people coping with psychiatric difficulties. *The Arts in Psychotherapy, 39*(5), 412–416. https://doi.org/10.1016/j.aip.2012.03.009

Besthorn, F. H. (2000). Toward a deep-ecological social work: Its environmental, spiritual and political dimensions. *Spirituality and Social Work Forum, 7*(2), 2–7.

Besthorn, F. H. (2012). Deep ecology's contributions to social work: A ten-year retrospective. *International Journal of Social Welfare, 21*(3), 248–259. https://doi.org/10.1111/j.1468-2397.2011.00850.x

Biehl, J. (1999). *The Murray Bookchin reader*. Black Rose Books.

Boetto, H. (2017). A transformative eco-social model: Challenging modernist assumptions in social work. *British Journal of Social Work, 47*(1), 48–67. https://doi.org/10.1093/bjsw/bcw149

Boetto, H. (2019). Advancing transformative eco-social change: Shifting from modernist to holistic foundations. *Australian Social Work, 72*(2), 139–151. https://doi.org/10.1080/0312407X.2018.1484501

Bookchin, M. (1990). *The philosophy of social ecology: Essays on dialectical naturalism*. Black Rose Books.

Bookchin, M. (2005). *The ecology of freedom: The emergence and dissolution of hierarchy*. AK Press.

Bookchin, M. (2006). *Social ecology and communalism*. AK Press.

Bookchin, M. (2015). *The next revolution: Popular assemblies and the promise of direct democracy*. Verso Books.

Bozalek, V., & Pease, B. (2021). *Post anthropocentric social work: Critical posthuman and new materialist perspectives*. Routledge.

Bullard, R. (1990). *Dumping in Dixie: Race, class and environmental quality*. Westview.

Case, R. A. (2016). Social work and the moral economy of water: Community-based water activism and its implications for eco-social work. *Critical Social Work, 17*(2), 60–81. https://doi.org/10.22329/csw.v17i2.5903

Case, R. A. (2017). Eco-social work and community resilience: Insights from water activism in Canada. *Journal of Social Work, 17*(4), 391–412. https://doi.org/10.1177/1468017316644695

Case, R. A., & Connor, L. (2023). From concern to action: The founding of the Wellington Water Watchers and the battle against water bottling in Ontario, Canada. *Local Environment, 28*(2), 218–232. doi.org/10.1080/13549839.2022.2134321

Coates, J. (2003). *Ecology and social work: Toward a new paradigm*. Fernwood.

Crawford, F., Agustine, S. S., Earle, L., Kuyini-Abubakar, A. B., Luxford, Y., & Babacan, H. (2015). Environmental sustainability and social work: A rural Australian evaluation of incorporating eco-social work in field education. *Social Work Education*, 34(5), 586–599. https://doi.org/10.1080/02615479.2015.1074673

Curnow, J., & Helferty, A. (2018). Contradictions of solidarity: Whiteness, settler coloniality, and the mainstream environmental movement. *Environment and Society*, 9(1), 145–163. https://doi.org/10.3167/ares.2018.090110

Dominelli, L. (2012). *Green social work: From environmental crises to environmental justice*. Polity.

Dominelli, L. (2013). Environmental justice at the heart of social work practice: Greening the profession. *International Journal of Social Welfare*, 22(4), 431–439. https://doi.org/10.1111/ijsw.12024

Environmental Registry of Ontario. (2021). *ERO# 019-2422: Proposal to require municipal support for new or increased bottled water takings*. https://ero.ontario.ca/notice/019-2422

Fletcher, T. H. (2003). *From Love Canal to environmental justice: The politics of hazardous waste on the Canada– US border*. Broadview.

Fortier, C., & Hon-Sing Wong, E. (2019). The settler colonialism of social work and the social work of settler colonialism. *Settler Colonial Studies*, 9(4), 437–456. https://doi.org/10.1080/2201473X.2018.1519962

Gibson-Wood, H., & Wakefield, S. (2013). "Participation," white privilege and environmental justice: Understanding environmentalism among Hispanics in Toronto. *Antipode*, 45(3), 641–662. https://doi.org/10.1111/j.1467-8330.2012.01019.x

Gobby, J. (2020). *More powerful together: Conversations with climate activists and Indigenous land defenders*. Fernwood.

Government of Ontario. (2020). *Regulation # 463.16: A regulation establishing a moratorium on the issuance of new or increasing permits to take water for water bottling*. Ontario Regulatory Registry. https://www.ontariocanada.com/registry/view.do?postingId=22948

Graeber, D., & Wengrow, D. (2021). *The dawn of everything: A new history of humanity*. Penguin.

Gray, M., & Coates, J. (2012). Environmental ethics for social work: Social work's responsibility to the non-human world. *International Journal of Social Welfare*, 21(3), 239–247. https://doi.org/10.1111/j.1468-2397.2011.00852.x

Gray, M., & Coates, J. (2015). Changing gears: Shifting to an environmental perspective in social work education. *Social Work Education*, 34(5), 502–512. https://doi.org/10.1080/02615479.2015.1065807

Greene, J. (2018). Bottled water in Mexico: The rise of a new access to water paradigm. *Wiley Interdisciplinary Reviews: Water*, 5(4), e1286. https://doi.org/10.1002/wat2.1286

Hansen, M. M., Jones, R., & Tocchini, K. (2017). Shinrin-yoku (forest bathing) and nature therapy: A state-of-the-art review. *International Journal of Environmental Research and Public Health, 14*(8), 851. https://doi.org/10.3390/ijerph14080851. Medline:28788101

Hawkins, G., Potter, E., & Race, K. (2015). *Plastic water: The social and material life of bottled water.* MIT Press.

Heinsch, M. (2012). Getting down to earth: Finding a place for nature in social work practice. *International Journal of Social Welfare, 21*(3), 309–318. https://doi.org/10.1111/j.1468-2397.2011.00860.x

Hetherington, T., & Boddy, J. (2013). Ecosocial work with marginalized populations: Time for action on climate change. In M. Gray, J. Coates, & T. Hetherington (Eds.), *Environmental social work* (pp. 46–61). Routledge.

Hiller, C., & Carlson, E. (2018). These are Indigenous lands: Foregrounding settler colonialism and Indigenous sovereignty as primary contexts for Canadian environmental social work. *Canadian Social Work Review/Revue canadienne de service social, 35*(1), 45–70. https://doi.org/10.7202/1051102ar

Ilyniak, N. (2014). Mercury poisoning in Grassy Narrows: Environmental injustice, colonialism, and capitalist expansion in Canada. *McGill Sociological Review, 4*, 43–66.

Isla, A. (2019). *Climate chaos: Ecofeminism and the land question.* Inanna/Education Inc.

Jaffee, D., & Case, R. A. (2018). Draining us dry: Scarcity discourses in contention over bottled water extraction. *Local Environment, 23*(4), 485–501. https://doi.org/10.1080/13549839.2018.1431616

Kemp, S. (2011). Recentring environment in social work practice: Necessity, opportunity, challenge. *British Journal of Social Work, 41*(6), 1198–1210. https://doi.org/10.1093/bjsw/bcr119

Krings, A., Victor, B. G., Mathias, J., & Perron, B. E. (2020). Environmental social work in the disciplinary literature, 1991–2015. *International Social Work, 63*(3), 275–290. https://doi.org/10.1177/0020872818788397

Leiss, W. (1994). *Domination of nature.* McGill-Queen's University Press.

Little Bear, L. (2000). Jagged worldviews colliding. In M. Battiste (Ed.), *Reclaiming Indigenous voice and vision* (pp. 77–85). UBC Press.

Mary, N. L. (2008). *Social work in a sustainable world.* Oxford University Press.

Mascarenhas, M. (2012). *Where the waters divide: Neoliberalism, white privilege, and environmental racism in Canada.* Lexington Books.

Matthies, A. L., & Närhi, K. (Eds.). (2016). *The ecosocial transition of societies: The contribution of social work and social policy.* Taylor & Francis.

McAdam, S. (2019). *Nationhood interrupted: Revitalizing Nêhiyaw legal systems.* Purich. (Original work published 2015)

McKinnon, J. (2013). The environment: A private concern or a professional practice issue for Australian social workers? *Australian Social Work, 66*(2), 156–70. https://doi.org/10.1080/0312407X.2013.782558

Miller, S. E., Hayward, R. A., & Shaw, T. V. (2012). Environmental shifts for social work: A principles approach. *International Journal of Social Welfare, 21*(3), 270–277. https://doi.org/10.1111/j.1468-2397.2011.00848.x

Muldoon, A. (2006). Environmental efforts: The next challenge for social work. *Critical Social Work, 7*(2). https://doi.org/10.22329/csw.v7i2.5729

Naranjo, N. R. (2020). Environmental issues and social work education. *British Journal of Social Work, 50*(2), 447–463. https://doi.org/10.1093/bjsw/bcz168

Nesmith, A., & Smyth, N. (2015). Environmental justice and social work education: Social workers' professional perspectives. *Social Work Education, 34*(5), 484–501. https://doi.org/10.1080/02615479.2015.1063600

Norton, C. L., & Watt, T. T. (2014). Exploring the impact of a wilderness-based positive youth development program for urban youth. *Journal of Experiential Education, 37*(4), 335–350. doi.org/10.1177/1053825913503

Nyahunda, L. (2021). Environmental social work practice. In V. Mabvurira, A. Fahrudin, & E. Mtetwa (Eds.), *Professional social work in Zimbabwe: Past present and the future* (pp. 264–296). National Association of Social Workers of Zimbabwe.

Pauli, B. J. (2019). *Flint fights back: Environmental justice and democracy in the Flint water crisis.* MIT Press.

Peeters, J. (2012). The place of social work in sustainable development: Towards ecosocial practice. *International Journal of Social Welfare, 21*(3), 287–298. https://doi.org/10.1111/j.1468-2397.2011.00856.x

Rambaree, K. (2020). Environmental social work. *International Journal of Sustainability in Higher Education, 21*(3), 557–574.

Ramsay, S., & Boddy, J. (2017). Environmental social work: A concept analysis. *British Journal of Social Work, 47*(1), 68–86. https://doi.org/10.1093/bjsw/bcw078

Robinson, M. (2019, June 13). Protesters demand Nestle cease and desist water-taking. *Wellington Advertiser.* https://www.wellingtonadvertiser.com/province-wide-days-of-action-mark-one-year-of-conservative-government/

Ross, D., Brueckner, M., Palmer, M., & Eaglehawk, W. (Eds.). (2019). *Eco-activism and social work: New directions in leadership and group work.* Routledge.

Schmitz, C. L., Matyók, T., Sloan, L. M., & James, C. (2012). The relationship between social work and environmental sustainability: Implications for interdisciplinary practice. *International Journal of Social Welfare, 21*(3), 278–286. https://doi.org/10.1111/j.1468-2397.2011.00855.x

Shaw, T. V. (2013). Is social work a green profession? An examination of environmental beliefs. *Journal of Social Work, 13*(1), 3–29. https://doi.org/10.1177/1468017311407555

Shimo, A. (2018, October 4). While Nestlé extracts millions of litres from their land, residents have no drinking water. *The Guardian.* https://www

.theguardian.com/global/2018/oct/04/ontario-six-nations-nestle-running
-water

Shiva, V., & Mies, M. (2014). *Ecofeminism*. Zed Books.

Shokane, A. L. (2016). Indigenous knowledge and social work in the context of climate change and older persons in rural areas. *Indilinga: African Journal of Indigenous Knowledge Systems, 15*(2), 105–122.

Sidenius, U., Stigsdotter, U. K., Varning Poulsen, D., & Bondas, T. (2017). "I look at my own forest and fields in a different way": The lived experience of nature-based therapy in a therapy garden when suffering from stress-related illness. *International Journal of Qualitative Studies on Health and Well-being, 12*(1), 1324700. https://doi.org/10.1080/17482631.2017.1324700. Medline:28534665

Simpson, L. R. (2004). Strategies for the recovery and maintenance of Indigenous knowledge. *American Indian Quarterly, 28*(3/4), 373–384. https://doi.org/10.1353/aiq.2004.0107

Six Nations Council. (2008). *The Haldimand Treaty of 1784*. Six Nations Land and Resources. http://www.sixnations.ca/LandsResources/HaldProc.htm

Smith, M., & Sterritt, A. (2010). Towards a shared vision: Lessons from collaboration between First Nations and environmental organizations to protect the Great Bear Rainforest and coastal First Nations. In L. Davis (Ed.), *Re/envisioning relationships: Indigenous–non-Indigenous alliances and coalitions for social and environmental justice* (pp. 131–148). University of Toronto Press.

Spronk, S., & Webber, J. (2007). Struggles against accumulation by dispossession in Bolivia: The political economy of natural resource contention. *Latin American Perspectives, 34*(31), 31–47. https://doi.org/10.1177/0094582X06298748

Tricks, M. (2021, November 19). How Nahua Indigenous communities in Mexico took on Danone in defence of water and life. *Shado*. https://shado-mag.com/act/how-nahua-indigenous-communities-in-mexico-took-on-danone-in-defence-of-water-and-life/

Varning Poulsen, D., Lygum, V. L., Djernis, H. G., & Stigsdotter, U. K. (2021). Nature is just around us! Development of an educational program for implementation of nature-based activities at a crisis shelter for women and children exposed to domestic violence. *Journal of Social Work Practice, 35*(2), 159–175. https://doi.org/10.1080/02650533.2019.1703659

White, L. (1967). The historical roots of our ecologic crisis. *Science, 155*(3767), 1203–1207. https://doi.org/10.1126/science.155.3767.1203

Williams, K. P. (2018). *Kayanerenkó: wa: The Great Law of Peace*. University of Manitoba Press.

WWW (Wellington Water Watchers). (2018). Water is for life, not profit. https://d3n8a8pro7vhmx.cloudfront.net/wellingtonwaterwatchers/pages/890/attachments/original/1566487665/WWW-Backgrounder-WaterForLifeNotForProfit.pdf

6 Nutritional Social Work: An Avenue for Teaching in Social Work Education about Sustainability and the Climate Emergency

ARIELLE DYLAN, JENNI CAMMAERT,
AND LEA TUFFORD

As outlined by the Canadian Association of Social Work Education (CASWE-ACFTS, 2021a, 2021b), the Canadian regulatory body of all schools of social work, social justice, however ill-defined, lies at the core of social work curricula and has a present and aspirational focus that aims to confront social, political, and economic inequalities (Nicotera, 2019). However, talk of human wellness, social and economic justice, and human rights is incomplete without inclusion of eco-realties, including nutritional considerations. Social work educators are in a key position to integrate eco-issues into the curricula and take a leading role in educating future social workers to respond to the diverse impacts of eco-crises as a central part of their professional purview. Guided by an anti-oppressive lens, nutritional social work advocates earth-friendly approaches. Nutritional concerns are linked with climate change and other contemporary eco-issues because food access, security, and nutritional quality are increasingly jeopardized in our climate emergency (Dylan & Cammaert, 2022; FEMA, 2020; Ziska et al., 2016). Social work has a history of operating from an ecological perspective, considering people in their environments (Bretzlaff-Holstein, 2018), and while several eco-social work scholars have made the case for expanding the term "environment" to encompass the natural environment, links with nutrition and the eco-crisis have largely been lacking (Besthorn, 2012, 2013a; Boddy et al., 2018; Boetto, 2017; Coates, 2005; Dominelli, 2012; Dominelli et al., 2018; Gray et al., 2013; Jones, 2010; Papadopoulos, 2019; Shaw, 2011; Teixeira & Krings, 2015). "Nutritional social work," a term recently coined in the eco-social work literature (Dylan & Cammaert, 2022), fills this theoretical gap because it is a critical concept that requires adopting nutritional considerations, at all levels of social work practice, as part of a robust social justice, human rights, and human wellness orientation. This chapter explores the important contribution nutritional social work can make to the process of greening social work, highlighting a variety of ways nutritional considerations can be incorporated into social work classrooms, inviting further interdisciplinary and community-based participatory research, and creating new field placement opportunities. The concept of nutritional social work has the potentiality to mobilize individuals, collectives, and institutions around the issue of sustainability and the climate emergency in concrete and transformative ways.

Eco-social Work

Social work has a history of considering persons in their environment: professional roots in the Settlement House movement are evidence of this (Martin, 2012). As Gal et al. (2020) explain, the Settlement House model usually involved the establishment of a building-based community in a low-income neighbourhood in which social workers resided and sought to work with the residents of the neighbourhood and to engage in the community, the purpose being to further residents' well-being. Intrinsic to this model was a focus on empowerment, advocacy, social reform, and public health. Indeed, this person-in-environment focus is, in many ways, what sets social work apart from other helping professions. In the late twentieth century and the turn of the twenty-first, social work had begun to look more specifically at the natural environment, expanding the professional metaphor beyond its social orientation (Besthorn & Canda, 2002; Coates, 2003; Hoff & McNutt, 1994). In the past two decades, a growing body of social work literature has explored the climate emergency and eco-crises from a variety of viewpoints, including green social work (Dominelli, 2012, 2019), sustainability (Bowles et al., 2016; Drolet et al., 2015; Mary, 2008; Peeters, 2012a, 2012b), deep ecology (Besthorn, 2003), eco-ontology (Zapf, 2009), education (Lysack, 2010), eco-justice (Erickson, 2018; Nesmith & Smyth, 2015; Teixeira & Krings, 2015), eco-spirituality (Coates, 2013; Dylan & Coates, 2012; Zapf, 2012), and other critical perspectives (Besthorn, 2013a; Boetto, 2017; Gray & Coates, 2012; Nähri & Matthies, 2018).

Nutritional Insecurity

While some of this scholarship highlights food security and the alarming increase in food insecurity resulting from a variety of ecological crises (e.g., desertification, topsoil erosion and salinization, other forms of contamination, biodiversity loss, and endangered bees, to name a few), none focuses on nutritional social work or the need to prioritize nutritional considerations as a core pillar in sound eco-social work and eco-justice practice. Nutritional social work, a concept centring the right to sound nutrition (not simply access to food but access to nutritious food) for all human beings, necessitates multilevel engagement operating at the policy, community, and direct-practice levels, nested within a holistic, critical eco-social work framework. In its broadest conceptualization, nutritional social work encompasses dietary needs of non-human species as their habitats are increasingly encroached on by human activity (Angus, 2016; Caputi, 2020).This requires using an eco-justice orientation, focused on systemic, intersecting forms of oppression and their connections to the natural world, together with traditional analytical, advocacy, and coalition-building skills to change the oppressive, discriminatory, short-sighted policy terrain (Jansson, 2018; Pawar, 2019) to better respond to the climate emergency and other eco-crises that have a direct bearing on nutritional outcomes. In a sense, nutritional social work does not point to something new but instead highlights an existing phenomenon, nutritional insecurity (Dominelli, 2012), that is entirely interdependent with ecological wellness (or lack thereof).

Community Engagement

Policy and welfare reform often hinge on community engagement, and the eco-social worker operating with a holistic understanding, where nutritional social work constitutes a central practice pillar, would necessarily be working in communities. Eco-social work entails assisting with community organizing and knowledge mobilization, collaborating in ways that foster a "mutually beneficial exchange of knowledge and resources" (Bhagwan, 2017, p. 316), and "engaging in participatory action research and the coproduction of solutions to contemporary problems, valuing Indigenous and local knowledges, and supporting research that produces benefits for all" (Dominelli, 2019, p. 233), including that explicitly targeting ecological challenges and eco-justice issues.

Anthropocentrism

While the CASWE-ACFTS has produced a position statement on climate change (Schibli, 2020) and the role social work has therewith, it sadly reproduces the same logic responsible, in part, for the climate emergency: anthropocentrism. The document states, "social workers have a very important role in humanizing climate change by highlighting the ways that it is intricately tied to social inequities and how that impacts individuals and communities at the most fundamental level – the right to be who you are" (Schibli, 2020, p. 16). Moreover, because the natural environment has been severely and anthropogenically degraded (Angus, 2016; Caputi, 2020), the ability for people to construct "a subjective reality of life" (Kraus, 2019, p. 100) has been compromised, contributing to experiences of anxiety, depression, and despair that compound the more physical concerns (e.g., hunger, thirst, lack of shelter, pandemics) stemming from stifling material conditions caused by climate change and ecological degradation. Thus, while it is true that humanizing climate change might be helpful, such conceptualizations fall short in not considering what Leopold (2013) described as the "biotic community," the community of all species of which humanity is just one part, and with which we are inextricably interdependent. This ontological error in thought leads to methodological errors when responding to eco-crises, the illustrious Operation Cat Drop, the airdropping of cats into a remote village in Borneo to remedy an overpopulation of rats, being a case in point (O'Shaughnessy, 2008). Coates (2003), Besthorn (2003), and others have identified anthropocentrism as an issue to be addressed by eco-social workers, but the CASWE-ACFTS climate change position paper neglected to include this line of thought. In addition, Bozalek and Pease (2021) highlight the need for social work education and practice to embrace a critical post-humanist framework, "developing an ethical sensibility that values entanglements of [more-than-human] life and the natural environment" (p. 2).

Environmental Racism and Injustice

Eco-social work literature has had a growing focus on environmental racism and environmental injustice, identifying the ways Black, Indigenous, and people of colour (BIPOC) and low-income peoples are differentially exposed to environmental toxins, disproportionately experiencing environmental hardships (Nesmith & Smyth, 2015; Rogge, 2008; Teixeira & Krings, 2015). While eco-social work scholarship has not been devoid of content pertaining to Indigenous peoples and realities, the focus has tended to be on the ways Indigenous knowledges and practices can be included within the scope of eco-social work. Largely absent has been a discussion of settler colonialism, with its goal of "ongoing appropriation of Indigenous lands and resources by and for the benefit of settlers" (Bacon, 2019, p. 59). Hiller and Carlson (2018) problematize the dearth of settler-colonial exploration in eco-social work scholarship and recommend centring "Indigenous sovereignty within environmental social work … recognizing, in the Canadian context, that we live and work in *treaty* territories" and that "treaty relationships entail responsibilities to learn to know and care for the land" (p. 61). Yellow Bird and Gray (2010) insist that nothing short of rejecting and disrupting settler privilege will suffice. Without a lens on settler colonialism, the various theories and methodologies proffered by eco-social work scholars risk perpetuating colonialism, what Bacon (2019) terms "colonial ecological violence" (p. 59). In its holistic framing, nutritional social work takes these important points under advisement and posits an approach that brings settler colonialism and its attendant ecological colonial violence into its scope in the context of multilevel social justice practice and eco-social relations.

Greening Social Work Education

Even though social workers are proactively engaged in working with the most disadvantaged and marginalized members of society, "they need to educate themselves and others about climate change and the opportunities for micro and macro practice interventions" (Hetherington & Boddy, 2012, p. 54). There are immediate food insecurity needs, including nutritional insecurity exacerbated by eco-crises, which disproportionally impact marginalized and disadvantaged populations (Dominelli, 2012). These significant social justice issues fall within the purview of social work practice and are often overlooked. As outlined in the emergent literature on nutritional social work (Dylan & Cammaert, 2022), "nutritional social work highlights the role for social workers at direct, community, and policy levels in ensuring all people, through participatory, democratizing, power-sharing, and equity-creating processes, have access to nutritious foods" (p. 336). Below, the authors provide a multilevel overview highlighting how nutritional social work can be integrated into direct practice, community, theory, policy, and curricula, potentially creating experiential learning opportunities in field education.

Greening Schools of Social Work

The responsibility for educating new social workers about the interrelationship between human nutritional security and the natural environment resides with schools of social work, who establish their approach to course development and administration, under the auspices of national accreditation standards (CASWE-ACFTS, 2021a). If schools do not have a vested interest in integrating this knowledge into the curricula, these issues will not inform future social work practice, furthering the impact of the eco-crisis on disadvantaged and marginalized members of society. The sentiment from eco-scholars (Besthorn, 2013a; Boddy et al., 2018; Boetto, 2017; Coates, 2005; Dominelli, 2012; Dominelli et al., 2018; Gray et al., 2013; Jones, 2010; Papadopoulos, 2019; Shaw, 2011; Teixeira & Krings, 2015) and practitioners is clear: social work curricula need to include knowledge of the extent and impact of ecological crises and relevant practice skills. For example, after surveying over 350 social workers in the United States, practitioners agreed that social workers wanted more curriculum content on the impact of the environmental crisis, stating a lack of existing practice knowledge on the subject (Shaw, 2011). Without sufficient knowledge and skill development regarding ecological practices, including nutrition, social workers are not able to address environmental injustices in practice, as social work codes of ethics preclude practising without competence in professional domains (CASWE-ACFTS, 2021).

Greening CASWE-ACFTS Accreditation Standards

While Canadian schools of social work have autonomy in approaches to course development and delivery, all schools must meet the accreditation standards established by the national social work education body, CASWE-ACFTS. (See Hillock's introduction in this volume, which details recent revisions to the CASWE-ACFTS accreditation standards that have finally recognized environmental social work as integral to the social work curriculum.) Internationally, the connection between humans and eco-social work has also been incorporated into some national educational and accreditation standards, such as the Council on Social Work Education in the United States (CSWE, 2015). CSWE's third competency, "Advance human rights and social, economic, and environmental justice," states that "social workers: apply their understanding of social, economic, and environmental justice to advocate for human rights at the individual and system levels; and engage in practices that advance social, economic, and environmental justice" (pp. 7–8). Inclusion of environmental justice is also an important step to move to a broader understanding and integration of eco-social work into curricula, and addresses the suggestion Boddy and colleagues (2018) have made to embed environmental content in contemporary social work curricula. However, the CSWE (2015) does not mandate that schools adopt this standard, stating that "programs may add competencies that are consistent with their mission and goals and respond to their context" (p. 7). Lacking clear direction and interest, this allows eco-content to be omitted from curricula and ultimately social work practice.

Clear direction to accredited social work programs on environmental justice is also largely missing in Australia. A content analysis by Papadopoulos and Hegarty (2017) on the inclusion of environmental content in the *Australian Social Work Education and Accreditation Standards* (ASWEAS, 2020) identified that, of the six mentions of environment in the standards, half related to student learning environments and the other half to person-in-environment or "the points where people integrate with their physical environments" (p. 360). However, the latter tends only to reference a person's social environment, lacking clear connection to the transverse impact of the physical environment. Without clear standards, the pragmatics of systematically integrating eco-social work across university curricula is uncertain and likely disjointed.

To attend to environmental justice and reduce the impact of the eco-crisis on the most marginalized and disadvantaged members of society, governing social work education bodies need to dedicate attention to the synergistic impact of the physical environment and create clear standards that direct multilevel curricula and field practice development consistently across schools of social work. Integration of this knowledge throughout the curriculum will build capacity amongst future social workers and situate social work at the crux of environmental change. It is imperative to align social justice with ecological realities, such as nutritional considerations, to meet the needs of all people and communities and reduce inequalities and continued environmental degradation.

Critical Nutritional Social Work: A Green Approach

Nutritional social work is conceptualized as inseparable from critical eco-social work, the kind of eco-praxis that foregrounds eco-justice, the struggle against settler colonialism (Wolfe, 2006), and rights and anti-oppressive approaches as they pertain to BIPOC realities and those experiences of other oppressed groups. Research indicates that Indigenous peoples (Roosvall & Tegelberg, 2015; Whyte, 2019), other racialized groups (Bullard, 2005; Bullard & Wright, 2012; Burke et al., 2015; Gosine & Teelucksingh, 2008), sexually diverse people (Frank, 2020), and women (Nagel, 2016; Nellemann et al., 2011) are differentially impacted by the climate emergency and other eco-issues because of colonialism, racism, and neo-liberal capitalism, and the way socioeconomic status and geopolitical location act as variables. These groups also experience more issues with access to nutritional food. Systemic racism creates structural barriers and inequities for racialized people that limit opportunities and produce outcomes that include food insecurity (Odoms-Young, 2018). A study investigating food insecurity in a remote First Nation located in the James Bay region found factors such as two-family dwellings, inordinately high grocery store prices, concerns that foods harvested on the land are contaminated, and lack of road access to more affordable foods (Skinner et al., 2014). These factors underscore the way race, class, and settler colonialism interweave to create unequal food access. Gates (2014) found food insecurity issues are more prevalent among "LGBT adults when compared to non-LGBT adults across several national surveys, and across gender, age, racial/ethnic, and education level groups," and women and bisexual and racialized persons within the LGBTQ community are even more likely to experience food insecurity.

Understanding how the climate emergency, and related eco-crises, produce differential outcomes is central to sound critical nutritional social work, which involves multilevel praxis from a social justice orientation. Czyzewski and Tester (2014) have rightly identified the need for non-Indigenous persons (e.g., social workers, researchers, and others) to meaningfully engage with colonialism and its persistent harms. Anishinaabe/Ojibway scholar John Borrows (2018) asserts that reconciliation in the Canadian context involves not only repairing the relationship between Indigenous peoples and the Crown but also reconciling with the Earth. Indigenous peoples have long had relationships with their lands that involve reciprocity and "cultures of gratitude" for "the gifts provided by Mother Earth" (Kimmerer, 2011, p. 257). The damage and waste created by dissociated practices of agribusiness and factory farming characteristic of the dominant culture are antithetical to an Indigenous worldview. For Indigenous peoples food sovereignty is not simply about rights but involves the "cultural responsibilities and relationships that Indigenous peoples have with their environment … [and] examining the efforts being made by Indigenous communities to restore these relationships through the revitalization of their Indigenous foods and ecological knowledge systems as they assert control over their own wellbeing" (Coté, 2016, p. 59).

For nutritional social work, addressing colonial injustices such as restricting access to traditional hunting grounds for Indigenous peoples means recognizing the Indigenous lands on which social work activities occur, seeking ways to disrupt settler colonialism, seeking to avoid committing colonial ecological violence, and working to transform the neo-liberal state into a more socially just polity. As Haley (2020) argues, "neoliberalism supports White settler nation-state structures" (p. 221), which in turn reinforce racial and other inequities and the persistence of associated social issues. Some of the ways to unsettle settler colonialism include investigating one's settler location and its objectionable impacts (Kouri, 2020), exploring the ways society reproduces settler-colonial privilege and power (Haley, 2020), examining cultural and pedagogical narratives for how they counter or reinscribe settler-colonial perspectives (Clark et al., 2014), supporting community-based participatory research involving Indigenous peoples and communities to centre and mobilize Indigenous knowledges and understandings, and other practices that decentre settler-colonial epistemologies and ontologies.

Because nutritional social work addresses issues of food security and the more nuanced issue of nutritional security, it is unquestionably an eco-social work issue, as food security hinges so firmly on the health of the planet, which is becoming increasingly precarious. Talk of nutritional social work without a settler-colonial lens is incomplete, for it misses the power relations enacted on the land, overlooks the Crown's unilateral assertion of sovereignty (Turner, 2006), and neglects to interrogate the privileges and benefits that have accrued and continue to accrue to settlers, with considerable consequences for Indigenous peoples. Indigenous responses and acts of resistance are also ignored in an eco-calculus that does not problematize settler colonialism. Nutritional social work, operating with an understanding of settler-colonial society and seeking to decolonize social work, would support Indigenous food sovereignty and self-determination, recognizing, as Ahern (2020, p. 243) says, "that nutritious, affordable, culturally appropriate food is inextricably linked to cultural, spiritual, and ecological well-being, concepts that also resonate with human rights thinking and holistic" and critical eco-social work.

Nutritional social work needs also to be aware of and sensitive to the experiences of other groups that are differentially impacted by the climate emergency, such as those identified above. If we are to maintain our social justice mantle, then all groups that are more vulnerable in the climate emergency warrant focused critical eco- and nutritional social work care. Nutritional social work looks at the politics of nutrition and nutritional access, recognizes the interdependency of nutrition with planetary, and often bioregional, wellness, and explicitly seeks to address systemic, structural, and institutional arrangements that oppress groups socially, ecologically, and nutritionally. To graduate students who have skills, competency, and experience in nutritional social work, it is imperative that the social work curricula, including learnings in both classroom and field placements, include content in this important social justice area.

Application of Nutritional Social Work in the Social Work Curricula

Social work is an academic discipline and a practice-based profession evolving from a contextual understanding of human existence with a professional obligation to create conditions for a more just living environment for all. This requires social workers to consider the synergistic influence of nutritional wellness and security within our multilayered practice. This translation of knowledge requires a foundational shift in social work curricula to include a more critical understanding of these eco-realities. In 1991, seventeen principles of environmental justice were adopted by the First National People of Colour Leadership Summit in the United States. The resulting document contained a "call for the education of present and future generations with an emphasis on environmental issues, including reforms to education around interconnectedness versus compartmentalization and specialization and ecological education in schools" (Miller et al., 2012, p. 275).When this is linked to social work practical applications, like nutritional social work, students will shift to an understanding of the interdependent relationship between person and environment. Encouraging students to build knowledge of equity and social justice requires active, practice-based learning, which may be obtained through the field education portion of the curriculum (Kolb, 1984). Dressel and Marcus (1982) identified that significant learning occurs "when an individual not only knows but is also able to interpret, understand, and use words, concepts, and symbols to facilitate their thought processes and judgments" (p. 25). This section provides an overview of how knowledge of equity and social justice via nutritional social work can be integrated throughout social work curricula, including field education, which has long been recognized as the signature pedagogy within social work education (CSWE, 2015).

Direct Practice with Individuals, Families, and Groups

The links between poor nutritional quality and mental health issues have been explored by various scholars outside of social work (Dylan & Cammaert, 2022), creating a call to integrate this knowledge into prevention and intervention strategies. Considering social work's utilization of person-in-environment, incorporating nutritional considerations into direct-level curricula with individuals, families, and groups is part of evidence-based practice. To incorporate nutritional considerations, students will need to accrue an understanding of nutritional terminology and basic processes of food growth (Cederholm et al., 2016) to help service users navigate food choices and ensure individual and family health and well-being. Accompanying this foundational knowledge is the appreciation of the diversity of eating patterns that contribute to a healthy diet (Jahns et al., 2018). Students need to be provided with ample critical knowledge on the nutritional and physical/mental health connection that highlights the importance of interdisciplinary planning around interventions, nutritional food offerings, and meal planning. Nutrition education not only pertains to food itself but encompasses the perceptions, beliefs, attitudes, meanings, and social norms of food (Contento, 2016), essential knowledge for direct practice.

With respect to direct practice courses such as social work communication and skills and social work practice with families and groups, nutritional considerations regarding individual and family food security and decision-making around food acquisition can be integrated throughout teaching about assessment, intervention planning, and program development. Further, by situating nutritional considerations within questions of availability, economic and geographic accessibility, cultural practices and sustainability, students can be taught how to use critical reflective skills on a tangible topic. For example, course content around social work assessments (e.g., individual, family, and group) can include a nutritional component by inquiring about current food practices, consumption patterns, and culturally specific food needs and preferences.

Within direct practice theory courses, it is essential that students are taught to critically examine how to help service users overcome barriers related to the structural and systemic forces that shape food accessibility and availability. This refers not only to the many ways intersecting oppressions reduce food access and security, but also how the industrial, neo-liberal agribusiness model of food production leads to destructive economic policies and practices that render small-scale farming impracticable and separate growers from lands and seeds, resulting in marginalization and exploitation (Coté, 2016; Shiva, 2016). Against this sociopolitical backdrop, students can be taught the importance of encouraging people to take ownership of their health and well-being through reconnecting with food production in their local region and integrating fresh food, while minimizing their overall carbon footprint through reduced involvement with food transportation.

Community Practice and Engagement

Applying nutritional security to community-level curricula involves an understanding of community organizing, engagement, awareness, and capacity building, which are the historical foundation of social work practice (Stall & Stoecker, 1998). As such, neighbourhood revitalization and resilience, advocating for food and ecological security, and raising awareness of building local healthy environments can easily be integrated into course content and provide students with practical application examples of community practice. Critical examination of community practice on nutritional security requires students to question barriers to accessing nutritional security, including the role of power dimensions, historical contexts, political pedagogy, and the influence of capitalism and big agribusinesses, all the while examining opportunities for more equitable, democratic, ecological, and culturally and contextually relevant food production, distribution, and consumption practices.

Practical application of nutritional social work during community-level courses will allow students to understand how to improve physical and mental health outcomes through sharing nutrition knowledge. Dylan and Cammaert (2022) noted that this includes examining how "grassroots development of community kitchens, community gardens, vertical gardens, networking with local farmers, integrating fresh food into pantries and food banks (with a view to eliminating their need), mapping out access points, transforming green spaces into viable growing spaces, and coalition building pertaining to food security and food justice" represent key practices of nutritional social work (p. 334).

Policy

Social work students are required to engage in policy, or indirect practice curriculum, during their professional degrees. By integrating nutritional security through discussion and case study into policy-level courses, student will have an opportunity to gain and critically apply knowledge on the personal becoming political (Riger, 1993). Social workers have an ethical responsibility to integrate structural understanding of the contexts, histories, and power relations that shape social arrangements and social suffering. This includes social movements and policy changes linked to nutritional insecurity.

Considering the vast impact of nutritional insecurity on the individual, social, cultural, economic, and ecological dimensions of the profession, indirect social work practice curricula need to teach students how to push the political agenda for inclusive policies. Without a commitment to integrate nutritional security within an ecological lens into mainstream education, nutrient quality decline and barriers to access to nutritious foods will increase due to the impact of extreme weather events and rising levels of carbon dioxide (Ziska et al., 2016). Practically speaking, social work curricula can include modules of green political initiatives that promote sustainable agriculture, decreased food waste, and clean power (Drolet et al., 2015; Melekis & Woodhouse, 2015). In addition, critical discussions around rural and urban challenges to accessibility and cultural and ecological needs, and conceptualizing ways to reduced economic barriers including advocating for living-wage policies (Biddix & Park, 2008; Chandler, 2009), will provide students a way to meaningfully engage with the course material.

Field Education

Field education is universally recognized as the key curriculum component where students learn to apply the knowledge, values, and skills of their particular profession, develop professional use of self, integrate theory and practice, and function in community organizations (Bogo, 2010; Shulman, 2005). Although traditional practicum sites in health care, social services, and child welfare continue to dominate the landscape, non-traditional placement opportunities are beginning to flourish as exemplified by the increased usage of placements within students' existing social service employment (Pelech et al., 2009), online counselling services (Mishna et al., 2013), and web-based models of field education (Zuchowski, 2015). In conjunction with these innovative and unique placements, we propose that social work students could equally benefit from placements with a focus on nutritional social work such as community kitchens, community gardens, vertical gardens, pantries, and food banks. These largely unexplored field placement sites are congruent with the twin priorities of social and environmental justice coupled with human and environmental rights (Androff, 2016).

For example, the past quarter century has witnessed the rise of community gardens (Chen & Gregg, 2017; Himmelheber, 2014). These community-based operations allow participation in food production and foster community building, agency, and empowerment (Kaiser & Hermsen, 2015; Peeters, 2012b; Ragan & Dimitropoulos, 2017) while reducing psychological distress associated with food insecurity. Community gardens can be established in multiple urban locations where students complete practicum placements, including shelters for women and children fleeing intimate partner violence and for persons experiencing homelessness. Shelters have long been criticized for neglecting the health and wellness of their residents and promulgating the risk of malnutrition, substance abuse, and mental illness (Wiecha et al., 1991). Successful shelters, on the other hand, enhance the internal relationships between members along with external relationships with the wider community (Walsh et al., 2009). These community gardens allow residents access to green space, which can ameliorate their relationship to the natural environment.

Since the 1990s, schools of social work have decried the undersupply of appropriate field placement opportunities (Fook & Cleak, 1994; Gushwa & Harriman, 2019) that allow students to grow in their professional development and understanding as well as work to ameliorate the lives of oppressed and marginalized populations. We strenuously argue that field placements in the area of nutritional social work are viable opportunities to fill this gap in the social work field education landscape. Integrating nutritionally focused field placement opportunities into the existing repertoire of field placement sites offers students additional avenues to explore for their future social work practice.

Field placements focusing on nutritional social work are also congruent with the Canadian Association of Social Workers' *Guidelines for Ethical Practice* (2005), which notes, "social workers endeavour to advocate for a clean and healthy environment and advocate for the development of environmental strategies consistent with social work principles and practices." Jones (2010) notes that individual, family, and community well-being are rooted in the broader environment, which also includes environmental problems, such as disasters, pollution, and lack of access to nutritious food (Dominelli, 2012).

The application of theory to practice is a central focus of the field education experience. Practicum sites with an emphasis on nutritional social work see students witness oppression theory (Robbins, 2017) firsthand, through the grossly unequal distribution of wealth in the current neo-liberal landscape, with specific impacts on lone-parent mothers, those living in poverty, and marginalized groups (Raphael, 2016). At the same time, community gardens and kitchens along with vertical farming may be a conscientizing and mobilizing force as exemplified by service users' increased knowledge about food issues and the involvement of a diversity of community members (Besthorn, 2013b). These sites see communities come together to make decisions, share space, supplies, and equipment, and work together for a common goal. Service users have more control and choice over food selection and increased management of their food needs, which is supportive of empowerment theory (Lee & Hudson, 2017), along with resilience theory (Gilligan, 2017) and hope theory (Polgar, 2017).

Conclusion

This chapter has argued the need to foreground nutritional social work in the development of professional theorizing and practice responses to the climate emergency. The recommendations outlined throughout have been designed to be transferrable and applicable to schools of social work internationally, beyond the Canadian context. Nutritional social work promotes Earth- and species-friendly approaches that are informed by an anti-oppressive lens and a critique of settler colonialism. As this chapter has demonstrated, nutritional social work can make an important contribution to the process of greening social work education. Indeed, the social work profession needs to expand its current curricular parameters to incorporate more critical eco-social work content into classrooms, field placements, research, and scholarship, if it is to persist with its social justice claims. When a new concept is introduced into any discipline, it typically takes time for the concept to be adopted and used broadly. Integrating understandings of nutritional insecurity into foundational elements of social work pedagogy (e.g., classroom theory, practice, critical reflection, and field) facilitates uptake of this concept in day-to-day social work practice. If social work fails now to respond in an informed and skilful manner to the variety of injustices produced by the climate emergency, then the professional assertion of social justice is hollow. This chapter has explored how nutritional social work is essential to the greening of social work process and has outlined ways nutritional social work can enhance social work education and practice in multilevel contexts, potentially mobilizing individuals, collectives, and institutions with respect to the climate emergency in concrete and transformative ways.

REFERENCES

Ahern, E. S. (2020). Resistance and renewal: How native food sovereignty movements should guide human rights and social work. *Journal of Human Rights and Social Work, 5*(4), 236–245. https://doi.org/10.1007/s41134-020 -00122-4

Androff, D. (2016). *Practicing rights: Human rights-based approaches to social work practice.* Routledge.

Angus, I. (2016). Tipping points, climate chaos, and planetary boundaries. In *Facing the Anthropocene: Fossil capitalism and the crisis of the Earth system* (pp. 59–77). Monthly Review Press.

Australian Association of Social Workers. (2020). *Australian social work education and accreditation standards*. Retrieved from https://www.aasw.asn .au/document/item/6073

Bacon, J. M. (2019). Settler colonialism as eco-social structure and the production of colonial ecological violence. *Environmental Sociology, 5*(1), 59–69. https://doi.org/10.1080/23251042.2018.1474725

Besthorn, F. (2003). Radical ecologisms: Insights for educating social workers in ecological activism and social justice. *Critical Social Work, 3*(1), 66–106.

Besthorn, F. H. (2012). Deep ecology's contributions to social work: A ten-year retrospective. *International Journal of Social Welfare, 21*(3), 248–259. https:// doi.org/10.1111/j.1468-2397.2011.00850.x

Besthorn, F. H. (2013a). Radical equalitarian ecological justice: A social work call to action. In M. Gray, J. Coates, & T. Hetherington (Eds.), *Environmental social work* (pp. 31–45). Routledge.

Besthorn, F. H. (2013b). Vertical farming: Social work and sustainable urban agriculture in an age of global food crises. *Australian Social Work, 66*(2), 187–203. https://doi.org/10.1080/0312407X.2012.716448

Besthorn, F. H., & Canda, E. R. (2002). Revisioning environment: Deep ecology for education and teaching in social work. *Journal of Teaching in Social Work, 22*(1–2), 79–101. https://doi.org/10.1300/J067v22n01_07

Bhagwan, R. (2017). Community engagement within a social work programme in rural India. *Social Work, 53*(3), 315–329. https://doi.org/10.15270 /53-3-572

Biddix, J., & Park, H. W. (2008). Online networks of student protest: The case of the living wage campaign. *New Media & Society, 10*(6), 871–891. https:// doi.org/10.1177/1461444808096249

Boddy, J., MacFarlan, S., & Greenslade, L. (2018). Social work and the natural environment: Embedding content across curricula. *Australian Social Work, 71*(3), 367–375. https://doi.org/10.1080/0312407X.2018.1447588

Boetto, H. (2017). A transformative eco-social model: Challenging modernist assumptions in social work. *British Journal of Social Work, 47*(1), 48–67. https://doi.org/10.1093/bjsw/bcw149

Bogo, M. (2010). *Achieving competence in social work through field education*. University of Toronto Press.

Borrows, J. (2018). Earth-bound: Indigenous resurgence and environmental reconciliation. In M. Asch, J. Borrows, & J. Tully (Eds.), *Resurgence and reconciliation: Indigenous-settler relations and earth teachings* (pp. 49–81). University of Toronto Press.

Bowles, W., Boetto, H., Jones, P., & McKinnon, J. (2016). Is social work really greening? Exploring the place of sustainability and environment in social work codes of ethics. *International Social Work, 61*(4), 503–517. https://doi .org/10.1177/0020872816651695

Bozalek, V., & Pease, B. (2021). *Post-anthropocentric social work: Critical posthuman and new materialist perspectives*. Routledge.

Bretzlaff-Holstein, C. (2018). The case for humane education in social work education. *Social Work Education, 37*(7), 924–935. https://doi.org/10.1080/02615479.2018.1468428

Bullard, R. (2005). *The quest for environmental justice*. Sierra Club Books.

Bullard, R., & Wright, B. (2012). *The wrong complexion for protection: How the government response to disaster endangers African American communities*. NYU Press.

Burke, M., Hsiang, S. M., & Miguel, E. (2015). Global non-linear effect of temperature on economic production. *Nature, 527*(7577), 235–239. https://doi.org/10.1038/nature15725. Medline:26503051

Canadian Association for Social Work Education (CASWE-ACFTS). (2021a). *Educational policies and accreditation standards for Canadian social work education*. Retrieved from https://caswe-acfts.ca/wp-content/uploads/2021/04/EPAS-2021.pdf

Canadian Association for Social Work Education. (2021b). *Standards for accreditation*. Retrieved from https://caswe-acfts.ca/wp-content/uploads/2013/03/CASWE-ACFTS.Standards-11-2014-1.pdf

Canadian Association of Social Workers (CASW). (2005). *Guidelines for ethical practice*. Retrieved from https://www.casw-acts.ca/files/attachements/casw_guidelines_for_ethical_practice_e.pdf

Caputi, J. (2020). *Call your "mutha": A deliberately dirty-minded manifesto for the Earth Mother in the Anthropocene*. Oxford.

Cederholm, T., Barazzoni, R., Austin, P., Ballmer, P., Biolo, G., Bischoff, S., Compher, C., Correia, I., Higashiguchi, T., Holst, M., Jensen, G., Malone, A., Muscaritoli, M., Nyulasi, I., Pirlich, M., Rothenberg, E., Schindler, K., Schneider, S., de van der Schueren, M. A., … Singer, P. (2016). ESPEN guidelines on definitions and terminology of clinical nutrition. *Clinical Nutrition, 36*(1), 49–64. https://doi.org/10.1016/j.clnu.2016.09.004. Medline:27642056

Chandler, S. (2009). Working hard, living poor: Social work and the movement for livable wages. *Journal of Community Practice, 17*(1–2), 170–183. https://doi.org/10.1080/10705420902856159

Chen, T., & Gregg, E. (2017). *Food deserts and food swamps: A primer*. National Collaborating Centre for Environmental Health.

Clark, V., Pacini-Ketchabaw, V., & Hodgins, B. D. (2014). Thinking with paint: Troubling settler colonialisms through early childhood art pedagogies. *International Journal of Child, Youth, and Family Studies, 5*(4.2), 751–781. https://doi.org/10.18357/ijcyfs.clarkv.5422014

Coates, J. (2003). *Ecology and social work: Toward a new paradigm*. Fernwood.

Coates, J. (2005). The environmental crisis: Implications for social work. *Journal of Progressive Human Services, 16*(1), 25–49. https://doi.org/10.1300/J059v16n01_03

Coates, J. (2013). Eco spiritual approaches: A path to decolonizing social work. In M. Gray, J. Coates, M. Yellow Bird, & T. Hetherington (Eds.), *Decolonizing social work* (pp. 93–109). Ashgate.

Contento, I. (2016). *Nutrition education: Linking research, theory, and practice* (3rd ed.). Jones and Bartlett Learning.

Coté, C. (2016). "Indigenizing" food sovereignty: Revitalizing Indigenous food practices and ecological knowledges in Canada and the United States. *Humanities, 5*(3), 57–71. https://doi.org/10.3390/h5030057

Council on Social Work Education (CSWE). (2015). *Educational policy and accreditation standards.* Retrieved from http://www.cswe.org/File.aspx?id =81660

Czyzewski, K., & Tester, F. (2014). Social work, colonial history, and engaging Indigenous self-determination. *Canadian Social Work Review, 32*(2), 211–226.

Dominelli, L. (2012). *Green social work: From environmental crises to environmental justice.* Polity.

Dominelli, L. (2019). Green social work, political ecology and environmental justice. In S.A. Webb (Ed.), *The Routledge handbook of critical social work* (pp. 233–243). Routledge.

Dominelli, L., Nikku, B. R., & Ku, H. B. (2018). Conclusions: Towards a green society and mainstreaming green social work in social work education and practice. In L. Dominelli (Ed.), *The Routledge handbook of green social work* (pp. 569–572). Taylor and Francis-Balkema.

Dressel, P. L., & Marcus, D. (1982). *On teaching and learning in college: Reemphasizing the roles of learners and the disciplines.* Jossey-Bass.

Drolet, J., Wu, H., Taylor, M., & Dennehy, A. (2015). Social work and sustainable social development: Teaching and learning strategies for "green social work" curriculum, *Social Work Education, 34*(5), 528–543. https://doi.org/10.1080 /02615479.2015.1065808

Dylan, A., & Cammaert, J. (2022). Nutritional social work: What it is and why it matters. *Journal of Social Work, 22*(2), 323–344. https://doi.org /10.1177/14680173211008367

Dylan, A., & Coates, J. (2012). The spirituality of justice: Bringing together the eco and the social. *Journal of Religion and Spirituality in Social Work, 31*(1/2), 128–149. https://doi.org/10.1080/15426432.2012.647895

Erickson, C. L. (2018). Social work's foundational concepts: Values and skills for environmental justice. In *Environmental justice as social work practice* (pp. 25–42). Oxford.

Federal Emergency Management Agency (FEMA). (2020). *2020 National Preparedness Report.* https://www.hsdl.org/c/2020-national-preparedness-report/

First National People of Color Environmental Leadership Summit. (1991). *Principles of environmental justice.* United Church of Christ Commission for Racial Justice.

Fook, J., & Cleak, H. (1994). The state of field education in Australia: Results of a national survey. In J. Ife, S. Leitmann, & P. Murphy (Eds.), *Advances in social work and welfare education – National conference papers, Perth* (p. 29). AASWWE/School of Social Work, University of Western Australia.

Frank, T. (2020). LGBTQ people are at higher risk in disasters: A federal report about vulnerability focuses on historically disadvantaged people for the first time. *Scientific American*. https://www.scientificamerican.com/article/lgbtq-people-are-at-higher-risk-in-disasters/

Gal, J., Köngeter, S., & Vicary, S. (2020). *The Settlement House movement revisited: A transnational history*. Policy Press.

Gates, G. (2014). *LGBT people are disproportionately food insecure*. Williams Institute.

Gilligan, R. (2017). Resilience theory and social work practice. In F. Turner (Ed.), *Social work treatment: Interlocking theoretical approaches* (6th ed., pp. 441–451). Oxford University Press.

Gosine, A., & Teelucksingh, C. (2008). *Environmental justice and racism in Canada: An introduction*. Emond.

Gray, M., & Coates, J. (2012). Environmental ethics for social work: Social work's responsibility for the non-human world. *International Journal of Social Welfare*, 21(3), 239–347. https://doi.org/10.1111/j.1468-2397.2011.00852.x

Gray, M., Coates, J., & Hetherington, T. (2013). Overview of the last ten years and typology of ESW. *Environmental Social Work*, 1–28.

Gushwa, M., & Harriman, K. (2019). Paddling against the tide: Contemporary challenges in field education. *Clinical Social Work Journal*, 47(1), 17–22. https://doi.org/10.1007/s10615-018-0668-3

Haley, J. M. (2020). Intersectional and relational frameworks: Confronting anti-Blackness, settler colonialism, and neoliberalism in US social work. *Journal of Progressive Human Services*, 31(3), 210–225. https://doi.org/10.1080/10428232.2019.1703246

Hetherington, T., & Boddy, J. (2012). Ecosocial work with marginalized populations: Time for action on climate change. In M. Gray, J. Coates, & T. Hetherington (Eds.), *Environmental social work* (pp. 46–61). Routledge.

Hiller, C., & Carlson, E. (2018). These are Indigenous lands: Foregrounding settler colonialism and Indigenous sovereignty as primary contexts for Canadian environmental social work. *Canadian Social Work Review*, 35(1), 45–70. https://doi.org/10.7202/1051102ar

Himmelheber, S. (2014). Examining the underlying values of food security programming: Implications for the social work profession. *Journal of Progressive Human Services*, 25(2), 116–132. https://doi.org/10.1080/10428232.2014.898203

Hoff, M., & McNutt, J. (Eds.). (1994). *The global environmental crisis: Implications for social welfare and social work*. Avebury.

Jahns, L., Davis-Shaw, W., Lichtenstein, A. H., Murphy, S. P., Conrad, Z., & Nielsen, F. (2018). The history and future of dietary guidance in America. *Advances in Nutrition, 9*(2), 136–147. https://doi.org/10.1093/advances/nmx025

Jansson, B. (2018). *Becoming an effective policy advocate: From policy practice to social justice*. Brooks/Cole.

Jones, P. (2010). Responding to the ecological crisis: Transformative pathways for social work education. *Journal of Social Work Education, 46*(1), 67–84. https://doi.org/10.5175/JSWE.2010.200800073

Kaiser, M. L., & Hermsen, J. (2015). Food acquisition strategies, food security, and health status among families with children using food pantries. *Families in Society, 96*(2), 83–90. https://doi.org/10.1606/1044-3894.2015.96.16

Kimmerer, R. (2011). Restoration and reciprocity: The contributions of traditional ecological knowledge. In D. Egan, E. Hjerpe, & J. Abrams (Eds.), *Human dimensions of ecological restoration: Integrating science, nature, and culture* (pp. 257–276). Island Press.

Kolb, D. (1984). *Experiential learning: Experience as the source of learning and development*. Prentice-Hall.

Kouri, S. (2020). Settler education: Acknowledgement, self-location, and settler ethics in teaching and learning. *International Journal of Child, Youth and Family Studies, 11*(3), 56–79. https://doi.org/10.18357/ijcyfs113202019700

Kraus, B. (2019). Relational constructionism and relational social work. In S. A. Webb (Ed.), *The Routledge handbook of critical social work* (pp. 93–104). Routledge.

Lee, J. A. B., & Hudson, R. E. (2017). Empowerment approach to social work treatment. In F. Turner (Ed.), *Social work treatment: Interlocking theoretical approaches* (6th ed., pp. 142–165). Oxford University Press.

Leopold, A. (2013). *A Sand County almanac & other writings on ecology and conservation*. Oxford University Press.

Lysack, M. (2010). Environmental decline, loss, and biophilia: Fostering commitment in environmental citizenship. *Critical Social Work, 11*(3), 48–66. https://doi.org/10.22329/csw.v11i3.5832

Martin, M. (2012). Philosophical and religious influences on social welfare policy in the United States: The ongoing effect of reformed theology and social Darwinism on attitudes toward the poor and social welfare policy and practice. *Journal of Social Work, 12*(1), 51–64. https://doi.org/10.1177/1468017310380088

Mary, N. (2008). *Social work in a sustainable world*. Lyceum.

Melekis, K., & Woodhouse, V. (2015). Transforming social work curricula: Institutional supports for promoting sustainability. *Social Work Education, 34*(5), 573–585. https://doi.org/10.1080/02615479.2015.1066325

Miller, S. E., Hayward, R. A., & Shaw, T. V. (2012). Environmental shifts for social work: A principles approach. *International Journal of Social Welfare, 21*(3), 270–277. https://doi.org/10.1111/j.1468-2397.2011.00848.x

Mishna, F., Levine, D., Bogo, M., & Van Wert, M. (2013). Cyber counselling:
An innovative field education pilot project. *Social Work Education*, *32*(4),
484–492. https://doi.org/10.1080/02615479.2012.685066

Nagel, J. (2016). *Gender and climate change: Impacts, science, policy.* Routledge.

Närhi, K., & Matthies, A.-L. (2018). The ecosocial approach in social work
as a framework for structural social work. *International Social Work*, *61*(4),
490–502. https://doi.org/10.1177/0020872816644663

Nellemann, C., Verma, R., and Hislop, L. (Eds). (2011). *Women at the frontline
of climate change: Gender risks and hopes, a rapid response assessment.* United
Nations Environment Programme, GRID-Arendal.

Nesmith, A., & Smyth, N. (2015). Environmental justice and social work
education: Social workers' professional perspectives. *Social Work Education*,
34(5), 484–501. https://doi.org/10.1080/02615479.2015.1063600

Nicotera, A. (2019). Social justice and social work, a fierce urgency:
Recommendations for social work social justice pedagogy. *Journal of Social
Work Education*, *55*(3), 460–475. https://doi.org/10.1080/10437797.2019
.1600443

Odoms-Young, A. (2018). Examining the impact of structural racism on food
insecurity: Implications for addressing racial/ethnic disparities. *Family &
Community Health*, 41, S3–S6. https://doi.org/10.1097/FCH
.0000000000000183. Medline:29461310

O'Shaughnessy, P. (2008). Parachuting cats and crushed eggs: The controversy
over the use of DDT to control malaria. *American Journal of Public Health*,
98(11), 1940–1948. https://doi.org/10.2105/ajph.2007.122523

Papadopoulos, A. (2019). Integrating the natural environment in social work
education: Sustainability and scenario-based learning. *Australian Social
Work*, *72*(2), 233–241. https://doi.org/10.1080/0312407X.2018.1542012

Papadopoulos, A., & Hegarty, K. (2017). Moving beyond the metaphor,
reaching beyond the rhetoric: Social work education in a changing
environment. *Journal of Cleaner Production*, *168*, 357–365. https://doi.org
/10.1016/j.jclepro.2017.08.204

Pawar, M. (2019). Social work and social policy practice: Imperatives
for political engagement. *International Journal of Community and Social
Development*, *1*(1), 15–27. https://doi.org/10.1177/2516602619833219

Peeters, J. (2012a). Social work and sustainable development: Towards a socio-
ecological practice model. *Journal of Social Intervention: Theory and Practice*,
21(3), 5–26. https://doi.org/10.18352/jsi.316

Peeters, J. (2012b). The place of social work in sustainable development:
Towards ecosocial practice. *International Journal of Social Welfare*, *21*(3),
287–98. https://doi.org/10.1111/j.1468-2397.2011.00856.x

Pelech, W. J., Barlow, C., Badry, D. E., & Elliott, G. (2009). Challenging
traditions: The field education experiences of students in workplace

practica. *Social Work Education, 28*(7), 737–749. https://doi.org/10.1080/02615470802492031

Polgar, A. T. (2017). Hope theory and social work treatment. In F. Turner (Ed.), *Social work treatment: Interlocking theoretical approaches* (6th ed., pp. 266–275). Oxford University Press.

Ragan, E., & Dimitropoulos, G. (2017). A critical look at food security in social work: Applying the socio-ecological lens. *Journal of Undergraduate Research in Alberta, 6,* 40–50.

Raphael, D. (2016). *Social determinants of health: Canadian perspectives* (3rd ed.). Canadian Scholars.

Riger, S. (1993). What's wrong with empowerment. *American Journal of Community Psychology, 21*(3), 279–292. https://doi.org/10.1007/BF00941504

Robbins, S. P. (2017). Oppression theory and social work treatment. In F. Turner (Ed.), *Social work treatment: Interlocking theoretical approaches* (6th ed., pp. 376–386). Oxford University Press.

Rogge, M. (2008). Environmental justice. In T. Mizrahi & L. E. Davis (Eds.), *The encyclopedia of social work* (e-reference ed.). Oxford University Press.

Roosvall, A., & Tegelberg, M. (2015). Media and the geographies of climate justice: Indigenous peoples, nature, and the geopolitics of climate change. *tripleC: Journal for a Global Sustainable Information Society, 13*(1), 39–54. https://doi.org/10.31269/triplec.v13i1.654

Schibli, K. (2020). *CASW: Climate change and social work, 2020 position statement.* Canadian Association of Social Workers.

Shaw, T. (2011). Is social work a green profession? An examination of environmental beliefs. *Journal of Social Work, 13*(1), 3–29. https://doi.org/10.1177/1468017311407555

Shiva, V. (2016). *Biopiracy: The plunder of nature and knowledge.* North Atlantic Books.

Shulman, L. S. (2005). Signature pedagogies in the professions. *Dædalus,* 53–59.

Skinner, K., Hanning, R., & Tsuji, L. (2014). Prevalence and severity of household food insecurity of First Nations people living in an on-reserve, sub-Arctic community within the Mushkegowuk Territory. *Public Health Nutrition, 17*(1), 31–39. https://doi.org/10.1017/S1368980013001705

Stall, S., & Stoecker, R. (1998). Community organizing or organizing community? Gender and the crafts of empowerment. *Gender & Society, 12*(6), 729–756. https://doi.org/10.1177/089124398012006008

Teixeira, S., & Krings, A. (2015). Sustainable social work: An environmental justice framework for social work education. *Social Work Education, 34*(5), 513–527. https://doi.org/10.1080/02615479.2015.1063601

Turner, D. (2006). *This is not a peace pipe: Towards a critical Indigenous philosophy.* University of Toronto Press.

Walsh, C., Graham, J., & Shier, M. (2009). Toward a common goal for shelter service. *Social Development Issues, 31*(2), 57–69.

Whyte, K. (2019). Way beyond the lifeboat: An Indigenous allegory of climate justice. In D. Munshi, B. Kum-Kum, J. Foran, and P. Kurian (Eds.), *Climate futures: Reimagining global climate justice* (pp. 11–27). Zed Books.

Wiecha, J., Dwyer, J., & Dunn-Strohecker, M. (1991). Nutrition and health service needs among the homeless. *Public Health Reports, 106*(4), 364–374. Medline:1908587

Wolfe, P. (2006). Settler colonialism and the elimination of the native. *Journal of Genocide Research, 8*(4), 387–409. https://doi.org/10.1080/14623520601056240

Yellow Bird, M., & Gray, M. (2010). Indigenous peoples and the language of social work. In M. Gray, J. Coates, & M. Yellow Bird (Eds.), *Indigenous social work around the world: Towards culturally relevant education and practice* (pp. 59–70). Ashgate.

Zapf, M. K. (2009). *Social work and the environment: Understanding people and place*. Canadian Scholars.

Zapf, M. K. (2012). Profound connections between person and place: Exploring location, spirituality, and social work. In J. R. Graham, J. Coates, B. Swartzentruber, & B. Ouellette (Eds.), *Spirituality and social work: Selected Canadian readings* (pp. 229–242). Canadian Scholars.

Ziska, L., Crimmins, A., Auclair, A., DeGrasse, S., Garofalo, J. F., Khan, A. S., Loladze, I., Pérez de León, A. A., Showler, A., Thurston, J., & Walls, I. (2016). Food safety, nutrition, and distribution. In A. Crimmins, J. Balbus, J. L. Gamble, C. B. Beard, J. E. Bell, D. Dodgen, R. J. Eisen, N. Fann, M. D. Hawkins, S. C. Herring, L. Jantarasami, D. M. Mills, S. Saha, M. C. Sarofim, J. Trtanj, & L. Ziska (Eds.), *The impacts of climate change on human health in the United States: A scientific assessment* (pp. 189–216). US Global Change Research Program.

Zuchowski, I. (2015). Being the university: Liaison persons' reflections on placements with off-site supervision. *Social Work Education, 34*(3), 301–314. https://doi.org/10.1080/02615479.2015.1005070

7 The War-Climate Nexus: Educating Future Social Workers about the Global Adversities Related to War, Climate Change, and Environmental Degradation

BREE AKESSON

The first two decades of the twenty-first century have been characterized by an overwhelming number of social challenges related to social ills, including poverty, war, political instability, climate change, and environmental degradation. Today's global crises have forced 79.5 million people to flee their homes or countries (United Nations High Commissioner for Refugees (UNHCR), 2020). Among their devastating consequences, displacement ruptures families' protective social systems (e.g., family, peers, community networks, and governance structures) and physical environments (e.g., homes, schools, neighbourhoods, and hospitals) necessary for healthy development and well-being (Akesson, 2017; Boehm et al., 2011; Boothby et al., 2006). Although at this time it is unclear how the COVID-19 pandemic will affect the trajectory of today's major wars, if at all, the pandemic precipitated a global economic crisis, driving an additional 150 million people below the extreme poverty line (Malley, 2020). Although there is no direct correlation between income levels and conflict, there is evidence that violence is more likely during periods of economic volatility (Malley, 2020).

In addition to mass numbers of displaced persons and increased poverty related to the COVID-19 pandemic, climate change poses another significant threat to the world. Climate change describes long-term (e.g., decades or centuries) change in average weather patterns (Masson-Delmotte et al., 2018), whereas climate variability refers to fluctuations in weather patterns within a smaller period of time such as months, seasons, or years (International Committee of the Red Cross [ICRC], 2020, p. 13). While the effects of climate change and climate variability are often discussed as something that will happen in the future, some of the most vulnerable populations in the world are already feeling those effects and dealing with the fallout (Jackson, 2017).

As the other chapters in this book explain, the world is facing an existential climate crisis, which shares a relationship with other pressing social challenges such as war, injustice, and poverty. Social work has a professional and ethical responsibility to address these new, ever-changing, and urgent issues. This chapter will focus on yet another aspect of the climate crisis – its relationship with political instability, violence, and war – and how future social workers can be prepared to tackle this complex issue through education in theory, practice, and policy.

The War-Climate Nexus

Researchers have mixed views on whether climate change contributes to a rise in armed conflict. The relationship is much more complex than simply cause and effect. Some have described the causal chain as circuitous (Malley, 2020) and context specific (International Crisis Group, 2021, para. 1). One thing that is clear, however, is that climate change worsens instability and conflict beyond what we have seen in the past (Taylor, 2017). In other words, climate change is a threat-multiplier adding stress to already stressed societies and therefore serving as a catalyst for conflict, violence, and war. Increased instances of extreme weather events – drought, heat waves, hurricanes, monsoons, floods – exacerbate food insecurity, water scarcity, and resource competition while disrupting livelihoods and spurring migration (International Crisis Group, 2021). This struggle for basic resources such as water and fertile land may contribute to potential future conflict (M. Cronin & Jones, 2015; Dominelli & Hackett, 2012).

Countries that are already mired in conflict tend to be disproportionately affected by climate change. They are less able to cope with climate change because their ability to adapt is weakened by conflict (ICRC, 2020). The Notre Dame Global Adaptation Initiative (ND-Gain) Index identified twenty countries most vulnerable to climate change, according to the country's ability to improve resilience (Chen et al., 2015; ND-GAIN, 2021). Sixty per cent of those twenty countries are currently experiencing armed conflict. For example, the current war in Yemen, the origins of which can be traced back to the Arab Spring of 2011, has been characterized as a politically motivated competition for power with underlying tensions related to scarcity of water (Douglas, 2016). Another example is Mali, which since 2012 has experienced severe political instability, with over three hundred thousand people displaced from their homes (Bisimwa, 2021). In addition to violence, Mali has faced rising temperatures alongside increasingly frequent periods of drought and flooding, further displacing people and contributing to high rates of morbidity and mortality. Migrating families tend to move south where there is pasture for their animals. But this creates further tensions between communities over who has access to fertile land and water, which can escalate into localized violence (ICRC, 2020).

At the same time, conflict and instability are contributing to climate change through increased environmental degradation. According to the ICRC (2020), "environmental degradation is a process through which the natural environment is compromised. This can be an entirely natural process, or it can be accelerated or caused by human activities" (p. 13). There are a range of ways that environmental degradation is related to conflict. Militaries are notorious for engaging in environmentally damaging practices such as building bases on ecologically important areas (Benton et al., 2008), using large amounts of fossil fuels (Belcher et al., 2020), creating chemical and noise pollution (Gillies et al., 2010; Waitz et al., 2005), and dumping surplus munitions and waste at sea (Beldowski et al., 2020). During conflict, landscapes may be damaged from pollution, weapons, or conflict rubble (Garrity, 2014), while scorched-earth tactics – intended to destroy anything that might be useful to "the enemy" – leaves large swaths of land completely obliterated (Leebaw, 2014). These tactics of war are so damaging to the environment that they have been labelled as environmental war crimes (Drumbl, 2009). Increased access to small arms and light weapons has also led to increases in hunting and poaching, thereby harming wildlife conservation efforts and relationships with local communities (Brito et al., 2018; Daskin & Pringle, 2018). As conflict displaces large numbers of people from their homes, camps and settlements are hastily created with little to no attention to essential services such as access to water or sanitation and waste management (Hamani, 2019; Weir, 2019). Displaced families may be constrained to gather local resources such as firewood in order to cook, putting additional pressure on the environment (Gonzalez, 2020). Before long, there are no resources available for these families, illustrating how environmental degradation wrought by conflict has vast implications for people as well as ecosystems (Weir, 2020).

The Human Consequences of the War-Climate Nexus

Distinctions have been made between conflict-induced and disaster-induced displacement. The former is typically categorized as resulting from the actions of humans, whereas disaster-induced displacement is categorized as stemming from natural causes (Global Migration Data Analysis Centre, 2021). While this delineation is useful and important when addressing displacement, the lines between the terms are quite blurry. As discussed above, conflicts may arise due to fighting over natural resources, and human activity is a major contributing factor to natural disasters.

Amplified natural disasters related to climate change, intersecting with ongoing political conflict, continue to displace vulnerable populations at an unprecedented rate. The number of those displaced worldwide has rapidly increased in recent years. In 2019, 25 per cent of the 33.4 million new internal displacements across 145 countries and territories were due to conflict and violence, while 75 per cent of new internal displacements were due to disasters (Internal Displacement Monitoring Centre, 2020). Individuals, families, and communities often reluctantly flee their homes of origin, due to impending violence or because they face a range of hardships such as food insecurity, resulting from the war-climate nexus.

The war-climate nexus also contributes to mixed migration or cross-border movements of people, including refugees, victims of trafficking, and people seeking better lives and opportunities. Mixed migration – a hallmark of the war-climate nexus – is becoming more common, complicating how social workers and others address forced migration. While those who flee their countries due to a well-founded fear of persecution are afforded broad legal protections under the 1951 Refugee Convention (United Nations, 1951), the designation, legal status, and rights of those who are displaced by environmental factors are unclear and contested:

> People migrating for environmental reasons do not fall squarely within any one particular category provided by the existing international legal framework. Terms such as "environmental refugee" or "climate change refugee" have no legal basis in international refugee law. There is a growing consensus among concerned agencies ... that their use is to be avoided. (Borràs-Pentinat, 2021, p. 111)

These categorizations may be misleading, because they do not capture the complexity of mixed migration. Therefore, their use has the potential to undermine international legal protections for refugees. This leads to increased vulnerability for these populations.

Combined, the pressing and overlapping forms of adversity that result from the war-climate nexus negatively affect the overall well-being of individuals, families, and communities. Already-vulnerable populations – such as women (especially pregnant and nursing mothers), children (particularly those under the age of five), the elderly, and persons with disabilities – are even more burdened by the intersections of violent conflict, climate change, and environmental degradation (Ryan et al., 2014). Those most vulnerable are those who are the most likely to lack resources to reconstruct their homes and communities (Gaillard et al., 2017). They are therefore forced to migrate to survive. As these populations move, they face additional struggles as their safety and status may be further marginalized during their journey to seek safety (Powers et al., 2018, p. 1029).

Once those displaced as a result of the war-climate nexus have a place of temporary or permanent refuge, they may still struggle with a myriad of challenges. Though initially intended to serve as a short-term solution for displaced populations, camps for displaced populations tend to transition into semi-permanent cities with the average duration of a camp standing at over ten years (Devictor, 2019). While refugee camps serve to protect refugees, conditions in refugee camps are extremely challenging for children and families. There is often substandard sanitation (A. A. Cronin et al., 2008) and scarce electricity (Lehne et al., 2016). Organized crime and violence also contribute to an insecure environment (Glenny, 2015). Furthermore, reports indicate that displaced populations face greater risk of war-related mental health conditions (Scharpf et al., 2021), early marriage (Yaman, 2020), and child labour (Meyer et al., 2020). The displaced face another challenge in the camp context: boredom and rolelessness (Gharahaghi & Anderson-Nathe, 2014; Vitus, 2010). For example, among Syrian refugees in Jordan, even though there are educational programs for children coordinated by non-governmental organizations, low attendance rates lead to fears of an illiterate "lost generation" following the crisis (Beste, 2015, p. 1). Everyday mobilities – such as access to home, school, play spaces, and social networks – are also severely disrupted and compromised by life in refugee camps. Families may have decreased access to education (Akesson, 2015; Davies, 2004) and health services (Sousa et al., 2020), as well as to extended peer and social networks, which may compromise their physical and mental well-being as they find themselves trapped in their own homes (Akesson, 2014). The levels and layers of loss are countless for these populations: loss of friends, family, home, community, culture, language, legal protection, and livelihoods, among many others.

Case Study: Rohingya Refugees in Bangladesh

The example of Rohingya refugees in Bangladesh illustrates the complexity and insidiousness of the war-climate nexus. The Rohingya are a stateless ethnic group and one of the most persecuted minorities in the world, experiencing an ethnic cleansing campaign consisting of horrific acts of violence, burning of homes and villages, and sexual violence at the hands of the Myanmar military and local Buddhist population ("Who are the Rohingya?" 2018; Amnesty International, 2018; Human Rights Watch, 2018; MacLean, 2019). By August 2018, over seven hundred thousand Rohingya had fled their homes – or the remains of their homes – in Myanmar's Rakhine state, where many had lived for generations (International Organization for Migration, 2018). The majority of these individuals sought refuge just across the border in southern Bangladesh, leading to one of the largest and fastest movements of people in recent history. Today, there are approximately one million displaced Rohingya living in southern Bangladesh's overcrowded camps in Cox's Bazar (International Organization for Migration, 2018).

In addition, Bangladesh has been referred to as ground zero for the global climate crisis (Cons, 2018). It is one of the most densely populated countries in the world with 1,265 people per square kilometre (World Bank, 2020). And as the population grows, Bangladesh's land mass decreases: an area larger than Manhattan is being washed away every year (McDonnell, 2019). Its low elevation (only seven feet above sea level) makes it extremely vulnerable to severe floods that result from an increasing number of extreme weather events (Szczpanski et al., 2018),

Many of the refugee camps in southern Bangladesh are the size of large cities but with none of the basic infrastructure to support the large number of Rohingya families who are displaced there ("The Rohingya," 2019). The population density for most camps is less than fifteen square metres per person, which is far below the minimum thirty to forty metres per person required for housing in refugee camps as recommended by the internationally recognized *Humanitarian Charter and Minimum Standards in Humanitarian Response* (Sphere Project, 2018). Most Rohingya families live in temporary bamboo structures covered with only a plastic sheet (Beaubien, 2018). The Bangladesh floodplains and hillsides are the only sites that the Bangladeshi government has made available for Rohingya families to build their homes ("The Rohingya," 2019). But these sites are highly vulnerable to acute climate-related disasters. Aid organizations have argued that monsoon and cyclone floods – which peak between May and October – have the potential to submerge up to one-third of all of the Rohingya camps (K. Ahmed, 2019; Loy, 2018). This means that Rohingya refugees in Bangladesh are even more vulnerable due to bureaucratic policies that will put them at risk of losing their homes yet again, as a result of climate change.

Furthermore, the large and quick influx of Rohingya refugees from Myanmar into Bangladeshi camps has led to environmental degradation both within the camps and in the surrounding communities (Mukul et al., 2019). Research has found that over two thousand hectares of forest has been lost in the Cox's Bazar region (Hassan et al., 2018). The expansion of the Kutupalong camp to accommodate the growing numbers of refugees led to the blockage of an important corridor for the endangered Asian elephant, leaving forty-five elephants stranded (M. S. Ahmed et al., 2017) and amplifying human-elephant conflict (McVeigh & Peri, 2018). The elephants that have survived face dwindling resources from high rates of deforestation due to refugees cutting down trees for fuelwood (Rahman, 2019).

The human impact of the Rohingya's displacement is also dire. The environment within which Rohingya refugees live plays a major role in their well-being. Acute malnutrition rates remain high, with aggravating factors including poor water-sanitation facilities, substandard housing, and rainy seasons (Nutrition Sector, 2018). One study found that prevalence of negative mental health outcomes such as depression, post-traumatic stress disorder (PTSD), and suicidal ideation among Rohingya in Bangladesh was mediated by daily environmental stressors such as quality of housing and exposure to the elements (Riley et al., 2017).

As in other contexts of vulnerability, social workers are at the forefront of the war-climate nexus in Bangladesh (Ali et al., 2013). Today, social workers continue to support local populations impacted by climate change – including the Rohingya refugee population – while also advocating at the policy level for legislation to both support refugees and mitigate the impacts of climate change.

The Role of Social Work Education in Addressing the War-Climate Nexus

Social work's response to the war-climate nexus is as complicated as trying to resolve the challenge itself. The complexity of this issue dares social work educators to think beyond unidimensional interventions that may only serve as a temporary salve to affected populations. What is needed are major efforts: significant systemic and structural changes, political will, competent government support, human and financial investment, technical knowledge, and a shift in mindset (ICRC, 2020, p. 43). And social work education is perfectly suited to spearhead these major efforts.

As described elsewhere in this volume, in 2015 the Council on Social Work Education (CSWE) expanded the definition of human rights and social and economic justice to also include environmental justice (CSWE, 2015). (See Hillock's introduction to this volume for pertinent details concerning recent environmental standards issued from Canada's social work education accrediting body.) Green educational policies such as those developed by CSWE help ensure that social work students are prepared to address environmental issues – and their intersections with other global adversities – once they are practising. This section will explore how social work education can promote addressing the war-climate nexus through theory, practice, and policy. The following serves as a guide for areas where social work educators can integrate knowledge about the war-climate nexus in the classroom, while preparing their students to meet the complex needs of vulnerable populations most affected.

Greening Theory

Social work education requires a new level of theoretical thinking for social workers to address the adversities faced by populations impacted by the war-climate nexus. While attuning itself to a person-in-environment model (Akesson et al., 2017), social work has traditionally emphasized the social environment over the physical environment. However, to truly address the complexities posed by the war-climate nexus, the person-in-environment model should be revised to emphasize the natural and built environments (Akesson et al., 2017). Such an emphasis will provide a framework for social work to increasingly recognize that everything is connected in the world, a useful approach when considering the war-climate nexus and its myriad impacts on vulnerable populations. As Powers et al. (2018) explain, "life on earth is not just composed of interactions between humans, but also includes the connectedness of humans, entire ecosystems, and the physical environment" (p. 232). A renewed emphasis on the natural and built environments within the person-in-environment framework can help social work expand beyond individual-focused models towards place-based and community-focused models (see, for example, Crimeen et al., 2017; Ham & Alderwick, 2015) that are more responsive to addressing environmental issues and the connections to war and violence.

In this vein, social work has also begun to engage theoretically in environmental issues, expanding educational approaches, so that the environment has become a part of the social work discourse (Coates, 2003; Coates & Gray, 2012; Dominelli, 2012; McKinnon & Alston, 2016; Zapf,

2009). Other environment-focused theories that have gained traction in social work theory include deep ecology (Besthorn, 2011; Besthorn & Canda, 2002), which emphasizes the inherent worth of all living beings regardless of perceived utility, and eco-feminism (Besthorn & McMillen, 2002; Klemmer & McNamara, 2020), which uses the lens of gender to understand the relationship between humans and nature. Social work has also drawn from Indigenous perspectives and knowledge to better understand the relationship between humans, non-humans, and the environment (Billiot et al., 2019; Muldoon, 2006). As an example, Powers et al. (2018) suggests that social work education embrace a biophilia framework (Wilson, 1984), which "involves an awareness of the interconnectedness of nature and understands the role of humans as only one aspect in nature" (Powers et al., 2018, p. 1028). In relation to the war-climate nexus, a biophilia framework helps to uncover how the damaging and destruction of the environment can impact humans physically, psychologically, and spiritually (Kellert & Wilson, 1995). Consequently, theories informed by Indigenous knowledge and the biophilia framework have the potential to help future social workers engage with holistic, collective, and complex theories that provide a foundation for effective practice and advocacy.

Greening Practice

ASSESSING AND ADDRESSING
Social work is committed to supporting the most vulnerable populations in the world, such as those impacted by the war-climate nexus. To do so, social workers should take a comprehensive and holistic approach to assessing the realities and the needs of those impacted by the war-climate nexus. Thus, social workers must be taught to move beyond what is visible (Bunn et al., 2023) and expand their assessments to include past experiences, current capacities, and future goals. Inquiring into past experiences includes listening to people who have experienced loss of home, family, community, and even country due to war or disaster. At the same time, it is critical for social workers to always keep the strengths, resilience, and capacities of vulnerable populations in mind, especially when assessing their present circumstances and co-creating a plan to move forward with a focus on people's future goals.

To assess and address the issues facing populations impacted by the war-climate nexus, social work educators should include training for students in a range of crisis practice activities such as providing psycho-social support to families fleeing conflict, coordinating shelter for the displaced whose temporary homes were destroyed during a climate-related event such as flooding or monsoon, and reunifying family members separated while fleeing their countries of origin to seek safety. These practical skills could be taught within a social work curriculum or in partnership with other helping profession disciplines that address humanitarian issues such as public health, social services, medicine, nursing, community psychology, and refugee studies.

It is important to note that social workers themselves may have been forced to leave their homes and communities, thereby experiencing some of the same issues as the populations they are serving. Indeed, in contexts of disasters and crises, local social workers may be employed by humanitarian and development agencies (Bartley & Beddoe, 2018; Bartley & Fronek, n.d.; Beddoe et al., 2011; Danso, 2015), and the task of assessing and addressing the needs of impacted populations may also include providing support to those who are tasked with helping the most vulnerable. By assessing and addressing the needs of those most impacted by the war-climate nexus, social workers can also learn to recognize and support people's human rights. That is, social workers can engage in activities that promote people's right to migrate, to resettle or to go back to their homelands, and to pursue a safe and secure future.

(RE)SETTLE, (RE)BUILD, (RE)ESTABLISH

Social workers play an important role in helping those affected by the war-climate nexus to (re)settle, (re)build, and (re)establish their lives. The most effective interventions that can be taught to future practitioners are those that promote connection and socialization to forge new links and (re)establish a sense of community (Bunn et al., 2023), which may have been seriously compromised or even destroyed in the course of war or disaster. In addition to facilitating collective healing, encouraging face-to-face interactions among people through community organization methods helps them (re)establish community ties and (re)connect to place and home (Gamble & Weil, 2010). Social work educators may wish to turn to the work of Gamble and Weil (2010), who have outlined community organization methods – all which are relevant skills that should be taught as part of a comprehensive social work education – including activities such as planning, engaging in effective communication, encouraging community participation, facilitating collective decision-making, involving groups and organizations, mobilizing resources, and advocating at the government level.

Teaching about community organizing, as well as participatory approaches, can ensure the meaningful participation of those impacted has the capacity to contribute more powerfully to healing processes, and can assist social workers to more easily recognize individual, family, and community strengths, as a means of helping to facilitate community resilience (Ellis & Abdi, 2017). Future social workers can also be taught community organization methods as a means to address the roots of the war-climate nexus, for example, bringing people together to advocate for policies and action that stop environmental degradation, protects the natural and built environment (and its flora and fauna), and restores lands to their community caretakers.

VOICE AND STORYTELLING

While populations impacted by the war-climate nexus confront multiple and interrelated adversities, they also have individual and collective assets such as agency, resilience, and the potential for healing, which can be uncovered via storytelling (Moore, 2017). Storytelling can be as simple as asking an individual, family, or community to share their history, experiences, and dreams of the future. Future social workers can be encouraged to use multimedia approaches – such as comics (Akesson, 2012), audio recordings, photography, or video – that can be used as a memento for the storyteller or to share with others as a means of community building, education, and advocacy.

To emphasize the importance of the voices of affected populations, social work educators may wish to teach their students about various participatory storytelling methods. Narrative storytelling can be supported by drawings, audio recordings, and photography (Moore, 2017). Digital storytelling is one such participatory method that combines these creative elements and can be used to not just tell one's story of overcoming adversity but also underscore strengths and produce a counter-narrative that challenges often erroneous assumptions of victimhood (Lenette et al., 2015; Marshall et al., 2022).

Due to the complexity of life and experience, telling one's story may also include memories that evoke sadness, loss, stress, harm, and trauma. There is a concern that the retelling can result in re-traumatization (Bell, 2001). However, a systematic review of therapies for post-traumatic stress disorder that involved such retelling found that any arising distress is short term (American Psychological Association, 2017). In the longer term, retelling in a safe and conversational context may be psycho-educational, relieving, and an important part of symptom reduction. In fact, the retelling of distressing events, combined with supportive therapy, is associated with positive outcomes (Gwozdziewycz & Mehl-Madrona, 2013; Hijazi et al., 2014).

For many individuals, families, and communities impacted by the war-climate nexus, their stories are formative parts of their past, present, and future. The opportunity to share – and the act of sharing itself – provides a venue to highlight the voices of those most impacted by the war-climate nexus, to encourage (re)settlement, (re)building, and (re)establishing individual identity, a sense of purpose, and connections to places, both in the past and future.

Greening Policy

ADVOCACY

Social work practitioners and educators have the capacity to provide leadership on climate advocacy and action, drawing links between climate change and conflict, and contributing to policy that can mitigate environmental change. Social workers also have a responsibility to advocate for environmental justice and to address the war-climate nexus through education, advocacy, community outreach, and research (Jackson, 2017). The *Global Agenda for Social Work and Social Development* (2012), developed in collaboration among the International Federation of Social Workers, International Association of Schools of Social Work, and International Council on Social Welfare, instructs social workers and social work educators to recognize how pressing environmental issues such as natural resource depletion and environmental degradation undermine both people and planet and complicate social work's goal of achieving a just society. The *Global Agenda* calls for social workers and social work educators to promote social and economic equality, promote the dignity and worth of people, work towards environmental sustainability, and recognize the importance of human relationships. The *Agenda* thereby provides an advocacy framework via which social work educators can respond to the war-climate nexus, while still addressing social work's core commitment to human rights and social justice.

Under the *Agenda*, social workers have an ethical responsibility to advocate for laws and policies that support affected populations. For example, although the environmental crisis and war are often interwoven, persons displaced due to disaster/climate crises have few legal protections under international humanitarian law. In Canada, social workers should advocate for the Canadian Immigration and Refugee protection Act (IRPA) to grant permanent residency to applicants who are seeking protection due to climate-related events in their country of origin. In cases where the 1951 Refugee Convention does not apply, permanent residency could be granted on humanitarian and compassionate grounds.

Other specific areas of social work advocacy that social work educators could include in their curricula include holding Canada accountable for its contribution to the war-climate nexus. As the tenth-largest climate polluter in the world (Friedrich et al., 2020), Canada remains complicit in its role in the climate crisis. It has benefitted from the growing fossil fuel industry and could use that wealth to address climate change and accommodate populations impacted by the war-climate nexus. Social workers should therefore advocate for policies and laws that both decrease Canada's fossil fuel emissions and reinforce mechanisms to help support refuge-seeking populations.

COLLABORATION

Finally, in order to address such a complex issue as the war-climate nexus, social work must facilitate collaboration at multiple levels. Fortunately, social work is a profession that comfortably manoeuvres among multiple systems and disciplines. While technical solutions (e.g., reducing environmental degradation at sites of displacement, creating drought-resistant crops, and facilitating conflict resolution between refugee and host communities) to address the war-climate nexus are critical, social solutions are equally important, but often overlooked (Mason, as cited in Jackson, 2017). Accordingly, an interdisciplinary lens is important, as social workers should work alongside colleagues from other disciplines in the social and natural sciences, as well as practice communities around the globe, to prevent and address the impact of climate change, environmental degradation, and war (Powers et al., 2018). One such opportunity is the United Nations' movement to prevent the exploitation of the environment in war and armed conflict, which offers an opportunity for social workers to engage in multidisciplinary partnerships with others committed to expanding the UN's sustainable development goals. Thus, social work educators must encourage multidisciplinary thinking among colleagues and students by shifting social work from a siloized profession towards a networking profession that remains open to new and innovative solutions (Frost, 2017).

Conclusion

As the current volume exhibits, social work education has begun to recognize that climate change and environmental degradation greatly affect individuals, families, and communities. Yet there is less recognition regarding the intersections between environmental issues and war, which results in deleterious impacts upon some of the world's most vulnerable populations.

Fortunately, the profession of social work is well suited to address the complexity of the war-climate nexus. Social workers meet people "where they are at," in order to better understand the adversities they face and the strengths available to address such challenges. Social workers understand and see value in the person-in-environment framework, which is a significant lens by which to examine the human relationship with the natural and built environment. Social workers emphasize the voices of those most affected by adversity. Social workers are agents of change. Social workers understand the importance of human relationships and collaboration in addressing some of the biggest issues facing our planet today.

There is a need for social work leadership and education at all of these levels: theory, practice, and policy. Social work educators have a responsibility to train the future generation of social workers to take up the challenge and address the war-climate nexus, thereby joining a global community of leaders committed to addressing and ameliorating this pressing global crisis.

REFERENCES

Ahmed, K. (2019, April 18). Rohingya camps run out of time as Bangladesh storm season arrives. *The New Humanitarian.* https://www.thenewhumanitarian.org/news/2018/04/18/rohingya-camps-run-out-time-bangladesh-storm-season-arrives

Ahmed, M. S., Haque, M. A., Islam, H., & Motaleb, M. A. (2017). *Atlas: Elephant routes and corridors in Bangladesh.* IUCN. https://portals.iucn.org/library/sites/library/files/documents/2016-072.pdf

Akesson, B. (2012, May). *Using graphic narratives in the international social work classroom.* Canadian Association of Social Work Education.

Akesson, B. (2014). Castle and cage: Meanings of home for Palestinian children and families. *Global Social Welfare, 1*(2), 81–95. https://doi.org/10.1007/s40609-014-0004-y

Akesson, B. (2015). School as a place of violence and hope: Tensions of education in post-intifada Palestine. *International Journal of Educational Development, 41*, 192–199. https://doi.org/10.1016/j.ijedudev.2014.08.001

Akesson, B. (2017). Refugee youth affected by war and displacement: A socio-ecological approach. In S. Wilson-Forsberg & A. Robinson (Eds.), *Immigrant youth in Canada* (pp. 361–377). Oxford University Press.

Akesson, B., Burns, V., & Hordyk, S.-R. (2017). The place of place in social work: Rethinking the person-in-environment model in social work education and practice. *Journal of Social Work Education, 53*(3), 372–383. https://doi.org/10.1080/10437797.2016.1272512

Ali, I., Azman, A., & Hatta, Z. A. (2013). Transforming the local capacity on natural disaster risk reduction in Bangladeshi communities: A social work perspective. *Asian Social Work and Policy Review, 8,* 1–9. https://doi.org/10.1111/aswp.12023

American Psychological Association. (2017). *Clinical practice guidelines for the treatment of posttraumatic stress disorder (PTSD) in adults.*

Amnesty International. (2018). *"We will destroy everything": Military responsibility for crimes against humanity in Rakhine State* (ASA 16/8630/2018).

Bartley, A., & Beddoe, L. (Eds.). (2018). *Transnational social work: Opportunities and challenges of a global profession.* Policy Press.

Bartley, A., & Fronek, P. H. (n.d.). *Migrant social workers crossing borders: In conversation with Allen Bartley* (No. 61) [Podcast]. http://www.podsocs.com/podcast/migrant-social-workers-crossing-borders/

Beaubien, J. (2018, August 25). Forced to flee Myanmar, Rohingya refugees face monsoon landslides in Bangladesh [Radio broadcast]. National Public Radio. https://www.npr.org/2018/08/25/641568806/forced-to-flee-myanmar-rohingya-refugees-face-monsoon-landslides-in-bangladesh

Beddoe, L., Fouché, C., Bartley, A., & Harington, P. (2011). Migrant social workers' experience in New Zealand: Education and supervision issues. *Social Work Education, 31*(8), 1012–1031. https://doi.org/10.1080/02615479.2011.633600

Belcher, O., Bigger, P., Neimark, B., & Kennelly, C. (2020). Hidden carbon costs of the "everywhere war": Logistics, geopolitical energy, and the carbon boot-print of the US military. *Transactions of the Institute of British Geographers, 45*(1), 65–80. https://doi.org/10.1111/tran.12319

Beldowski, J., Brenner, M., & Lehtonen, K. (2020). Contaminated by war: A brief history of sea-dumping of munitions. *Marine Environmental Research, 162,* 105189. https://doi.org/10.1016/j.marenvres.2020.105189. Medline:33126113

Bell, P. (2001). The ethics of conducting psychiatric research in war-torn contexts. In M. Smyth & G. Robinson (Eds.), *Researching violently divided societies: Ethical and methodological issues* (pp. 184–192). UN University Press/Pluto.

Benton, N., Ripley, J. D., & Powledge, F. (Eds.). (2008). *Conserving biodiversity on military lands: A guide for natural resource managers.* NatureServe. http://www.dodbiodiversity.org

Beste, A. (2015). *Education provision for Syrian refugees in Jordan, Lebanon and Turkey: Preventing a "lost generation"* (UNU-GCM Policy Reports). UNU-GCM. https://collections.unu.edu/view/UNU:5524

Besthorn, F. (2011). Deep ecology's contributions to social work: A ten-year retrospective. *International Journal of Social Welfare, 21*(3), 248–259. https://doi.org/10.1111/j.1468-2397.2011.00850.x

Besthorn, F., & Canda, E. R. (2002). Revisioning environment: Deep ecology for education and teaching in social work. *Journal of Teaching in Social Work*, 22(1–2), 79–101. https://doi.org/10.1300/J067v22n01_07

Besthorn, F., & McMillen, D. P. (2002). The oppression of women and nature: Ecofeminism as a framework for an expanded ecological social work. *Families in Society: The Journal of Contemporary Social Services*, 83(3), 221–232. https://doi.org/10.1606/1044-3894.20

Billiot, S., Beltrán, R., Brown, D., Mitchell, F. M., & Fernandez, A. (2019). Indigenous perspectives for strengthening social responses to global environmental changes: A response to the social work grand challenge on environmental change. *Journal of Community Practice*, 27(3–4), 296–316. https://doi.org/10.1080/10705422.2019.1658677. Medline:33013154

Bisimwa, L. (2021, February 18). *Mali's invisible front line: Climate change in a conflict zone*. International Committee for the Red Cross. https://www.icrc.org/en/document/mali-invisible-front-line-climate-change-conflict-zone

Boehm, D. A., Hess, J. M., Coe, C., Rae-Espinoza, H., & Reynolds, R. R. (2011). Children, youth, and the everyday ruptures of migration. In C. Coe, R. R. Reynolds, D. A. Boehm, J. M. Hess, & H. Rae-Espinoza (Eds.), *Everyday ruptures: Children, youth and migration in global perspective*. Vanderbilt University Press.

Boothby, N., Strang, A., & Wessells, M. (2006). Introduction. In N. Boothby, A. Strang, & M. Wessells (Eds.), *A world turned upside down: Social ecological approaches to children in war zones* (pp. 1–18). Kumarian.

Borràs-Pentinat, S. (2021). Environmental refugees: Reshaping the borders of migration in the EU. In M. C. Eritja (Ed.), *The European Union and global environmental protection: Transforming influence into action* (pp. 109–131). Routledge.

Brito, J. C., Durant, S. M., Pettorelli, N., Newby, J., Canney, S., Algadafi, W., Rabeil, T., Crochet, P.-A., Pleguezuelos, J. M., Wacher, T., Smet, K. de, Gonçalves, D. V., Silva, M. J. F. da, Martínez-Freiría, F., Abáigar, T., Campos, J. C., Comizzoli, P., Fahd, S., Fellous, A., & Carvalho, S. B. (2018). Armed conflicts and wildlife decline: Challenges and recommendations for effective conservation policy in the Sahara-Sahel. *Conservation Letters*, 11(5), e12446. https://doi.org/10.1111/conl.12446

Bunn, M., & Samuels, G., & Higson-Smith, C. (2023). Ambiguous loss of home: Syrian refugees and the process of losing and remaking home. *Wellbeing, Space and Society*, 4. https://doi.org/10.1016/j.wss.2023.100136

Chen, C., Noble, I., Hellmann, J., Coffee, J., Murillo, M., & Chawla, N. (2015). *University of Notre Dame global adaptation (ND-Gain) index: Country index technical report*. University of Notre Dame. https://gain.nd.edu/our-work/country-index/

Coates, J. (2003). *Ecology and social work: Towards a new paradigm*. Fernwood.

Coates, J., & Gray, M. (2012). The environment and social work: An overview and introduction. *International Journal of Social Welfare, 21*(3), 230–238. https://doi.org/10.1111/j.1468-2397.2011.00851.x

Cons, J. (2018). Staging climate security: Resilience and heterodystopia in the Bangladesh borderlands. *Cultural Anthropology, 33*(2), 266–294. https://doi.org/10.14506/ca33.2.08

Council on Social Work Education. (2015). *Educational policy and accreditation standards for baccalaureate and master's social work programs.* https://www.cswe.org/getmedia/23a35a39-78c7-453f-b805-b67f1dca2ee5/2015-epas-and-glossary.pdf

Crimeen, A., Bernstein, M., Zapart, S., & Haigh, F. (2017). *Place-based interventions: A realist informed literature review.* Centre for Health Equity Training, South Western Sydney Local Health District/UNSW Australia.

Cronin, A. A., Shrestha, D., Cornier, N., Abdalla, F., Ezard, N., & Aramburu, C. (2008). A review of water and sanitation provision in refugee camps in association with selected health and nutrition indicators – The need for integrated service provision. *Journal of Water and Health, 6*(1), 1–13. https://doi.org/10.2166/wh.2007.019. Medline:17998603

Cronin, M., & Jones, D. N. (2015). Social work and disasters. In J. D. Wright (Ed.), *International encyclopedia of the social and behavioral sciences* (2nd ed., pp. 753–760). Elsevier.

Danso, R. (2015). Migration studies: Resuscitating the casualty of the professionalisation of social work. *British Journal of Social Work, 46*(6), bcv111. https://doi.org/10.1093/bjsw/bcv111

Daskin, J. H., & Pringle, R. M. (2018). Warfare and wildlife declines in Africa's protected areas. *Nature, 553*(7688). https://doi.org/10.1038/nature25194

Davies, L. (2004). *Education and conflict: Complexity and chaos.* Routledge Falmer.

Devictor, X. (2019, December 9). *2019 update: How long do refugees stay in exile? To find out, beware of averages.* World Bank Blogs. https://blogs.worldbank.org/dev4peace/2019-update-how-long-do-refugees-stay-exile-find-out-beware-averages

Dominelli, L. (2012). *Green social work: From environmental crises to environmental justice.* Polity.

Dominelli, L., & Hackett, S. (2012). Social work responses to the challenges for practice in the 21st century. *International Social Work, 55*(4), 449–453. https://doi.org/10.1177/0020872812440784

Douglas, C. (2016). *A storm without rain: Yemen, water, climate change, and conflict* (No. 40). Center for Climate and Security.

Drumbl, M. A. (2009). *Accountability for property crimes and environmental war crimes: Prosecution, litigation, and development.* International Center for Transitional Justice.

Ellis, H. B., & Abdi, S. (2017). Building community resilience to violent extremism through genuine partnerships. *American Psychologist, 72*(3), 289–300. https://doi.org/10.1037/amp0000065. Medline:28383981

Friedrich, J., Ge, M., & Pickens, A. (2020). *This interactive chart shows changes in the world's top 10 emitters.* World Resources Institute. https://www.wri.org/insights/interactive-chart-shows-changes-worlds-top-10-emitters

Frost, N. (2017). From "silo" to "network" profession: A multi-professional future for social work. *Journal of Children's Services, 12*(2), 174–183. https://doi.org/10.1108/jcs-05-2017-0019

Gaillard, J. C., Sanz, K., Balgos, B. C., Dalisay, S. N. M., Gorman-Murray, A., Smith, F., & Toelupe, V. (2017). Beyond men and women: A critical perspective on gender and disaster. *Disasters, 41*(3), 429–447. https://doi.org/10.1111/disa.12209. Medline:27654026

Gamble, D. N., & Weil, M. (2010). *Community practice skills: Local to global.* Columbia University Press.

Garrity, A. (2014). *Conflict rubble: A ubiquitous and under-studied toxic remnant of war.* Conflict and Environment Observatory. https://ceobs.org/conflict-rubble-a-ubiquitous-and-under-studied-toxic-remnant-of-war/

Gharahaghi, K., & Anderson-Nathe, B. (2014). No place for a child: The refugee camp experience. *Child & Youth Services, 35*, 1–3. https://doi.org/10.1080/0145935X.2014.893737

Gillies, J. A., Etyemezian, V., Kuhns, H., Moosmüller, H., Engelbrecht, J., King, J., Uppapalli, S., Nikolich, G., McAlpine, J. D., Zhu, D., Skiba, M., Gilette, D. A., Shaw, W., & Hashmonay, R. (2010). *Final report: Particulate matter emissions factors for dust from unique military activities* (SERDP Project SI-1399). Strategic Environmental Research and Development Program.

Glenny, M. (2015, September 21). The refugee crisis has produced one winner: Organized crime. *New York Times.* https://www.nytimes.com/2015/09/21/opinion/the-refugee-crisis-has-produced-one-winner-organized-crime.html

Global Migration Data Analysis Centre. (2021, March 30). *Forced migration or displacement.* Migration Data Portal. https://migrationdataportal.org/themes/forced-migration-or-displacement

Gonzalez, A. (2020, April 15). *How tree growing can mitigate the environmental impact of displacement.* Forests News. https://forestsnews.cifor.org/65093/how-tree-growing-can-mitigate-the-environmental-impact-of-displacement?fnl=

Gwozdziewycz, N., & Mehl-Madrona, L. (2013). Meta-analysis of the use of narrative exposure therapy for the effects of trauma among refugee populations. *Permanente Journal, 17*(1), 70–76. https://doi.org/10.7812/TPP/12-058. Medline:23596375

Ham, C., & Alderwick, H. (2015). *Place-based systems of care: A way forward for the NHS in England.* The King's Fund.

Hamani, S. (2019). *Protecting the environment in humanitarian responses to population displacement*. United Nations Environmental Programme. https://www.unep.org/news-and-stories/story/protecting-environment-humanitarian-responses-population-displacement

Hassan, M. M., Smith, A. C., Walker, K., Rahman, M. K., & Southworth, J. (2018). Rohingya refugee crisis and forest cover change in Teknaf, Bangladesh. *Remote Sensing, 10*(5), 689. https://doi.org/10.3390/rs10050689

Hijazi, A., Lumley, M., Ziadni, M., Haddad, L., Rapport, L., & Arnetz, B. (2014). Brief narrative exposure therapy for posttraumatic stress in Iraqi refugees: A preliminary randomized clinical trial. *Journal of Traumatic Stress, 27*(3), 314–322. https://doi.org/10.1002/jts.21922. Medline:24866253

Human Rights Watch. (2018, August 5). *"Bangladesh is not my country": The plight of Rohingya refugees from Myanmar*. https://www.hrw.org/report/2018/08/05/bangladesh-not-my-country/plight-rohingya-refugees-myanmar

Internal Displacement Monitoring Centre. (2020). *2020 Global report on internal displacement*. https://www.internal-displacement.org/publications/2020-global-report-on-internal-displacement

International Committee of the Red Cross. (2020). *When rain turns to dust: Understanding and responding to the combined impact of armed conflicts and the climate and environment crisis on people's lives* (No. 4487/002). ICRC's Division of Policy and Humanitarian Diplomacy.

International Crisis Group. (2021). *Climate change and conflict*. https://www.crisisgroup.org/future-conflict/climate

International Federation of Social Workers, International Association of Schools of Social Work, & International Council on Social Welfare. (2012). *The global agenda for social work and social development commitment to action*. https://www.ifsw.org/wp-content/uploads/ifsw-cdn/assets/globalagenda2012.pdf

International Organization for Migration. (2018, July 13–19). *Rohingya humanitarian crisis response – External update*. https://www.iom.int/sites/g/files/tmzbdl486/files/situation_reports/file/bangladesh_sr_20180713-19.pdf

Jackson, K. (2017). Climate change and public health: How social workers can advocate for environmental justice. *Social Work Today, 17*(6), 10.

Kellert, S. R., & Wilson, E. O. (1995). *The biophilia hypothesis*. Shearwater/Island Press.

Klemmer, C. L., & McNamara, K. A. (2020). Deep ecology and ecofeminism: Social work to address global environmental crisis. *Affilia, 35*(4), 503–515. https://doi.org/10.1177/0886109919894650

Leebaw, B. (2014). Scorched earth: Environmental war crimes and international justice. *Perspectives on Politics, 12*(4), 770–788.

Lehne, J., Blyth, W., Lahn, G., Bazilian, M., & Grafham, O. (2016). Energy services for refugees and displaced people. *Energy Strategy Reviews, 13–14*, 134–146. https://doi.org/10.1016/j.esr.2016.08.008

Lenette, C., Cox, L., & Brough, M. (2015). Digital storytelling as a social work tool: Learning from ethnographic research with women from refugee backgrounds. *British Journal of Social Work, 45*(3), 988–1005. https://doi.org/10.1093/bjsw/bct184

Loy, I. (2018, February 5). Mapped: How monsoon rains could submerge Rohingya refugee camps. *The New Humanitarian*. https://www.thenewhumanitarian.org/maps-and-graphics/2018/02/05/mapped-how-monsoon-rains-could-submerge-rohingya-refugee-camps

MacLean, K. (2019). The Rohingya crisis and the practices of erasure. *Journal of Genocide Research, 21*(1), 83–95. https://doi.org/10.1080/14623528.2018.1506628

Malley, R. (2020, December 30). *10 conflicts to watch in 2021*. International Crisis Group. https://www.crisisgroup.org/global/10-conflicts-watch-2021

Marshall, D. J., Smaira, D., & Staeheli, L. A. (2022). Intergenerational place-based digital storytelling: A more-than-visual research method. *Children's Geographies, 20*(1), 109–121. https://doi.org/10.1080/14733285.2021.1916436

Masson-Delmotte, V., Zhai, P., Pörtner, H.-O., Roberts, D., Skea, J., Shukla, P. R., Pirani, A., Moufouma-Okia, W., Péan, C., Pidcock, R., Connors, S., Matthews, J. B. R., Chen, Y., Zhou, X., Gomis, M. I., Lonnoy, E., Maycock, T., Tignor, M., & Waterfield, T. (2018). *Global warming of 1.5°C: An IPCC special report on the impacts of global warming of 1.5°C above pre-industrial levels and related global greenhouse gas emission pathways*. IPCC.

McDonnell, T. (2019, January 24). Climate change creates a new migration crisis for Bangladesh. *National Geographic*. https://www.nationalgeographic.com/environment/article/climate-change-drives-migration-crisis-in-bangladesh-from-dhaka-sundabans

McKinnon, J., & Alston, M. (Eds.). (2016). *Ecological social work: Towards sustainability*. Palgrave.

McVeigh, K., & Peri, D. (2018, May 9). Fatal elephant attacks on Rohingya refugees push Bangladesh to act. *The Guardian*. https://www.theguardian.com/global-development/2018/may/09/fatal-elephant-attacks-on-rohingya-refugees-push-bangladesh-to-act

Meyer, R., Yu, G., Rieders, E., & Stark, L. (2020). Child labor, sex and mental health outcomes amongst adolescent refugees. *Journal of Adolescence, 81*, 52–60. https://doi.org/10.1016/j.adolescence.2020.04.002. Medline:32361065

Moore, T. (2017). Strengths-based narrative storytelling as therapeutic intervention for refugees in Greece. *World Federation of Occupational Therapists Bulletin, 73*(1), 45–51. https://doi.org/10.1080/14473828.2017.1298557

Mukul, S. A., Huq, S., Herbohn, J., Nishat, A., Rahman, A. A., Amin, R., & Ahmed, F. U. (2019, April 12). Rohingya refugees and the environment. *Science, 364*(6436), 138. https://doi.org/10.1126/science.aaw9474

Muldoon, A. (2006). Environmental efforts: The next challenge for social work. *Critical Social Work, 7*(2). https://doi.org/10.22329/csw.v7i2.5729

ND-GAIN. (2021). *Country index.* https://gain.nd.edu/our-work/country-index/

Nutrition Sector. (2018). *Emergency nutrition assessment: Preliminary results (April 28–May 28, 2018).*

Powers, M. C. F., Schmitz, C. L., Nsonwu, C. Z., & Mathew, M. T. (2018). Environmental migration: Social work at the nexus of climate change and global migration. *Advances in Social Work, 18*(3), 1023–1040. https://doi.org/10.18060/21678

Rahman, M. H. (2019). Rohingya refugee crisis and human vs. elephant (Elephas maximus) conflicts in Cox's Bazar district of Bangladesh. *Journal of Wildlife and Biodiversity, 3*(3), 10–21. https://doi.org/10.22120/jwb.2019.104762.1057

Riley, A., Varner, A., Ventevogel, P., Taimur Hasan, M. M., & Welton-Mitchell, C. (2017). Daily stressors, trauma exposure, and mental health among stateless Rohingya refugees in Bangladesh. *Transcultural Psychiatry, 54*(3), 304–331. https://doi.org/10.1177/1363461517705571. Medline:28540768

Ryan, J. M., Buma, A. P. C. C., & Beadling, C. W. (2014). *Conflict and catastrophe medicine: A practical guide.* Springer.

Scharpf, F., Kaltenbach, E., Nickerson, A., & Hecker, T. (2021). A systematic review of socio-ecological factors contributing to risk and protection of the mental health of refugee children and adolescents. *Clinical Psychology Review, 83*, 101930. https://doi.org/10.1016/j.cpr.2020.101930. Medline:33186775

Sousa, C., Akesson, B., & Badawi, D. (2020). "Most importantly, I hope God keeps illness away from us": The context and challenges surrounding health for Syrian refugees in Lebanon. *Global Public Health, 15*(11), 1617–1626.

Sphere Project. (2018). *The Sphere handbook: Humanitarian charter and minimum standards in humanitarian response.* https://handbook.spherestandards.org/en/sphere/#ch001

Szczpanski, M., Sedlar, F., & Shalant, J. (2018, September 13). *Bangladesh: A country underwater, a culture on the move.* NRDC. https://www.nrdc.org/onearth/bangladesh-country-underwater-culture-move

Taylor, M. (2017, November 2). Climate change will create world's biggest refugee crisis. *The Guardian.*

The Rohingya. (2019, March 25). *The New Humanitarian.* https://www.thenewhumanitarian.org/in-depth/myanmar-rohingya-refugee-crisis-humanitarian-aid-bangladesh

United Nations. (1951). *The 1951 refugee convention.* United Nations High Commissioner for Refugees. http://www.unhcr.org/1951-refugee-convention.html

United Nations High Commissioner for Refugees. (2020). *Figures at a glance.* https://www.unhcr.org/figures-at-a-glance.html

Vitus, K. (2010). Waiting time: The de-subjectification of children in Danish asylum centres. *Childhood, 17*(1), 26–42. https://doi.org/10.1177/0907568209351549

Waitz, I. A., Lukachko, S. P., & Lee, J. J. (2005). Military aviation and the environment: Historical trends and comparison to civil aviation. *Journal of Aircraft, 42*(2), 329–339. https://doi.org/10.2514/1.6888

Weir, D. (2019). *How Yemen's conflict destroyed its waste management system.* Conflict and Environment Observatory.

Weir, D. (2020). *How does war damage the environment?* Conflict and Environment Observatory.

Who are the Rohingya? (2018, April 18). *Al Jazeera.* https://www.aljazeera.com/indepth/features/2017/08/rohingya-muslims-170831065142812.html

Wilson, E. O. (1984). *Biophilia.* Harvard University Press.

World Bank. (2020). *Population density (people per sq. km of land area) – Bangladesh.* https://data.worldbank.org/indicator/EN.POP.DNST?locations=BD

Yaman, M. (2020). Child marriage: A survival strategy for Syrian refugee families in Turkey? In L. Williams, E. Coşkun, & S. Kaşka (Eds.), *Women, migration and asylum in Turkey: Developing gender-sensitivity in migration research, policy and practice* (pp. 213–233). Springer International. https://doi.org/10.1007/978-3-030-28887-7_10

Zapf, M. K. (2009). *Social work and the environment: Understanding people and place.* Canadian Scholars.

8 Finding a Place for Animals in Green Social Work Education and Practice

JASMINE TIFFANY FERREIRA, ATSUKO MATSUOKA,
AND JOHN SORENSON

Human relationships with other animals are constantly changing. Companion animals (pets) are increasingly valued as family members in homes across Canada. At the same time, meat consumption is rising rapidly (Whitnall & Pitts, 2019), mass farming of animals for human consumption has been identified as a leading contributor to climate change (Lazarus, McDermid, & Jacquet, 2021), and animal species are being driven into extinction. While these conflicting realities for non-human animals are rarely considered in the context of social work practice, they are shaped by foundational philosophies about hierarchies of life, such as the great chain of being, a persisting Western belief from the classical period of a universal ranked order of beings (see Lovejoy, 1964). These ideas are deeply rooted in our thinking and are embedded in larger systems of violence that contribute to environmental destruction. By examining how non-human animals are defined, erased, and neglected within green social work literature, green social work education and practice can challenge structural inequality, promote social justice, and actively contribute to decolonization. In this chapter, we highlight the importance of challenging anthropocentric assumptions that, left unquestioned, sustain the oppressive systems that should be dismantled in pursuit of justice. Taking a Critical Animal Studies approach (Nocella et al., 2014), we demonstrate how green social work can better contribute to eliminating structural violence that perpetuates injustice and oppression for all.

Green Social Work

Green social work has gained popularity in recent years and is rooted in anti-oppressive practice principles (Ramsay & Boddy, 2017) and environmental justice frameworks (Dominelli, 2013). Much of the practice research in this area is global in scope, concentrating on disaster relief, migration, and equitable distribution of resources (Dominelli & Ku, 2017). Through these areas of focus, green social work has provided important critiques on global and systemic impacts of climate change and how social workers can address these impacts through community mobilizing, education, interprofessional and collaborative advocacy work, and participating in policy. Dominelli (2012) writes:

> Green social work adopts a political stance in that it recognizes that power relations shape human interactions and these are rooted in an ethics of care whereby people care for one another and the environment in sustainable ways to ensure that all living things will survive now and for generations to come. (p. 437)

Generally focused on macro and policy-based interventions, studies have highlighted innovative community-led approaches such as targeting reduction of carbon emissions as alternatives to bureaucratic change (Bay, 2013). Critiques of these macro policies and community methods, however, condemned slowness and inconsistent outcomes and argued that often they are not meaningful to all persons involved (Appleby et al., 2017).

Green social work research has made significant contributions to understanding how capitalist systems impact society in complex and diversely oppressive ways (Perkins, 2019). Hawkins (2010) highlights that "in the current climate of global capitalism, concern for human safety and environmental protection are consistently subjugated to economic growth and maintenance of inefficient patterns of production and consumption" (p.76). Importantly, these Euro-Western modernist ideals, including capitalism (Philip & Reisch, 2015), neo-liberalism (Coates & Gray, 2012), globalization (Norton, 2012), and consumerism do not promote or value the well-being of the environment or humans (Muldoon, 2006). The socio-economic values that modernity espouses include limitless consumerism and progress that can only end with total exhaustion of the world's resources (Besthorn, 2014). Connecting modernity to postmodernist theory, Muldoon (2006) highlights the contradiction between consumption and production that ultimately results in the destruction of what is needed for our own survival. Some of the strongest critiques of anthropocentrism in Euro-Western social work highlight the domination of modernist philosophies that underpin the social work profession (Besthorn, 2002; Besthorn, 2012; Ryan, 2011), namely, that goals of supporting individuals in increasing production or contributing to neo-liberal ideas of success may always be in opposition to achieving sustainability or non-exploitative relationships with the non-human world (Boetto, 2019). An additional concern with the dualistic worldview of modernity is the limitations of binaries that are hierarchal and prioritize unending growth while subjugating environmental ethics of care, and even human rights (Philip & Reisch, 2015). New alternatives that challenge capitalist systems are needed (Noble, 2016).

Critical Animal Studies

The interdisciplinary field of Critical Animal Studies (CAS) offers important criticisms of social work's anthropocentric speciesist foundations, from which green social work can learn. A key concept for CAS is anthropocentrism: the material and discursive construction of a sharp ontological and ethical division between humans and other forms of life, a conviction that humans are exceptional and distinct from all other beings, possessing morally relevant qualities absent in other living organisms. Anthropocentrism places humans above other beings but also is associated with construction of hierarchies among humans, classifying some groups, for instance women and racialized peoples, as closer to non-human animals. Although often overlooked, anthropocentrism is the basis of enslavement, killing, displacement, and extinction of other species (Kim, 2015) and is institutionalized in the animal industrial complex (Noske, 1986), an essential structural component of globalized capitalism. While anthropocentrism regards the natural world as a repository of resources for humans and regards non-human animals as instruments for human ends, CAS acknowledges them as sentient beings with intrinsic value and whose interests should be recognized. For utilitarian philosophers such as Singer (1975), the sentience of other beings necessitates at least the moral requirement to minimize human-imposed suffering. CAS takes it further. For CAS, sentience is the basis for recognizing the personhood of non-human beings and treating them with compassion, respect, and justice.

Importantly, CAS rejects the anthropocentric assumption of human exceptionalism that a single species has higher moral value than all others and instead promotes the idea of trans-species social justice (Matsuoka & Sorenson, 2014, 2021; Matsuoka et al., 2020). Rather than adopting a view of justice limited to distributing goods equitably among humans, trans-species social justice recognizes individuals of other species as subjects of moral consideration and deserving justice. CAS helps green social work to reconceptualize animals by incorporating their rights to an environment conducive to their flourishing. As Nussbaum (2006) maintains, it is unjust if non-human animals are not allowed to flourish in their own way and to live with dignity, which entails realization of their capabilities in terms of freedom of movement, social relations, stimulation, access to suitable habitat, and the opportunity to experience the full complexity of their own lives. Within a trans-species social justice framework, justice can be achieved by realizing institutional conditions free from domination and oppression. Methodologically, this calls for examination of power relations, specifically domination and oppression (Matsuoka & Sorenson, 2014; Nocella et al., 2014).

Another key concept in CAS is speciesism, a term coined by Richard Ryder (1970) to denote prejudice against other species. By introducing the concept, CAS can uncover taken-for-granted anthropocentrism in social work. This gives deeper understanding of the intersectionality of oppression and that continued exploitation, subjugation, and violence towards other animals by humans is interconnected with all forms of oppression, including violence towards humans (Adams, 2000; Fitzgerald, Barrett, et al., 2009; Fitzgerald, Kalof, & Dietz, 2009; Matsuoka & Sorenson, 2013, 2014, 2018; Sanbonmatsu, 2011; Sorenson & Matsuoka, 2019). Inclusion of the concept of speciesism offers greater insight for ecological justice and helps social workers to incorporate animals in education and practice.

Moreover, speciesism is an ideology that is rarely visible and understood. It distorts our perception of ethical problems and requires an innovative concept such as "truncated narratives" (Kheel, 1993, p. 255) to unveil it. Kheel explains that "wrenching an ethical problem out of its embedded context severs the problem from its roots" (p. 255). Truncated narratives "present the problem in an incomplete or distorted form" and thus "we need to find out what is severed" (Koleszar-Green & Matsuoka, 2018, p. 345). This concept helps contextualize problems, particularly ethical problems, that green social workers often face.

Animals in Green Social Work

Rethinking our relationships to the natural environment and non-human inhabitants is essential to find lasting solutions to many of our moral, social, and environmental issues (Irvine, 2007). Much of how animals have, or have not, been considered in green social work is informed by existing social constructions of nature that tend to define things in relation to human needs (White, 2003) and consumption. Even critical approaches demonstrate this anthropocentric hierarchy. For example, green social work literature has examined everyday and long-term impacts of climate change and environmental disasters, referred to as "slow violence" (p. 134) or "micro disasters" (p. 139), and considered how rising temperatures result in less visible seasonal shifts that change the livability of lands through drought or flooding and impact vulnerable populations in different ways (Willett, 2019). These terms have generally been applied to habitability for humans but should be extended to other living beings that often experience the impact of slow violence before humans do. This reframing helps highlight the reality of some of climate change's less recognized impacts. Hidden and less observable changes require awareness and understanding for the benefit of all living beings.

Critiques of green and environmental social work for being anthropocentric (Faver, 2013) are not new and have been a focus of eco-social work in recent decades. Some green social work scholars recognize anthropocentrism as a limitation and acknowledge that "nature and other beings" have intrinsic value requiring moral consideration (Erickson, 2018, p. 68), yet, they have stopped short of considering how social work should support the rights of non-human animals. Moreover, when justice is considered in relation to nature in green social work, it is usually in terms of environmental justice, the idea that various human groups should not be exposed to differential environmental harms and that they should have equal access to natural "resources."

Largely absent is the idea that nature and, in particular, non-human animals are themselves owed justice. In contrast, the eco-centric perspective of Critical Animal Studies emphasizes that non-human animals have intrinsic moral value, not simply instrumental value. Therefore, in responding to existing critiques of green social work as being anthropocentric, we can begin examining how animals are conceptualized within environmental advocacy and the pursuit of ecological justice in social work education and practice by applying a CAS perspective. Below, we select three areas to examine animals in green social work: animals as "wild," as domestic, and as food.

Animals as "Wild"

Perhaps not surprisingly, throughout environmental studies and green social work literature, conceptualizations of animals are most often absorbed into the idea of nature as "wilderness." However, the origin of this term "wilderness" is an English word meaning "the place of wild beasts" (Akhurst, 2010, p. 296), intended to describe places without human presence or activity. This idea, combined with anthropocentric perspectives that view humans as separate from and superior to nature, initially served as justification for colonialism. Equating wilderness with emptiness or a lack of "civilization" represented land, animals, and Indigenous humans as free-for-the-taking resources to claim. This ideology ensured the success of modern, capitalist, imperial, and colonial projects. These in turn contributed to a particular version of nature, a concept of "wild" animals separate from "civilized" humans, creating a category of "others" that can be owned, consumed, or protected depending on colonial human needs or desires. This politically, economically, and socially constructed perspective of the non-human world as wild continues to undergird oppressive, hierarchical human relationships and beliefs about what types of nature warrant benevolent protection (Forkey, 2000), perpetuating anthropocentrism as the norm and ideal.

Taken-for-granted anthropocentrism neglects the fact that non-human animals, along with plants, constitute biodiversity, the diversity of life that maintains the functioning of planetary systems essential for the survival of all. Since Rachel Carson's ground-breaking work *Silent Spring* (1962), we are more aware that our livelihoods and well-being depend on nature; rather than being separate from nature and other animals, humans are dependent upon them. Other forms of life, even the smallest and seemingly most insignificant, interact with the physical environment to create the foundations of human existence, such as a breathable atmosphere and a habitable climate. Despite biodiversity's central role, human activities are destroying it at unprecedented rates. The WWF's (2020) *Living Planet Report* described our "broken" relationship with nature (p. 4), noting that the number of non-human animals inhabiting the planet had more than halved since 1970 and that population sizes of amphibians, birds, fish, mammals, and reptiles had declined 68 per cent (p. 16). Dirzo et al. (2014) warned that "systematic defaunation clearly threatens to fundamentally alter basic ecological functions and is contributing to push us toward global scale 'tipping points' from which we may not be able to return" (p. 405), while Ceballos et al. (2017, p. E6089) described the situation starkly as "biological annihilation." "Biological annihilation" is significant for social work as it threatens the very basis of our existence, livelihoods, and well-being. Thus, we believe that green social work can make a profound contribution through examinations of normative expectations, anthropocentrism, and interlocking structural inequality, including speciesism.

Animals as "Domestic"

While companion animals are generally absent from green social work literature, animal-assisted therapies (AAT) and other forms of animal-human relations have been increasingly written about and studied in social work (Heinsch, 2012). Current trends have focused on inclusion of therapy or companion animals in direct practice for therapeutic value (Gee & Mueller, 2019; Hughes et al., 2020; Risley-Curtiss, 2010), as they can promote human well-being and welfare. Typical frameworks supporting inclusion of companion animals in social work practice include attachment theories, one health, and post-humanism, which assume benign co-constitutive relationships, overlooking individual and structural levels of power imbalance stemming from unchecked speciesism and anthropocentrism. In addition, few articles critically consider the fact that utilizing animals, even with some consideration of their welfare, still constitutes objectification of living beings as resources for human benefit; very few AAT articles have connected with broader ideas of nature and ecology in social work (Gray & Coates, 2012), generally overlooking animals who live in their natural habitat and the fact that they do have agency. There appears to be a conceptual disconnect when it comes to animals in social work practice as being "domestic" and therefore not associated with ideas of wilderness and environment. Conveniently and uncritically compartmentalizing animals into wild and domestic (pets and farmed animals) obfuscates oppression such as violence, exploitation, and cultural imperialism towards non-human animals (Sorenson & Matsuoka, 2019). Again, it is important to utilize the concept of truncated dominant narratives to recognize what has been neglected and how these categorizations of companion animals are also socially constructed in relation to oppression and colonization. It helps us understand how anthropocentric and speciesist conceptualizations block us from realizing that non-human animals are not resources for humans to use, regardless of how we choose to categorize them.

Animals as "Food"

In discussing food production, green social work acknowledges negative impacts of agribusiness on human well-being, ranging from damaged ecological systems to health implications from fast food consumption (Dominelli, 2012). In addition, green social work literature has highlighted the devastating impacts of "natural" disasters on farming and food security (Kaiser et al., 2015). These issues are especially relevant as climate changes increase the frequency and severity of drought and extreme weather events globally. Importantly, green social work has highlighted that the harmful human impacts of these events are not experienced equitably. Many see sustainable agricultural practices that attend to poverty and food distribution as important issues for social work and communities around the world (Besthorn, 2013). However, animals are noticeably "disappeared" from these conversations on both food and farming, absorbed into "agriculture," as one of many nameless commodities. This erasure is problematic not only because it ignores the personhood of individual sentient beings but also because animal farming practices have been recognized as leading contributors to biodiversity loss, climate change, colonization, and structural inequality (Benton et al., 2021; Cohen 2017; Ficek 2019; Matsuoka & Sorenson 2014; Nibert 2013). Significantly, the effects of these practices negatively affect human and non-human animals alike.

Eating of animals is a topic that historically has been avoided by environmentalists and thus has not been at the forefront of environmental social work academia (Gordon, 2017). Thus, animals are notably missing from their narratives. In reality, our use and treatment of non-human animals as food is not a secondary issue, but of utmost concern. The main driver of biological annihilation, for example, is human activity, primarily changes in land use for animal agriculture and industrial fishing in the oceans. More recently, there has been a significant surge in wildlife farming and use of wild animals for food (Intergovernmental Science-Policy Platform on Biodiversity and Ecosystem Services, 2020). Essentially, demand for meat is destroying planetary life, not only because of greenhouse gas emissions from "livestock" but because of deforestation, habitat destruction, biodiversity loss, pollution of air, soil, and water, ocean acidification and eutrophication, and waste production (Ilea, 2009).

With the world still recovering from the COVID-19 pandemic, we should note that 60 per cent of known infectious diseases and 75 per cent of newly emerging diseases are zoonotic (i.e., transmitted from animals), with increasing danger of such diseases driven by increased meat demand, factory farming, greater exploitation of wildlife, habitat destruction, global transportation systems, and processing in wet markets and slaughterhouses (United Nations Environment Programme and International Livestock Research Institute, 2020). We can no longer afford to ignore that animal agriculture is directly responsible for massive deforestation, catastrophic biodiversity loss, pollution of air, soil and water, and many other destructive environmental impacts (Benton et al., 2021; Cohen 2017; Ficek 2019; Matsuoka & Sorenson 2014; Nibert 2013). In addition, animal agriculture, especially meat and dairy production, is a major source of greenhouse gas emissions and climate crisis. The current catastrophic biodiversity losses are now recognized as the sixth great extinction, which also entails the collapse of so-called ecosystem services, the ecological processes that enable human life (Ceballos et al., 2017, p. E6095).

The UN's Intergovernmental Science-Policy Platform on Biodiversity and Ecosystem Services warned in May 2019 of accelerating biodiversity extinctions, that essential ecosystems for human survival are deteriorating rapidly, and that "we are eroding the very foundations of our economies, livelihoods, food security, health and quality of life worldwide" (para. 2). In December 2020, UN secretary General António Guterres acknowledged that even the inadequate commitments made in the 2016 Paris Agreement to limit global temperature rise were far from being met and urged political leaders globally to declare a state of climate emergency (United Nations, 2020, para. 1). In January 2021, a report by seventeen leading international scientists based on over 150 studies stated that the crisis is worse than experts had thought, and that human activity was destroying the planet's biodiversity and the basis for civilization as well as the very "ability to support complex life" (Bradshaw et al., 2021, p. 1). The Intergovernmental Panel on Climate Change February 2022 report further listed drastic and immediate changes needed to keep from exceeding the 1.5-degree-Celsius threshold of climate change, indicating that we are not on track and headed towards irreversible and devastating impacts to communities and ecosystems globally.

The capacity for social work to address the impacts of climate change is closely linked with how we conceptualize social welfare. Social welfare in capitalist society functions to allocate resources to amend negative effects of market economies (Gilbert, 1985). Social workers working in various systems contribute by attempting to implement fair and equitable access to resources to meet human needs, such as fair access and distribution of food; however, goals such as food security cannot be fully realized through this conceptualization of social welfare without unlimited resources. This suggests that our concept of social welfare requires further analysis of capitalist systems, which are rooted in commodification and exploitation.

Focusing on instrumental use of animals as food, Matsuoka and Sorenson (2013) demonstrated that social welfare should be redefined to include other animals in its analysis. Examining use of animals as food – from production, transport, slaughter, processing, and consumption – they showed that every stage had serious adverse outcomes not only for non-human animals but for human's health and their environment. They revealed a truncated narrative: "concomitant with institutionalized animal exploitation is exploitation of workers, and oppression of women and indigenous peoples" (p. 23). They contend that "unless we include industrialized institutional animal exploitation into analysis of social welfare, we will not recognize the full costs, which are serious and growing" (p. 23). Oppression of other animals is intertwined with human oppression, and conceptualizations of social welfare must reflect this understanding, for social welfare should contribute to social justice. However, a socially just allocation of resources cannot be achieved without analysis of intertwined systemic oppression of other animals and humans, as this analysis of animals as food has explicated. In other words, if green social work addresses everyday injustice, justice should not be limited to the human species but beyond, that is, trans-species social justice.

Moreover, CAS scholar David Nibert (2013, p. 6) identifies animal domestication (which he calls "domesecration" to highlight the ethical transgression of enslaving other beings) as foundational to the development of global capitalism. Commodification of non-human animals under capitalism means institutionalized violence with intensified and concentrated production to ensure maximum profits. For example, in slaughterhouses the drive to process ever-greater numbers means that even minimal standards requiring animals to be stunned before they are killed are ignored, so that many are torn to pieces while fully conscious, and human workers suffer negative physical and psychological impacts (Boggs 2011; Eisnitz 2006). Recognition that production of non-human animals for food is not just a massive system of speciesist oppression but a key contributor to biodiversity and climate crises should inspire green social work to adopt an anti-speciesist approach and promote adoption of plant-based food systems as a vital means of addressing the most serious problems facing the world today.

Bringing CAS into Green Social Work Education and Practice

Education

Building on green social work's contribution, we propose shifting conceptualizations of justice from calls for equitable distribution of natural resources to justice that recognizes the intrinsic value of all individual living beings and the natural world. Accordingly, non-human animals and nature are not viewed as mere resources but as co-inhabitants on the planet. Thus, CAS promotes alternative understandings of non-human animals that avoid anthropocentrism and evaluation of other beings based solely on their utility to humans. For example, educators introducing topics such as disasters (Drolet et al., 2015) and food insecurity (Kaiser et al., 2015), as ways of "greening" social work education, might consider how a CAS approach can further help social workers critically examine our conceptualization of animals, including humans.

To do this, social work students might reflect on the following questions: Are non-human animals considered inferior or mere resources? If they are valued, on what basis and for whom? Do we acknowledge their intrinsic value? Do we recognize that other animals do not wish to be killed, eaten, or tortured? Furthermore, CAS encourages expanding our epistemological ground to include affect knowledge; if we do, social workers can quickly relate to statements like "We should not kill, eat, torture, and exploit animals because they do not want to be so treated, and we know that. If we listen, we can hear them" (Donovan, 1990, p. 375), and also realize that this is not sentimentality but foundational knowledge to be included in social work practice and education.

In addition, critical analysis of language is essential in order to make lasting and transformative changes to social work education. For example, when we consider food security, agribusiness, and meat production, we are discussing animals' lives, not "meat" – not "bacon" but pigs, not "veal" but calves. Accurate language is essential for critical analysis, and euphemisms such as these function to support truncated narratives that are convenient for maintaining exploitation and global capitalism today. Questioning such narratives, along with those concerning "wild" and "domesticated" animals, enables green social work education to interrogate anthropocentric assumptions in social work education and practice.

Finally, these insights could be brought into social work curricula as a way to reflect on our own and service users' ontology and epistemology: that is, what people consider reality and important facts is not limited to human relationships and knowledge alone. Such awareness and reflection are foundational to building non-anthropocentric social work practices.

Practice

Beginning to integrate green social work with a Critical Animal Studies approach in practice requires operationalizing the theoretical tenets discussed above. This chapter highlights how analyses of anti-anthropocentrism and anti-speciesism and an expanded analysis of the intersectionality of oppression with speciesism can be useful practice tools. In the case of violence against women (VAW), for example, for a quarter-century studies documented the importance of supporting both women and their companion animals, yet very few VAW shelters do so. A recent study found that professionals in VAW shelters who accommodated both women and their companion animals seemed to have adopted perspectives of anti-anthropocentrism, anti-speciesism, and the inter-sectionality of oppression within their practice framework. By doing so, they recognized women as actively exercising a feminist ethics of care/responsibility towards non-human family members, maintaining their mutually respectful reciprocal relationships, and countering abusers' coercive control and intersectional hierarchical relations with women and companion animals (Matsuoka & Sorenson, 2023).

In a different example, examining limited access to public housing for older adults with companion animals through a CAS lens revealed that practices and public housing policies unwittingly maintained domi-nant discourses of classism and speciesism (Matsuoka et al., 2020). As a result, some older adults delayed moving into public housing, choos-ing to live in less-than-desirable housing with their trans-species family member(s). Another case example investigated anti-immigrant policies and activism countering them, utilizing CAS to understand the inter-sectionality of racism and speciesism, which allowed the authors to assert the importance of anti-anthropocentrism and anti-speciesism to challenge such policies (Matsuoka & Sorenson, 2021). Just as Wroe et al. (2018) highlight the need for green social work to challenge our under-standing of social justice for humans across borders, CAS offers impor-tant additional considerations as environmental impacts increasingly displace both human and non-human animals. All of these examples demonstrate how a CAS lens allows for more complex understanding of green social work applications and how social workers can engage in anti-speciesist practice.

Social workers are increasingly incorporating nature into clinical practice (Heinsch, 2012; Ramsay & Boddy, 2017), which further dem-onstrates the need for an ontological shift. Consider that "clients" may consider some animals as significant others and see nature not just as "the environment" but in terms of significant relations. Engaging a CAS viewpoint can also support social workers in asking deeper reflex-ive questions about clients and all animals as they engage in nature-based activities. For example, social workers who take nature walks with service users might ask themselves: How are "wild" animals we observe or interact with being considered differently from "farmed" animals? What hierarchies are being reproduced by privileging some animal lives (including humans) and well-being over others? Non-Indigenous social workers might reflect on the intersecting oppression of non-human animals and humans as an opportunity to interrogate settler-colonial contexts and challenge dominant Western anthropocen-tric ontologies, thus contributing to decolonizing social work. In these ways, CAS can support applications of green social work in reaching beyond individualist therapeutic techniques in practice by considering all animals (including humans) and connecting to broader goals of eradicating all forms of oppression and violence.

Intersectional Oppression

Bringing CAS into green social work acknowledges non-human animals as sentient beings deserving justice and addresses foundations of intersectional oppressions such as racism, classism, and sexism. This includes "environmental racism," which Bullard (1993) first theorized concerning corporations found dumping toxic waste near and within racialized communities without their knowledge or consent, which has had significant negative impacts on their physical environment and health (Dominelli, 2013; Philip & Reisch, 2015). It has long been recognized that exploited and racialized communities are inequitably exposed to pollution and toxic waste from factory farms and that individuals from such groups suffer high rates of injuries from working in slaughterhouses (Human Rights Watch, 2004; Leibler & Perry 2017). Understanding that the oppressions of human and non-human animals intersect allows a more comprehensive understanding of terms such as "food justice," recognizing that structural racism has subjected under-resourced and racialized communities to unhealthy diets, with generational impacts of higher rates of diabetes, heart disease, and high blood pressure (Howard et al., 2018; McMichael et al., 2017).

Importantly, CAS acknowledges that food preferences may be created historically as a response to social conditions that deplete any control over food choices and economic and social advantage. For example, higher-proportion Black neighbourhoods in the United States have both increased density of fast food restaurants (Kwate, 2008) and decreased access to grocery stores, often referred to as "food deserts" (Karpyn et al., 2019, p. 1). This disparity in access to food sources has been linked to a complex web of disproportionality in economic, community and individual health and well-being (James et al., 2014; Karpyn et al., 2019). In *Sistah Vegan*, Breeze Harper (2010) offers important perspectives from Black women utilizing veganism in response to concerns about anti-Black racism, animal well-being, and the environment. Advocacy for plant-based diets and vegan activism offer important intersectional and anti-oppressive opportunities to further challenge structural food systems by ensuring that non-human animals will not be killed for food, and that the health of human communities will be improved (Crimarco et al., 2020). Developing better knowledge about the colonial history, politics, and economics behind food justice, social workers have solid ground to advocate for all oppressed animals, including humans.

Furthermore, CAS sees speciesism as an important foundation for racism in its construction of the binary identities "human" and "animal," with the latter depicted as lacking qualities providing eligibility for moral consideration. Through discourses of "animalization," various human groups are depicted as being "like animals" and thus suitable for exploitation (Matsuoka & Sorenson, 2021). Consequently, CAS contends that various forms of oppression are mutually constitutive and reinforcing, and to truly confront oppression it is necessary to challenge the hierarchical conceptual framework, rather than rearrange positions within it. Thus, addressing speciesism, which supplies a conceptual framework for various forms of hierarchal human oppression, is critical for green social work to challenge the roots of structural violence and move towards transformative practice.

A New Ethical Paradigm

Non-anthropocentric and anti-speciesism practice challenges green social workers to review current practices, enabling "do no harm" ethical commitments. Such practice (including direct practice, policy, and program development) deepens appreciation for the fact that human well-being must be grounded in more positive, respectful, and compassionate interactions with non-human animals and nature in general. Dominelli (2013) importantly highlights the "ethics of care" (p. 437) as a central position to understanding power relations in the context of green social work for the well-being of all living things. This emphasis, along with CAS's view on the personhood of non-human beings, is congruent with Ryan's (2011) transformative proposal for a social work code of ethics that expands beyond anthropocentrism. Such fundamental changes in perspective would set clear ethical frameworks for green social work education and practice to move progressively forward. Societies based on exploitation, violence, and instrumental use of non-human animals can only reinforce other forms of exploitation and violence towards humans. Encouraging positive, respectful relationships with non-human animals in social work practice not only helps overcome individual issues, but can improve the quality of social life and well-being of this planet.

Conclusion

Essential for challenging systemic issues is a recognition that anthropocentric and instrumentalist views are not only detrimental to those species deemed as resources, pets, or food but are among the primary contributors to the climate crisis and oppression for humans as well. The global COVID-19 pandemic is simply one indication of this vital truth. Rather than limiting understanding of social justice to relations among humans and their surrounding environment, trans-species social justice is a more vital perspective (Ross et al., 2021) as it challenges the devastating impact of anthropocentric, speciesist worldviews and justifies efforts to avoid the collapse of planetary ecosystems and biodiversity. Thus, trans-species social justice reveals truncated narratives contained in concepts such as food justice that only consider human access to resources rather than more complex forms of intertwined oppression, including exploitation of non-human others under capitalist, patriarchal, and colonial systems.

We contend that a CAS approach is indispensable in strengthening green social work education and practice, providing critical concepts such as speciesism, anthropocentrism, and truncated narratives, acknowledging affect knowledge such as compassion and peaceful attitudes towards all animals, and setting the goal of trans-species social justice. Unpacking and challenging language and histories of the environmental perspectives rooted in human-focused concerns prevents social workers from being unwittingly complicit in the oppressive systems we seek to dismantle. Just as forms of injustice exacerbate one another, addressing all forms of exploitation and violence will help to promote justice for all living beings.

REFERENCES

Adams, C. (2000). *The sexual politics of meat*. Continuum.
Akhurst, J. (2010). Exploring the nexus between wilderness and therapeutic experiences. *Implicit Religion*, 13(3), 295–305. https://doi.org/10.1558/imre.v13i3.295
Appleby, K., Bell, K., & Boetto, H. (2017). Climate change adaptation: Community action, disadvantaged groups and practice implications for social work. *Australian Social Work*, 70(1), 78–91. https://doi.org/10.1080/0312407X.2015.1088558
Bay, U. (2013). Transition town initiatives promoting transformational community change in tackling peak oil and climate change challenges. *Australian Social Work*, 66(2), 171–186. https://doi.org/10.1080/0312407X.2013.781201
Benton, T. G., Bieg, C., Harwatt, H., Pudasaini R., & Wellesley, L. (2021). *Food system impacts on biodiversity loss*. Chatham House. https://www

.chathamhouse.org/sites/default/files/2021-02/2021-02-03-food-system
-biodiversity-loss-benton-et-al_0.pdf

Besthorn, F. H. (2002). Radical environmentalism and the ecological self: Rethinking the concept of self-identity for social work practice. *Journal of Progressive Human Services, 13*(1), 53–72. https://doi.org/10.1300/J059v13n01_04

Besthorn, F. H. (2012). Deep ecology's contribution to social work: A ten-year retrospective. *International Journal of Social Welfare, 21*(3), 248–259. https://doi.org/10.1111/j.1468-2397.2011.00850.x

Besthorn, F. H. (2013). Vertical farming: Social work and sustainable urban agriculture in an age of global food crises. *Australian Social Work, 66*(2), 187–203. https://doi.org/10.1080/0312407X.2012.716448

Besthorn, F. H. (2014). Ecopsychology, meet ecosocialwork: What you might not know – A brief overview and reflective comment. *Ecopsychology, 6*(4), 8. https://doi.org/10.1089/eco.2014.0024

Boetto, H. (2019). Advancing transformative eco-social change: Shifting from modernist to holistic foundations. *Australian Social Work, 72*(1), 139–151. https://doi.org/10.1080/0312407X.2018.1484501

Boggs, C. (2011). Corporate power, ecological crisis and animal rights. In J. Sanbonmatsu (Ed.), *Critical theory and animal liberation* (pp. 71–96). Rowman and Littlefield.

Bradshaw, C. J. A., Ehrlich, P. R., Beattie, A., Ceballos, G., Crist, E., Diamond, J., Dirzo, R., Ehrlich, A. H., Harte, J., Harte, M. E., Pyke, G., Raven, P. H., Ripple, W. J., Saltré, F., Turnbull, C., Wackernagel, M., & Blumstein, D. T. (2021). Underestimating the challenges of avoiding a ghastly future. *Frontiers of Conservation Science, 1*(615419). https://doi.org/10.3389/fcosc.2020.615419

Bullard, R. D. (1993). Environmental racism and invisible communities. *West Virginia Law Review, 96*, 1037–1050.

Carson, R. (1962). *Silent spring.* Houghton Mifflin.

Ceballos, G., Erlich, P. R., & Dirzo, R. (2017). Biological annihilation via the ongoing sixth mass extinction signaled by vertebrate population losses and declines. *Proceedings of the National Academy of Sciences of the United States of America, 114*(30), E6089–E6096. https://doi.org/10.1073/pnas.1704949114

Coates, J., & Gray, M. (2012). The environment and social work: An overview and introduction. *International Journal of Social Welfare, 21*(3), 230–238. https://doi.org/10.1111/j.1468-2397.2011.00851.x

Cohen, M. (2017). "Animal colonialism: The case of milk." *American Journal of International Law Unbound, 111*, 267–271. https://doi.org/10.1017/aju.2017.66

Crimarco A., Turner-McGrievy, G. M., Botchway, M., Macauda, M., Arp Adams, S., Blake, C. E., & Younginer, N. (2020). "We're not meat shamers. We're plant pushers": How owners of local vegan soul food restaurants promote healthy eating in the African American community. *Journal of Black Studies, 51*(2), 168–193. https://doi.org/10.1177/0021934719895575

Dirzo, R., Young, H. S., Galetti, M., Ceballos, G., Isaac, N. J. B., & Collen, B. (2014). Defaunation in the Anthropocene. *Science, 345*(6195), 401–406. https://doi.org/10.1126/science.1251817. Medline:25061202

Dominelli, L. (2012). *Green social work: From environmental crises to environmental justice.* Polity.

Dominelli, L. (2013). Environmental justice at the heart of social work practice: Greening the profession. *International Journal of Social Welfare, 22*(4), 431–439. https://doi.org/10.1111/ijsw.12024

Dominelli, L., & Ku, H. (2017). Green social work and its implications for social development in China. *China Journal of Social Work, 10*(1), 3–22. https://doi.org/10.1080/17525098.2017.1300338

Donovan, J. (1990). Animal rights and feminist theory. *Signs, 15*(2), 350–375. https://www.jstor.org/stable/3174490

Drolet, J., Wu, H., Taylor, M., & Dennehy, A. (2015). Social work and sustainable social development: Teaching and learning strategies for "green social work" curriculum. *Social Work Education, 34*(5), 528–543. https://doi.org/10.1080/02615479.2015.1065808

Eisnitz, G. A. (2006). *Slaughterhouse: The shocking story of greed, neglect, and inhumane treatment inside the US meat industry.* Prometheus.

Erickson, C. L. (2018). *Environmental justice as social work practice.* Oxford University Press.

Faver, C. A. (2013). Environmental beliefs and concern about animal welfare: Exploring the connections. *Journal of Sociology & Social Welfare, 40*(4), 149–168. https://scholarworks.wmich.edu/jssw/vol40/iss4/9

Ficek, R. E. (2019). Cattle, capital, colonization: Tracking creatures of the Anthropocene in and out of human projects. *Current Anthropology, 60* (Suppl. 20), S260–S271. https://doi.org/10.1086/702788

Fitzgerald, A. J., Barrett, B. J., Stevenson, R., & Cheung, C. H. (2009). Animal maltreatment in the context of intimate partner violence: A manifestation of power and control? *Violence Against Women, 25*(15), 1806–1828. https://doi.org/10.1177%2F1077801218824993. Medline:30714886

Fitzgerald, A. J., Kalof, L., & Dietz, T. (2009). Slaughterhouses and increased crime rates: An empirical analysis of the spillover from "the Jungle" into the surrounding community. *Organization & Environment, 22*(2), 158–184. https://doi.org/10.1177%2F1086026609338164

Forkey, N. S. (2000). *Canadians and the natural environment to the twenty-first century.* University of Toronto Press.

Gee, N., & Mueller, M. (2019). A systematic review of research on pet ownership and animal interactions among older adults. *Anthrozoös, 32*(2), 183–207. https://doi.org/10.1080/08927936.2019.1569903

Gilbert, N. (1985). The commercialization of social welfare. *Journal of Applied Behavioral Science, 21*(4), 365–376. https://doi.org/10.1177%2F0021886 38502100403

Gordon, H. L. (2017). Climate change and food: A green social work perspective. *Critical and Radical Social Work, 5*(2), 145–162. https://doi.org/10.1332 /204986017X14933953111184

Gray, M., & Coates, J. (2012). Environmental ethics for social work: Social work's responsibility to the non-human world. *International Journal of Social Welfare, 21*(3), 239–247. https://doi.org/10.1111/j.1468-2397.2011.00852.x

Harper, A. B. (Ed.). (2010). *Sistah vegan*. Lantern Books.

Hawkins, C. A. (2010). Sustainability, human rights, and environmental justice: Critical connections for contemporary social work. *Critical Social Work, 11*(3), 68–81. https://doi.org/10.1155/2013/837432

Heinsch, M. (2012). Getting down to earth: Finding a place for nature in social work practice. *International Journal of Social Welfare, 21*(3), 309–318. https:// doi.org/10.1111/j.1468-2397.2011.00860.x

Howard, G., Cushman, M., Moy, C. S., Oparil, S., Muntner, P., Lackland, D. T., Manly, J. J., Flaherty, M. L., Judd, S. E., Wadley, V. G., Long, D. L., & Howard, V. J. (2018). Association of clinical and social factors with excess hypertension risk in Black compared with White US adults. *Journal of the American Medical Association, 320*(13), 1338–1348. https://doi.org/10.1001 /jama.2018.13467

Hughes, M. J., Verreynne, M. L., Harpur, P., & Pachana, N. A. (2020). Companion animals and health in older populations: A systematic review. *Clinical Gerontologist, 43*(4), 365–377. https://doi.org/10.1080/07317115 .2019.1650863

Human Rights Watch. (2004). *Blood, sweat and fear: Workers' rights in US meat and poultry plants*. https://www.hrw.org/sites/default/files/reports /usa0105.pdf

Ilea, R. C. (2009). Intensive livestock farming: Global trends, increased environmental concerns, and ethical solutions. *Journal of Agricultural and Environmental Ethics, 22*, 153–167. http://doi.org/10.1007/s10806-008-9136-3

Intergovernmental Panel on Climate Change. (2022). *Climate change 2022: Impacts, adaptation, and vulnerability*. Contribution of Working Group II to Sixth Assessment Report of the IPCC. Cambridge University Press.

Intergovernmental Science-Policy Platform on Biodiversity and Ecosystem Services. (2020). *Workshop report on biodiversity and pandemics of the intergovernmental platform on biodiversity and ecosystem services*. IPBES Secretariat.

Irvine, L. (2007). Social justice and the animal question. *Humanity and Society, 31*(4), 299–304. https://doi.org/10.1177%2F016059760703100401

James, P., Arcaya, M. C., Parker, D. M., Tucker-Seeley, R. D., and Subramanian, S. V. (2014). Do minority and poor neighbourhoods have higher access

to fast-food restaurants in the United States? *Health and Place*, *29*, 10–17.
https://doi.org/10.1016/j.healthplace.2014.04.011. Medline:24945103

Kaiser, M. L., Himmelheber, S., Miller, S., & Hayward, R. A. (2015). Cultivators of change: Food justice in social work education. *Social Work Education*, *34*(5), 544–557. https://doi.org/10.1080/02615479.2015.1063599

Karpyn, A. E., Riser, D., Tracy, T., Wang, R., & Shen, Y. E. (2019). The changing landscape of food deserts. *UNSCN Nutrition*, *44*, 46–53. Medline:32550654

Kheel, M. (1993). "From heroic to holistic ethics: The ecofeminist challenge." In G. Gaard (Ed.), *Ecofeminism: Women, animals, nature* (pp. 243–271). Temple University Press.

Kim, C. J. (2015). *Dangerous crossings: Race, species, and nature in a multicultural age*. Cambridge University Press.

Koleszar-Green, R., & Matsuoka, A. (2018). Indigenous worldviews and critical animal studies: Decolonization and revealing truncated narratives of dominance. In A. Matsuoka & J. Sorenson (Eds), *Critical animal studies: Toward trans-species social justice* (pp. 333–349). Rowman and Littlefield. https://www.rowmaninternational.com/book/critical_animal_studies/3-156-8606c11f-3a7d-4a69-9f66-b5ab28e57336

Kwate, N. O. A. (2008). Fried chicken and fresh apples: Racial segregation as a fundamental cause of fast food density in black neighbourhoods. *Health and Place*, *14*(1), 32–44. https://doi.org/10.1016/j.healthplace.2007.04.001. Medline:17576089

Lazarus, O., McDermid, S., & Jacquet, J. (2021). The climate responsibilities of industrial meat and dairy producers. *Climatic change*, *165* (1–2), 1–21. https://doi.org/10.1007/s10584-021-03047-7

Leibler, J. H., & Perry, M. J. (2017). Self-reported occupational injuries among industrial beef slaughterhouse workers in the midwestern United States. *Journal of Occupational and Environmental Hygiene*, *14*(1), 23–30. https://doi.org/10.1080/15459624.2016.1211283. Medline:27715500

Lovejoy, A. O. (1964). *The Great Chain of Being: A study of the history of an idea*. Harvard University Press.

Matsuoka, A., & Sorenson, J. (2013). Human consequences of animal exploitation: Needs for redefining social welfare. *Journal of Sociology & Social Welfare*, *40*(4), 8–23. https://doi.org/10.15453/0191-5096.3759

Matsuoka, A., & Sorenson, J. (2014). Social justice beyond human beings: Trans-species social justice. In T. Ryan (Ed.), *Animals in social work: Why and how they matter* (pp. 94–119). Palgrave Macmillan.

Matsuoka, A., & Sorenson, J. (Eds.). (2018). *Critical animal studies towards trans-species social justice*. Rowman and Littlefield.

Matsuoka, A., & Sorenson, J. (2021). Like an animal – Tropes for delegitimization. In N. Khazaal and N. Almiron (Eds.), *Like an animal: Critical animal studies approaches to borders, displacement, and othering* (pp. 101–124). Brill.

Matsuoka, A., & Sorenson, J. (2023). Inclusive approaches by VAW shelters: Respecting women's choice to be together with companion animals. *Affilia: Feminist Inquiry in Social Work. 38*(3), 466–482. https://doi.org/10.1177/08861099221097758

Matsuoka, A., Sorenson, J., Graham, T., & Ferreira, J. (2020). No pets allowed: A trans-species social justice perspective to address housing issues for older adults and companion animals. *Aotearoa New Zealand Social Work, 32*(4), 55–64. https://doi.org/10.11157/anzswj-vol32iss4id793

McMichael, A. J., Powles, J. W., Butler, C. D., & Uauy, R. (2017). Food, livestock production, energy, climate change, and health. *The Lancet, 370*(9594), 1253–1263. https://doi.org/10.1016/S0140-6736(07)61256-2

Muldoon, A. (2006). Environmental efforts: The next challenge for social work. *Critical Social Work, 7*(2), 1–6. https://doi.org/10.22329/csw.v7i2.5729

Nibert, D. (2013). *Animal oppression & human violence: Domesecration, capitalism, and global conflict.* Columbia University Press.

Noble, C. (2016). Green social work – the next frontier for action. *Social Alternatives, 35*(4), 14–19.

Nocella II, A. J., Sorenson, J., Socha, K., & Matsuoka, A. (Eds.). (2014). *Defining critical animal studies: An intersectional social justice approach.* Peter Lang.

Norton, C. L. (2012). Social work and the environment: An ecosocial approach. *International Journal of Social Welfare, 21*(3), 299–308. https://doi.org/10.1111/j.1468-2397.2011.00853.x

Noske, B. (1986). *Humans and other animals: Beyond the boundaries of anthropology.* Black Rose Books.

Nussbaum, M. C. (2006). *Frontiers of justice: Disability, nationality, species membership.* Harvard University Press.

Perkins, P. E. (2019). Climate justice, commons, and degrowth. *Ecological Economics, 160* (February), 183–190. https://doi.org/10.1016/j.ecolecon.2019.02.005

Philip, D., & Reisch, M. (2015). Rethinking social work's interpretation of "environmental justice": From local to global. *Social Work Education, 34*(5), 471–483. https://doi.org/10.1080/02615479.2015.1063602

Ramsay, S., & Boddy, J. (2017). Environmental social work: A concept analysis. *British Journal of Social Work, 47*, 68–86. https://doi.org/10.1093/bjsw/bcw078

Risley-Curtiss, C. (2010). Social work practitioners and the human companion animal bond: National study. *Social Work, 55*(1), 38–47. https://doi.org/10.1093/sw/55.1.38. Medline:20069939

Ross, D., Bennett, B., & Menyweather, N. (2021). Towards a critical posthumanist social work: Trans-species ethics of ecological justice, nonviolence and love. In V. Bozalek & B. Pease (Eds.), *Post-anthropocentric social work: Critical posthuman and new materialist perspectives* (pp. 175–186). Routledge.

Ryan, T. (2011). *Animals and social work: A moral introduction.* Palgrave and Macmillan.

Ryder, R. (1970). *Speciesism* [Leaflet].

Sanbonmatsu, J. (Ed). (2011). *Critical theory and animal liberation.* Rowan and Littlefield.

Singer, P. (1975). *Animal liberation.* Ecco.

Sorenson, J., & Matsuoka, A. (Eds). (2019). *Dog's best friend?: Rethinking human-canid relations.* McGill-Queen's University Press.

United Nations. (2019, May 6). *UN report: Nature's dangerous decline "unprecedented"; species extinction rates "accelerating."* https://www.un.org/sustainabledevelopment/blog/2019/05/nature-decline-unprecedented-report/

United Nations. (2020, December 12). *Press conference by Secretary-General António Guterres at United Nations headquarters* [Press release]. https://www.un.org/press/en/2020/sgsm20499.doc.htm

United Nations Environment Programme & International Livestock Research Institute. (2020). *Preventing the next pandemic: Zoonotic diseases and how to break the chain of transmission.* https://www.ilri.org/publications/preventing-next-pandemic-zoonotic-diseases-and-how-break-chain-transmission

White, D. (2003). Hierarchy, domination, nature. *Organization and Environment, 16*(1), 34–65. https://www.jstor.org/stable/26161783

Whitnall, T., and Pitts, N. (2019). *Meat consumption: Analysis of global meat consumption trends.* Government of Australia, Department of Agriculture, Fisheries and Forestry. https://www.agriculture.gov.au/abares/research-topics/agricultural-outlook/meat-consumption

Willett, J. (2019). Micro disasters: Expanding the social work conceptualization of disasters. *International Social Work, 62*(1), 133. https://doi.org/10.1177%2F0020872817712565

World Wide Fund for Nature. (2020). *Living planet report.* https://livingplanet.panda.org/en-us/

Wroe, L., Ng'andu, B., Doyle, M., & King, L. (2018). Positioning Social Workers Without Borders within green social work. In L. Dominelli (Ed.), *The Routledge handbook of green social work* (pp. 321–331). Routledge.

PART THREE

Greening Social Work Education: Practical Application

SUSAN HILLOCK

This final section of the book presents practical applications and concrete examples of what Canadian educators and activists in the field are currently doing in terms of teaching this knowledge and content, incorporating environmentalism and sustainability into their curricula, and mobilizing students and colleagues to climate/global justice. The following section also explores key environmental theoretical viewpoints; highlights Indigenous approaches, community-based models, eco-feminism, and eco-socialism; demonstrates how environmental rights and social action can be incorporated into social work, community practice, and field education; and introduces the first ever "Red-Green Manifesto for Greening Social Work Education."

National and Provincial Perspectives

Chapters 9 and 10 respectively examine the current state of affairs nationally in Canadian social work education and explore what is happening provincially within the Quebec context. In Chapter 9, "Towards a Radical Ecological Grounding in Social Work Education," James P. Mulvale explores our progress (or lack thereof) in integrating a radical ecological perspective within Canadian undergraduate social work education. His chapter highlights the need for fundamental transformation in political processes and economic structures, as well in existing relations of domination and exclusion, especially in regard to Indigenous, racialized, and other marginalized peoples. Mulvale posits that shifts like this are necessary if we want to effectively address rapidly expanding global warming, mass extinctions, and other Anthropocenic environmental crises.

Accordingly, this chapter explores how insights from radical ecology and a commitment to fundamental social-ecological transition could be more deeply integrated within Canadian BSW curricula. Drawing from the ecological social work literature, Mulvale provides a critical overview of the current state of Canadian "green" social work education and makes recommendations about how to further incorporate (especially radical) ecological perspectives into BSW curriculum. To accomplish this, he also highlights three additional data sources:

- a survey of ecology-focused courses and course content that are currently on offer in BSW programs in Canada, as indicated in social work schools' web-based program descriptions;
- key informant interviews (n = 5 or 6) with recognized leaders in the development of ecologically focused curriculum in social work education in Canada; and
- focus group discussions with senior undergraduate students at the University of Manitoba to gather their experiences, questions, and insights in regard to ecologically focused content in the BSW curriculum.

Reflective of the diverse Canadian social work landscape, Chapter 10, "Reimagining Environmental-Ecological Social Work in Québec," by Sue-Ann MacDonald and Jeanne Dagenais-Lespérance, offers a unique perspective about what is currently happening in Quebec in terms of this book's main themes. Informed by a feminist critical pedagogy framework (Freire, 2017; hooks, 1991) and inspired by insider action research (Coghlan & Shani, 2008), this chapter illuminates what is happening in terms of greening social work education and practice in Québec. To make their argument, the authors outline preliminary results of a qualitative study with social work students in Québec, related to the existence (or not) and significance of environmental concepts and content in social work education. They also examine the creation of various knowledge-exchange activities about greening social work in practice milieus. Although many have argued that social work should be concerned with the intersection of social justice and the environment, and indeed have become principal actors of a shift to "greener" social work education and practice (Besthorn, 2012a, 2012b; Besthorn & Canda, 2002; Bexell et al., 2019; Krings et al., 2018; Ramsay & Boddy, 2017), the authors found that the impact of rapid environmental changes on social work practice and education remains relatively unexplored.

An International Perspective: Green Field Placements

Along with highlighting the need for multi/inter-disciplinary approaches, it is important to acknowledge that this is a global crisis: climate emergencies have no borders. Given this, it is worthwhile to hear from an author from our closest geographical neighbour, the United States. Accordingly, Chapter 11, "Greening Social Work Education: Teaching Environmental Rights in Community Practice" by David Androff, offers a glimpse into innovative environmental projects that are happening in American social work education. His chapter also provides excellent examples of how to apply a sustainability and environmental rights approach in community-based practice and to field education, an area that is extremely underdeveloped in the social work literature.

Like our Canadian authors, Androff posits that green issues such as protecting environmental rights and promoting sustainability are starting to grow in importance to social work practice but continue to be largely ignored in social work curricula. Of particular significance to this book because of the paucity of practical field education examplars in the literature, this chapter uses comparative case studies of two student-led community projects to illustrate how environmental rights can be incorporated into social work, community practice, and field education. Lessons from these successful student projects – creating community gardens in homeless shelters and political advocacy against mining – reveal the interconnection of human and environmental rights as well as social and environmental justice. The author concludes by discussing implications for social work education.

Concluding Thoughts: Starting a Revolution

My concluding chapter, "The Red-Green Manifesto for Greening Social Work Education," briefly highlights key themes that are interwoven across the book: the belief that coverage of sustainability and the environment should be added/increased in social work education and the helping professions, the merits of multi/inter-disciplinary approaches to teaching this content, and the need to utilize innovative new and inclusive theories and approaches that interrogate capitalism, anthropocentrism, over-consumption/production, fossil fuel reliance, and environmental degradation. Accordingly, Chapter 12 presents the first ever Red-Green Manifesto for Greening Social Work Education to assist the social work profession to mainstream these ideas and incorporate this content. From the research, literature, and my personal and professional experiences, this manifesto summarizes the top ten things that I think social work education needs to do to green itself from the inside out. Rounding out the book, the appendix offers additional green educational resources, including books, software applications, websites, films/videos, and hopeful news stories about successful climate action.

REFERENCES

Besthorn, F. H. (2012a). Deep ecology's contributions to social work: A ten-year retrospective. *International Journal of Social Welfare, 21*(3), 248–259. https://doi.org/10.1111/j.1468-2397.2011.00850.x

Besthorn, F. H. (2012b). Radical equalitarian ecological justice: A social work call to action. In M. Gray, J. Coates, & T. Hetherington (Eds.), *Environmental Social Work* (pp. 31–45). Routledge. http://doi.org/10.4324/9780203095300-8

Besthorn, F. H., & Canda, E. R. (2002). Revisioning environment: Deep ecology for education and teaching in social work. *Journal of Teaching in Social Work, 22*(1–2), 79–101. https://doi.org/10.1300/J067v22n01_07

Bexell, S. M., Decker Sparks, J. L., Tejada, J., & Rechkemmer, A. (2019). An analysis of inclusion gaps in sustainable development themes: Findings from a review of recent social work literature. *International Social Work, 62*(2), 864–876. https://doi.org/10.1177/0020872818755860

Coghlan, D., & Shani, A. B. (Rami). (2008). Insider action research: The dynamics of developing new capabilities. In *The Sage handbook of action research* (pp. 643–655). Sage. http://doi.org/10.4135/9781848607934.n56

Freire, P. (2017). *Pedagogy of the oppressed*. Penguin.

hooks, b. (1991). Theory as liberatory practice. *Yale Journal of Law and Feminism, 4*(1), 1–12. https://heinonline.org/HOL/P?h=hein.journals/yjfem4&i=7

Krings, A., Victor, B. G., Mathias, J., & Perron, B. E. (2018). Environmental social work in the disciplinary literature, 1991–2015. *International Social Work, 63*(3), 275–290. https://doi.org/10.1177/0020872818788397

Ramsay, S., & Boddy, J. (2017). Environmental social work: A concept analysis. *British Journal of Social Work, 47*(1), 68–86. https://doi.org/10.1093/bjsw/bcw078

9 Towards a Radical Ecological Grounding in Social Work Education

JAMES P. MULVALE

The academic literature on ecological social work has been growing steadily over the last two decades and more (e.g., Coates, 2003; Besthorn, 2012; Boetto, 2017; Dominelli, 2012; Gray & Coates, 2015; Mulvale, 2017; Zapf, 2009). Given this development, this chapter considers progress (or lack thereof) in the implementation of ecologically focused curriculum in social work education in Canada. In other words, how well are social work educators doing in imparting essential values, knowledge, and skills to students related to environmental sustainability and the ecological practice of social work? Based on qualitative data collected in early 2021 on social work courses specifically focused on social work and ecology/environment, and on the observations of four social work academics who have been engaged in the "greening" of social work education, this chapter offers a snapshot of progress on ecologically focused social work curriculum in Canada.

In this chapter, I use the term "eco-social work" that is found in numerous sources in the academic literature on social work and ecology (e.g., Boetto, 2017; Case, 2017; Hetherington & Boddy, 2013). This term denotes theorizing, researching, teaching, and practising social work in ways that incorporate a profound commitment to environment and ecology, as well as social justice and ecological sustainability; these operate to situate what social workers do in their political, economic, and social milieux; and this takes a critically reflective approach to all levels and aspects of practice. Similar terms found in the literature are "green social work" (Dominelli, 2012) and "deep ecological social work" (Besthorn, 2012). Dominelli maintains that her green social work model ties critical thinking about the environment to critical analysis of the political and economic structures of globalized capitalism. She contends (I believe unfairly) that this element is missing in Besthorn's thinking (cf. Besthorn, 2012, p. 253).

I am using the term "environment" above and throughout this chapter to refer to the natural and physical settings that human beings and societies inhabit, and that are affected by various challenges and risks such as climate change, pollution, loss of biodiversity, and resource depletion. I use "ecology" as a broader concept that encompasses the very complex set of interrelationships between and among the elements of the natural world (composed of its flora, fauna, and inanimate material) *and* the elements of human societies (our purposely constructed settings, activities, and artifacts related to production and reproduction necessary for continued human life). From this ecological perspective, human beings are viewed as one species among countless others that inhabit the biosphere of planet Earth. However, human beings have created societies and economies that have – especially over the last five centuries – overexploited, despoiled, and taken for granted the natural world upon which all life (including human life) depends.

This lack of balance with, and respect for, the natural world has resulted in the age in which we now live being labelled the Anthropocene (Pavid, n.d., para. 4). It has taken shape over the last six decades as a result of the "Great Acceleration" of "carbon dioxide emissions, global warming, ocean acidification, habitat destruction, extinction and widescale natural resource extraction [that] are all signs that we have significantly modified our planet." *Homo sapiens* has "fundamentally altered the physical, chemical and biological systems of the planet on which we and all other organisms depend" (para. 3).

This degradation of the Earth poses immediate *environmental* problems and threats. The Anthropocene also necessitates a new *ecological* understanding of the complex ways in which all life and systems (including human societies) are interrelated and mutually dependent, and an imperative for radical action to restore ecological balance and health. Social work education must enable students both to understand these immediate environmental problems *and* to develop a deep and broad ecological consciousness and critique.

As discussed in this volume's introduction, the importance of an environmental/ ecological grounding in the education of future social workers has recently been articulated by our national accreditation body for university-based social work programs (CASWE, 2021). (See Hillock's introduction for detail on recent changes.) An evidence-informed argument is made below that there is much work still to do in implementing this new national accreditation standard in Canadian social work education. In this endeavour, it is possible to draw on a large and rapidly growing literature on eco-social work curriculum and pedagogy. For example, in Europe there is a focus on educating students on social work's role in responding to and preventing disasters induced by ecological, natural, and social forces (Cuadra & Eydal, 2018); in Aotearoa/New Zealand, social work field students are learning about sustainable social work grounded in Indigenous (specifically Maori) values (Ellis et al., 2018); and in Australia, a comprehensive approach to greening social work education and practice has been advanced (Nipperess & Boddy, 2018).

Data Gathered from Social Work Programs

To gather data for this chapter, an email communication went out to all anglophone social work programs accredited with the Canadian Association for Social Work Education inviting their participation in this study. The author and a research assistant sought out two sources of information for this study: individual academics who are engaged in thinking about and developing ecologically focused social work curriculum and who would be willing to be interviewed as key informants; and information on eco-social work curriculum in use as found in program overviews, course outlines, or other documents. An Internet search was also undertaken independently for online and publicly available curricular material on the websites of social work programs in Canada.

The time available for data collection for this project was short, but our outreach yielded four key informant interviews and some relevant documentation from social work programs. General findings from the key informant interviews are summarized in the next section. What follows immediately below are examples of ecologically focused social work courses that were on offer in early 2021 in university-based programs in Canada.

First, the BSW program at MacEwan University in Edmonton, Alberta, has as a hallmark of its curriculum a focus on "sustainability – how social, environmental and economic issues interrelate, and how we fit into the larger community" (MacEwan University, n.d. a). All MacEwan BSW students are required to take two courses (MacEwan University, n.d. b): SOWK 302 – Indigenous Knowledge: Contributions to Sustainable Social Work Practice; and SOWK 303 – Social Work and Sustainability.

Second, a number of social work programs at other Canadian universities offer optional or elective courses specifically focused on ecology/ environment and social work. Examples include the following:

- University of Calgary: SOWK 557-S05 – Climate Change and Sustainable Social Development and SOWK 557.42 S01 – Trauma/Healing: Person/Planet;

- University of Regina: SW 855 – Social Work and the Environment;
- McMaster University: SOC WORK 4G03/6G03 (Special Topics in Social Work) – Social Justice Responses to Climate Change and the Environment;
- Université de Montréal: SVS 3517 – Travail Social et Environnement; and
- St. Thomas University: SCWK-5823 – Ecology and Social Justice.

These courses are taught at the undergraduate level as BSW courses, with two exceptions: the University of Regina course is a graduate-level MSW elective course and the McMaster course is cross-listed as an undergraduate and graduate offering.

In addition to offering free-standing courses focused on eco-social work, it is possible to infuse or integrate green content in other social work courses across the curriculum. Environmental problems and ecological perspectives can in principle be addressed in a variety of established courses, including those focused on theories and models of practice, social policy, human behaviour in the social environment, and research methods for social work. Eco-social work approaches can also be an integral component in field education. Students can be challenged to think about ecological models of practice in integrative seminars during their placements. Social work programs can also offer students field placement opportunities in environmental advocacy organizations or in agencies that employ eco-social work approaches in their programs for service users (e.g., wilderness treks for youth or animal-mediated therapy). All of these possibilities for the integration of green content across social work curricula are eminently worthy of further development and evaluation.

Key Informant Interviews

Four individuals at four different university-based social work programs in Canada were interviewed for this study. Each of these key informants had a keen interest in and various ideas about building ecologically focused social work curriculum. Their input is summarized below, grouped under four general themes that emerged across the interviews.

1. ECO-SOCIAL WORK IS FUNDAMENTALLY LINKED
WITH INDIGENOUS KNOWLEDGES
This theme was strongly emphasized by all key informants. The centrality of Indigenous knowledges to eco-social work is based on a connection to the lands of Turtle Island (a name Indigenous peoples

use to refer to North America and sometimes the planet) and to the natural environments within which Indigenous peoples have survived and thrived from time immemorial. Indigenous practices of living in harmony with the land, and acting as stewards rather than dominators and exploiters, can model a better ecological future for settlers and for leaders in political and economic institutions. Unfortunately, Indigenous voices are often marginalized or ignored on environmental questions, a point that was consistently made in the interviews. As one person put it:

> The capitalistic world has just commodified everything – air, water, soil, plants, animals, microbes, DNA – it's killing the spirit of life. Our only way out is to return to our Indigenous roots.

This point echoes what has been found in academic literature related to the connection between Indigenous worldviews and the ecological health of Mother Earth (e.g., Fenelon & Hall, 2008; Huseman & Short, 2012; Kimmerer, 2013).

In addition, key informants stated that Indigenous knowledges can teach all of us about stewardship, protection, and spiritual connection with the natural world, but that these lessons can only be conveyed effectively in the context of full implementation of treaty rights and meaningful political sovereignty and economic self-determination of Indigenous peoples. A key informant also stressed how Indigenous knowledges connect us to sacred places and to the beyond-the-human world, and that these connections can facilitate individual and collective healing from the traumas associated with colonization and racism. Such healing can arguably help us to move towards authentic truth-telling, respect, and reconciliation between Indigenous peoples and settlers as envisioned by the Truth and Reconciliation Commission of Canada (2015). McGregor (2018) states, "we cannot talk about reconciliation without also speaking of Indigenous environmental justice" (p. 224).

Key informants also stressed that Indigenous knowledges are not elements to be "added into" social work curriculum. They must be foundational. When it comes to environmental questions, Indigenous knowledge and experience can instruct settlers and guide collective efforts to protect and preserve the land, air, water, other species, and sacred spaces. Seeing Mother Earth from an Indigenous perspective can help us understand the ravages and injustices of colonialism and racism, including settler populations grabbing land and pillaging resources (Whyte, 2016) while at the same time failing to provide Indigenous communities the basic necessities such as safe drinking water

(Cecco, 2021). Informants therefore believed that ecologically focused social work curriculum can help educate minds and change hearts to enable the flourishing of individuals, communities, and all species in Turtle Island.

2. ECO-SOCIAL WORK IS RELATED TO INTERVENTION AT THE MICRO- LEVEL OF SOCIAL WORK PRACTICE, AS WELL AS AT THE BROADER LEVELS OF MEZZO- AND MACRO-PRACTICE

We are confronting many "big" ecological issues such as minimizing and adapting to climate change, abating and cleaning up toxic and non-recyclable waste, and preserving natural spaces to ensure a diversity of species. In thinking about and responding to these big issues, it is natural to think about mezzo-level social work strategies such as neighbourhood and community mobilization and macro-level strategies such as social activism and public policy design and advocacy. However, the key informants in this study consistently stressed that eco-social work must also be an integral part of micro-practice with individuals and families.

Numerous aspects of an eco-social work approach at the micro-level were mentioned, including the following:

- the importance of a strong connection with, and ready access to, the natural environment and green space as a determinant of good physical and mental health;
- environmental threats as contributors to anxiety and stress among students and service users;
- loss of our connection to nature and other species as a source of grief among service users;
- ecological aspects of practice in specific fields such as mental health and child welfare;
- an ecological focus as a necessary part of doing bio-psycho-social assessment; and
- specific approaches such as "decolonizing trauma work" with service users (e.g., Linklater, 2020) and crisis and disaster counselling (e.g., Dass-Brailsford, 2009) as aspects of micro-level eco-social work practice.

One key informant underlined the importance of linking micro-level practice with a radical ecological commitment in social work more generally. This informant posed the question:"What's the point of teaching people to do talk therapy or to comfort people as survivors of capitalism, if we are all dead?"

3. ECO-SOCIAL WORK INCORPORATES RELIEF EFFORTS AND
SOCIAL RECONSTRUCTION RELATED TO NATURAL
AND ENVIRONMENTAL DISASTERS

A significant focus in eco-social work is the role that practitioners play in supporting communities and populations that have experienced natural, environmental, and other disasters (Alston et al., 2019; Bauwens & Naturale, 2017). As discussed in Hillock's introduction to this volume, social work and allied professions are often on the ground in the immediate aftermath of disasters such as floods, earthquakes, forest fires, drought, toxic waste spills, and severe weather related to global warming. Beyond the emergency provision of food, shelter, health care, and material aid, social workers can make longer-term and more creative contributions to community and social reconstruction in post-disaster settings. The goal becomes not just the alleviation of immediate suffering and deprivation, but the restoration of community agency and a sense of hope for the future.

One key informant outlined how eco-social work curriculum can address the profession's role in post-disaster scenarios in regard to both reconstructing physical infrastructure *and* restoring social cohesion and community viability within affected populations. This informant observed that local officials, national governments, and international aid organizations frequently assume that *they* know what is required in the aftermath of disasters. But their assumptions frequently do not align with the wishes, knowledge, and capabilities of the communities who have been directly affected. An example of this mentality that "the experts know best" was described by an informant in relation to the reconstruction of housing. This housing may be designed by engineers and built by contractors assisting in post-disaster relief without any consultation with those who have been made homeless. The result might be new physical structures that do not provide disaster survivors with a sense of *being at home* in the new dwellings they had no part in designing or building.

Social workers can also bring their understanding of social recovery and adaptive social protection to bear in such situations. They can use social work tools and strategies such as community engagement and mobilization (Ledworth, 2020), participatory action research (Healy, 2001), and political advocacy (Mosley, 2013). In these ways, social workers can accentuate the voice of survivors and help ensure that local and national leaders and international aid organizations are listening to survivors and are acting in accountable ways.

In communities that have not experienced but are at risk of disaster, a key informant indicated that social workers can use these same strategies and skills in efforts to prevent future calamities. They can engage proactively with local communities to address issues such as threats by developers to farmland and natural habitat, the unwise exploitation of natural resources, and the failure of polluters and environmental regulators to clean up contamination of the natural world that threatens human and ecological health. A key informant also noted that Canadian social workers may be advantageously positioned to play roles in disaster relief and environmental advocacy around the globe. Our country is a wealthy one with a diversity of Indigenous and newcomer cultures and languages. Many recent immigrants to Canada have roots and social connections in other countries around the globe. As Canadian social workers and allied professionals, we can employ our material, intellectual, cultural, and social capital in responding to emergencies and in helping to rebuild communities around the world that have experienced environmental calamity, forced migration, or armed conflict.

4. EFFECTIVE PEDAGOGY IN ECO-SOCIAL WORK

The key informants noted a variety of challenges, questions, and possibilities in regard to how to deliver curriculum on eco-social work in ways that engage students and shape their professional knowledge, skills, and values. These ideas included the following:

- Introduce eco-social work ideas early in the program and come back to this topic over the students' course of studies, thereby facilitating deepening awareness and understanding. It may be helpful to have one or more social work courses specifically focused on eco-social work. But whether or not programs have such dedicated courses, eco-social work should be suffused throughout the curriculum. This includes field education – with eco-social work approaches being integrated in a variety of field practice settings, and some field placement opportunities being made available to students wanting to work directly with environmental organizations and advocates (see Chapter 11 of this volume for exemplars).
- Situate the social work program's emphasis on eco-social work in relation to relevant ecologically focused assets in the broader university, such as institutional commitments to Indigenization and environmental sustainability. This strategy could include partnerships with other programs and centres at one's institution that address ecology and environment.
- Tap into student anxiety and angst about the health of the environment in sensitive and supportive ways. Students (who are mostly

young people with most of their lives still ahead of them) are already very conscious of the environmental risks and dangers facing them. This awareness can be channelled into learning about and practising eco-social work as a constructive response to the ecological crisis.

• Make connections between environmental threats and social-structural injustices related to both *economic exploitation* (based on social class divisions and the concentration of wealth and power) and *social oppression* (based on the often-intersecting categories of race, ethnicity, gender, sexuality, ability, religion, and so on).

Making connections between economic exploitation and social oppression, as mentioned in the point immediately above, could be concretized in the classroom through focusing on specific topics. For instance, social work educators could focus on the racialization of exposure to hazardous contaminants where one lives and works (Tuncak, 2020) or on colonialist dispossession of Indigenous peoples of their territory in the interests of capitalist economic growth (Bird, 2013).

Additional specific topics were mentioned by key informants as ones that can "hook" student interest in eco-social work and resonate with students' own experience and curiosity. These topics (also covered in various chapters of this volume) include Indigenous activism to protest pipelines and other carbon-intensive developments; food security, including the environmental impacts of food production and distribution and the exploitation of migrant farm workers; social work micro-practices that use inter-species connections with pets or farm animals to enhance healing and wellness for service users; and the role of social work internationally in addressing global environmental problems and supporting people through local and regional disasters resulting from environmental or other causes.

Green Models for Moving Forward

Incorporating the above aspects of eco-social work curriculum into BSW and MSW programs is no small task. As social work educators, we only have students with us for a limited time. It is a challenge during this brief period to equip them with the values, knowledge, and skills that they need to be competent and dedicated practitioners in a variety of areas, whether as generalists coming out of a BSW program or as specialists with an MSW. Eco-social work is an absolutely essential part of their professional education, but there are many other necessary components in social work education that must fit into time-limited programs that have finite resources for carrying out their educational mission.

Various scholars have suggested useful ideas for "greening" social work teaching, educational sites, and curricula (e.g., Drolet et al., 2015; Philip & Reisch, 2015: Rambaree, 2020). Within the confines of this brief chapter, two approaches to building green social work curriculum will be examined: Boetto (2017) provides a very helpful way of conceptualizing ecologically focused social work curriculum, and Jones (2018) provides some useful suggestions on implementation and pedagogy for greening social work education. The key ideas of these two scholars are presented here, but of course, social work academics must take up and apply these approaches in ways that make sense and will work well in their own particular settings. The overall goal is to develop and implement ecologically focused social work curriculum that will equip our students to practice green social work and contribute to the struggle for an ecologically sustainable and just world.

Conceptualizing Green Social Work Curriculum

Boetto (2017) helps us *conceptualize* eco-social work education in a way that facilitates its mapping on to social work curriculum in clear and efficient ways. Boetto calls for a "transformative eco-social model" of social work education and practice that is conceptualized as three concentric circles (p. 52, Fig. 1):

1. the innermost circle is *ontology* (who we are as social work practitioners, educators, and students);
2. the middle circle is *epistemology* (the knowledge that we must have in relation to ecology and social work); and
3. the outermost circle is *methodology* (what we must do to enact eco-social work understandings and practices with service users, in knowledge generation and dissemination, and in broader processes of social change).

At an ontological and very personal level, according to Boetto (2017, p. 52), "how we understand and relate to the natural environment is central to a transformative eco-social approach to practice." Our way of being in social work is "made up of personal morals, beliefs and attitudes" (p. 52), and the orientation of each individual social worker to the natural environment will shape their professional identity and practice. She points to eco-feminism, deep ecology, eco-spirituality, and Indigenous worldviews as groundings for social workers as they move towards "a conceptualisation of the 'self' as a relational part of a much larger system" (p. 53). She expands on these and other ideas in discussing the epistemological foundations of an eco-social work orientation (pp. 53–58):

- a holistic conception of *ecological justice* that encompasses all living organisms, and that recognizes that in human societies it is the poor and the marginalized who suffer disproportionately from environmental hazards and ecological degradation;
- *ecological literacy* that commits social workers to learning about the ever-developing science of environmental challenges and ecological interdependence;
- *Indigenous perspectives* that are about "living in harmony with the natural world, based on spiritual beliefs, holism, collectivism and connection with the land," and that call for cultural humility on the part of non-Indigenous social workers as they work to decolonize the profession and deconstruct white privilege in their practice settings and in social policies;
- *eco-feminism and critical theory* that make the "connections between the domination of nature and the exploitation of women" and that trace environmental decline to root causes in "social and political systems which cause exploitation, disadvantage and unequal power relationships";
- a *global perspective* in social work that understands the global North's environmental victimization of the global South, the need to advance towards ecological justice on the international level, and the contributions of social work in the global South to "new perspectives on micro and macro practice and the relationship between them"; and
- a radical understanding of *sustainability* that includes a commitment to *degrowth* – if we are to achieve ecological justice on a finite and endangered planet, we must curb consumption in wealthy countries and classes and scale back overall economic activity, especially in carbon-intensive industries.

The degrowth imperative is of particular interest to social workers and those working in the broader social and health service sector. The welfare state as we know it in industrialized democratic countries such as Canada is largely the result of rapid economic growth bolstered by Keynesian economic policies during the middle decades of the twentieth century (Mulvale, 2017). To ensure a society that is both sustainable and just, it will be necessary to delink the future development of the welfare state from the imperative of economic growth. In the past, welfare state expansion has been financed in large measure by increased tax revenue resulting from economic growth. The time has now come to reverse four decades of neo-liberal tax cuts for wealthy individuals and profitable corporations and to create a new *welfare society* that goes far beyond the welfare state (Lightman & Lightman, 2017, pp. 319–324). Hoppner and Theuer (2019) argue that such a society could be based on democratically determined economic degrowth, a fundamental redistribution of wealth, and the provision of universal basic income and universal basic services.

At the methodological or "doing" level, Boetto (2017, pp. 58–63) provides a plethora of "eco-social practice strategies" that social workers can employ to strive for ecological justice with the individuals, groups, and communities that they serve. These strategies and techniques (pp. 61–62, Table 2) revolve around the following:

- personal growth towards connectedness with the natural environment;
- a notion of "human well-being" that goes beyond material consumption and wealth and that embraces a holistic understanding of human fulfilment rooted in positive social connections, affinity with nature and other species, and collective efforts to make life better for all;
- the development of "communities of practice and organisational change" in the social work profession and in our workplaces to advance ecological and social justice;
- mobilization of communities and networks, "to develop local knowledge and cross-cultural learning about sustainability practices and perspectives" that can bring about practical and positive change close to home; and
- engagement in "social action to facilitate economic and political change" with broad and diverse constituencies, using various means such as public meetings, social media campaigns, community education, alliances with Indigenous and other social movements, and peaceful political protest.

Implementation

Jones (2018) also provides guidance on how to implement eco-social work curriculum in programs with multiple and sometimes conflicting demands for new or revised content. He argues that the incorporation of eco-social content into social work education requires us to go beyond "bolting on" (adding in new content or courses) or "embedding" (infusing existing courses with new material) (p. 560). He does not dismiss these methods, but he also recognizes that social work educators must navigate multiple and often competing demands for the inclusion of new ideas and new research into an already "crowded" curriculum. Jones steps back and calls for a more fundamental *transformation* in the foundations and orientation of social work education. Educators in eco-social work must move

> away from a traditional, modernist and anthropocentric orientation towards a set of concepts and values which are grounded in recognition of the interdependent nature of humans' relationship with the environment and oriented towards sustainability. (p. 562)

Two Alternative Pedagogical Approaches

Jones (2018) points to a means of realizing such a transformed vision through two "alternative pedagogical approaches" (p. 562). The first is "transformative learning theory" (p. 563), which can guide social work educators in enabling critical reflection by students on their "relationship with, and place in, the natural world." Such reflection can result in students understanding ecology in new ways and taking them beyond "anthropocentric, individualised, [and] patriarchal" frames of reference (p. 563).

The second pedagogical approach that Jones (2018) recommends is "education for sustainability" – "what we need to know, across all fields of human knowledge and action, in order to live sustainably" (p. 563). This pedagogy would necessarily take social work students (and instructors) well beyond traditional fields of study such as theories of intervention, human behaviour in the social environment, fields of social work practice, and social policy narrowly conceived as distinct from broader environmental and economic policy. Education for sustainability is interdisciplinary and would connect social work education with environmental science and engineering (McClain-Meeder, 2019), the moral and political dimensions of ecological theory (Besthorn, 2012), Indigenous knowledges (Masoga & Shokane, 2019), and the liberal arts and humanities (Holm et al., 2015).

How Social Work Educators Can Green Their Teaching and Curricula

As social work educators, we shape students' knowledge, skills, and values in the classroom, in field education, and as role models through our beliefs and everyday behaviours. Social work education at the BSW level aims to prepare graduates for generalist practice. We can build on this generalist intellectual scaffolding, in order to enhance students' abilities to work in interdisciplinary ways on environmental issues with others from non-social work professions and backgrounds (Forbes et al., 2016). It is notable in this regard that Bozalek and Pease (2021) call for the building of a "post-anthropocentric social work" that can be achieved in part through joining other "disciplines and professions engaging with posthumanism, new materialism and affect theory" (p. 6). We can also have students in existing social work research courses undertake investigations of local environmental crises and challenges in order to make eco-social work real and immediate to them (Forbes et al., 2016).

Another potentially valuable resource in such a transformation to an eco-social model for social work education would be a professional grouping that is devoted to the mobilization of eco-social work knowledge among practitioners, academics, students, professional regulatory bodies, and service delivery agencies. Such a body could be fashioned to some extent after groups in allied professions such as the Canadian Association of Physicians for the Environment (www.cape.ca/about -us), Ecojustice (led by lawyers; www.ecojustice.ca/about-us), and the Canadian Association of Nurses for the Environment (www.cane-aiie .ca/who-we-are).

As social work educators, we have a professional and moral responsibility, and an exciting opportunity, to transform social work curriculum from an anthropocentric to an eco-centric project. We can equip future social workers (as well as current ones through continuing education) to be mediators and connectors between service users and the natural world at all levels of practice. We can play a prominent role in advocacy for ecological justice that incorporates social justice, working towards this goal with allies who also strive for sustainability, universal economic security, decolonization, and the ending of anthropocentrism, patriarchy, racism, and heteronormativity. Social work educators are well positioned to contribute to ecological viability linked to social justice as we navigate beyond the Anthropocene and work to ensure not just the survival but the flourishing of all species.

Acknowledgment

I am grateful to Hyelee Jo, MSW, who worked as a research assistant on this project during her studies at the University of Manitoba.

REFERENCES

Alston, M., Hazeleger, T., & Hargreaves, D. (2019). *Social work and disasters: A handbook for practice*. Routledge.

Bauwens, J., & Naturale, A. (2017). The role of social work in the aftermath of disasters and traumatic events. *Clinical Social Work Journal, 45,* 99–101. https://doi.org/10.1007/s10615-017-0623-8

Besthorn, F. (2012). Deep ecology's contributions to social work: A ten-year retrospective. *International Journal of Social Welfare, 21,* 248–259. https://doi.org/10.1111/j.1468-2397.2011.00850.x

Bird, J. (2013). *Aboriginal dispossession and proletarianization in Canadian industrial capitalism: Creating the right profile for the labour market* [Master's thesis]. University of Regina. https://ourspace.uregina.ca/

Boetto, H. (2017). A transformative eco-social model: Challenging modernist assumptions in social work. *British Journal of Social Work, 47,* 48–67. https://doi.org/10.1093/bjsw/bcw149

Bozalek, V., & Pease, B. (2021). Towards post-anthropocentric social work. In V. Bozalek & B. Pease (Eds.), *Post-anthropocentric social work: Critical posthuman and new materialist perspectives* (pp. 1–13). Routledge.

Canadian Association for Social Work Education (CASWE). (2021). *Educational policies and accreditation standards for Canadian social work education*. https://caswe-acfts.ca/wp-content/uploads/2021/04/EPAS-2021.pdf

Case, R. A. (2017). Eco-social work and community resilience: Insights from water activism in Canada. *Journal of Social Work, 17*(4), 391–412. https://doi.org/10.1177/1468017316644695

Cecco, L. (2021, April). Dozens of Canada's First Nations lack drinking water: "Unacceptable in a country so rich." *The Guardian.* https://www.theguardian.com/world/2021/apr/30/canada-first-nations-justin-trudeau-drinking-water

Coates, J. (2003). *Ecology and social work: Towards a new paradigm*. Fernwood.

Cuadra, C. B., & Eydal, G. B. (2018). Towards a curriculum in disaster risk reduction from a green social work perspective. In L. Dominelli (Ed.), *The Routledge handbook of green social work* (pp. 522–534). Routledge.

Dass-Brailsford, P. (Ed.). (2009). *Crisis and disaster counseling: Lessons learned from Hurricane Katrina and other disasters*. Sage.

Dominelli, L. (2012). *Green social work: From environmental crises to environmental justice*. Polity.

Drolet, J., Wu, H., Taylor, M., & Dennehy, A. (2015). Social work and sustainable social development: Teaching and learning strategies for "green social work" curriculum. *Social Work Education, 34*(5), 528–543. http://doi.org/10.1080/02615479.2015.1065808

Ecojustice. (n.d.). *We're building the case for a better earth*. https://ecojustice.ca/about-us/

Ellis, L. M., Napan, K., & O'Donoghue, K. (2018). Greening social work education in Aotearoa/New Zealand. In L. Dominelli (Ed.), *The Routledge handbook of green social work* (pp. 535–546). Routledge.

Fenelon, J., & Hall, T. D. (2008). Revitalization and Indigenous resistance to globalization and neoliberalism. *American Behavioral Scientist* (Beverly Hills), *51*(12), 1867–1901. https://doi.org/10.1177/0002764208318938

Forbes, R., Nesmith, A., Powers, M., & Schmitz, C. (2016, April 11). Environmental justice (No. 189) [Audio podcast episode] [Interviewer: Louanne Bakk]. In *inSocialWork*. University of Buffalo School of Social Work. http://www.insocialwork.org/episode.asp?ep=189

Gray, M., & Coates, J. (2015). Changing gears: Shifting to an environmental perspective in social work education. *Social Work Education, 34*(5), 502–512. http://doi.org/10.1080/02615479.2015.1065807

Healy, K. (2001). Participatory action research and social work: A critical appraisal. *International Social Work, 44*, 93–105. https://doi.org/10.1177/002087280104400108

Hetherington, T., & Boddy, J. (2013). Ecosocial work with marginalized populations: Time for action on climate change. In M. Gray, J. Coates, & T. Hetherington (Eds.), *Environmental social work* (pp. 46–61). Taylor & Francis.

Holm, P., Adamson, J., Huang, H., Kirdan, L., Kitch, S., McCalman, I., Ogude, J., et al. (2015). Humanities for the environment: A manifesto for research and action. *Humanities, 4*(4), 977–992. http://dx.doi.org/10.3390/h4040977

Hopp, J., & Theuer, L. (2019). *Bidding farewell to growth: How to provide welfare in a degrowth society*. Exploring Economics. https://www.exploring-economics.org/en/discover/bidding-farewell-growth-how-provide-welfare-degrow/

Huseman, J., & Short, D. (2012). "A slow industrial genocide": Tar sands and the Indigenous peoples of northern Alberta. *International Journal of Human Rights, 16*(1), 216–237. https://doi.org/10.1080/13642987.2011.649593

Jones, P. (2018). Greening social work education: Transforming the curriculum in pursuit of eco–social justice. Chap. 46 in L. Dominelli (Ed.), *The Routledge handbook of green social work* (1st ed.). Routledge. https://doi.org/10.4324/9781315183213

Kimmerer, R. W. (2013). *Braiding sweetgrass: Indigenous wisdom, scientific knowledge and the teachings of plants*. Milkweed.

Ledworth, M. (2020). *Community development: A critical and radical approach* (3rd ed.). Policy Press.

Lightman, E., & Lightman, N. (2017). *Social policy in Canada* (2nd ed.). Oxford University Press.

Linklater, R. (2020). *Decolonizing trauma work: Indigenous stories and strategies*. Fernwood.

MacEwan University. (n.d.-a). *Social work – Bachelor of social work. Overview.* https://calendar.macewan.ca/programs/degree-programs/bsw-social -work/#admissionscriteriatext

MacEwan University. (n.d.-b). *Social work – Bachelor of social work. Program requirements.* https://calendar.macewan.ca/programs/degree-programs /bsw-social-work/#programrequirementstext

Masoga, M. A., & Shokane, A. L. (2019). Indigenous knowledge systems and environmental social work education: Towards environmental sustainability. *Southern African Journal of Environmental Education, 35,* 1–11. https://doi.org/10.4314/sajee.v35i1.14

McClain-Meeder, K. (Host). (2019, April 22). Social work research on global environmental change: Past, present, and future directions (No. 262) [Audio podcast episode]. In *inSocialWork.* University of Buffalo School of Social Work. https://www.insocialwork.org/episode-262-dr-lisa-reyes-mason-social-work -research-on-global-environmental-change-past-present-and-future-directions/

McGregor, D. (2018) Reconciliation and environmental justice, *Journal of Global Ethics, 14*(2), 222–231. https://doi.org/10.1080/17449626.2018.1507005

Mosley, J. (2013) Recognizing new opportunities: Reconceptualizing policy advocacy in everyday organizational practice. *Social Work, 58*(3), 231–239. https://doi.org/10.1093/sw/swt020. Medline:24032304

Mulvale, J. (2017). Reclaiming and reconstituting our understanding of "environment" in social work theory. *Canadian Social Work Review, 34*(2), 169–186. https://doi.org/10.7202/1042887ar

Nipperess, S., & Boddy, J. (2018). Greening Australian social work practice and education. In L. Dominelli (Ed.), *The Routledge handbook of green social work* (pp. 547–557). Routledge.

Pavid, Katie. (n.d.). *What is the Anthropocene and why does it matter?* Natural History Museum (UK). https://www.nhm.ac.uk/discover/what-is-the -anthropocene.html

Philip, D., & Reisch, M. (2015). Rethinking social work's interpretation of "environmental justice": From local to global. *Social Work Education, 34*(5), 471–483. http://doi.org/10.1080/02615479.2015.1063602TT

Rambaree, K. (2020). Environmental social work: Implications for accelerating the implementation of sustainable development in social work curricula. *International Journal of Sustainability in Higher Education, 21*(3), 557–574. http://doi.org/10.1108/IJSHE-09-2019-0270

Truth and Reconciliation Commission of Canada. (2015). *Honouring the truth, reconciling for the future: Summary of the final report of the Truth and Reconciliation Commission of Canada.* http://www.trc.ca/assets/pdf /Executive_Summary_English_Web.pdf

Tuncak, B. (2020, November 27). *Visit to Canada: Report of the special rapporteur on the implications for human rights of the environmentally sound management and disposal of hazardous substances and waste.* Human Rights Council, United Nations. https://undocs.org/A/HRC/45/12/Add.1

Whyte, K. P. (2016). *Indigenous experience, environmental justice and settler colonialism.* http://doi.org/10.2139/ssrn.2770058

Zapf, M. K. (2009). *Social work and the environment: Understanding people and place.* Canadian Scholars.

10 Reimagining Environmental-Ecological Social Work in Québec

SUE-ANN MACDONALD AND
JEANNE DAGENAIS-LESPÉRANCE

Climate change has been identified as the biggest challenge facing humanity in the twenty-first century (Dominelli, 2018; IPCC, 2021; WHO, 2021), and yet the field of social work has lagged in its response to the climate emergency (Bowles et al., 2018). Unprecedented climate fluctuations, worsened by human-induced environmental damage, increasingly give rise to disasters (e.g., rising temperatures, droughts, floods, and famines) that harm already vulnerable communities, further deepening social inequalities and triggering social work interventions (Dagenais-Lespérance & MacDonald, 2019; Powers & Engstrom, 2020). Recently, the increase in human-generated environmental degradation has triggered the spread of zoonotic diseases, increasing the probability of pandemics (Cox, 2021). Historically, environmental degradation and toxic environments (dumps, reduced green space, heat domes, etc.) have been disproportionately located in poorer, racialized communities, affecting their health and well-being (Philip & Reisch, 2015, p. 476). Unsurprisingly, these communities are disproportionately affected by climate change (Boddy, 2018; Centemeri, 2017; Dominelli, 2018). Increasing awareness of the human-environment relationship is growing as the layered impacts of environmental degradation increase (Dylan, 2013), in the face of an escalating climate emergency (Cox, 2021). Social work on the whole, however, has been slow to recognize the importance of environmental considerations on well-being and social inequalities and has generally reflected a binary approach to the human-nature relationship (Jones, 2013, 2018). The challenge for social work is immense, yet the current absence of a nuanced social work understanding of the importance of environmental considerations, and the social and intersectional impacts of rapid environmental degradation and the climate crisis, are largely absent in knowledge and training in Québec.

Many social work scholars have claimed that the discipline should be concerned with the intersection of social justice and the environment, and in fact become a principal agent of a shift to "greener" social work education and practice (Besthorn & Canda, 2008; Krings et al., 2020; Ramsay & Boddy, 2017). Some argue that despite the "call to action" by academics (Besthorn, 2013, p. 31), empirical studies are still too rare (Bexell et al., 2019). Moreover, social work's knowledge base has not significantly shifted to greener forms of thinking and training; it has not brought environmental-ecological considerations into its centre of analysis and action despite the growing climate emergency. We argue that this is all the more true of social work education and practice in Québec, where green initiatives are rarely evoked. Drawing on several sources of inspiration, this chapter will first review the different sectors identified by scholars as suitable for a paradigm shift and then reflect upon how these are enacted (or forgotten) in social work education and practice in Québec.

We point briefly to the literature to underscore the importance of the environment-ecology and climate change in social work education and practice. Taking Québec as our case example, we will provide a brief overview of current environmental social work training, or rather, demonstrate its absence, and underline this gap by illustrating student perspectives. We then showcase the development of different knowledge exchange activities about greening social work in practice milieus in Québec. We undertake this endeavour by situating our respective engagements from two perspectives: as a student who is currently conducting her master's project on this topic (Dagenais-Lespérance), and as a professor who is also director of field education for the largest Bachelor of Social Work program in a francophone university in Canada (MacDonald). Our reflections are informed by a feminist and critical pedagogy posture (Freire, 2017; Keating, 2006) and inspired by insider action research (Coghlan & Shani, 2008). Finally, we will suggest some thoughts on the possibilities of renewing social work education with an environmental shift in Québec.

Renewing Social Work Education Globally

During the last decade, English-language literature highlighting the importance of integrating the environment-ecology into social work education and practice has increased (Dominelli, 2012, 2018; Gray, Coates & Hetherington, 2013; Hawkins, 2010; Mason et al., 2017; Miller & Hayward, 2014; Texeira & Krings, 2015), and more recently, social work education has been considered a privileged space to rethink the profession in relation to environmental issues and the climate crisis (McKinnon & Alston, 2017). It is important to note that several terms are used to refer to social work from environment-ecological perspectives; these include "deep ecology" and "environmental justice" (Besthorn, 2013); "ecological social work" (Ungar, 2002) or "eco-social" work (Jones, 2018; Lysack, 2011); and "green social work" (Dominelli, 2012, 2013). While each term has its nuances, an eco-social approach has become a broad umbrella term and has an "understanding of ecology (i.e. recognition of the interconnected nature of all living and non-living elements) and society, and which sees human well-being as inherently and inextricably linked to a healthy and sustainable natural environment" (Jones, 2018, p. 559). Green social work as developed by Dominelli (2012) is "a form of holistic professional social work practice" that focuses on the interdependencies, interactions, and relationships between people and their habitats and a profound transformation in how people conceptualize these "relationships with each other, living things and the inanimate world" (p. 25). Scholars (e.g., Dominelli, 2012, 2018; Gray, Coates, & Hetherington, 2013; Holbrook et al., 2019) present a range of micro, mezzo, and macro environmental social work practices, including crisis and post-disaster intervention with individuals, families, and communities; sustainable community development projects; and social-environmental policy development and advocacy.

Historically and philosophically, social work has developed within modernist thinking, embedded in a capitalist paradigm reposing upon a binary separating nature and people (Bell, 2021; Coates, 2003; Nicholson, 2021). Green, environmental-ecological, and eco-social work approaches fundamentally invert, epistemologically and ontologically, these modernist assumptions. Several schools of thought regarding greening social work education exist. One is to simply add on content to encourage environmental thinking (Beltrán et al., 2016) and eco-social concepts within existing social work programs (still situated within an anthropocentric lens (Boetto, 2017; Jones, 2018). Another is to be more transformative and transversal (Jones, 2018), infusing an eco-social work lens across all aspects of curricula (Powers et al., 2019) and the development of ecological literacy and practices (Jones, 2013, 2018), that is, to fundamentally re-centre what we know, teach, and practice by acknowledging our interrelationship, interdependence, and interconnectedness with nature (Besthorn, 2012, 2013; Dominelli, 2012; Peeters, 2012; Powers et al., 2019). Coates (2003) outlines five guidelines underpinning the transformative worldview required towards a sustainable future: wisdom in nature, becoming, diversity, relationship in community, and change. Dominelli (2012) draws on Indigenous, eco-feminist, and transdisciplinary perspectives to develop social work scholarship and practices that examine structural and gender inequalities. Gray and Coates (2015) propose to develop social work curricula with eco-centric environmental principles including conservation, degrowth, diversity, sustainability, spirituality, and restoration. Boetto (2017) mobilizes eco-feminism and deep ecology to argue for a new set of values with a focus on sustainability, including values of degrowth, collectivism, ecological justice, and global citizenship. In a similar vein, Bozalek (2021) suggests applying slow food movement principles to inspire a "slow social work" anti-capitalist movement, wherein relationships between people and the environment are fundamentally respectful, reciprocal, and meaningfully maintained. Others (Drolet et al., 2015; Firang, 2020; Mary, 2008; Schmitz et al., 2013) have argued for the importance of making sustainability central.

Ramsay and Boddy (2017) argue that environmental social work is a challenge to the traditional person-in-environment model of practice (Germain, 1979), wherein the environment is conceived through a human-social prism. They emphasize the importance of shifting to different values or new ways of being and acting to incorporate the physical environment. Zapf (2009) introduces the idea of "people as place," the spiritual aspect of belonging to a locality (p. 188). Billiot et al. (2019) argue that "Indigenous peoples are particularly susceptible to and affected by climate change due to their close ties to the land and its resources" (p. 296). Several scholars point to Indigenous knowledge and non-violent spiritual practices as inspirations to shift knowledge and practice (Bell, 2021; Besthorn, 2012, 2013; Lysack, 2010), enticing social workers to anchor interventions in outside environments, with a decolonial framework in mind (Powers & Engstrom, 2020).

Moreover, 80 per cent of the world's biodiversity exists within recognized Indigenous lands and territories; the result of "millenia of stewardship founded in deep, spiritual connections with our lands and territories and not predicated on modern economic systems" (Indigenous Climate Action, 2019, as cited in Cox, 2021, p. 81). Territories are indeed contested colonial, political spaces; decolonial practices are identified as ways to critically engage with the environment in both social work practice and education (Gray, Coates, & Yellowbird, 2013; Harris, 2006, Moeke-Pickering, 2014). Environmental justice has emerged as a powerful concept for practice (Erickson, 2018; Nesmith & Smyth, 2015; Schlossberg, 2007) as "communities most affected by environmental injustices are often the same communities where social workers are entrenched in service provision at the individual, family, and community level" (Teixeira & Krings, 2015, p. 513). Environmental injustice occurs when vulnerable people shoulder more of the burdens caused by environmental degradation and disasters, and paradoxically do not have sufficient resources, or access thereto, to buffer the harms and risks associated with these events (Bullard, 1993), for example, "inequitable exposure of communities of color, and communities in poverty, to environmental risks due primarily to their lack of recognition and political power" (Agyeman et al., 2016, p. 322). In Québec, social work has not necessarily joined up with prominent Indigenous voices such as Watt-Cloutier (2016), who equates environmental destruction with human trauma (Schibli, 2020).

According to Rambaree et al. (2019), there is not one pedagogical or practice approach way of integrating green or eco-social work in education and practice. However, there is a recognition of the interconnectedness of all life forms and that the goal is the fair and sustainable use of resources to promote well-being. Boddy (2018) argues for an extension of Tronto's (1993) "ethics of care" perspective, encouraging the inclusion of interdependence with the natural environment. Critical caring perspectives also join up with Indigenous ways of knowing and practising critical social work, reposing on reciprocity, respect, honouring and caring for the natural world, a recognition that we are not separate from it, evoking stewardship but also fundamental obligations to the land and future generations (Bozalek & Pease, 2021; Green, 2018). This too provokes an awareness of the relationship and intertwinement of colonization and environmental exploitation, that these forms of oppression cannot be separated but are deeply connected to capitalism and intersecting forms of oppression.

Social work has largely developed within a settler-colonialism standpoint (Billiot et al., 2019). To the best of our knowledge, Québec scholarship on how to infuse the environment-ecology, social work, and decolonial or post-colonial approaches within practice is non-existent. In the following sections, we will use the different principles and elements described above as lenses to examine social work education in Québec. We argue that these elements could provide a way to nourish the development of environmental-ecological social work in Québec and inspire a fundamental practice shift. We have found that students' needs echo the reflections found in the literature.

Contextualizing the Place of the Environment-Ecology in Social Work in Québec

As in the rest of the country, the ten universities offering social work programs in Québec are accredited by the Canadian Association of Social Work Educators – Association canadienne pour la formation en travail social (CASWE-ACFTS), which has recently included a new environmental accreditation standard. (See Hillock's introduction to this volume for details.) However, in Québec, as we will demonstrate, the shift required to implement this new standard is seismic, as environmental crises are rarely evoked in relation to social work education and practice.

In Québec, the profession of social work is regulated by the Order of Social Workers and Therapists of Québec (known as the Ordre des travailleurs sociaux et des thérapeutes conjugaux et familiaux du Québec [OTSTCFQ]). It does make mention of the environment in recognizing inequalities, stating that "action on the social determinants of health is part of the strategies to achieve [the reduction of inequalities], including action on living conditions (housing, security, income, transportation, environment, etc.) and access to basic services (educational, social health-related)" (our translation, OTSTCFQ, 2012, p. 10). Furthermore, in outlining its competencies' framework, it notes the importance of having "knowledge of the social determinants, i.e., the structural determinants and living conditions that are at the root of health inequalities" (p. 22). Despite not specifically naming climate change or the place of the environment in social work practice, the OTSTCFQ is fostering links about how the environment affects health and social inequalities in practice settings. However, the place of the environment and climate change in Québec professional practice is cursory at best.

In relation to the environment, Québec social work scholarship in disaster contexts deserves special mention, where it is principally led by Danielle Maltais (and her team), who holds a research chair in traumatic events, mental health, and resilience at the Université du Québec à Chicoutimi (UQAC) (Maltais & Gauthier, 2008; Maltais, Bolduc, et al., 2015; Maltais & Rheault, 2005; Maltais, Robichaud, & Simard, 2000, 2012; Maltais, Tremblay, & Côté, 2006; Maltais et al., 2020; Maltais, Tremblay, et al., 2019; Robichaud et al., 2001). She focuses on psycho-social interventions in the wake of disasters, in terms in individual interventions post-event but also community resilience. Drawing from experiences of the Saguenay region flooding in 1996 (Maltais, Robichaud, & Simard, 2000; Robichaud et al., 2001), her research explores, for example, the redefining of home by survivors, given the physical change to their environment after landslides due to the increased water level. She has also studied the train disaster in the town of Lac-Mégantic in 2013, where the derailment of seventy-two tanks of crude oil caused a massive explosion, assessing the resilience of the community and of its senior population, and showcasing the importance of social support for post-traumatic growth (Maltais, 2020; Maltais, Tremblay, et al., 2019).

We argue that applying Dominelli's green social work framework (2012, 2013) to disaster situations could be an interesting lens to bridge and shape this knowledge, highlighting and incorporating several key topics:

> assessing need; coordinating and delivering goods and services; assisting in family reunification; supporting individuals and communities to rebuild their lives, developing resilience and building capacity to minimize future risks; and advocating, lobbying, and mobilising for changes that safeguard the environment and prevent future disasters. (2013, p. 438)

This kind of work, often spearheaded by social workers, is rarely captured within a climate crisis and decolonizing framework. Despite the important links that have been made between injustice, social inequalities, and climate change, briefly discussed above, as well as the elements mentioned by OTSTCFQ and CASWE-ACFTS, we argue that these connections do not often trickle down into social work training.

Indeed, in the four largest schools of social work in Québec (Université de Montréal, Université Laval, McGill University, and Université du Québec à Montréal), there are currently few courses that specifically explore the links between the environment and social inequalities, or climate justice. From our research, the only course that stands out is a "Social Work and the Environment" course offered in the Bachelor of Social Work program at the Université de Montréal (MacDonald et al., 2018).

A brief search of the research interests of faculty members at the four universities mentioned above, using the keywords "climate," "environment," or "ecology," yields meagre results. Only one professor from UQAM mentions "eco-citizenship" in her areas of expertise, while a professor at the Université de Montréal includes "global health and climate change" in his profile. As mentioned above, one professor at the Université du Québec à Chicoutimi lists expertise on disasters and their impact on mental health. Also, the Université du Québec en Outaouais clearly positions itself through its social work department's mission statement: "[social work education] aims to develop critical thinking and an ethical posture of social solidarity that recognizes the structural aspects related ... to social and ecological discrimination and inequality" (Université de Québec en Outaouais, 2018, para. 3). A more in-depth study of course outlines from social work education programs in Québec might reveal how climate change or ecological concepts are incorporated into courses; however, this information is not readily available, and we remind readers that this is not an exhaustive analysis.

Admittedly, this is an insufficient overview of the state of environmental social work thought in Québec schools, but it does parallel a study of American social workers. Indeed, Nesmith and Smyth's (2015) research with 373 social workers shows that the vast majority of them consider that they face situations of inequality and environmental injustice in their practice, but they believe their training to be inadequate in preparing them for these realities. They do not feel well equipped to intervene and believe that the environment should be addressed more in social work education. The researchers also state that the environment remains a subject that is not sufficiently addressed in the scientific social work literature, which is far from helpful in educating future social workers (Coates, 2003; Coates, Gray, & Hetherington, 2013; Schmitz et al., 2013; Zapf, 2009). In the francophone social work literature, there are only a few small contributions of notable interest specifically targeting the environment and social work (Centemeri, 2017; Joly and Lebarbier, 2009; Maldonado-Gonzalez, 2009), which makes the construction of a French-language bibliography challenging, impeding the development of curriculum in our province's official language.

Students' Perspectives

In the absence of adequate francophone knowledge on this topic, Jeanne (the student co-author) embarked on a master's thesis project exploring this very question. She asked: what is the place accorded to the environment in students' social work training? As a community organizer active in intercultural organizations, she was often frustrated by the siloing of actions in the community sector. For instance, some community organizations were fighting poverty or exclusion and others were concerned with environmental issues, but these interrelated issues were not taken up within a more global understanding or connectedness. Jeanne was working in neighbourhoods with noise and air pollution, and inadequate access to green space and community gardens. The neighbourhood was mobilizing for increased access to green space and community gardens to promote social connections through the building of community spaces, but the city and other organizations were responding with food banks and limited material resources. The response was a stark mismatch to the needs (material and symbolic) of the community.

This division was further reinforced when Jeanne entered a social work program, where the topics of capitalism, neo-liberalism, colonization, gender discrimination, and violence were thoroughly explored, but the links between the ongoing colonial violence of territorial exploitation, social inequality, and environmental justice remained under-problematized. Climate change was barely mentioned as a topic, even though heat waves were recognized as forms of "social murder," killing the most vulnerable, the elderly, isolated, and poor (Macfarlane, 2019). As a white person from a privileged socio-economic background, Jeanne wondered how her research posture was linked to her social position and pondered the question: how could she invest in this object of study that appeared too distant from the immediate needs of vulnerable and marginalized people, but that clearly had long-term impacts? Anchored in the critical methodology of feminist ethnography (Abu-Lughod, 2000; Buch & Staller, 2013; Naples, 2003), she decided to explore the links between the environment and social work emerging from students' experiences: her own peers. She conducted three focus groups among master's students (n = 15; pseudonyms are used to report on students' perceptions) to gather data to add to her own insider's experience. This next section reports on her preliminary results based on a thematic analysis, informed by a borderland framework (Anzaldúa, 2002). Borderland theory is principally a decolonial non-binary lens that invites us to deconstruct and to blur boundaries, to look at the in-between spaces and the "view from the cracks" (Anzaldúa, 2015, p. 83), to transform our knowledge. We present these preliminary results from these in-between spaces to flesh out how the environment and climate change are taken up within social work education in Québec from a student perspective.

1. The Difficult Emotional Journey of Thinking about the Future

Students mentioned a real sense of fear and anxiety regarding the prospect of an apocalyptic future:

> Like they say that if we don't do something about the environment and we keep polluting the planet we're going to disappear with the Earth. So I'm scared. Because I want to live. (MS)[1]

> You were talking about eco-anxiety, every time I start to get more involved in the environment, it's as if I'm awakening this anxiety, this concern. (Gabrielle)

Anger was also communicated in the focus groups, mostly about social work programs that are perceived as static, antiquated, as if stuck in old paradigms. Several participants responded with: "What is the social

---

1 All translations from the French are the authors'.

work faculty waiting for?" Students expressed a sense of exasperation, urgency, and a shared preoccupation about the lack of environmental discourse in their education.

When environmental issues were brought forward by the rare educator or peers, students found it particularly enlightening and motivating, resulting in a fundamental change in their way of thinking and conceptualizing practice possibilities:

> I found the insights we had from a rural community worker [*travailleuse de rang*] really important, it really resonated with me, the impact of the environment on well-being. It kind of changed my view of social work. And yet, you know, it's kind of obvious with my rural origins, where I come from, the way my family earns its living, you know ... And yet it should have been obvious to me that you know, social work wasn't just happening in the urban centres of Montreal! (Véronique)

It should be noted, however, that these reflections were due to a few individual initiatives; overall, the environment and climate change did not occupy a systematic or fundamental place in students' social work education.

2. A Lack of Preparation and Training

The feeling of being unprepared for (natural) disasters was a recurring topic. The links with COVID-19 repeatedly arose, with students noting that the pandemic gave humanity a taste of the social upheaval climate change could cause. Participants cited the dearth of training for large-scale crises, noting the lack of preparation in social work education for all types of disasters:

> Even in relation to natural disasters. We have no training ... take COVID, it's not really related to climate change directly, but like, we're not really prepared to deal with big social crises. We're really more prepared to work with individuals, or small systems. (Lou)

> Well, I think we can visualize what will happen with the environmental crisis, that it will exacerbate social inequalities, just like with the current COVID crisis. (Bi)

> We are not equipped. Our systems, our infrastructures are not equipped ... our hospitals, our health and social service centres [CIUSSS], they can't handle a natural disaster. We are in these situations like lock-down because

our medical systems cannot handle this type of virus ... And I think that we are very ill equipped for our present and very imminent future and how climate change is impacting health. (Imola)

Participants also reflected on the lack of training in collective action and its importance for practicing environmental social work. Individual practice was only mentioned in connection to eco-anxiety:

It's a crisis that requires mobilization and that's how I think people are going to feel better and that we're going to be able to make concrete changes by mobilizing together. And not only by managing, by doing individual actions directly with people who live with eco-anxiety for example. So the change is on a larger scale. And we have to take that into account. (Laurence)

3. Trained to "Patch the Holes of Broken Pots": The Depoliticization of Social Work

Reflections on social work and neo-liberalism resulted in the sentiment that students' training prepared them to respond to the symptoms of problems but not the underlying causes. Students used the metaphor of "patching up the holes of broken pots" (a common French expression). This raised an ethical and ultimately unanswerable question: are we condemned to apply Band-aids to deep-seated problems and structural inequalities?

So we can bury our heads in the sand, but the fact is, it's going to catch up with us. Is it possible to rethink current neo-liberal approaches in social work that simply apply Band-aids to open wounds? Can we not instead work upstream to develop preventive strategies? ... I'm not saying that it would be easy or anything ... But I think we need to have this idea in mind when we revise the curricula. (Frédéric)

And the climate inequalities are there, we're already in a period of climate change, and it's the social worker who deals with the aftereffects, after the damage is done. (MGF)

4. Reflecting on Privilege in the Face of Inequality

Privilege was a common topic, but it was understood in a myriad of ways. We noted two complementary trends. Students felt privileged because they had the space to think about environmental issues and had the "luxury" of not having to be concerned with pressing issues (e.g., poverty). Further, they described this privilege as having the ability to "see the storm coming," which reinforced a sense of responsibility to act:

> The fact that we are privileged enough to sit down and talk about the environment is a reality ... climate change will enormously increase social inequalities. And that's where social work comes in. And it's really, in our mandate, these inequalities, and to defend vulnerable people that will be more affected by them. (Frédéric)

> I see a host of ethical issues with climate change, because it will exacerbate social inequalities. But on top of that, it's the people with the most resources who are going to be the least affected, but who cause the most problems. Right there we have an incredible imbalance. And I think that social work has a duty as a profession to denounce this and to look for solutions. Yeah, I see it more as a duty of the profession, because we're supposed to fight for social justice, and that's a big blind spot that we don't really address. (Gabrielle)

Echoing the literature presented earlier in this chapter, participants described an urgency to act on climate change and environmental issues as a professional and ethical responsibility within an understanding of social inequalities (Powers, 2017). Moreover, disasters were seen as catalysts for reflection and action, forcing students to think and act differently. COVID-19 was repeatedly brought up as a case in point of unprepared disaster planning and execution, demonstrating educational gaps related to addressing complex social problems (as mentioned by Lou) and natural disasters. Furthermore, the wealth of recent Québec scholarship on disaster social work Maltais, 2020; Maltais, Bolduc, et al., 2015; Maltais, Robichaud, & Simard, 2012; Maltais, Tremblay, et al., 2019) does not seem to percolate into classrooms. Also, participants made connections with neo-liberal logics and bio-medical analyses that operate by responding to symptoms and deficiencies (downstream) but deplored the lack of structural analyses and preventative (upstream) interventions. Participants suggested moving beyond the individual-society dichotomy to integrate the environment in their knowledge base and ultimately transform practices. Many of the elements raised by students supported what we gleaned from the literature (Gray, Coates, & Hetherington, 2013; Ramsay & Boddy, 2017) and also seemed to underline the students' need to have collective discussions, for social and emotional support. Participants noted the following at the end of a focus group:

> I am so happy to see other people being interested by it … I think that creating links is important for these issues. (MGF)

> I tell myself that we may not be that many, but it is starting to bubble … Because it hits us in the guts. With emotions guiding us, we can initiate actions with great passion. (K)

Caution: Green-Washing

Including the environment in social work education does come with a caveat. While this shift is important, as social work becomes more interested in the bio-physical environment we have to be careful not to reproduce binary ways of thinking, and the white scripts endemic to social work perspectives reinforcing oppressive structures (Finn, 2016). In Jeffery's (2015) excellent critique about the colonizing potential of such a shift, she states that "there is nothing natural about nature" (p. 495). Moreover, she warns that

> unproblematized concepts of and assumptions about "Indigeneity" tend to function in much of the social work discourse that lays out a rationale and practice direction. Representations of native and nature seem to easily slide into nostalgia and depoliticized longing for a premodern self. (p. 494)

These are grave warnings; social work educators must not forget the political dimensions wrapped up in occupying different ontological and epistemological spaces and the risk of reproducing colonialist paradigms or seemingly apolitical ways of thinking. Similar to our participants' understandings, Alston (2013) argues that in order to make the shift to greener forms of social work, we need to do just the opposite and repoliticize our work.

Leading Change

We close this chapter by presenting a recent initiative about centring climate justice and the environment in social work practices in Québec. We were members of a scientific committee that planned and hosted the OTSTCFQ's 2021 fall conference with the theme "Climate Justice and Social Inequalities." This was a first for Québec. The scientific committee was composed of social workers, therapists, academics, educators, and students. We established five priority themes:

1. climate crisis and international social work, sustainable development, climate migration, and gendered impacts;
2. international global perspectives;
3. the environment and Indigenous worldviews and practices;
4. climate change in Québec – impacts on individuals and families, mental health, food security, community resilience, collective mobilization, intersectoral approaches; and
5. the history of crisis intervention in Quebec: what have we learned?

The planning committee brainstormed several topics related to climate change and social inequalities, including individual impacts on mental health (e.g., eco-anxiety and grief) and psychosocial interventions; disproportionate impacts based on gender but also on marginalized peoples (i.e., people experiencing homelessness), who have the least resources to cope with extreme weather events; coping mechanisms and practices, individual and collective; natural disasters and crisis interventions; community mobilizing and resilience; the roles and responsibilities of government; and transforming social work practices. While constructing the conference program, we were surprised at the limited knowledge base about environmental social work and the dearth of practical examples of green social work practices in Québec (i.e., accessible and published). In the absence of locally grounded research and education practices, to build the conference program we turned to the writings of Dominelli (2012, 2018), Jones (2018), Jeffery (2015), and Coates (2003) about the roles social work could and should play in leading change.

Conclusion

The myriad implications outlined above help us to reflect upon the place taken up by the environment in social work education and practice in Québec. This raises the question of whether forms of environmental social work may in fact be happening in Québec but simply have not been captured from these perspectives. Even though the institutional bodies (CASWE-ACFTS, OTSTCFQ) appear to be fertile ground for environmental-ecological social work practice, social work education is slow to take up this challenge, as evidenced by our preliminary curriculum reviews and focus groups.

As we enter a new post-COVID era, social work in Québec will be faced with a major ethical challenge: how do we prioritize climate change and push for developing practices and shifting knowledge bases that necessitate an ecological transition when the pandemic further exacerbated social inequalities? Moreover, taking up the environment as politicized and contested space, how can we integrate it responsibly and justly? Thus, we believe critical discussions are needed to think about social work's roles and responsibilities in environmental crises and recognize that they are deeply linked to the capitalist colonial state in which we live, where territories and people are exploited for the desires and needs of the present, without thinking about the storm our actions are fuelling for the generations to come.

REFERENCES

Abu-Lughod, L. (2000). Locating ethnography. *Ethnography, 1*(2), 261–267. https://doi.org/10.1177/14661380022230778

Agyeman, J., Schlossberg, D., Craven, L., & Matthews, C. (2016). Trends and directions in environmental justice: From inequity to everyday life, community, and just sustainabilities. *Annual Review of Environmental Resources, 41*, 321–340.

Alston, M. (2013). Environmental social work: Accounting for gender in climate disasters. *Australian Social Work, 66*(2), 218–233. https://doi.org/10.1080/0312407X.2012.738366

Anzaldúa, G. (2002). Now let us shift … The path of conocimiento … Inner work, public acts. In *This bridge we call home: Radical visions for transformation* (pp. 540–578). Taylor & Francis. http://ebookcentral.proquest.com/lib/umontreal-ebooks/detail.action?docID=1487197

Anzaldúa, G. (2015). Geographies of selves – Reimagining identity: Nos/otras (us/other), las nepantleras, and the new tribalism. In *Light in the dark/Luz en lo oscuro: Rewriting identity, spirituality, reality*, edited by AnaLouise Keating (pp. 65–94). Duke University Press. https://doi.org/10.1515/9780822375036-006

Bell, K. (2021). A philosophy of social work beyond the Anthropocene. In V. Bozalek & B. Pease (Eds.), *Post-anthropocentric social work: Critical posthuman and new materialist perspectives* (pp. 58–67). Routledge.

Beltrán, R., Hacker, A., & Begun, S. (2016). Environmental justice is a social justice issue: Incorporating environmental justice into social work practice curricula. *Journal of Social Work Education, 52*(4), 493–502. https://doi.org/10.1080/10437797.2016.1215277

Besthorn, F. H. (2013). Radical equalitarian ecological justice: A social work call to action. In M. Gray, J. Coates, & T. Hetherington (Eds.), *Environmental Social Work* (pp. 31–45). Routledge. https://doi.org/10.4324/9780203095300-8

242   Sue-Ann MacDonald and Jeanne Dagenais-Lespérance

Besthorn, F. H., & Canda, E. R. (2008). Revisioning environment: Deep ecology for education and teaching in social work. *Journal of Teaching in Social Work*, 22(1–2), 79–101. https://doi.org/10.1300/J067v22n01_07

Bexell, S. M., Decker Sparks, J. L., Tejada, J., & Rechkemmer, A. (2019). An analysis of inclusion gaps in sustainable development themes: Findings from a review of recent social work literature. *International Social Work*, 62(2), 864–876. https://doi.org/10.1177/0020872818755860

Billiot, S., Beltrán, R., Brown, D., Mitchell, F. M., & Fernandez, A. (2019). Indigenous perspectives for strengthening social responses to global environmental changes: A response to the social work grand challenge on environmental change. *Journal of Community Practice*, 27(3–4), 296–316. https://doi.org/10.1080/10705422.2019.1658677. Medline:33013154

Boddy, J. (2018). The politics of climate change: The need for a critical ethics of care in relation to the environment. In B. Pease, A. Vreugdenhil, & S. Stanford (Eds.), *Critical ethics of care in social work: Transforming the politics and practices of caring* (pp. 219–228). Routledge.

Boetto, H. (2017). A transformative eco-social model: Challenging modernist assumptions in social work. *British Journal of Social Work*, 47(1), 48–67. https://doi.org/10.1093/bjsw/bcw149

Bowles, W., Boetto, H., Jones, P., & McKinnon, J. (2018). Is social work really greening? Exploring the place of sustainability and environment in social work codes of ethics. *International Social Work*, 6(4), 503–517. https://doi.org/10.1177/0020872816651695

Bozalek, V. (2021). Propositions for slow social work. In V. Bozalek & B. Pease (Eds.), *Post-anthropocentric social work: Critical posthuman and new materialist perspectives* (pp. 83–94). Routledge.

Bozalek, V., & Pease, B. (2021). *Post-anthropocentric social work: Critical posthuman and new materialist perspective*. Routledge.

Buch, E. D., & Staller, K. M. (2013). What is feminist ethnography? In S. H. Biber (Ed.), *Feminist research practice: A primer* (2nd ed.). Sage.

Bullard, R. (Ed.). (1993). *Confronting environmental racism: Voices from the grassroots*. South End.

Centemeri, L. (2017). Crise écologique et dynamique locale: Un avenir pour les métiers du social? In C. Bolzman, J. Libois, & F. Tschopp (Eds.), *Le travail social à la recherche de nouveaux paradigmes: Inégalités sociales et environnementales* (pp. 125–145). Éditions IES. http://books.openedition.org/ies/391

Coates, J. (2003). *Ecology and social work: Toward a new paradigm*. Fernwood.

Coates, J., Gray, M., & Hetherington, T. (2013). *Environmental social work* (1st ed.). Routledge. https://www.taylorfrancis.com/books/9781136212826

Coghlan, D., & Shani, A. B. (Rami). (2008). Insider action research: The dynamics of developing new capabilities. In P. Reason & H. Bradbury, *The*

Sage handbook of action research (pp. 643–655). Sage. https://doi.org/10.4135/9781848607934.n56

Cox, S. (2021). *The path to a livable future: A new politics to fight climate change, racism, and the next pandemic.* City Lights Books.

Dagenais-Lespérance, J., & MacDonald, S.-A. (2019). La justice environnementale: Dans l'angle mort de la formation en travail social? *Intervention, 150,* 113–119. https://revueintervention.org/numeros-en-ligne/150/la-justice-environnementale-dans-langle-mort-de-la-formation-en-travail-social

Dominelli, L. (2012). *Green social work: From environmental crises to environmental justice.* Wiley.

Dominelli, L. (2013). Environmental justice at the heart of social work practice: Greening the profession. *International Journal of Social Welfare, 22,* 431–439. https://doi.org/10.1111/ijsw.12024

Dominelli, L. (2018). *The Routledge handbook of green social work.* Routledge. https://ebookcentral.proquest.com/lib/umontreal-ebooks/detail.action?docID=5331755

Drolet, J., Wu, H., Taylor, M., & Dennehy, A. (2015). Social work and sustainable social development: Teaching and learning strategies for "green social work" curriculum. *Social Work Education, 34*(5), 528–543. https://doi.org/10.1080/02615479.2015.1065808

Dylan, A. (2013). Environmental sustainability, sustainable development, and social work. In M. Gray, J. Coates, & T. Hetherington (Eds.), *Environmental Social Work* (1st ed.). Routledge.

Erickson, C. L. (2018). *Environmental justice as social work practice.* Oxford University Press.

Finn, J. L. (2016). *Just practice: A social justice approach to social work* (3rd ed.). Oxford University Press.

Firang, D. (2020). Joining the call to incorporate sustainability into the Canadian social work profession. *Canadian Social Work Review, 37*(2), 27–50. https://doi.org/10.7202/1075110ar

Freire, P. (2017). *Pedagogy of the oppressed.* Penguin.

Germain, C. B. (Ed.). (1979). *Social work practice: People and environments, an ecological perspective.* Columbia University Press.

Gray, M., & Coates, J. F. (2015). Changing gears: Shifting to an environmental perspective in social work education. *Social Work Education, 34*(5), 502–512. https://doi.org/10.1080/02615479.2015.1065807

Gray, M., Coates, J. F., & Hetherington, T. (2013). *Environmental social work.* Routledge.

Gray, M., Coates, J. F., & Yellow Bird, M. (2013). *Decolonizing social work.* Ashgate.

Green, S. (2018). Aboriginal people and caring within a colonised society. In B. Pease, A. Vreugdenhil, & S. Stanford (Eds.), *Critical ethics of care in social work: Transforming the politics and practices of caring* (pp. 139–147). Routledge.

Harris, B. (2006). A First Nations' perspective on social justice in social
 work education: Are we there yet? (a post-colonial debate). *Canadian
 Journal of Native Studies, 26*(2), 229–263. https://search.proquest.com
 /docview/218101225/abstract/A8D9AFE4339940AEPQ/1
Hawkins, C. A. (2010). Sustainability, human rights, and environmental
 justice: Critical connections for contemporary social work. *Critical Social
 Work, 11*(3). https://doi.org/10.22329/csw.v11i3.5833
Holbrook, A. M., Akbar, G., & Eastwood, J. (2019). Meeting the challenge of
 human-induced climate change: Reshaping social work education. *Social
 Work Education, 38*(8), 955–967. https://doi.org/10.1080/02615479.2019
 .1597040
IPCC (Intergovernmental Panel on Climate Change). (2021) *Climate change
 2021: The physical science basis. Contribution of Working Group I to the sixth
 assessment report of the Intergovernmental Panel on Climate Change.* Cambridge
 University Press.
Jeffery, D. (2015). Green encounters and Indigenous subjectivity: A cautionary
 tale. In C. Janzen, K. Smith, & D. Jeffery, *Unravelling encounters: Ethics,
 knowledge, and resistance under neoliberalism* (pp. 71–93). Wilfrid Laurier
 University Press. https://ebookcentral.proquest.com/lib/umontreal
 -ebooks/detail.action?docID=3297888
Joly, F., & Lebarbier. M. (2009). Écologie du social ou socialité de l'écologie?
 Le sociographe, 2(29), 59–66. https://www.cairn.info/revue-le-sociographe
 -2009-2-page-59.htm
Jones, P. (2013). Transforming the curriculum: Social work education and
 ecological consciousness. In M. Gray, J. Coates, & T. Hetherington (Eds.),
 Environmental social work (pp. 213–230). Routledge.
Jones, P. (2018). Greening social work education: Transforming the curriculum
 in pursuit of eco–social justice. In L. Dominelli, *The Routledge handbook of green
 social work* (pp. 558–568). Routledge. https://doi.org/10.4324/9781315183213
Keating, A. (2006). From borderlands and new mestizas to nepantlas and
 nepantleras: Anzaldúan theories for social change. *Human Architecture:
 Journal of the Sociology of Self-Knowledge, 4,* 5–16.
Krings, A., Victor, B. G., Mathias, J., & Perron, B. E. (2020). Environmental
 social work in the disciplinary literature, 1991–2015. *International Social
 Work, 63*(3), 275–290. https://doi.org/10.1177/0020872818788397
Lysack, M. (2010). Environmental decline and climate change: Fostering social
 and environmental justice on a warming planet. In N. Negi & R. Furman
 (Eds.), *Transnational social work* (pp. 52–75). Columbia University Press.
Lysack, M. (2011). Building capacity for environmental engagement and
 leadership: An ecosocial work perspective. *International Journal of Social
 Welfare, 21*(3), pp. 260–269. https://doi.org/10.1111/j.1468-2397.2011
 .00854.x

MacDonald, S-A., Carlton, R., Jetté, C., & Cloos, P. (2018). Plan cadre, SVS 3517. In *Travail social et environnement* [course]. École de travail social, Université de Montréal. https://travail-social.umontreal.ca/public/FAS /travail_social/Documents/1-Programmes-cours/1-cycle/2018A_SVS3517 _Travail_social_et_environnement.pdf

Macfarlane, J. (2019). *Montreal expects more brutal heat waves, vows to improve response.* CBC. https://www.cbc.ca/news/canada/montreal/montreal -public-health-extreme-heat-plan-1.5136993

Maldonado-Gonzalez, A.-L. (2009). Que peut faire le travail social en environne-ment au Québec? *Le sociographe, 2*(29), 83–91.https://www.cairn.info /revue-le-sociographe-2009-2-page-83.htm

Maltais, D., Bolduc, V., Gauthier, V., & Gauthier, S. (2015). Les retombées de l'intervention en situation de crise, de tragédie ou de sinistre sur la vie professionnelle et personnelle des intervenants sociaux des CSSS du Québec. *Revue Intervention, 142*, 51–64. https://revueintervention.org /wp-content/uploads/2015/07/intervention_142_6_les-retombees-de -l-intervention.pdf

Maltais, D., & Gauthier, S. (2008). Les catastrophes dites naturelles: Un construit social. In *Comptes rendus de la 4e Conférence canadienne sur les géorisques: Des causes à la gestion*, pp. 1–8. https://cgs.ca/docs/geohazards /GeoHazards4/geohazard/0_Keynotes/Maltais.pdf

Maltais, D., Lansard, A-L., Roy, M., Généreux, M., Fortin, G., Cherblanc, J., Bergeron-Leclerc, C., & Pouliot, E. (2020). Post-disaster health status of train derailment victims with posttraumatic growth. *Australasian Journal of Disaster and Trauma Studies, 24*(1), 51–63.

Maltais, D., & Rheault, M.-A. (2005). *L'intervention sociale en cas de catastrophe.* Presses de l'Université du Québec. http://international.scholarvox.com /book/88801460

Maltais, D., Robichaud, S., & Simard, A. (2000). Redéfinition de l'habitat et santé mentale des sinistrés suite à une inondation. *Santé mentale au Québec, 25*(1), 74–94. https://doi.org/10.7202/013025ar

Maltais, D., Robichaud, S., & Simard, A. (2012). *Sinistres et intervenants: Essai.* J.-M. Tremblay. http://doi.org/10.1522/030566275

Maltais, D., Tremblay, A.-J., Labra, O., Fortin, G., Généreux, M., Roy, M., & Lansard, A.-L. (2019). Seniors who experienced the Lac-Mégantic train derailment tragedy: What are the consequences on physical and mental health? *Gerontology and Geriatric Medicine, 5*, 2333721419846191. https:// doi.org/10.1177/2333721419846191. Medline:31192276

Maltais, D., Tremblay, S., & Côté, N. (2006). *Intervention en situation de désastre: Connaître les conséquences de l'exposition aux catastrophes pour mieux intervenir.* Groupe de recherche et d'intervention régionales. https://constellation .uqac.ca/2847/

Mary, N. L. (2008). *Social work in a sustainable world*. Lyceum Books.

Mason, L. R., Shires, M. K., Arwood, C., & Borst, A. (2017). Social work research and global environmental change. *Journal of the Society for Social Work and Research, 8*(4), 645–672. https://doi.org/10.1086/694789

McKinnon, J., & Alston, M. (2017). *Ecological social work: Towards sustainability*. Red Globe.

Miller, S. E., & Hayward, R. A. (2014). Social work education's role in addressing people and a planet at risk. *Social Work Education, 33*(3), 280–295. https://doi.org/10.1080/02615479.2013.805192

Moeke-Pickering, T., & Partridge, C. (2014). Service social autochtone – Incorporer la vision autochtone du monde dans les stages pratiques en service social. *Reflets, 20*(1), pp. 150–169. https://www.erudit.org/fr/revues/ref/2014-v20-n1-ref01469/1025800ar/

Naples, N. A. (2003). *Feminism and method: Ethnography discourse analysis and activist research*. Routledge.

Nesmith, A., & Smyth, N. (2015). Environmental justice and social work education: Social workers' professional perspectives. *Social Work Education, 34*(5), 484–501. https://doi.org/10.1080/02615479.2015.1063600

Nicholson, A. (Host). (2021, June 3). Eco-social work from a professional training perspective [Audio podcast episode]. In *Eco social work in Australia*. HOPE. https://newworldviews.podbean.com/e/eco-social-work-from-a-professional-training-perspective/

OTSTCFQ. (2012). Ordre des travailleurs sociaux et des thérapeutes conjugaux et familiaux du Québec. *Référentiel de compétences des travailleuses sociales et des travailleurs sociaux*. https://www1.otstcfq.org/sites/default/files/referentiel_de_competences_des_travailleurs_sociaux.pdf

Peeters, J. (2012). The place of social work in sustainable development: Towards eco-social practice. *International Journal of Social Welfare, 21*(1), 105–107. https://doi.org/10.1111/j.1468-2397.2011.00856.x

Philip, D., & Reisch, M. (2015). Rethinking social work's interpretation of "environmental justice": From local to global. *Social Work Education, 34*(5), 471–483. https://doi.org/10.1080/02615479.2015.1063602

Powers, M. C. F. (2017). Transforming the profession: Social workers' expanding response to the environmental crisis. In A.-L. Matthies & K. Narhi, *The ecosocial transition of societies: The contribution of social work and social policy* (pp. 286–300). Routledge. https://www.taylorfrancis.com/books/9781317034605

Powers, M. C. F., & Engstrom, S. (2020). Radical self-care for social workers in the global climate crisis. *Social Work, 65*(1), 29–37. https://doi.org/10.1093/sw/swz043. Medline:31828329

Powers, M. C. F., Schmitz, C., & Beckwith Moritz, M. (2019). Preparing social workers for ecosocial work practice and community building. *Journal of*

Community Practice, 27(3–4), 446–459. https://doi.org/10.1080/10705422
.2019.1657217

Rambaree, K., Powers M. C. F., & Smith, R. J. (2019). Ecosocial work and
social change in community practice. *Journal of Community Practice, 27*(3–4),
205–212. https://doi.org/10.1080/10705422.2019.1660516

Ramsay, S., & Boddy, J. (2017). Environmental social work: A concept analysis.
British Journal of Social Work, 47(1), 68–86. https://doi.org/10.1093/bjsw
/bcw078

Robichaud, S., Maltais, D., Lalande, G., Simard, A., & Moffat, G. (2001). Les
inondations de juillet 1996: Une série d'événements stressants. *Service social,
48*(1), 16–33. https://doi.org/10.7202/006875ar

Schibli, K. (2020). *Climate change and social work: 2020 position statement.*
Canadian Association of Social Workers. https://www.casw-acts.ca/files
/documents/SW_and_Climate_Change_Final_PDF.pdf

Schlossberg, D. (2007). *Defining environmental justice: Theories, movements and
nature.* Oxford University Press.

Schmitz, C. L., Matyok, T., James, C. D., & Sloan, L. M. (2013). Environmental
sustainability: Educating social workers for interdisciplinary practice. In M.
Gray, J. Coates, & T. Hetherington (Eds.), *Environmental social work*
(pp. 260–279). Routledge.

Teixeira, S., & Krings, A. (2015). Sustainable social work: An environmental
justice framework for social work education. *Social Work Education, 34*(5),
513–527. https://doi.org/10.1080/02615479.2015.1063601

Tronto, J. C. (1993). *Moral boundaries: A political argument for an ethic of care.*
Routledge.

Ungar, M. (2002). A deeper, more social ecological social work practice. *Social
Service Review, 76*(3), 480–497. https://doi.org/10.1086/341185

Université de Québec en Outaouais. (2018). Department of Social Work
Mission Statement. https://uqo.ca/dep/travail-social/enonce-mission

Watt-Cloutier, S. (2015). *The right to be cold: One woman's story of protecting her
culture, the Arctic and the whole planet.* Penguin Random House Canada.

Watt-Cloutier, S. (2016, September 13). *Human trauma and climate trauma as one*
[Video]. Youtube. https://www.youtube.com/watch?v=5nn-awZbMVo

WHO (World Health Organization). (2021, October 30). *Climate change and
health.* https://www.who.int/news-room/fact-sheets/detail/climate-change
-and-health

Zapf, M. K. (2009). *Social work and the environment: Understanding people and place.*
Canadian Scholars

11 Greening Social Work Education: Teaching Environmental Rights in Community Practice

DAVID ANDROFF

In April 2014, United States secretary of state John Kerry declared climate change to be the challenge of a generation – as great a social problem as poverty (Kerry, 2014). The *Global Agenda for Social Work and Social Development* included environmental sustainability as a core pillar (Jones & Truell, 2012). The US Council on Social Work Education's (CSWE) 2015 Education and Policy Accreditation Standards included advancing environmental justice as a core competency. Emphasis upon the environment has grown within social work professional organizations, at conferences, and in the academic literature (Gray & Coates, 2012; Hessle, 2012). Green social work is an emerging priority area for social work practice (Dominelli, 2012, 2018). This chapter offers a US perspective on greening social work education.

Background

Social work and environmental issues are linked through shared priorities of social and environmental justice and human and environmental rights (McKinnon, 2008). Concern for people's social environment has been a distinguishing element of social work. Recent work has drawn attention to the negative social consequences of environmental problems, such as disasters, pollution, lack of access to food and clean water, and climate change. Although vulnerable, oppressed, and marginalized populations suffer disproportionately from environmental crises, social workers have not taken a leading role in these issues (Jones, 2010; McKinnon, 2008).

A growing body of environmental social work literature (Besthorn, 2001, 2002; Coates, 2003; Rogge, 1998) has advanced systems-based arguments for the adoption of an ecologically oriented model of social work within mainstream practice (Jones, 2010). Besthorn (2001, 2002, 2012) established connections between social work and deep ecology. Coates (2003) addressed modernity, ecology, and social work. Rogge (1998) explored the social consequences of environmental toxins.

Green social work (Dominelli, 2012, 2018) is an approach that seeks to shift the social work paradigm towards environmental action to promote environmental rights and justice, by engaging the profession through connections to social justice and human rights. Dominelli (2012, 2018) calls upon social work to respond to environmental crises by addressing the social inequalities and disparities resulting from scarce natural resources and patterns of globalization, consumption, and industrialization. Green social work is a holistic approach to integrate the interdependencies between people and the sociocultural, economic, and physical environments as a means of protecting the environment and improving people's overall well-being.

These developments represent an opportunity for social work to expand its professional capacity in a world increasingly affected by environmental changes. Despite the pressing nature of environmental challenges, however, they have not been widely incorporated into social work education in the United States (Pillai & Gupta, 2013). If social workers are to provide solutions, they must be educated on environmental issues (Besthorn, 2012). If social workers are to work with communities responding to climate change, green social work must be addressed in the curricula (Borrell et al., 2010). The greening of social work education requires explicit links between social justice and environmental justice (McKinnon, 2008), and pedagogical approaches that highlight ecological literacy, social sustainability, and models of action and activism (Jones, 2010; McKinnon, 2008).

Pedagogical Framework

Community practice, focused on working with communities to address social, economic, and political forces, is a natural point to integrate green social work (Dominelli, 2012, 2018; Weil, 2013). This chapter utilizes a comparative case study approach to demonstrate how environmental rights can be incorporated within a community practice course.

According to Yin (2003), a case study design is appropriate when the focus of the study is to answer "how" or "why" research questions. To demonstrate how the topic of environmental rights can best be incorporated into macro community practice social work curricula, this chapter focuses on two case studies drawn from a required, semester-long class for MSW students, specializing in macro practice in a large public university in the south-western United States. The year-long macro practice concentration prepares students to engage in planned approaches to social change via coursework on program planning, program evaluation, administrative practice, and policy practice. The community practice course teaches community practice models (Weil, 2013), social change theories (Meenaghan et al., 2005), and community-organizing practice skills, including framing (Lakoff, 2004), strategic planning (Bobo et al., 2010), tactics, and recruitment (Alinsky, 1971).

In a community participation class project, students engage in partnership with a community organization and contribute community practice skills. In small groups, students explore community change opportunities in which they can participate and apply practice skills. They are encouraged to select their own groups and partners and to submit project proposals for the instructor's review. Students are expected to incorporate theoretical perspectives in their projects, which culminate in a final presentation and paper.

Green Social Work Case Studies

The two case studies discussed in this chapter are drawn from student projects that addressed social facets of environmental issues and applied community practice models to mobilize communities to respond to environmental challenges. Each case study is described below in six parts, with an overview, the community change opportunity, description of the community partner, description of the project, and summary of outcomes. Table 11.1 indicates the background issue, the population affected, the environmental right(s) at risk, the associated social work ethical principle, and the community change opportunity.

Case 1: Building a Community Garden with Unhoused Families

This project focused on unhoused families' lack of access to green space in shelters. Students partnered with a temporary housing shelter, Vista Colina (https://www.azhousinginc.org/vista-colina.html), that serves unhoused families. Residents of the shelter rarely interacted with each other, or with neighbourhood residents surrounding the shelter facility; the institutional nature of the temporary shelter contained no green spaces for the residents. The project aimed to use a community development model (Weil, 2013) to foster relationship building between shelter residents, build a sense of community among residents, and create a green space in the form of a community garden. Community gardens are an important tool for green social work, with many community

Table 11.1. Case Studies

Issue	Population	Environmental Right	Social Work Principle	Change Opportunity
1 Lack of community in shelter housing	Unhoused families	The right to sustainable development	Dignity and worth of the person	Lack of green space in temporary shelter
2 Environmental destruction, open-pit mining	Rural residents	The right to preservation	Participation	Lack of control over local resources

Source: Adapted from Androff, Fike, & Rorke (2017), p. 401.

benefits (Teig et al., 2009), and community building is a key community practice strategy (Androff, 2018).

UNHOUSED FAMILIES AND COMMUNITY GARDENS
There are an estimated 77,157 unhoused families in the United States, representing 37.8 per cent of the total unhoused population (National Alliance to End Homelessness [NAEH], 2013). Despite reductions in the number of people experiencing chronic lack of housing, the population of unhoused families continues to increase, as does the number of unhoused children in families (NAEH, 2013). Traditional models of shelter and service delivery have been criticized for neglecting the health and wellness of shelter residents, increasing the risk of malnutrition, substance abuse, and mental illness (Wiecha et al., 1991). Attending to residents' dignity has been linked to optimum shelter service delivery (Shier et al., 2007), as has enhancing relationships within shelters, including with the neighbouring community (Walsh et al., 2009). The built environment of shelters also influences service delivery and service users' experiences; access to green space is a critical element in how the built environment shapes resident health and activity (Shier et al., 2007).

Community development is a promising approach for working with unhoused people (Uzo, 2006). Community variables such as civic engagement, social networks, and collective efficacy have been linked to community members' health and quality of life (Hanna, 2000; Teig et al., 2009). Community gardens are an important community and environmental tool (Besthorn, 2013; Delgado, 2000), and are associated with participants' health (Litt et al., 2011; Saldivar-Tanaka & Krasny, 2004). They have been identified as a community practice intervention with special relevance for rebuilding communities in urban settings, with the potential to increase community engagement and "urban environmentalism" (Delgado, 2000, p. 89; Hanna, 2000). The community development benefits of community gardens include decreased isolation, increased socialization, a sense of community, and increased local control over shared resources (Delgado, 2000). Communities benefit from community gardens, regardless of engagement, through recreational opportunities, ecological preservation, and improved air quality (Saldivar-Tanaka & Krasny, 2004).

CENTRAL ARIZONA SHELTER SERVICES AND VISTA COLINA

Central Arizona Shelter Services (CASS) has operated as a non-profit since 1984 to meet the temporary housing needs of unhoused people, and is the largest provider of shelters and services in the state, with a mission to empower people and end homelessness through shelter and supportive services (www.cassaz.org). CASS programs include shelters, employment services, case management, accredited childcare programs, a dental clinic, a street outreach program, and a veterans' program. Its three shelters nightly house over one thousand people.

CASS opened a family shelter, Vista Colina, in 1993 to meet the unique needs of unhoused families. Vista Colina provides apartment housing for ninety days, serving thirty-nine families at a time or about eight hundred people annually. Residents work with case managers and employment specialists and have access to supportive services during their stay and after they exit the shelter. CASS and Vista Colina rely heavily upon volunteers and community donations for their programming and to provide residents with necessities.

COMMUNITY GARDENS

The student project aimed to help residents build a closer community through planting a community garden at Vista Colina. Project goals included giving residents access to green space within their shelter, an opportunity to learn gardening skills, and participation in a stress-relieving activity. The garden was also geared towards improving community relations and promoting trust with shelter resident neighbours, as unhoused families often suffer from negative social perceptions that contribute to community distrust (Karim et al., 2006). Students applied a community development model of practice (Weil, 2013) and utilized the theory of community building (Weil, 1996) to engage shelter administrators, staff, residents, and neighbours and promote their participation. Students recruited volunteer gardeners, solicited donations, and coordinated the planting.

ENGAGING STAKEHOLDERS, FRAMING, OUTREACH, AND RECRUITMENT

The students applied community practice tactics of engaging stake-holders, framing, fundraising, and recruitment (Alinksy, 1971; Bobo et al., 2010; Lakoff, 2004). Students began their initiative with consultations with shelter stakeholders, including agency staff, shelter residents, and neighbours. They met with the CASS administrators, including the volunteer coordinator, and secured approval for their project and access to the organization's database of volunteers. Student consultations with residents, as the primary constituency, were the most extensive, assessing their need for community building and access to green space – particularly for their children. Student consultations with the shelter's neighbours focused on highlighting positive perceptions of the shelter and securing in-kind donations to support the garden.

In order to maximize their outreach, recruitment, and fundraising efforts, the students constructed a message to communicate the project's goal and its value to the community: "Building a community garden helps families to build relationships with neighbours, and gives them something to work toward for the future." The students consciously avoided using the frame of "homelessness" when identifying shelter residents as the beneficiaries of the garden, to combat the negative stereotypes of the residents as needy, weak, and undeserving. This message prevented the alienation of potential supporters by avoiding politically divisive or polarizing language (Lakoff, 2004). Instead, they used the more generalized and socially acceptable frame of family, which invoked positive associations and empathy. The use of both "family" and "work" frames in the message presented shelter residents to neighbours and donors as hard working and deserving, worthy of dignity, respect, and support. These ideas about family and rewarding people for hard work appeal to both conservative and liberal political ideologies (Lakoff, 2004).

Students increased awareness and support for their project by publicizing the garden through word of mouth and by distributing flyers among shelter residents, organization staff, and neighbours. This was supplemented with a letter-writing campaign informing potential donors about the project and requesting donations of gift cards, plants, and tools to build the garden. The students targeted potential donors from nearby businesses, nurseries, and neighbourhood community members, then made initial contact through in-person meetings and hand delivery of letters, and followed up in person with each business and community member. Additional flyers were distributed to recruit resident and neighbour participation in the garden-planting event.

OUTCOMES

The project was successful in the creation of a community garden at Vista Colina. The community garden was built by resident families, neighbours, and students. The students were successful in obtaining nursery donations and conducted additional research about seeds, soil, and planting techniques. Vista Colina's resident and neighbourhood children spread the soft mulch while shelter and neighbourhood adults and the students performed the hard labour of pick-axing the tough desert caliche soil. The planting brought together children and parents from different families to participate in planting their own community garden.

The in-kind donations from targeted businesses were critical to the garden's success, as they provided the raw materials required to create the garden. The donations were secured due to the in-person follow-up with donors. This reveals a powerful community practice strategy, as potential donors may have more difficulty refusing an in-person request to help the local community than an impersonal email contact (Bobo et al., 2010). Securing the in-kind donations was effective in encouraging participation from residents, who showed interest in joining the project once the tools, soil, and plants were visible. Students were more successful in soliciting donations from smaller local nurseries; they were unable to solicit resources from large retail chains. The small scale of the project meant that a few donations from a few sources was sufficient to complete the planned tasks. However, students spent a disproportionate amount of time pursuing donations from large retailers that did not materialize.

Case 2: Community Organizing for Environmental Rights

This case study comprises a traditional grass-roots community-organizing campaign (Alinksy, 1971) to mobilize political action against powerful corporate interests threatening environmental preservation. When a mining company threatened to degrade the local ecosystem on public lands, students partnered with an environmental rights group, Save the Scenic Santa Ritas (www.scenicsantaritas.org) to organize a grass-roots campaign to block the mine. Community organizing and advocacy are fundamental components of community practice (Ezell, 2001), and in this case study students were able to implement political and social action (Weil, 2013). The environmental movement has a long history of community organizing, political advocacy, and coalition building (Pilisuk et al., 1996); macro social work practitioners can collaborate with environmental activists and advocate for environmental protection and sustainability and against the destruction and depletion of natural resources (Dominelli, 2012, 2018).

OPEN-PIT MINING AND ENVIRONMENTAL PRESERVATION

Open-pit mining, also known as surface or strip mining, involves significant negative environmental consequences, including destruction and degradation of land, generation of excessive noise and dust, release of poisonous gases, and water pollution (Dudka & Adriano, 1997). Open-pit mining physically transforms the environment, through drilling and blasting, transportation of machinery and raw materials, and corrosion, and the resultant waste – toxic materials and acidic water – creates an environmental concern for residents in proximity to the mining activities, who have to live with the effects of the activity long after operations cease (Monjezi et al., 2009). This can leave permanent negative impacts on the topography, soil, vegetation, fresh waters, and ecosystems. Thus, opposition to such mining efforts is not only a matter of local advocacy, but also fits the universal definition of environmentalism.

In 2005, a mining company proposed an open-pit copper mine over a mile wide and over two thousand feet deep on a public/private land swath in southern Arizona, threatening the environmental preservation of the Santa Rita and Patagonia mountain ranges (*Our national forests at risk*, 2007). The company's proposed mining operations were expected to last for twenty years, and further environmental destruction could have resulted from inadequate reclamation or restoration of the land and ecosystem to a natural or usable state. Local residents were suddenly faced with the prospect of environmental devastation, degradation, and waste brought on by a foreign company, and those in opposition needed a unified and collaborative voice to stave off a large corporate interest with deep pockets.

SAVE THE SCENIC SANTA RITAS

Save the Scenic Santa Ritas (SSSR) is a volunteer-based, non-profit organization formed in 1996 by residents of the Santa Rita mountain range to block previous open-pit mining. Local residents formed an environmental preservation coalition with the Sierra Club (www.sierraclub.org), Audubon Society (www.audubon.org), and League of Conservation Voters (www.lcv.org) and successfully fought the proposal, which was withdrawn in 1998. Buoyed by their success, SSSR continued to conduct outreach efforts to protect the Santa Rita mountain range from future mining propositions. Individual members of SSSR represent communities from southern Arizona along the US–Mexico border; their communities tend to be small, rural, diverse, and economically reliant upon tourism. SSSR's mission is to "protect the scenic, aesthetic, recreational, environmental and wildlife values" of the mountains through education, outreach, and protection from degradation (www.scenics antaritas.org/about-us/, para. 2). While SSSR works to prevent environmental destruction through mining, the organization's long-term goal is to secure permanent protection for the mountain and valley regions of the south-west. Their goal of environmental preservation is critical to maintaining their communities' economic and social health and preventing the intrusion of outside companies that may exacerbate social inequality in the region.

ENVIRONMENTAL ACTIVISM AS SOCIAL WORK

Students collaborated with SSSR on an environmental activism campaign to increase the participation of the southern Arizona communities most affected by the mine, primarily through grass-roots community organizing. Students extended the SSSR community education program by developing media contacts, increasing volunteer participation, fundraising, and working on the sustainability of SSSR beyond their current campaign. They employed a political action model of practice (Weil, 2013) for their advocacy project, which was based on the theoretical premise of community organizing (Alinsky, 1971). Participation of local communities in the decisions that affect their welfare is a key social work value and central purpose of community practice (Bobo et al., 2010; Weil, 2013). In order to build the capacity of SSSR and to build support for its environmental advocacy in southern Arizona, students engaged in coalition building, recruitment, and fundraising.

COALITION BUILDING, RECRUITING VOLUNTEERS, AND FUNDRAISING

In consultation with SSSR leadership and staff, students developed a project to build public support for the SSSR campaign against the mining proposition, by increasing community participation in advocacy and the political process – two elements that would increase the visibility and viability of the opposition effort. They employed tactics of coalition building, volunteer recruitment, and fundraising to accomplish their project goals. The students used coalition building to broaden support for environmental preservation of the region's natural resources and beauty with business and community interests that were not purely environmentalism based and thus had not been approached by SSSR. They recruited local businesses to join with SSSR to voice and advertise their opposition to the mine, community members to serve as volunteers, and donors for fundraising. Students coordinated volunteers to conduct community-organizing techniques such as gathering petition signatures, tabling events, phone banking, and organizing demonstrations. They maintained supporter and donor lists to raise financial resources to combat the pro-mine contingent's expensive media campaign.

In addition, students worked to reframe the issue of mining in southern Arizona, nicknamed the "Copper State" for the industry's role in its history. Through an extensive radio and television media campaign, pro-mine supporters promoted the mine as creating opportunity for new jobs and economic development for rural residents. The students worked with SSSR to reframe the mine as unfair to existing businesses in the community by depleting resources and ravaging the natural beauty that attracts tourism and investment. This framing strategy (Lakoff, 2004) was designed to influence public opinion while at the same time establishing the issue as relevant to a wide spectrum of community members and encouraging their participation in the organization regardless of their propensity for environmentalism (Bobo et al., 2010). The students communicated their framework through press releases, media contacts, active kiosk displays at events, and email blasts.

OUTCOMES

Students were successful in implementing community-organizing tactics to generate community support to block the proposed mine. The tactics were strategically chosen to increase community participation as well as minimize cost, as they had no official budget. Fundraising was a particular strength, as SSSR was able to draw donations from local business and community supporters. The engagement of local businesses was also essential to diversification of stakeholders. The development and coordination of SSSR's volunteer network was also critical to facilitate the community-organizing effort. The students' project strengthened SSSR's coalition and partnerships and increased community participation.

Discussion

These case studies demonstrate that students can successfully apply community practice skills to environmental issues. Table 11.2 shows how environmental rights were incorporated into macro social work education.

The case studies reveal how green social work can fit community practice models, theoretical perspectives, and applied skills such as outreach and recruitment, engaging stakeholders and furthering coalition building, fundraising, framing, research, and organizational reform

Table 11.2. Community Practice Dimensions

Project	Model of Practice	Theoretical Basis	Tactics	Outcome
1 Building a community garden	Community development	Community building	Engaging stakeholders, fundraising, recruitment	Organized shelter residents to plant community garden using in-kind donations
2 Environmental activism as social work	Political action	Community organizing	Coalition building, fundraising, recruitment	Conducted advocacy campaign against pro-mining proposition

Source: Adapted from Androff, Fike, & Rorke (2017), p. 409.

(Alinsky, 1971; Bobo et al., 2010; Ezell, 2001; Schultz, 2003). While each project faced challenges and was limited by the scope of the assignment, the semester time frame, and student resources, both were successful in making progress towards community partners' goals of protecting environmental rights. Thus, students learned how environmental rights are linked to social justice.

Implications

These case studies are excellent examples of green social work. They illustrate the interconnection of social justice, human rights, and environmental rights in the fields of health, poverty, and community practice (Coates, 2003; Dominelli, 2012, 2018). One essential key to the projects' success was students partnering with local organizations. This allowed students to quickly engage with ongoing community change efforts. Another lesson is the important role of narrative framing and community education for green social work (Androff, 2018; Lakoff, 2004). These projects also combatted negative stereotypes by constructing messages to communicate the organizations' values and facilitate outreach and recruitment. Future efforts should include social media skills development to amplify campaign messages, recruitment, and impact.

In addition, more research is required to support the greening of social work education. Future studies should also survey contemporary social work curricula in the United States to investigate what, if any, green content is being included in social work classes. For example, social work education research should measure social work students' attitudes towards, knowledge of, interest in, and experiences with environmental issues and green social work concerns. A promising model could be similar to the scales developed by McPherson and Abell (2012) to study social work students' exposure to and depth of knowledge of human rights. Such measurement would help to identify a baseline of social work student knowledge of and interest in green issues, which could be used for developing social work curriculum adaptations and extensions to incorporate awareness of green issues, ecological literacy (Jones, 2010), and green social work practice interventions promoting social sustainability (McKinnon, 2008).

Ultimately, these cases reveal that social workers can strengthen communities' capacity to respond to environmental issues. They represent an initial step towards "an ecological revolution in social work education" (Jones, 2010, p. 72). Using community project assignments for students to explore environmental issues and develop practice skills that advance environmental rights is a promising approach to greening social work education (McKinnon, 2008). Supplemented with green course material, such experiences are likely to make explicit for students the links between social and environmental justice, between human and environmental rights, and the growing interdependence between social work practice and environmental sustainability.

Acknowledgment

This chapter is adapted and reprinted with permission from Androff, D., Fike, C., & Rorke, J. (2017), Greening social work education: Teaching environmental rights and sustainability in community practice, *Journal of Social Work Education, 53*(3), 399–413.

REFERENCES

Alinsky, S. (1971). *Rules for radicals: A pragmatic primer for realistic radicals.* Random House.

Androff, D. (2018). A case study of a grassroots Truth and Reconciliation Commission from a community practice perspective. *Journal of Social Work, 18*(3), 273–287. https://doi.org/10.1177/1468017316654361

Androff, D., Fike, C., & Rorke, J. (2017). Greening social work education: Teaching environmental rights and sustainability in community practice. *Journal of Social Work Education, 53*(3), 399–413. https://doi.org/10.1080/10437797.2016.1266976

Besthorn, F. (2001). Is it time for a new ecological approach to social work: What is the environment telling us? *Spirituality and Social Work Forum, 9,* 2–5.

Besthorn, F. (2002). Radical environmentalism and the ecological self. *Journal of Progressive Human Services, 13*(1), 53–72. https://doi.org/10.1300/J059v13n01_04

Besthorn, F. (2012). Deep ecology's contributions to social work: A ten-year retrospective. *International Journal of Social Welfare, 21*(3), 248–259. https://doi.org/10.1111/j.1468-2397.2011.00850.x

Besthorn, F. (2013). Vertical farming: Social work and sustainable urban agriculture in an age of global food crises. *Australian Social Work, 66*, 187–203. doi:10.1080/0312407X.2012.716448

Bobo, K., Kendall, J., & Max, S. (2010). *Organizing for social change: Midwest Academy manual for activists* (4th ed.). Forum.

Borrell, J., Lane, S., & Fraser, S. (2010). Integrating environmental issues into social work practice: Lessons learnt from domestic energy auditing. *Australian Social Work, 63*(3), 315–328. https://doi.org/10.1080/03124070903061669

Coates, J. (2003). *Ecology and social work: Toward a new paradigm*. Fernwood.

Delgado, M. (2000). *Community social work practice in an urban context: The potential of a capacity-enhancement perspective*. Oxford University Press.

Dominelli, L. (2012). *Green social work: From environmental crises to environmental justice*. Polity.

Dominelli, L. (Ed.). (2018). *The Routledge handbook of green social work*. Taylor and Francis.

Dudka, S., & Adriano, D. (1997). Environmental impacts of metal ore mining and processing: A review. *Journal of Environmental Quality, 26*(3), 590–602. https://doi.org/10.2134/jeq1997.00472425002600030003x

Ezell, M. (2001). *Advocacy in the human services*. Brooks/Cole.

Gray, M., & Coates, J. (2012). Environmental ethics for social work: Social work's responsibility to the non-human world. *International Journal of Social Welfare, 21*(3), 239–247. https://doi.org/10.1111/j.1468-2397.2011.00852.x

Hanna, A., & Oh, P. (2000). Rethinking urban poverty: A look at community gardens. *Bulletin of Science, Technology & Society, 20*(3), 207–216. https://doi.org/10.1177/027046760002000308

Hessle, S. (2012). Editorial. *International Journal of Social Welfare, 21*(3), 229.

Jones, D., & Truell, R. (2012). The Global Agenda for Social Work and Social Development: A place to link together and be effective in a globalized world. *International Social Work, 55*(4), 454–472. https://doi.org/10.1177/0020872812440587

Jones, P. (2010). Responding to the ecological crisis: Transformative pathways for social work education. *Journal of Social Work Education, 46*(1), 67–84. https://doi.org/10.5175/JSWE.2010.200800073

Karim, K., Tischler, P., Gregory, P., & Vostanis, P. (2006). Homeless children and parents: Short-term mental health outcome. *International Journal of Social Psychiatry, 52*(5), 447–458. https://doi.org/10.1177/0020764006066830. Medline:17278346

Kerry, J. (2014). *Remarks on climate change.* http://www.state.gov/secretary/remarks/2014/02/221704.htm

Lakoff, G. (2004). *Don't think of an elephant!: Know your values and frame the debate.* Chelsea Green Publishing.

Litt, J., Soobader, M., Turbin, M., Hale, J., Buchenau, M., & Marshall, J. (2011). The influence of social involvement, neighborhood aesthetics, and community garden participation on fruit and vegetable consumption. *American Journal of Public Health, 101*(8), 1466–1473. https://doi.org/10.2105/AJPH.2010.300111. Medline:21680931

McKinnon, J. (2008). Exploring the nexus between social work and the environment. *Australian Social Work, 61*(3), 256–268. https://doi.org/10.1080/03124070802178275

McPherson, J., & Abell, N. (2012). Human rights engagement and exposure in social work: New scales to challenge social work education. *Research in Social Work Practice, 22*, 704–713. https://doi.org/10.1177/1049731512454196

Meenaghan, T., Gibbons, W., & McNutt, J. (2005). Working with communities. In *Generalist practice in larger settings: Knowledge and skill concepts* (pp. 39–66). Lyceum Books.

Monjezi, M., Shahriar, K., Dehghani, H., & Namin, F. (2009). Environmental impact assessment of open pit mining in Iran. *Environmental Geology, 58*, 205–216. https://doi.org/10.1007/s00254-008-1509-4

National Alliance to End Homelessness (NAEH). (2013). *The state of homelessness in America 2013.* http://b.3cdn.net/naeh/bb34a7e4cd84ee985c_3vm6r7cjh.pdf

Our national forests at risk: The 1872 mining law and its impact on the Santa Rita Mountains of Arizona. Oversight Field Hearing before the Subcommittee on Energy And Mineral Resources, joint with the Subcommittee on Natural Resources of the US House of Representatives, 110th Cong. (2007). http://www.gpo.gov/fdsys/pkg/CHRG-110hhrg33608/html/CHRG-110hhrg33608.htm

Pilisuk, M., McAllister, J., & Rothman, J. (1996). Coming together for action: The challenge of contemporary grassroots community organizing. *Journal of Social Issues, 52*(1), 15–37. https://doi.org/10.1111/j.1540-4560.1996.tb01359.x

Pillai, V., & Gupta, R. (2013). *The greening of social work.* Council on Social Work Education, Global Commission. http://www.cswe.org/CentersInitiatives/KAKI/50754/66942.aspx

Rogge, M. (1998). Toxic risk, resilience, and justice in Chattanooga. In M. Hoff (Ed.), *Sustainable community development: Studies in economic, environmental, and cultural revitalization* (pp. 105–122). Lewis.

Saldivar-Tanaka, L., & Krasny, M. E. (2004). Culturing community development, neighborhood open space, and civic agriculture: The case of Latino community gardens in New York. *Agriculture and human values, 21*(4), 399–412. https://doi.org/10.1023/B:AHUM.0000047207.57128.a5

Shultz, J. (2003). *The democracy owners' manual: A practical guide to changing the world.* New Brunswick, NJ: Rutgers University Press.

Shier, M., Walsh, C., & Graham, J. (2007). Conceptualizing optimum homeless shelter service delivery: The interconnection between programming, community, and the built environment. *Canadian Journal of Urban Research, 16*(1), 58–75.

Teig, E., Amulya, J., Bardwell, L., Buchenau, M., Marshall, J., & Litt, J. (2009). Collective efficacy in Denver, Colorado: Strengthening neighborhoods and health through community gardens. *Health & Place, 15*(4), 1115–1122. https://doi.org/10.1016/j.healthplace.2009.06.003. Medline:19577947

Uzo, A. (2006). When a bed is a home: The challenges and paradoxes of community development in a shared-housing program for homeless people. *Canadian Review of Social Policy, 58,* 62–83.

Walsh, C., Graham, J., & Shier, M. (2009). Toward a common goal for shelter service. *Social Development Issues, 31*(2), 57–69.

Weil, M. (1996). Community building: Building community practice. *Social Work, 41*(5), 481–499

Weil, M. (Ed.) (2013). *The handbook of community practice* (2nd ed.). Sage.

Wiecha, J., Dwyer, J., & Dunn-Strohecker, M. (1991). Nutrition and health service needs among the homeless. *Public Health Reports, 106*(4), 364–374. Medline:1908587

Yin, R. (2003). *Case study research and methods* (3rd ed.). Sage.

12 The Red-Green Manifesto for Greening Social Work Education

SUSAN HILLOCK

The 1997 Tbilisi Intergovernmental Conference on Environmental Education's sustainability educational objectives (Shephard, 2010) were the first attempt to develop standards for incorporating environmental content into higher education. Congruent with this philosophical lens, this book has highlighted key issues, debates, and concepts that provide us with the facts, knowledge, research, and critical analyses that can help social work educators teach this content and transform our curricula. Contributors have also presented useful ideas related to innovative interdisciplinary theoretical approaches, analyses, and constructs that firmly land within a green, eco-critical, ecological/social justice, and anti-oppressive lens, a perspective that this book's contributors agree is necessary to achieve well-being for all humans, animals, plants, and the Earth.

In this final chapter, I pick up on these major themes to discuss how we, as social work educators, can best contribute in terms of initiating and supporting the social and cultural paradigm shifts required to save humanity, "more-than-humans" (Abram, 1996, p. 24), and the planet. To meet this goal and assist the social work profession to mainstream these ideas and incorporate this content, I present the first ever Red-Green Manifesto for Greening Social Work Education. Based upon the research, the literature, and my personal and professional experience, this manifesto summarizes the top ten things that I think social work education needs to do (now) to green itself from the inside out.

Greening Social Work: A Moral and Ethical Imperative

This collection joins the vastly increasing number of publications and research in this area and supports the ever-growing demand for radical change within the social work profession. One of the biggest challenges facing the environmental movement is: how can we motivate ourselves (and others) to make the paradigm shifts and macro-, mezzo-, and micro-level changes that are necessary to live more cooperatively to save humanity and the planet? And, if we accept that a shift in how we view things, treat others, and behave is a fundamental step required to create healthy egalitarian societies that can live in harmony with other humans, the flora and fauna, and Earth, what are the practical steps needed to move in that direction?

As I mentioned in this book's introduction, I think that this moral and ethical dilemma speaks to the pivotal role of education as a critical (re)socialization tool and process that can shift consciousness and help humanity move towards sustainability. Martins, Mata, and Costa (2006) agree, stating that "to achieve sustainability one needs to increase people's awareness about aspects like poverty, economic development, democracy and peace" (p. 32). Indeed, two of the fundamental purposes of this book are to raise consciousness to create a "new ethic for social work" (Berger & Kelly, 1993, p. 524; Richardson & Langford, 2022) and to explore how we can introduce, learn, and teach a more humane, ecology-centred, and communitarian/collectivist lifestyle and philosophy to mobilize communities, students, and colleagues to climate action.

In addition, there are many reasons why the book's contributors think social work as a profession needs to think about and incorporate ecology and sustainability into its lexicon. A primary one is the belief that environmentalism and social work are congruent because a major part of our work includes an ethic of care, human rights and social justice approaches, community organization, a moral/ethical mandate to serve vulnerable populations, and an assessment paradigm that rests on a person-in-environment approach. If we truly support serving vulnerable populations, dismantling oppression, and promoting justice for all – what I see as essential parts of our professional identity – then saving the planet must become our mission. Eco-social work – or what Dominelli (2012) calls "green social work" – with its critique of modernity (that leaves many people behind) and recognition of the need for inclusion of environmental justice within discourses of social justice, provides a way forward. Consequently, I believe that to "green" social work, that is, to ensure that the protection of the flora, fauna, and planet become primary concerns for all, it is essential that social workers understand climate change and the relevant science to develop ecological literacy and effectively teach this content.

However, the bottom line is, if the window for making necessary change is already closed (or closing), the oceans are going to die, and most of humanity may expire by the end of this century, the time for talk therapy and counselling, as our primary professional modality, is long past and a new direction for our profession is overdue. I would argue that teaching students how to be "masters of empathy" (Brown, 1988, p. 130), "comfort victims of social issues" (Mullaly, 2006, p. 145), and perform "talk therapy" not only does a disservice to both students and future service users but is simply not adequate preparation for these coming dark times.

Instead, in this chapter, I propose that what the social work profession needs most is to make radical paradigm shifts, start a revolution, and train to become ecological warriors. To accomplish this, I call for a radical shift in social work education – far away from conventional approaches like cognitive behavioural therapy (CBT), conventional systems theory, and psychoanalysis – to education that centres Indigenous knowledges, sustainability, climate action/justice, renewable energy, and eco-critical progressive approaches (such as eco-feminism and eco-socialism) that challenge the basic tenets and underlying assumptions of capitalism, patriarchy, and colonialism.

The Red-Green Manifesto: A Radical Shift

One way to accomplish this radical shift is to build new frameworks to transform social work education and the helping professions. Based upon the research, literature, and my own personal and professional experience, I have developed the Red-Green Manifesto for Greening Social Work Education (Box 12.1) summarizing the top ten things that I think social work education needs to do (now) to make necessary paradigm shifts as well as mainstream environmental and sustainability content. It is my hope that this type of declaration might be a useful tool to help social work educators gain confidence to start greening their teaching, curricula, and institutions, and to motivate social workers to become climate warriors.

Greening Social Work Education

Before I explain the manifesto's recommendations, it is important to define what is meant by "greening." Congruent with what Dominelli (2012) calls "green social work," the term "greening" refers to social work curriculum design, content, and teaching that not only critique modernity and recognize the need for inclusion of environmental justice within social justice discourses, but also ensure that the protection of the flora, fauna, and planet is paramount (Hoff & McNutt, 1998; Stein, 2004). To accomplish this, it is essential that social workers first understand climate change and the relevant science to develop ecological literacy and effectively teach this content. To effectively green social work education, I believe that we also need to ensure that our curricula, teaching methods, and content are informed by three major concepts: intersectionality, a critical red-green perspective, and Indigenous leadership. These new ways of thinking about and acting upon the world, can be utilized to form a new educational framework for social work, similar to what Wallace (2018) calls a red-green perspective.

INTERSECTIONALITY

To be effective and relevant, this chapter (and volume) maintains, an eco-green educational approach must be intersectional, anti-racist, and feminist. Intersectional analysis encourages awareness of the differential impacts of climate change on various marginalized groups, for instance the manifestation of environmental racism as seen in the water crisis in Flint, Michigan (see Chapter 5). As discussed in this book's introduction, those who are poor, racialized, Indigenous, disabled, female, very young or old, or from the Global South are more likely to be at risk and face harsher and more longer lasting climate change conditions and outcomes, including displacement, poverty, trauma, and illness/injury, than dominant groups (Dominelli, 2018). Correspondingly, eco-feminists have been at the forefront of promoting anti-oppressive social justice values, beliefs, and approaches that are essential to saving the planet. Examples include advocating for women's reproductive, property, voting, literacy, and numeracy rights; stopping violence; and celebrating women's ways of knowing (Klemmer & McNamara, 2020; Noble, 2021). Additionally, anti-racist activists have been key to identifying environmental racism, pointing out the disparities between the Global North and South and fighting for clean air, food, and water for marginalized populations (Finney, 2014; Isla, 2019; Wallace, 2018).

A CRITICAL RED-GREEN PERSPECTIVE

To this intersectional green lens, I believe that a red perspective should be added. If we are truly concerned with the root causes of human suffering and with eradicating oppression, then I suggest we have much to learn from the left (commonly referred to as "the Reds"), that is, structural/radical, eco-feminist, anti-colonial/racist, and socialist/Marxist critical theorists (Baines, 2017). They have been instrumental in pointing out that most forms of education have been complicit in supporting neo-liberalism, "perpetuating unsustainable environmental practices" (Shepherd, 2010, p. 15), and acting as a training ground for capitalism, patriarchy, and colonialism (Bigelow, 1996).

Incorporating a socialist or "red" view (Wallace, 2018) – which means identifying and dismantling the structural forces that harm humans (and more-than-humans) – eco/green social work challenges the way we look at the world, confronting such notions as the need for expansion and progress at all cost, "man's" innate right to control and commodify the planet, viewing of humans and animals solely as objects/labourers/consumers, a for-profit mindset at the expense of all others, and reliance on fossil fuels (Dominelli, 2018; Fogel et al., 2016; Gray et al., 2013; Närhi & Matthies, 2018).

INDIGENOUS LEADERSHIP: WALKING THE RED ROAD
Central to this red-green worldview that is quintessentially feminist, anti-racist, and socialist/Marxist are Indigenous understandings of stewardship, wholism, interdependence, and connectedness in terms of our relationships with each other, nature, and the Earth (Cajete, 1994; Bigelow & Swinehart, 2014; Isla, 2019; Skwiot, 2008). Some have described this as "walking the red road" (Spirit Horse Nation, 2022). Taking this path requires educators to centre Indigenous approaches (Carlson-Manathara & Rowe, 2021), implement Canada's Truth and Reconciliation Commission's *Calls to Action* (2015), embrace Elder traditions, employ "the 5 Rs – relationship, respect, responsibility, reciprocity and restoration" (Evering & Longboat, 2013, p. 245), and learn from/adapt Indigenous ways of knowing and being (Rich, 2012).

The Red-Green Manifesto for Greening Social Work Education

Before going further, I want to be clear that what follows is not meant be a "one size fits all" cookie-cutter formula; there will (and should) be tremendous variation in what works best in specific contexts. I also want to acknowledge the postmodernist critique related to the perils of priorizing a specific set of recommendations, values, beliefs, and theories (Jones, 2008, 2010). However, when it comes to saving the planet, I stand with Carniol's (2005) modernist conclusion:

> It is self-evident that when it comes to certain values, there are indeed universal truths. For example, real democracy is better than tyranny; respecting human beings is better than killing them; protection of our environment is better than poisoning our air, water and soil; caring about others is better than indifference, prejudice, hatred or contempt. Such universal values based as they are on reducing harm to people are consistent with social work values that seek to optimize human well-being. (p. 155)

Box 12.1. The Red-Green Manifesto for Greening Social Work Education

1. Know and teach the scientific facts.
2. Make radical paradigm shifts.
3. Adopt a multi/inter-disciplinary approach.
4. Adapt/develop green teaching approaches, methods, and skills and implement green curriculum/content changes.
5. Find, develop, adapt, and share green teaching resources.
6. The personal is political: take action at the micro and mezzo levels.
7. The structural is personal: take action at the macro level.
8. Stronger together: organize, take collective action, and resist.
9. Become climate justice/action leaders.
10. Do not give up: find and teach hope.

Consistent with these value positions, consider this manifesto (Box 12.1) as a take-away from this book that summarizes what social work educators can adapt from other disciplines and learn from the literature, community activists, and this book's contributors about how to green our content and curricula.

1. Know and Teach the Scientific Facts

In the introduction to this book, I explored the basic scientific facts that social work educators need to know to increase their ecological literacy, understand what is happening in terms of global warming and climate crises, and effectively teach this information. To briefly review, burning carbon-based fossil fuels produces carbon dioxide, a greenhouse gas that overheats the planet. If we are unable to keep global temperature under 1.5 degrees Celsius (which is now extremely unlikely), a series of cascading catastrophic climate events is likely to occur. The solution? At a minimum, humanity must cut "emissions of carbon dioxide by 45% by 2030" (McGrath, 2019, para. 3).

To accomplish this goal, a concerted effort – from all countries, governments, corporations, and peoples of the world – is required. Unfortunately, many authors suggest that the political and economic will required to make these necessary changes just does not exist, and so instead, they call for a huge groundswell of grass-roots mobilization, civil and constitutional litigation, and activism to force the hands of politicians and corporations (Coates, 2003; Dominelli, 2012; Klein, 2014; Zapf, 2009). If radical changes are not made soon, scientists warn that these increasing greenhouse effects and extreme weather events as well as continuing overconsumption, overpopulation, deforestation, destruction of flora and fauna habitat, and pollution are "incompatible with an organized global community" and "would be devastating to the majority of ecosystems" (Cockburn, 2019, p. 6). Sadly, even if we somehow manage to meet the above target, it may be too late to avoid the worst impacts of climate crises, as many argue that the window to change the most devastating outcomes has already closed (Klein, 2014). As a starting point, Section 1 in the appendix presents resources to help instructors understand the necessary scientific climate facts (and possible solutions) and begin to appreciate the benefits of incorporating environmental education.

2. Make Radical Paradigm Shifts

To accomplish the transformation required to save the planet and humanity, the social work profession needs to begin by "challenging existing paradigms, critically evaluating emerging alternatives, and encouraging action grounded in new ways of understanding the world" (Jones, 2010, p. 68). We also need to uncover the most effective ways to quickly transform our philosophies, teaching methods, field instruction, and curricula. Consequently, several suggestions for transforming current social work paradigms have been featured across this volume. In Section 2 of the appendix, anti-oppressive educational approaches and green teaching tools that support transformational teaching/learning are also listed. Additionally, Box 12.2 identifies important paradigm shifts necessary for global change.

Along with the these paradigm shifts, the following approaches provide direction in terms of greening social work education.

CENTRING INDIGENOUS APPROACHES
To facilitate the necessary paradigm shifts we do not have to begin from scratch, as we have already been provided a clear vision of how to proceed. We can begin by supporting and implementing Canada's Truth and Reconciliation Commission's (TRC) *Calls to Action* (2015). Relevant to the helping professions, several TRC recommendations focus on how to transform social welfare, education, and health systems. Centring Indigenous approaches, implementing the TRC's Calls To Action,

---

Box 12.2. Paradigm Shifting: Recommendations

1. *Reconceptualizing* the traditional person (in/with/as) environment assessment and intervention framework to foreground natural and human-built environments in concert with humanity's interests (Besthorn, 1997; Coates, 2003; Dominelli, 2012, 2018: Zapf, 2009).
2. *Teaching* about social/climate justice from an intersectional standpoint that interrogates (and seeks to dismantle) systemic inequality and environmental racism (Hetherington & Boddy, 2013), thus reaching towards a "deep justice" that "expands from justice between humans to a new way of thinking about the entire universe" where humans are part and parcel of nature and place (Närhi & Matthies, 2018, p. 498).
3. *Building* a "deep ecology," what Naess (1973) designated as "echosophy" (as cited in Zapf, 2009, p. 101), that is grounded in the profound "connection between human and natural ecological systems" (Devall & Session, 1985, as cited in Besthorn, 2018, p. 72) and an "ecology spirituality" that "integrates a transpersonal or spiritual awareness with ecological sensitivity and social justice" (ibid., p. 99).
4. *Developing* a red-green discourse to express our vision and motivate citizens. Part of our work as academics and community activists necessitates finding new language and concepts – in other words, a red-green discourse – to capture essential meaning, clearly express ourselves, and fire up the public's imagination.
5. *Privileging* eco-critical theoretical frameworks that are more congruent with environmentalism. Of course, this implies that these theories first need to critically re-examine their philosophical and conceptual assumptions to become less anthropocentric and more inclusive of natural and built environments, before they can be reconciled to congruence and utility within a green social work education framework (Mulvale, 2017; Ramsay & Boddy 2017).

---

embracing Elder traditions, and learning from and adapting Indigenous ways of knowing (and being) (Rich, 2012) are likely the most effective ways for us to save humanity and the planet. To this end, Chapter 1 in this book presents key ideas that can help social work implement the above strategies. In Chapter 2, Hill, Rutherford, and Wilkes also propose that "employing an IESS approach of the 5 Rs – relationship, respect, responsibility, reciprocity and restoration" (Evering & Longboat, 2013) can help students "to (re)consider the symbiosis of environmental repair and Indigenous cultural revitalization as an essential aspect of social work education" (Chapter 2, p. 78). Furthermore, if survival is our goal (and I presume it is), then whatever our political or theoretical stripes it is imperative, as explained above, that we incorporate a red-green perspective. It makes sense that the best way to do this is take guidance from Indigenous peoples – who have the lowest carbon footprints on the planet – and start emulating their practices.

STARTING A REVOLUTION: A RED-GREEN APPROACH

As explained earlier, incorporating a socialist or "red" view (Wallace, 2018) – that is, identifying and dismantling the structural forces that harm humans (and more-than-humans) – means challenging the way we look at the world. To accomplish this, activists and scholars make the case that social work must adopt an "earth-first" (Waldron, 2018, p. 144), "global and local" (Närhi & Matthies, 2018, p. 495) and "critical environmental justice" framework (Waldron, 2018, p. 7) to understand the climate crisis and mobilize students and colleagues for climate change/justice and green social work education. Related to these goals, see Box 12.3 for green teaching suggestions and the appendix for supportive green resources.

As outlined in Box 12.2, it is also important for social work to develop a new red-green discourse to express our vision and motivate people. For example, some have argued that to "fight" climate change, we need to use the thinking, strategies, and language of war, for instance, by recruiting humanity to fight against the "great evil" – climate change – and rallying, recruiting, and rationing like most countries did during World Wars I and II ("The ongoing search," 2021). Although we certainly do want to draw people together, mobilize, and fund climate action similar to past war efforts, the problem with this masculinized, violent language of war is that it is derived from the same worldviews and dominant discourses that created the climate problem in the first place. As Freire (1970) indicated, we risk becoming oppressors ourselves when we choose to use the tools of the oppressor, or as Lorde (1984) proclaimed, "the master's tools will never dismantle the master's house" (p. 112). So, part of our work as academics and community activists is to find new language and concepts – in other words, a red-green discourse – to capture essential meaning, clearly express ourselves, and ignite the public's imagination.

DEVELOPING A NEW MORAL AND ETHICAL IMPERATIVE

As explained in this book's introduction, to further build momentum I believe that the social work profession must establish a new moral and ethical imperative, one that holds the Global North and multinational corporations responsible for causing this extensive damage and joins the demand that wealthy countries rectify the damage by paying for a massive cleanup (Gray, 2013; Klein, 2014; Zapf, 2009). Activists have gone as far as to suggest that oil and gas's corporate profits "are so illegitimate that they deserve to be appropriated and re-invested in solutions to the climate crisis" (Klein, 2014, p. 355). Making the worst climate offenders pay makes perfect sense. Congruently, recent advances in this area include the December 2022 global biodiversity agreement at the COP15 United Nations Biodiversity Conference in Montreal that includes a "pledge to reduce subsidies deemed harmful to nature by at least $500 billion by 2030, while having developed countries commit to providing developing countries with at least $20 billion per year by 2025, and $30 billion per year by 2030" ("Biodiversity agreement," 2022, para. 6). However, enforcement of this moral and ethical imperative becomes a challenge, one with which activists will need to grapple, especially as global capital controls police and military power.

REVISIONING OF SOCIAL WORK'S MISSION, PURPOSE,
CURRICULA, AND PROGRAMS

I believe that it is not enough for social work schools and programs to simply add a smattering of content about, or maybe a course or two on, sustainability and climate justice. That is the bare minimum one might expect to meet the new Canadian accreditation standard, and is the *very* least that we can do. Instead, I am talking about encouraging a massive buy-in from our profession for a radical re-envisioning of our entire purpose, mission, philosophy, and teaching in terms of how we operate and what our role is globally and locally, how we can best support vulnerable communities both in theory and in practice, and how, as a result of integrating a red-green perspective, all of our strategic planning and decisions must now always include a consideration of potential environmental impacts.

This analysis should not be limited to simply changing instructional practices and identifying concerns about negative environmental impacts, but should also involve thoughtful discussion and proactive policies and behaviour that aim to green "both the work and the workplace" (Okaka, 2016, para. 1) and improve/ensure everyone's (and every living thing's) well-being. This means not simply teaching environmentalism and sustainability as selected topics but thinking ecologically and more broadly about how and what we teach, that is, considering "what understandings, knowledge and skills are needed to live sustainably, before explaining how the answer to this question might inform and shape the social work curriculum" (Jones, as cited in Dominelli, 2018, p. 561).

STOP TRAINING "MASTER THERAPISTS"
Thus, I am not suggesting that we simply offer students a broader and deeper selection of topics. Instead, to adequately prepare for the next century of our profession and the intensifying climate emergency, I want us to transform and radically shift social work education away from training "master therapists" (Brown, 1988) to a brave new "place-based education" frontier (Beltran et al., 2016, p. 494), where *we* become ecological justice, migration, and disaster-training experts/activists and begin to lead the social sciences field in this area. Ungar (2003) has even suggested that we change our title to "professional social ecologists" to "reposition" us "on the leading edge of progressive ecological thought" (p. 5). To develop this expertise, potential innovative topics that we could feature in social work programs include ecological grief and anxiety, environmental ethics, racism/justice, and intersectional analysis of climate crises, trauma-informed practice, disaster-preparedness, community risk assessment, eco-spirituality, international work with climate refugees, and effective climate action.

3. Adopt a Multi/Inter-disciplinary Approach

As discussed in this book's introduction, not only does social work need to quickly develop an interest in finding solutions to climate crises and building better relationships with other humans and the planet (and its flora and fauna), but it must also recognize that, in order to be effective, this work has to be done in concert with other academic disciplines, as well as community activists and social justice groups, initiatives, and movements (Schmitz et al., 2012). According to Närhi and Matthies (2018), in order to successfully transform we must unite a host of "different disciplines and societal actors to look for a holistic model of sustainable development that would distance itself from the present model committed to economic growth" (p. 496).

Therefore, social work needs to ask itself what it can learn from other academic disciplines and community activists in terms of *what* to teach and *how* to teach this content. Chapters 1 to 4 in this volume offer useful interdisciplinary guidance that can help social work grow in these aforementioned areas. We can begin by identifying relevant connection/foci between other disciplines and the helping professions; advocating for social work to take an equal place at the environmental table; contributing what we can bring to the discussion (as demonstrated in Chapters 5 to 11: community networking and organizing, grief work, risk assessment, etc.); and creating opportunities for training and leadership development within the field. Other possibilities for teaching/applying this content and integrating this material into our work/curricula include working with colleagues to develop cross-listed courses that are open to students from multiple disciplines; co-teaching/researching opportunities; general introductory environmental science courses made relevant for the social sciences; and innovative undergraduate and graduate degrees that offer interdisciplinary specializations and/or streaming options in social sciences–focused environmental education. Another useful resource that could be adapted for social work is Vincent, Roberts, and Mulkey's (2015) guide, which offers recommendations on best practices in terms of developing and supporting "IES (interdisciplinary environmental and sustainability) programs" (p. 423).

4. Adapt/Develop Green Teaching Approaches, Methods, and Skills and Implement Green Curriculum/Content Changes

Since, as a profession, we are still at the beginning stage of this greening of social work education process, there are several critical questions that social educators need to consider as they start greening their work. For instance, how do we know if our approaches or methods are green? How can we choose the most effective methods to bring about the transformation that we are seeking? And how do we go about mainstreaming this content?

MAINSTREAMING: FIRST STEPS

Higher education instructors from all disciplines can start by advocating for the inclusion of environmental education. They can engage with other faculty members, in their own departments as well as across campuses, to examine where and how sustainability is already being taught and where it should be introduced across the university and curriculum, and to consider various approaches to "include the main aspects of sustainability in the university curricula in a coherent way" (Martins et al., 2006, p. 34). Questions about format, process, structure, and content are sure to follow.

For instance, what general content about climate change should be offered? What key terms, authors, theories, books, and articles should be featured? What content and methods are appropriate for different levels and years of instruction as well as best suited for undergraduate versus graduate education? Should environmental content be taught in specific required courses, situated solely as part of elective offerings, infused across all courses, or offered in stand-alone courses? Should this content be included across all courses, programs, and disciplines or set in specific departments? What discipline-specific content should be taught? And, even if the motivation, interest, and necessary knowledge are present in our teaching body and schools, how much support and funding for green initiatives are available from the institutions and communities in which we live and work?

Obviously, these questions can all be applied to social work education. Alas, Besthorn (2014) and Crawford et al. (2015) found that there is little empirical research on best practices in this area, as the "doing" aspect of green social work is still in its infancy. From the research, mainstreaming recommendations include implementing a bolt-on approach where a course or two is added or relevant topics are added to specific courses in the curriculum (Jones, 2010, 2018); the infusion/integration model where we add environmental principles and thinking to most aspects of our programming, processes, and courses (Van Berkel, 2000); or a more transformative approach (the view promoted in this book), meaning a revolutionary shift in terms of putting ecology and earth first and training social workers to become ecological warriors (Jones, 2010; Peeters, 2012).

Also, there is a critical need to develop content and support skill development specifically related to incorporating environmentalism/sustainability into field education. Most of the literature shows that this research is necessary and represents a large gap in training and scholarship across the helping professions (Rogge, 1993). Chapters 6 and 11 in this collection do provide some guidance in greening community practice and field education, but much more is needed. For future research, some related questions that should be considered are: How do we ensure sustainability/environmental content is covered in field practicum? What green placement sites can we establish? How should field instructors teach/cover this content? How should students be supervised and evaluated for this content and learning? And what field activities are best for students to learn this content (Crawford et al., 2015)?

In many ways, the answers to these questions, at least in social work, are still in a nascent state. It is hoped that this collection can act as a catalyst for social work educators to build essential knowledge and find effective solutions, and thereby gain confidence, enter the climate justice arena, and start incorporating this content and material into their curricula and classrooms.

GREEN SOCIAL WORK EDUCATION IN CANADA

To review what aspects of green social work are being offered in Canadian schools of social work, see Chapters 9 and 10 of this volume, which provide the most recent research available about specific courses, approaches, and content. Not surprisingly, the conclusion of both is that the majority of social work programs do not cover environmental issues or content.

That is not to say that there no social work educators in Canada experimenting with green approaches in their courses. The reality is that, as environmental "advocates" and "role models" (Shepherd, 2010, p. 14), progressive instructors across Canada and the world have already started this work and are doing the best they can (albeit with limited support, training, or resources) to green their teaching. Unfortunately, those doing this type of innovative environmental work often stand alone. For these endeavours to be successful in mainstreaming this content and mobilizing millions of people, this work cannot be left solely to a small number of interested individuals.

Experts predict that "a maximum of 3.5% of the population needs to mobilize … for a peaceful mass movement to succeed" (Monbiot, 2019). Accordingly, given both social work's tendency to avoid major disruptions of dominant narratives and the general lack of "doing" research in this green area, broader philosophical questions remain to be tackled, including how best to teach social action and civil disobedience, make large-scale social change, mobilize enough critical mass to make a difference, and motivate people to act in time (Hillock, 2011, 2021, in press)?

GREENING CURRICULA AND TEACHING METHODS:
A GOOD FIT WITH SOCIAL WORK

So, how do we motivate ourselves and others to start this work? First, we know from this book's introduction that the literature and appropriate knowledge base to do this work already exist. Second, in terms of greening teacher education in general, Outlon and Scott (2005) found that environmental education (EE) teacher training must "contain two main elements, the theory and practice of EE, as well as personal experiences in EE" (as cited in Dobrinski, 2008, p. 21). Since the integration of theory and practice (i.e., thinking and doing), especially within field education, is fundamental to our profession, the aforementioned finding aligns well with the expertise and skills we already have in this area. Several exemplars of EE integration have been presented across this volume. Of particular note is Chapter 11, as it presents two green community case study examples that could be adapted for field courses.

Third, social work has an established history of using the person-in-environment approach (Germain & Gitterman, 1980), so, although the notion of "environment" has historically been narrowly defined as social environments, we could easily pivot to expand understandings of the person-in-environment model to include more-than-humans. Fourth, Beltran, Hacker, and Begun (2016) note that the "incorporation of environmental justice is especially suited to those courses that focus on issues of power, privilege, oppression, diversity, and multiculturalism" (p. 496). Thus, teaching from a critical red-green theoretical perspective, that is, challenging neo-liberalism, capitalism, and colonialism, and rethinking the nature of our relationships with all humans, more-than-humans, and the planet – central components to greening social work education – fits closely with the anti-oppressive analyses and content that many of us are already teaching. Hopefully, these parallels will reassure those who may not yet feel confident in trying these new approaches.

To help educators feel more confident about incorporating environmental material and content, Box 12.3 identifies suggestions to start greening curricula and teaching.

Box 12.3. Greening Curricula and Teaching Methods

1. Regularly engage with students in discussions about the environment, sustainability, and climate change/crisis, social and environmental justice, and action.
2. Present factual environmental and sustainability scientific content.
3. Critique and analyse capitalism, globalization, neo-liberalism, corporatization, and modernism.
4. Discuss structural oppression, systemic inequality, intersectionality, and environmental racism.
5. Critique conventional theories/dominant narratives and teach about progressive approaches/alternative narratives.
6. Expand students' understandings of the person-in-environment model to include more-than-humans.
7. Teach transformative, human rights, and social justice approaches to help build democratic citizenship.
8. Value affective learning domains and an ethic of caring for oneself, others, more-than-humans, and the planet.

9. Bring "gender [race, and climate] justice to the classroom" (hooks, 2000, p. 23) and explicitly discuss violence against humans, animals, habitats, and the planet.

10. Recognize spiritual connections to land, identify/know the status of local land treaties, expand teaching/learning beyond "the walls," and explore nature/wilderness therapies.

11. Invite Indigenous leaders and climate activists to guest lecture/co-teach (and pay them).

12. Integrate culturally relevant participatory teaching/learning methods.

13. Create innovative assignments that include green case studies, role play, and analysis, assessment, and intervention that also link green practice with field realities.

14. Review local, provincial, national, and international environmental policies.

15. Provide examples of successful social action strategies and campaigns.

16. Encourage students to envision what future social work could look like and to mobilize in terms of climate/social action.

Adapted from Baines (2017), Bigelow & Swinehart (2014), Campbell & Baikie (2012), Cohee (2004), hooks (2014), Hillock (2011, 2021, in press), Jones (2018), Mathieson (2002), Mezirow (2009), Miller & Hayward (2013), Okaka (2016), Richardson & Langford (2022), Shepherd (2010), and Waldron (2018).

5. Find, Develop, Adapt, and Share Green Teaching Resources

Social work educators need to find (but also start to create) the best available resources to green their teaching and curricula. Närhi and Matthies (2018) believe it is imperative that we focus on developing "definite tools for interfering structurally and proactively in social and physical living conditions" (p. 495) for both humans and "more-than-humans." In addition, we need to examine the literature and dialogue about what is already available, from other disciplines as well as community activists, that can be adapted to social work and the helping professions. To that end, the following recommendations are intended to direct readers to useful resources.

EXEMPLARS

A detailed literature and Internet search can reveal innovative course designs, outlines, and curricula exemplars that demonstrate what others are doing and that can be replicated and/or adapted (with permission, of course). For instance, Bartlett (2003) and Lucas-Darby (2011) provide detailed green course outline descriptions and Okaka (2016) describes green curriculum innovations and processes. Sauvé's (2005) environmental education mapping framework is also helpful. Powers and Rimball (2018) offer suggestions for transformative green teaching tools, including the "World Café/Gurteen Knowledge Café, Mind Mapping, and Doomsday Clock" (as cited in Ramabaree, 2020, p. 569). Additionally, journals such as the *Green Teacher* (https://greenteacher .com), *Canadian Journal of Environmental Education* (https://cjee.lake headu.ca), *International Electronic Journal of Environmental Education* (https://dergipark.org.tr/en/pub/iejeegreen), *Environmental Education Research* (https://www.tandfonline.com/loi/ceer20), *International Journal of Sustainability in Higher Education* (https://www.emerald .com/insight/publication/issn/1467-6370), and *The Trumpeter: Journal of Ecosophy* (http://trumpeter.athabascau.ca/index.php/trumpet) are excellent resources.

At the institutional level, the Australian Research Institute in Education for Sustainability (AIRES) (Shepherd, 2010) and Jain et al.'s (2013) description of TERI University's sustainability initiatives are good sources for policy, teaching, and practice suggestions for building ecological literacy, developing skills, and ensuring effective leadership. Junyent and Geli de Ciurana's (2008) ACES framework for greening higher education and its curricula is an excellent blueprint for universities to consider. In terms of practice, the Canadian Association of Social Workers (CASW) recently released a position statement on climate change and social work (Schibli, 2020) that is worth reading. Additionally, Miley et al.'s (2004) green assessment questions (as cited in Zapf, 2009, p. 53) provide practical examples for practitioners. (For more information on green resources, including recommended books, films/videos, communication technologies, software applications, and websites, see Sections 3 and 4 in the appendix.) And, of course, there is a plethora of significant research articles mentioned across this collection that readers can peruse at their leisure.

6. *The Personal Is Political: Take Action at the Micro and Mezzo Levels*

As mentioned across this book, and as evidenced by various contributors' personal and professional choices to green their lives and work, the notion that the personal is political (Levine, 1989) is central to taking action at the micro and mezzo levels, not only as social work educators and practitioners but also as global citizens. This gives new meaning to an older phrase – "think globally, act locally" (Mikulska, 2021). Indeed, this book is an invitation for readers to start thinking about what can they do, on the small (and large) scale, in their own lives, families, and communities.

At the micro level, the first stage, of course, is becoming aware and educated about the scientific facts, which hopefully, leads to cognitive and behavioural shifts that involve becoming more aware of our responsibilities as global citizens. There are tons of choices we can make: to buy only what we need (not what we want); stop overconsuming; reduce or cut out meat consumption; reuse, renew, and recycle; cut out single-use plastics; only invest in green funds and purchase from sustainable local producers; volunteer to help others; plant trees and build gardens, forests, and green spaces; turn the heat and air conditioner down; insulate our homes; use/support/buy green energies like solar panels, electric vehicles, and energy-efficient appliances; bicycle and walk more; decrease or cut out air travel; lobby our provincial MLAs and federal MPs to support carbon taxes; vote for green representation and policies; talk to friends; and join climate action groups.

At the mezzo level, we need to get involved! Vote; fundraise; use/support renewable solar, water, and wind power energies, electric transportation, and bicycle lanes; participate in urban planning; start or join anti-racism/anti-poverty campaigns, green political parties, democratic social movements, and cooperatives; insist on clean water for all; plant trees; expand parklands; build community gardens and green spaces; pick up garbage; hold politicians accountable; pressure governments to implement and support carbon pricing; and insist on divestment from fossil fuels in our pension and registered retirement saving plans.

7. The Structural Is Personal: Take Action at the Macro Level

We can no longer afford to pretend that what is happening "out there" somewhere, to "other people," is not soon coming our way and impacting all of the planet. Many of us have already been affected by extreme weather events and/or experienced housing/food insecurity. As citizens and employees, we work for, belong to, and affiliate/invest with several large institutions, companies, unions/associations, pension groups, and corporations. Therefore, I think that we have a duty to become more knowledgeable about the institutional infrastructures and investment practices of these organizations. We can research them, pressure them to divest from fossil fuels, identify issues, hold companies accountable and responsible for their choices, disrupt them if necessary, and lobby and advocate for green policy change, updates, regulation, and enforcement.

Regarding our Canadian governments, we can push them to implement and continue carbon pricing, honour the 2015 Paris Agreement (https://unfccc.int/process-and-meetings/the-paris-agreement/the -paris-agreement), give incentives for alternative energy use and home energy retrofits, make decisions and policies on an "Earth first" basis, eliminate billions of dollars in tax-free subsidies to multinational corporations and the fossil fuel industry, stop pipelines and the Alberta tar sands project, and provide clean water to all Indigenous and racialized/impoverished communities.

This work includes greening the departments, schools, and universities in which we work. The concept of a green university is not new. Indeed, the first ever higher education environmental education statement, the Talloires Declaration (http://ulsf.org/talloires-declaration/), was created in 1990 and included a ten-point action plan highlighting two main themes: "education for environmentally responsible citizenship" and "foster environmental literacy for all" (Shepherd, 2010, p. 15). However, just as international climate agreements suffer from a lack of compliance/enforcement, and similar to social work education's delay in mainstreaming environmental content, "many higher education institutions and many lecturers in higher education have not yet committed themselves to the concept of higher education for sustainability" (p. 16).

So, again, it is up to us to push our universities to become more sustainable by educating ourselves, students, and colleagues; maximizing energy efficiency; using/supporting renewable energies; reducing waste and carbon emissions; rejecting single-use plastics; advocating for increased social responsibility and good citizenship; broadening our missions and vision to incorporate an "Earth first" approach; greening our offices, processes, policies, teaching, materials, and research; partnering with local communities; and maximizing biodiversity on our campus grounds. We can also advocate for progressive policies that target discriminatory and unequal practices, processes, and behaviours as an essential part of transforming educational institutions.

Although they are not perfect evaluation systems, we can also pressure higher education institutions to join (and improve their rankings in) international sustainable ranking systems such as the UI Green Metric System (https://greenmetric.ui.ac.id) and the American Sustainability

Tracking, Assessment, & Rating System (STARS), "a transparent, self-reporting framework" that measures "sustainability performance" (2021, para. 1); rubrics such as Shi and Lai's (2013) criteria tree; and/or student-led initiatives, like the United Kingdom's People & Planet, that "rank higher education institutions … on campus sustainability" (Shepherd, 2010, p. 16).

8. Stronger Together: Organize, Take Collective Action, and Resist

Social workers can join as allies with existing activist groups in their communities to advocate for social change and climate justice (Dass-Brailsford, 2010; Fogel et al., 2016). We can also mobilize colleagues and students through associations and unions as well as municipal, provincial, and national politics and various professional and regulatory bodies like the CASW (https://www.casw-acts.ca), the Canadian Association of Social Work Education – Association canadienne pour la formation en travail social (CASWE-ACFTS, https://caswe-acfts.ca), and the International Association of Schools of Social Work (IASSW, https://www.iassw-aiets.org). One worthwhile example of union collectivism and activism on the environmental front is the Ontario Federation of Labour's (2019) creation of environmental policy resolutions.

As well, we can update and strengthen the environmental sustainability language (and enforcement) in our unions'/associations' collective agreements, codes of ethics, and accreditation standards. Social work educators – as citizens, investors, union/faculty association members, and employees – and students can join together to pressure our governments, associations/unions, institutions, and universities to divest from fossil fuels. Additionally, building inter/trans-disciplinarian networks and research across universities, disciplines, unions, student organizations, and social service/community organizations would be helpful in building alliances and working collectively with others who share progressive philosophies.

We also need to promote solidarity and dialogue among, across, and between academics, students, and field instructors who are attempting sustainability approaches within social work. Support groups for green workers, integrative field seminars, and an interactive website dedicated to green practitioners that allow us opportunities to discuss issues related to our theory, practice, field instruction, and research would help support green practitioners and educators. Social workers can advocate to their local, provincial, and national associations to hold workshops and conferences on greening social work practice and education. Attending, presenting, and sharing information and resources at these conferences are excellent ways to build a green social work education network. Readers can also lobby CASWE-ACFTS to have environmental social work featured as the major theme for future annual national conferences. Furthermore, a Canadian Association of Green Social Workers, Educators, and Programs and community and academic coalitions for interested professionals would be helpful and decrease the isolation and stress that green educators experience.

9. Become Climate Justice/Action Leaders

As this book is also aimed at professors and students who are interested in taking on a leadership role in this area, more effectively supporting others, and improving curriculum and the quality of the teaching of sustainability in social work education and the helping professions, we need to consider how we can best contribute to the climate discussion, action, and movement. What leadership skills do we still need to develop, and what expertise can we bring to the table? Although environmentalism may feel like new terrain for many of us (and likely requires a fairly steep learning curve at first), especially as we build a critical knowledge base about climate science, environmental racism, and disaster work, social work still has much to teach other disciplines about successfully working together, in teams, and in communities (Martins et al., 2006), especially in terms of the "transdisciplinarity and trans-sectorality" nature of much of our work (Närhi & Matthies, 2018, p. 497).

Social work continues to excel and can demonstrate leadership in several other key areas: risk assessment, emergency triage, and crisis intervention from our medical, foster care, community, and child protection experience; excellent emotional care work such as dealing with mental health issues like PTSD, anxiety, depression, trauma, and grief/loss; community development, organization, networking, and mobilization; and expertise in building capacity, strength, and resilience (Hetherington & Boddy 2013; Ungar, 2018).

10. Do Not Give Up: Find and Teach Hope

In my doctoral thesis work with social workers, respondents acknowledged that at times they felt hopeless. As a result, they identified the need for hope and optimism if one is to excel in the profession (Hillock, 2011). To inspire others, then, it is imperative that we demonstrate that the global situation is not hopeless (Kelsey, 2019). Consequently, Hawkins (2019) calls for a "change to the climate disaster script" and proclaims that "people need hope that things can change" (para. 1). Similarly, Solnit (2018) insists that "the climate fight is only over if you think it is" (para. 1). Social work educators need to do a better job of finding, teaching, and modelling successful examples of social movements, resistance strategies, and social action. Along with the examples that many of the contributors of this volume have already presented, Section 5 in the appendix offers examples of hope and good-news stories that have resulted from citizens banding together to make social change in the climate justice arena.

Obviously, the successes are still too few and far between and have not yet eliminated climate crises, but they are significant because they can give us renewed determination to fight for a decent quality of life for all species and a healthy planet for future descendants. Within this context, the author's hope is that this chapter sounds another clarion call to action and also gives social work educators the information and confidence they need to start including/teaching this interdisciplinary content, to help future social workers develop the necessary skills that are required to deal with the upcoming humanitarian and planetary crises.

On a final note, I offer hope to all social workers, helping professionals, activists, students, and caring individuals who are engaged in this revolutionary struggle all over the world. We are not alone. There are many people across the planet sharing our vision. Novelist Arundhati Roy's inspiring 2003 World Social Forum speech sums it up:

> We can re-invent civil disobedience in a million different ways ... becoming a collective pain in the ass ... Our strategy should be not only to confront empire but to lay siege to it. To deprive it of oxygen. To shame it. To mock it. With our music, our literature, our stubbornness, our joy, our brilliance, our sheer relentlessness ... The corporate revolution will collapse if we refuse to buy what they are selling – their ideas, their version of history, their wars, their weapons and their notion of inevitability. Remember this, we be many and they be few. They need us more than we need them. Another world is not only possible, she is on her way. On a quiet day, I can hear her breathing. (https://ratical.org/ratville/CAH/AR012703.html)

REFERENCES

Abram, B. (1996). *The spell of the sensuous: Perception and language in a more-than-human world.* New York: Vintage Books.

Baines, D. (Ed.). (2017). *Doing anti-oppressive practice: Social justice social work* (3rd ed.). Fernwood.

Bartlett, M. (2003). Two movements that have shaped a nation: A course in the convergence of professional values in environmental struggles. *Critical Social Work, 4*(1). https://ojs.uwindsor.ca/index.php/csw/issue/view/525

Baskin, C. (2011). *Strong helpers' teachings: The value of Indigenous knowledges in the helping professors.* Canadian Scholars.

Beltran, R., Hacker, A., & Begun, S. (2016). Environmental justice is a social issue: Incorporating environmental justice into social work practice curricula. *Journal of Social Work Education, 52*(4), 493–502. https://doi.org/10.1080/10437797.2016.1215277

Berger, R. M., & Kelly, J. J. (1993). Social work in the ecological crisis. *Social Work, 38*(5), 521–526. https://doi.org/10.1093/sw/38.5.521

Besthorn, F. H. (1997). *Reconceptualizing social work's person-in-environment perspective: Explorations in radical environmental thought* [Doctoral dissertation, University of Kansas]. UMI Microform 981157.

Besthorn, F. H. (2014). Eco psychology, meet ecosystem work: What you might not know – A brief overview and reflective comment. *Egopsychology, 6*(4), 199–206. https://doi.org/10.1089/eco.2014.0024

Besthorn, F. H. (2018). Radical ecologism: Insights for educating social workers in ecological activism and social justice. *Critical Social Work, 4,* 66–107.

Bigelow, B. (1996). How my schooling taught me contempt for the earth. *Rethinking Schools, 11*(10), 14–17.

Bigelow, B., & Swinehart, T. (Eds.). (2014). *A people's curriculum for the Earth: Teaching climate change and the environmental crises.* Rethinking Schools.

Biodiversity agreement to protect planet reached at UN conference in Montreal. (2022, December 19). CBC News. https://www.cbc.ca/news/science/cop15-montreal-biodiversity-agreement-1.6690667

Bozalek, V., & Pease, B. (2021). *Post-anthropocentric social work: Critical posthuman and new materialist perspectives.* Routledge.

Brown, C. (1988). Social work education as empowerment. In E. Chamberlain (Ed.), *Change and continuity in Australian social work* (pp. 129–141). Longman Cheshire.

Cajete, G. (1994). *Look to the mountains: An ecology of Indigenous education.* Kivaki.

Campbell, C. (2002). The search for congruency: Developing strategies for anti-oppressive social work pedagogy. *Canadian Social Work Review, 19*(1), 25–42.

Campbell, C., & Baikie, G. (2012). Beginning at the beginning: An exploration of critical social work. *Critical Social Work. 13*(1), 67–81. https://doi.org/10.22329/csw.v13i1.5849

Carlson-Manathara, E., & Rowe, G. (2021). *Living in Indigenous sovereignty.* Fernwood.

Carniol, B. (2005). *Case critical.* Between the Lines.

Coates, J. (2003). *Ecology and social work: Toward a new paradigm.* Fernwood.

Cockburn, H. (2019, June 5). "High likelihood of human civilisation coming to end" by 2050, report finds. *The Independent.* https://www.independent .co.uk/climate-change/news/climate-change-global-warming-end-human -civilisation-research-a8943531.html

Cohee, G. (2004). Feminist pedagogy. *The Teaching Exchange, 9*(1), 1–4.

Crawford, F., Sabine Augustine, S., Earle, L., Kuyini-Abubakar, A. B., Luxford, Y., & Babacan, H. (2015). Environmental sustainability and social work: A rural Australian evaluation of incorporating eco-social work in field education. *Social Work Education, 34*(5), 586–599. https://doi.org/10.1080 /02615479.2015.1074673

Dass-Brailsford, P. (2010). *Crisis and disaster counselling: Lessons learned from Hurricane Katrina and other disasters.* London: Sage.

Dobrinski, L. N. (2008). *Views of environmental educators on teaching environmental education* Unpublished master's thesis]. Queen's University.

Dominelli, L. (2012). *Green social work: From environmental crises to environmental justice.* Polity.

Dominelli, L. (2018). *The Routledge handbook of green social work.* Routledge. https://ebookcentral.proquest.com/lib/umontreal-ebooks/detail.action ?docID=5331755

Evering, B., & Longboat, D. R. (2013). An introduction to Indigenous environmental studies: From principles into action. In A. Kulnieks, D. R. Longboat, & K. Young (Eds.), *Contemporary studies in environmental and Indigenous pedagogies: A curricula of stories and place* (pp. 241–258). Sense.

Finney, C. (2014). *Black faces, white spaces: Reimagining the relationship of African Americans to the great outdoors.* University of North Carolina Press.

Fogel, S. J., Barkdull, C., & Weber, B. A. (2016). *Environmental justice: An issue for social work education and practice.* Routledge.

Freire, P. (1970). *Pedagogy of the oppressed.* Continuum.

Germain, C., & Gitterman, A. (1980). *The life model of social work practice.* Columbia University Press.

Gray, M., Coates, J., & Hetherington, T. (2013). *Environmental social work.* Routledge.

Hawkins, N. (2019, June 26). It's time to change the climate disaster script: People need hope that things can change. *The Guardian.* https://www .theguardian.com/commentisfree/2019/jun/26/climate-disaster-script -urgency-change

Hetherington, T., & Boddy, J. (2013). Ecosocial work with marginalized populations: Time for action on climate change. In M. Gray, J. Coates, & T. Hetherington (Eds.), *Environmental social work* (pp. 46–61). Routledge.

Hillock, S. (2011). *Conceptualizing oppression: Resistance narratives for social work* [Unpublished doctoral dissertation]. Memorial University of Newfoundland.

Hillock, S. (2021). Teaching from the margins: No good deed goes unpunished. In R. Csiernik & S. Hillock (Eds.), *Teaching social work: Reflections on pedagogy & practice* (pp. 248–264). University of Toronto Press.

Hillock, S. (in press). Eco-femagogy: Transforming social work education in a post-Covid world. In C. Noble, L. Harms Smith, S. Rasool, & G. Muñoz-Arce (Eds.), *Routledge's International Handbook on Feminisms and Social Work*. Routledge.

Hoff, M. D. (Ed.). (1998). *Sustainable community development: Studies in economic, environmental, and cultural revitalization*. Lewis.

hooks, b. (2000). *Feminist theory: From margin to centre* (2nd ed.). South End.

hooks, b. (2014). *Feminism is for everybody*. Routledge.

Isla, A. (2019). *Climate chaos: Ecofeminism and the land question*. Inanna/Education Inc.

Jain, S., Aggarwal, P., Sharma, N., & Sharma, P. (2013). Fostering sustainability through education, research and practice: A case study of TERI University. *Journal of Cleaner Production. 61*, 20–24. https://doi.org/10.1016/j.jclepro.2013.04.021

Jones, P. (2008). *Expanding the ecological consciousness of social work students: Education for sustainable practice* [Paper presentation]. EDU-COM International Conference, Edith Cowan University, Joondalup, Australia. https://ro.ecu.edu.au/cgi/viewcontent.cgi?article=1026&context=ceducom

Jones, P. (2010). Responding to the ecological crisis: Transformative pathways for social work education. *Journal of Social Work Education, 46*, 67–84. https://doi.org/10.5175/JSWE.2010.200800073

Jones, P. (2018). Greening social work education: Transforming the curriculum in pursuit of eco–social justice. In L. Dominelli (Ed.), *Handbook of green social work* (pp. 558–568). Routledge.

Junyent, M., & Geli de Ciurana, A. M. (2008). Education for sustainability in university studies: A model for reorienting the curriculum. *British Educational Research Journal, 34*(6), 763–782. https://doi.org/10.1080/01411920802041343

Kelsey, E. (2019). *Hope matters*. Greystone Books.

Klein, N. (2014). *This changes everything*. Vintage Canada.

Klemmer, C. L., & McNamara, K. A. (2020). Deep ecology and ecofeminism: Social work to address global environmental crisis. *Journal of Women and Social Work, 35*(4), 503–515.

Levine, H. (1989). The personal is political: Feminism and the helping professions. In G. Finn & A. Miles (Eds.), *Feminism from pressure to politics* (pp. 233–267). Black Rose Books.

Lorde, Audre. (1984). The master's tools will never dismantle the master's house. In *Sister outsider* (pp. 110–113). Crossing Press.

Lucas-Darby, E. (2011). The new colour is green: Social work practice and service learning. *Advances in Social Work, 12*, 113–125. https://doi.org /10.18060/1340

Martins, A. A., Mata, T. M., & Costa, C. A. V. (2006). Education for sustainability challenges and trends. *Clean Technology and Environmental Policy, 8*, 31–37. https://doi.org/10.1007/s10098-005-0026-3

Mathieson, G. (2002). Reconceptualizing our classroom practice: Notes from an anti-racist educator. In N. Nathaniel Wane, K. Deliovsky, & E. Lawson (Eds.), *Back to the drawing board: African Canadian feminisms* (pp. 158–74). Sumach.

McGrath, M. (2019, July 23). *Climate change: 12 years to save the planet? Make that 18 months.* BBC News. https://www.bbc.com/news/science -environment-48964736

Mezirow, J. (2009). Transformative learning theory. In J. Mezirow and E. W. Taylor (Eds), *Transformative learning in practice: Insights from community, workplace, and higher education* (pp. 18–32). Jossey-Bass.

Mikulska, A. (2021). *Think globally, act locally … thinking globally again.* Risk Management And Decision Processes Center, Wharton School. https:// riskcenter.wharton.upenn.edu/climate-risk-solutions-2/thinkglobally -act-locally-think-globally-again/

Miller, S. E., & Hayward, R. A. (2013). Social work education's role in addressing people and a planet at risk. *Social Work Education, 33*(3), 1–16. https://doi.org/10.1080/02615479.2013.805192

Monbiot, G. (2019, April 15). Only rebellion will prevent an ecological apocalypse. *The Guardian.* https://www.theguardian.com/commentisfree/2019/apr/15 /rebellion-prevent-ecological-apocalypse-civil-disobedience

Mullaly, B. (2006). *The new structural social work: Ideology, theory, practice.* Oxford University Press.

Mulvale, J. P. (2017). Reclaiming and reconstituting our understanding of "environment" in social work theory. *Canadian Social Work Review, 34*(2), 169–186. https://doi.org/10.7202/1042887art

Närhi, K., & Matthies, A. L. (2018). The ecosocial approach in social work as a framework for structural social work. *International Social Work, 6*(4), 490–502. https://doi.org/10.1177/0020872816644663

Noble, C. (2021). Ecofeminism to feminist materialism: Implications for Anthropocene feminist social work. In V. Bozalek & B. Pease (Eds.), *Post-anthropocentric social work: Critical posthuman and new materialist perspectives* (pp. 95–107). Routledge.

Okaka, W. T. (2016). *Developing green university curriculum innovations for sustainable education in Africa* [Paper presentation]. 11th European Conference on Social and Behavioral Sciences, Rome, Italy. https://www .researchgate.net/publication/308779446_Developing_Green_University _Curriculum_Innovations_for_Sustainable_Education_in_Africa

The ongoing search for the perfect climate change metaphor. (2021, April 16). CBC News. https://www.cbc.ca/news/science/what-on-earth-hydrogen-blue-green-1.5989192

Ontario Federation of Labour. (2019). *Environmental policy resolutions.* https://ofl.ca/wp-content/uploads/2019-OFL-Convention-2019-Policy-Resolutions-NEW.pdf

Peeters, J. (2012). The place of social work in sustainable development: Towards ecosocial practice. *International Journal of Social Welfare, 21*(3), 287–298. https://doi.org/10.1111/j.1468-2397.2011.00856.x

Rambaree, K. (2020). Environmental social work: Implications for accelerating the implementation of sustainable development in social work curricular. *International Journal of Sustainability in Higher Education, 21*(3), 557–574. https://doi.org/10.1108/IJSHE-09-2019-0270

Ramsay, S., & Boddy, J. (2017). Environmental social work: A concept analysis. *British Journal of Social Work, 47*(1), 68–86. https://doi.org/10.1093/bjsw/bcw078.

Rich, N. (2012). Introduction: Why link Indigenous ways of knowing with the teaching of environmental studies and sciences? *Environmental Studies and Sciences, 2*, 308–316.

Richardson, B., & Langford, R. (2022). Care-full pedagogy: Conceptualizing feminist care ethics as an overarching critical framework to interrupt the dominance of developmentalism within post-secondary early childhood education programs. *Contemporary Issues in Early Childhood, 23*(4), 408–420. https://doi.org/10.1177/14639491221120037

Rogge, M. E. (1993). Social work, disenfranchised communities, and the natural environment: Field education opportunities. *Journal of Social Work Education, 29*(1), 111–120. https://doi.org/10.1080/10437797.1993.10778803

Roy, A. (2003, January 27). Confronting empire. *World Social Forum.* https://ratical.org/ratville/CAH/AR012703.html

Sauvé, L. (2005). Currents in environmental education: Mapping a complex and evolving pedagogical field. *Canadian Journal of Environmental Education, 10*, 11–37.

Schibli, K. (2020). *Climate change and social work* [Position Statement of Canadian Association of Social Workers]. https://www.casw-acts.ca/files/documents/SW_and_Climate_Change_Final_PDF.pdf

Schmitz, C. L., Matyók, T., Sloan, L. M., & James, C. (2012). The relationship between social work and environmental sustainability: Implications for interdisciplinary practice. *International Journal of Social Welfare, 21*(3), 278–286. https://doi.org/10.1111/j.1468-2397.2011.00855.x

Shephard, K. (2010). Higher education's role in "education for sustainability." *Australia Universities' Review, 52*(1), 13–22.

Shi, H., & Lai, H. W. (2013). An alternative university sustainability rating framework with a structured criteria tree. *Journal of Cleaner Production, 61*, 59–69. https://doi.org/10.1016/j.jclepro.2013.09.006

Skwiot, R. (2008, Fall). Green dream: Environmental justice is emerging from the shadows. *Social Impact.* https://openscholarship.wustl.edu /socialimpact/6/.

Solnit, R. (2018, October). Don't despair: The climate fight is only over if you think it is. *The Guardian.* https://www.theguardian.com/commentisfree /2018/oct/14/climate-change-taking-action-rebecca-solnit

Spirit Horse Nation. (2022). *The red road.* https://www.spirithorsenation.org /the-red-road

Stein, R. (Ed.). (2004). *New perspectives on environmental justice: Gender, sexuality, and activism.* Rutgers University Press.

Sustainability Tracking, Assessment, & Rating System (STARS). (2021). Association for the Advancement of Sustainability in Higher Education. https://stars .aashe.org/

Truth and Reconciliation Commission of Canada. (2015). *Calls to action.* https:// www2.gov.bc.ca/assets/gov/british-columbians-our-governments /indigenous-people/aboriginal-peoples-documents/calls_to_action _english2.pdf

Ungar, M. (2003). The professional social ecologist: Social work redefined. *Canadian Social Work Review, 20*(1), 5–23.

Ungar, M. (2018). Systemic resilience: Principles and processes for a science of change in contexts of adversity. *Ecology and Society, 23*(4), 34. https://doi .org/10.5751/ES-10385-230434

Van Berkel, R. (2000). Integrating the environmental and sustainable development agendas into minerals education, *Journal of Cleaner Production, 8,* 413–423. https://doi.org/10.1016/S0959-6526(00)00045-7

Vincent, S., Roberts, J. T., & Mulkey, S. (2015). Interdisciplinary environmental and sustainability education: Islands of progress in a sea of dysfunction. *Journal of Environmental Studies and Sciences, 6,* 418–424. https://doi.org /10.1007/s13412-015-0279-z

Waldron, I. R. G. (2018). *There's something in the water: Environmental racism in Indigenous and Black communities.* Fernwood.

Wallace, V. (2018). *Red-green revolution: The politics and technology of eco-socialism.* Political Animal.

Zapf, M. K. (2009). *Social work and the environment: Understanding people and place.* Canadian Scholars.

Appendix: Greening Social Work Education Resources

SUSAN HILLOCK

Section 1: Climate Change Solutions and the Benefits of Environmental Education

RESOURCES

Biello, D. (2007, November 26). 10 Solutions for climate change. *Scientific American*. https://www.scientificamerican.com/article/10-solutions-for-climate-change/

Mitchell, A. (2019, July 11). Yes, climate change can be beaten by 2050. Here's how. *MacLean's*. https://www.macleans.ca/news/canada/yes-climate-change-can-be-beaten-by-2050-heres-how/

Nunez, C. (2019, January 24). Global warming solutions, explained. *National Geographic*. https://www.nationalgeographic.com/environment/article/global-warming-solutions

Suzuki, D. (2018, July 3). *Top 10 things you can do about climate change*. David Suzuki Foundation. https://davidsuzuki.org/what-you-can-do/top-10-ways-can-stop-climate-change/

Thompson, B. (2018, July 11). *The top 10 benefits of environmental education*. Green Prophet. https://www.greenprophet.com/2018/07/the-top-10-benefits-of-environmental-education/

Toth, S. (2016). *Top 10 benefits of environmental education*. Project Learning Tree. https://www.plt.org/educator-tips/top-ten-benefits-environmental-education/

Union of Concerned Scientists. (2021). *Climate hot map: Global warming effects around the world*. https://www.climatehotmap.org/global-warming-solutions/

Zafar, S. (2019, November 18). *Top 7 benefits of environmental education*. EcoMENA. https://www.ecomena.org/benefits-of-environmental-education/

Section 2: Supporting Transformational Teaching/Learning

Anti-oppressive Approaches

1. Democratic citizenship
2. Affective learning domains (Shepherd, 2010)
3. Service-based learning (Lucas-Darby, 2011)
4. Transformative perspectives (Jones, 2008, 2010; Mezirow, 1991)
5. Human rights and justice approaches
6. Culturally relevant participatory teaching/learning methods (Okaka, 2016; Waldron, 2018)

Green Teaching Tools

A. Role play, guest lectures, small group discussions, and case studies (e.g., Grassy Narrows and ENRICH from Chapter 1; Case, 2017; also see Chapter 11).
B. Ecological literacy assessments, "expanded eco-maps" (Miller & Hayward, 2013, p. 14), "journaling exercises," "political genograms," "eco-confessionals" (Besthorn, 2018, p. 72), "disorienting dilemma" experiences for students, and "ecological autobiography" assignments (Jones, 2010, pp. 75–77).
C. Beyond-classroom approaches, including nature/wilderness therapies (Bigelow, 1996; Miller & Hayward, 2013).
D. "Practical action" opportunities (Jones, 2010, pp. 75–76) and community-based field visits/work. As a case in point, Chapter 11 of this volume highlights the powerful contribution students can make and how their leadership skills can be enhanced (Lucas-Darby, 2011) when they work in partnership with community members.

RESOURCES

Besthorn, F. H. (2018). Radical ecologism: Insights for educating social workers in ecological activism and social justice. *Critical Social Work,* 4, 66–107.
Bigelow, B. (1996). How my schooling taught me contempt for the earth. *Rethinking Schools, 11*(10), 14–17.
Case, R. A. (2017). Community resilience and eco-social work praxis: Insights from water activism in Guelph, Ontario, Canada. *Journal of Social Work, 17*(4), 391–412. doi:10.1177/1468017316644695

Jones, P. (2008). Expanding the ecological consciousness of social work students: Education for sustainable practice. *EDU-COM International Conference*, Edith Cowan University, Perth, Australia, November 19–21, 2008. https://ro.ecu.edu.au/cgi/viewcontent.cgi?article=1026&context=ceducom

Jones, P. (2010). Responding to the ecological crisis: Transformative pathways for social work education. *Journal of Social Work Education, 46*, 67–84.

Lucas-Darby, E. (2011). The new colour is green: Social work practice and service learning. *Advances in Social Work, 12*, 113–125.

Mezirow, J. (1991). *Transformative dimensions of adult learning*. Jossey-Bass.

Miller, S. E., & Hayward, R. A. (2013). Social work education's role in addressing people and a planet at risk. *Social Work Education, 33*(3), 1–16.

Okaka, W. T. (2016). *Developing green university curriculum innovations for sustainable education in Africa*. https://www.researchgate.net/publication/308779446_Developing_Green_University_Curriculum_Innovations_for_Sustainable_Education_in_Africa

Shepherd, K. (2010). Higher education's role in "education for sustainability." *Australia Universities' Review, 52*(1), 13–22.

Waldron, I. R. G. (2018). There's something in the water: Environmental racism in Indigenous and Black communities. Fernwood.

Section 3: Recommended Books, Films, and Videos

Books

Carson's (1962) classic book *Silent Spring* is credited with jump-starting public awareness of environmental issues.

Among books that borrow and adapt from other disciplines, recommended ones include Cajete (1994), Finney (2014), Isla (2019), Kelsey (2019), Klein (2014), LaDuke (1999), Stein (2004), Sze (2020), Waldron (2018), and Wallace (2018).

In social work, the defining international green books are from Hoff and McNutt (1994, 1998) and Dominelli (2012, 2018). More recently, I would add Fogel, Barkdull, and Weber's (2016) and Bozalek and Pease's (2021) books to this list.

From Canada, key books include Baskin (2011), Carlson-Manathara and Rowe (2021), Coates (2003), Gray, Coates, and Hetherington (2013), and Zapf (2009).

RESOURCES

Baskin, C. (2011). *Strong helpers' teachings: The value of Indigenous knowledges in the helping professors*. Canadian Scholars.

Bozalek, V., & Pease, B. (2021). *Post-anthropocentric social work: Critical posthuman and new materialist perspectives*. Routledge.

Cajete, G. (1994). *Look to the mountains: An ecology of Indigenous education*. Kivaki.

Carlson-Manathara, E., & Rowe, G. (2021). *Living in Indigenous sovereignty*. Fernwood.

Carson, R. (1962). *Silent Spring*. Mariner Books.

Coates, J. (2003). *Ecology and social work: Toward a new paradigm*. Fernwood.

Dominelli, L. (2012). *Green social work: From environmental crises to environmental justice*. Polity.

Dominelli, L. (2018). *The Routledge handbook of green social work*. Routledge. https://ebookcentral.proquest.com/lib/umontreal -ebooks/detail.action?docID=5331755

Finney, C. (2014). *Black faces, white spaces: Reimagining the relationship of African Americans to the great outdoors*. University of North Carolina Press.

Fogel, S. J., Barkdull, C., & Weber, B. A. (2016). *Environmental justice: An issue for social work education and practice*. Routledge.

Gray, M., Coates, J., & Hetherington, T. (2013). *Environmental social work*. Routledge.

Hoff, M., & McNutt, J. (Eds.). (1994). *The global environmental crisis. Implications for social welfare and social work*. Ashgate.

Hoff, M. D. (Ed.). (1998). *Sustainable community development: Studies in economic, environmental, and cultural revitalization*. Boca Raton, FL: Lewis.

Isla, A. (2019). *Climate chaos: Ecofeminism and the land question*. Inanna Publications/Education Inc.

Kelsey, E. (2019). *Hope matters*. Greystone Books.

Klein, N. (2014). *This changes everything*. Vintage Canada.

LaDuke, W. (1999). *All our relations: Native struggles for life and land*. South End.

Stein, R. (Ed.). (2004). *New perspectives on environmental justice: Gender, sexuality, and activism*. Rutgers University Press.

Sze, J. (2020). *Environmental justice in a moment of danger*. University of California Press.

Waldron, I. R. G. (2018). *There's something in the water: Environmental racism in Indigenous and Black communities*. Fernwood.

Wallace, V. (2018). *Red-green revolution: The politics and technology of eco-socialism*. Political Animal.

Zapf, M. K. (2009). *Social work and the environment: Understanding people and place.* Canadian Scholars.

Films and Videos

In the book's Introduction, I have already suggested the BBC video *What Is Climate Change? A Really Simple Guide* as a good starting place and as a useful teaching tool: https://www.bbc.com/news /science-environment-24021772.

Beltran, Hacker, and Begun (2016) recommend the following videos as helpful teaching tools: "*The Story of Stuff* (Leonard, 2007), a Web video that critiques consumption" (https://www.youtube.com /watch?v=9Gorqroigqm), and "*Unnatural Causes* (Adelman, 2008)" (https://unnaturalcauses.org), a documentary that outlines "the connection between historical displacement, land destruction, and current health issues" (p. 499), while Klein (2014) suggests the "Academy award-nominated documentary on fracking, *Gasland*" (p. 217).

A recent 2019 Netflix documentary, *There's Something in the Water*, based on Waldron's (2018) book about environmental racism in Nova Scotia, is also worth watching.

Readers can check the following links for a list of the best environmental films and documentaries of all time: Burkhart (2020), https://www.treehugger.com/top-environmental-films-of-all-time -4868664, and Stubbs (2019), https://www.environmentshow.com /best-environmental-films/.

RESOURCES

Adelman, L. (2008). *Unnatural causes: Is inequality making us sick?* California Newsreel. https://unnaturalcauses.org

Beltran, R., Hacker, A., & Begun, S. (2016). Environmental justice is a social issue: Incorporating environmental justice into social work practice curricula. *Journal of Social Work Education, 52*(4), 493–502. https://doi.org/10.1080/10437797.2016.1215277

Burkhart, K. (2020, May 22). *The top ten environmental films of all time.* https://www.treehugger.com/top-environmental-films-of-all -time-4868664)

Klein, N. (2014). *This changes everything.* Vintage Canada.

Leonard, A. (2007). *The story of stuff* [Video]. Youtube. https://www .youtube.com/watch?v=9Gorqroigqm

Stubbs, P. (2019, January 21). *The best environmental films of all time.* https://www.environmentshow.com/best-environmental-films/.

Section 4: Green Technology, Software Applications, and Websites

Technology

In the ever-expanding world of social media, Internet, and software development and online learning platforms, it behooves instructors to explore innovative "information and communication technologies" (Martins et al., 2006, p. 34).

For instance, the University of Surrey has developed Internet environmental learning resources that "consist of a number of multidisciplinary case studies and supporting materials," and the Politecnico de Milano University offers "a collection of [online] tools and multimedia presentations which introduce students to the questions of sustainable production and consumption" (Martins et al., 2006, p. 34).

RESOURCES

Martins, A. A., Mata, T. M., & Costa, C. A. V. (2006). Education for sustainability challenges and trends. *Clean Technology and Environmental Policy, 8,* 31–37. https://doi.org/10.1007/s10098-005-0026-3

Apps and Websites

RESOURCES

Brown, S. (2020, April 22). *10 apps that help you be more sustainable in every area of life.* https://www.cnet.com/tech/services-and-software/10-apps-that-help-you-be-more-sustainable-in-every-area-of-life/

Cornish, N. (2018, November 21). 11 of the best eco-friendly apps to help you live a greener life: Reduce, reuse and recycle with a little help from your smartphone. *Country Living.* https://www.countryliving.com/uk/news/g24876084/best-eco-friendly-green-apps/

OISE, Environmental and Sustainable Education websites. https://www.oise.utoronto.ca/home/scan/get-involved/educators

Osborne, H. (2007, August 9). Top ten green websites. *The Guardian.* https://www.theguardian.com/environment/2007/aug/09/environment

7 Eco-Friendly apps to help you help the environment. (2020, February 25). Ecobnb. https://ecobnb.com/blog/2020/02/eco-friendly-apps/

Section 5: Hopeful Green Examples and Good News Stories

Legal Cases and Citizen Action

Across the planet, Indigenous peoples and youth have led the movement, through litigation, to enshrine the right to a healthy environment in constitutions and make governments legally responsible for protecting the environment. So far, they have engaged in successful lawsuits in Germany; France; Montana, United States; and Ontario, Canada, and there are several cases pending in multiple countries. Canadians also launched two more ongoing lawsuits: one against the federal government and the second against the government of British Columbia.

RESOURCES

Canada's constitution should include right to healthy environment, argues new book. (2021, June 10). CBC News. https://www.cbc.ca/news/science/what-on-earth-environmental-law-constitution-1.6060749

Casey, L. (2021, September 8). Ford government broke environmental law on public consultations, court rules. CBC News. https://www.cbc.ca/news/canada/toronto/ont-mzo-court-1.6169105

Court rules France failed to respect its climate change goal. (2021, February 3). CBC News. https://www.cbc.ca/news/science/france-climate-change-goal-1.5899025.

de Wit, E., Quinton, A., & Meehan, F. (2020, March 25). *Climate change litigation update.* Norton Rose Fulbright. https://www.nortonrosefulbright.com/en-au/knowledge/publications/0c9b154a/climate-change-litigation-update

Dyer, E. (2021, May 23). Young climate activists beat Germany's government in court. Could it happen here? CBC News. https://www.cbc.ca/news/politics/climate-change-emissions-carbon-canada-germany-youth-1.6029642

Hunter, J. (2022, March 31). Lawsuit challenges B.C. for failing to meet climate action targets. *Globe and Mail.* https://www.theglobeandmail.com/canada/british-columbia/article-lawsuit-challenges-bcs-missing-climate-action-targets/

Judge sides with youth climate activists in first-of-its-kind US lawsuit. (2023, August 14). CBC News. https://www.cbc.ca/news/science/montana-climate-lawsuit-1.6935978

Mangione, K. (2022, April 28). At-risk seabird used in old-growth forest fight as federal government targeted in lawsuit. CTV News (Vancouver). https://bc.ctvnews.ca/at-risk-seabird-used-in-old-growth-forest-fight-as-federal-government-targeted-in-lawsuit-1.5880595

Fossil Fuels and Emissions

Public and political pressure is increasing on multinational corporations and large capital funds to divest from fossil fuels. Recent good news includes the New York City state pension fund selling off its oil sands stake; BlackRock, the world's biggest asset-managing company, making environmental protection criteria central to its investment decisions; the Morgan Chase Bank ending fossil fuel loans for Arctic drilling and phasing out financial support of coal mining; Greenland banning all oil exploration; American president Joe Biden pausing oil drilling on public lands; and the Keystone XL pipeline being stopped. Even in Alberta, considered one of the bastions of fossil fuel support, oil and gas workers have recently voted to support stronger emission cuts, a hopeful sign that a cultural shift may be happening.

RESOURCES

Ambrose, J. (2020, February 25). JP Morgan to withdraw support for some fossil fuels. *The Guardian*. https://www.theguardian.com/business/2020/feb/25/jp-morgan-chase-loans-fossil-fuels-arctic-oil-coal

BlackRock, world's largest asset manager, changing its focus to climate change. (2020, January 14). CBC News. https://www.cbc.ca/news/business/blackrock-investment-climate-change-1.5426465

Greenland bans all oil exploration. (2021, July 16). CBC News. https://www.cbc.ca/news/business/greenland-oil-1.6105230

Keystone XL is dead, and Albertans are on the hook for $1.3 B. (2021, June 9). CBC News. https://www.cbc.ca/news/canada/calgary/keystone-xl-termination-1.6059683

Singh, I., & Hopton, A. (2021, April 27). Union representing energy workers backs stronger emission cuts – As long as there's a transition plan. CBC News. https://www.cbc.ca/news/science/climate-targets-transition-oil-energy-1.6000224

Subramanian, C., & King, L. (2021, January 27). Biden prioritizes climate change as national security concern, pauses oil drilling on public lands. *USA Today*. https://www.usatoday.com/story/news/politics/2021/01/27/joe-biden-sign-executive-actions-prioritizing-climate-change/4263775001/

Thurton, D. (2021, April 12). New York state pension fund says it's selling off a $7M stake in oilsands. CBC News. https://www.cbc.ca/news/politics/new-york-state-pension-oilsands-divestment-1.5983730

Carbon Taxing

Evidence demonstrates that carbon taxing/pricing works to reduce emissions, and many countries and their citizens seem to be accepting/ supporting these measures. Now even big oil companies have endorsed carbon taxes, and when they were challenged, Canada's Supreme Court ruled that the taxes were constitutional.

RESOURCES

Frank, B. (2019, July 28). Carbon pricing works. *Below 2C*. https://
below2c.org/2019/07/carbon-pricing-works/
Panetta, A. (2021, March 25). Carbon taxes win another endorsement –
From the US oil lobby. CBC News. https://www.cbc.ca/news
/world/carbon-tax-oil-lobby-1.5964181
Tasker, J. P. (2021, March 25). Supreme Court rules Ottawa's carbon
tax is constitutional. CBC News. https://www.cbc.ca/news/politics
/supreme-court-federal-carbon-tax-constitutional-case-1.5962687

Resistance and Citizen Mobilization

Large companies and corporations are being forced to consider environmental impacts either through required environmental risk assessments or social media campaigns and public pressure to not damage ecosystems. For example, even in my own backyard in the Durham region in Ontario, Canada, Amazon was looking to buy land to build a large warehouse on a designated wetland area. Although the provincial government was working behind the scenes to allow the corporation to bend and even break environmental regulations, the resistance, protests, and public outcry convinced Amazon to withdraw its bid. The hopeful message here is: if resistance and citizen mobilization to protect the environment is happening in my backyard, it can happen in everyone's backyard!

RESOURCES

McLeod, M. (2021, March 23). The rise and fall of Duffins Creek
MZO. *TVO Today*. https://www.tvo.org/article/the-rise-and
-fall-of-the-duffins-creek-mzo
Property developer valves to protect the Pickering wetland after
Amazon cancels warehouse. (2021, March 14). CBC News. https://
www.cbc.ca/news/canada/toronto/land-owner-vows-to-protect
-pickering-wetland-1.5949589

Coordinated Campaigns

The situation is not hopeless, as human beings have risen to the occasion before, by acting together to shift corporate and cultural behaviours to avert harm. Examples include the banning of chlorofluorocarbons (also called CfCs or freon) that were destroying the ozone layer, reducing rates of cigarette smoking in many countries, and decreasing drunk driving through the successful Mothers Against Drunk Driving (MADD) campaigns.

RESOURCES

Campbell, E. (2021, April 22). Carbon cutting strategy should take a couple pages from the campaign against smoking. CBC News. https://www.cbc.ca/news/opinion/opinion-carbon-emissions -smoking-1.5993185

Effectiveness of Mothers Against Drunk Driving. (2020, March 30). American Addiction Centers. https://www.alcohol.org/teens /mothers-against-drunk-driving/

Contributors

Editor

Susan Hillock (BA, BSW, MEd, PhD) is a full professor of social work at Trent University in Oshawa, Ontario. Her education, research, and direct service methods stem from and build upon experiential, liberation, and anti-oppressive theories, including feminist, anti-racist, and critical theory, structural social work, queer theory, and Marxism. In May 2022, she was awarded Trent's University Award for Education Leadership and Innovation, which recognizes sustained commitment over an extended period to the improvement of university teaching and learning; and in 2019 she received the Ontario Confederation of University Faculty Association (OCUFA)'s Status of Women and Equity Award of Distinction for outstanding contributions of members whose work has contributed meaningfully to the advancement of professors, academic librarians, and/or academic staff who are Indigenous, women, racialized, LGBTQ2S+, living with disabilities, and/or belong to other historically marginalized groups. Her solo-edited book *Teaching about Sex and Sexuality(ies) in Higher Education* (University of Toronto Press, 2021) and her two co-edited books *Teaching Social Work: Reflections on Pedagogy and Practice* (University of Toronto Press, 2021) and *Queering Social Work Education* (UBC Press, 2016) are the first of their kind in North America.

Other Contributors

Bree Akesson (BA, MPH, MSW, PhD) is an associate professor of social work at Wilfrid Laurier University, Waterloo, Ontario, and Canada Research Chair (Tier II) in Global Adversity and Well-being. Her program of research focuses on global social work issues, ranging from micro-level understandings of the experiences of war-affected families to macro-level initiatives to strengthen the global social service systems. She is currently the principal investigator for a study examining the socio-spatial experiences of refugee families living in Lebanon and Canada, for which she received Ontario's 2019 Early Career Researcher award. Her 2022 book, *From Bureaucracy to Bullets* (co-authored with Andrew Basso), explores the impact of home loss as a result of political violence. In addition to her research, Dr. Akesson continues to practise as a clinical treatment facilitator with the Global Psychiatric Epidemiology Group (GPEG), based at the New York State Psychiatric Institute at Columbia University.

David Androff (BA, MSW, PhD) is associate director for doctoral education and full professor in the School of Social Work at Arizona State University and a senior sustainability scholar with ASU's Julie Ann Wrigley Global Futures Laboratory. Dr. Androff earned his master's and doctorate in social welfare from the University of California, Berkeley. He studies human rights, immigrant and refugee rights, global social welfare, and social development. He is a founding member of the CSWE Committee on Human Rights and a research associate with the Centre for Social Development in Africa at the University of Johannesburg, and co-chaired the 21st International Consortium for Social Development conference in Yogyakarta, Indonesia, where he was visiting professor in the Department of Development and Social Welfare at the University of Gadjah Mada. He is the co-editor of the *Routledge International Handbook of Social Development, Social Work, and the Sustainable Development Goals* (Routledge, 2024) and the author of *Practicing Rights: Human Rights-Based Approaches to Social Work* (Routledge, 2016).

Jenni Cammaert (BA, BSW, MSW, PhD) is an associate professor in the School of Social Work at St. Thomas University in Fredericton, New Brunswick. Jenni's research is largely concerned with gender-based violence, structural understanding of eating disorder services, barriers to service utilization, nutritional social work, ecological sustainability, integrating research into social work education, and developing research and training opportunities.

Elizabeth (Liz) Carlson-Manathara's (BSW, MSW, PhD) ancestors settled on the sovereign lands of Anishinaabe and Omaha Nations. She is an associate professor of social work at Laurentian University in N'swakamok (Sudbury, Ontario). Her scholarship focuses on the anti-colonial and decolonial work of settlers, anti-colonial social work practice and research methodologies, and anti-colonial public education through film. As a settler scholar, Liz has an extensive background in direct social work practice and teaches both social change and direct practice courses. She is a treaty relative of the Robinson-Huron Treaty of 1850, a co-filmmaker of the *Stories of Decolonization* film project, and has recently published, with Gladys Rowe, *Living in Indigenous Sovereignty* (2021, Fernwood).

Robert A. Case (BA, BSW, MSW, PhD) is an associate professor of social development studies at Renison University College in Waterloo, Ontario, where he teaches courses on social policy, community organization, and social ecology. His research focuses on community organization and eco-social activism, with a particular focus on community-based water activism. Combining his scholarship with community service, Case has served on the board of directors of the water advocacy organization the Wellington Water Watchers since 2012 and as its chairperson from 2018 to 2021. His work on comparative analysis of water activism in two Canadian communities received the 2019 Marie O. Weil Award for outstanding scholarship, co-sponsored by the Association of Community Organizations and Social Administration (ACOSA) and Taylor & Francis Publisher (Case, R. A., & Zeglen, L. [2018]. Exploring the ebbs and flows of community engagement: The pyramid of engagement and water activism in two Canadian communities. *Journal of Community Practice, 26*[2], 184–203).

Jeanne Dagenais-Lespérance (BFA) is an MSW graduate from the Université de Montréal. She is an interdisciplinary student, seamstress, language teacher, artist, and activist with training in second-language teaching, social work, and theatre design. Feminist decolonial approaches, anti-oppressive practices, and critical pedagogy form the main inspiration for her work and teaching philosophy. Formerly a community organizer for an urban environmental organization, she is involved in environmental justice initiatives in her Parc-Ex neighbourhood in Montreal, which nourishes her present professional social work practice with asylum seekers. In her spare time, she loves to sew and embroider on scrap fabrics and test recipes for natural dyes, and finds inspiration in textile creation to facilitate grass-roots groupwork projects.

Arielle Dylan (BA, MA, MSW, PhD) is a full professor in the School of Social Work at St. Thomas University. Her research interests include critical and social justice explorations of eco-social work, spirituality and social work, contemplative practices, neuroscience, trauma, and Buddhism and social work. Arielle has completed positive neuroplasticity training, is nearing completion of her mindful self-compassion teacher training, and is currently enrolled in a Mind-fulness Meditation Teacher Certificate program.

Paul Elliott (BSc, PhD, PGCE) is an emeritus professor in the School of Education and Professional Learning at Trent University in Peterborough, Ontario. He is a faculty member of the Master of Education and Master of Arts in Sustainability Studies programs and the Canadian Studies and Interdisciplinary Social Research doctoral programs. He teaches MEd courses on well-being, sustainability, and experiential learning. In the Bachelor of Education program, he has taught courses in Indigenous, environmental, and sustainability education; science education; and an elective course in STEAM. Since 2010, he has co-hosted a program of workshops for pre-service teachers on how to become an eco-mentor. He has wide-ranging research interests that have included insect and bat ecology and various aspects of science education, mainly around the theme of scientific literacy. In recent years, his research, curriculum development, and advocacy have focused on environmental and sustainability education in teacher education. He co-founded an organization to promote this topic (see www.eseinfacultiesofed.ca) and serves on the board of the Canadian Network for Environmental Education and Communication (EECOM).

Jasmine Tiffany Ferreira (BA, MSW) is a PhD candidate at York University, Toronto, where her research is focused on the intersection of nature and mental well-being in social work practice through critical theory. She has led multi-year provincial and national projects in various non-profit settings over the past decade. Her professional experience has focused on gender-based violence in crisis, residential, and health-care settings. Additionally, she has taught sessional courses at the University of Windsor in the MSW for Working Professionals program and is an adjunct lecturer with the Factor-Inwentash Faculty of Social Work at the University of Toronto. Recent publications include *No Pets Allowed: A Trans-Species Social Justice Perspective to Address Housing Issues for Older Adults and Companion Animals* (2020).

Stephen Hill (PhD, BA, BSc, PEng) is an associate professor in the Trent School of the Environment. He is an active researcher in the areas of energy and climate policy, and community-based sustainability. Since 2003, he has coordinated Trent's core first-year course in environmental science and studies and was awarded Trent's Symons Award for Excellence in Teaching in 2011 and the CMHC Award for Excellence in Education in 2012.

Chris Hiller (BA, MA, PhD) is a settler Canadian of mixed European heritage who lives and works in Haudenosaunee, Anishinaabeg, and

Attawandaron territories (Guelph, Ontario). She is an assistant professor in social development studies at Renison University College – University of Waterloo. Chris teaches in the areas of critical social policy studies and anti-colonial education and social action, and her research explores pedagogical strategies for transforming settler consciousness, recognizing Indigenous sovereignty, and working towards decolonized futures.

Sue-Ann MacDonald (PhD, MSW, BA, International Development Studies) is an associate professor in the School of Social Work at the Université de Montréal, where she is director of field education (bachelor). She is also a researcher at CREMIS (Centre de recherche de Montréal sur les inégalités sociales et les discriminations), and co-responsible for the Homelessness axis. She worked for more than a decade as a social worker on mental health outreach teams. Her research program focuses on homelessness, mental health and judicialization, and the various tensions embedded in discourse and intervention practices (social, health, and judicial) affecting the lives of vulnerable and marginalized people. She also explores prevention efforts and community-based approaches as ways to combat structural inequalities. Prior to social work, she worked in international development from multidisciplinary socio-ecological perspectives.

Atsuko Matsuoka (BA, MA, PhD) is a full professor at the School of Social Work, York University, Toronto. She teaches courses in animals and social Work from a critical animal studies perspective. Her research has addressed the importance of understanding intersectionality of oppression among immigrants, ethnic older adults, and animals. In promoting consideration for animal-human relationships in social work, her current research, which is supported by the Social Sciences and Humanities Research Council of Canada, examines trans-species social justice (social justice beyond human animals) and social work. With Dr. John Sorenson, she co-edited *Dog's Best Friend? Rethinking Canid-Human Relations* (McGill/Queen's University Press, 2019); *Critical Animal Studies: Toward Trans-Species Social Justice* (Rowman & Littlefield International, 2018); and *Defining Critical Animal Studies: An Intersectional Social Justice Approach* (Peter Lang, 2014); and co-authored *Ghosts and Shadows: Constructions of Identity and Community in an African Diaspora* (University of Toronto Press, 2001).

James P. Mulvale (BA, MSW, MA, PhD, RSW) is a full professor in the Faculty of Social Work at the University of Manitoba in Winnipeg, Manitoba.

He teaches courses on social welfare policy and conducts research on universal basic income, social work theory, and digital pedagogical innovation in social work education. He was a founding member of the Basic Income Canada Network in 2008 and remains active in the basic income movement. He served on the steering group for the project Livelihoods, Incomes, and Community Resilience for a Net-Zero Canada, funded by Environment and Climate Change Canada. He practised social work prior to his academic career, doing community development work in Southwestern Ontario with organizations in the fields of developmental disability and mental health.

Karleen Pendleton Jiménez (BA, MFA, PhD) is a writer and full professor in education and gender and social justice at Trent University. Her research explores intersections of queerness, gender, race, and ethnicity through story and creative writing. Selected book chapters and journal articles include: "Start with the Land: Groundwork for Chicana Pedagogy"; "'I Will Whip My Hair" and "Hold My Bow": Gender-Creativity in Rural Ontario"; and "The Making of a Queer Latina Cartoon: Pedagogies of Border, Body, and Home." Her books *Tomboys and Other Gender Heroes: Confessions from the Classroom* and *"Unleashing the Unpopular": Talking about Sexual Orientation and Gender Diversity in Education* (co-edited with Isabel Killoran) explore queerness and homophobia in schools. Her new book *The Street Belongs to Us* (for eight years old and up) explores intersections of gender diversity, ethnicity, and relationships with the land. She also wrote the screenplay for the award-winning animated short film *Tomboy*.

Stephanie Rutherford (BA, MSc, PhD) is an associate professor in the Trent School of the Environment, and also teaches and advises in the MA and PhD programs in sustainability studies, cultural studies, and Canadian and Indigenous studies. Her work is similarly interdisciplinary, focusing on the intersections among the environmental humanities, animal studies, and environmental politics. She is the author or co-editor of three books that consider these themes and has a new book titled *Villain, Vermin, Icon, Kin: Wolves and the Making of Canada* (MQUP, 2022).

John Sorenson (BA, MA, PhD) is a full professor in the Department of Sociology, Brock University where he teaches critical animal studies. His past research was on war, nationalism, and refugees as an activist/scholar with various solidarity groups and relief work in Africa. From SSHRC-funded research on trans-species social justice, he co-edited with Dr. Atsuko Matsuoka *Dog's Best Friend? Rethinking Canid-Human Relations* (McGill-Queen's University Press, 2019); *Critical Animal Studies: Toward Trans-Species Social Justice* (Rowman & Littlefield International, 2018); and *Defining Critical Animal Studies: An Intersectional Social Justice Approach* (Peter Lang, 2014). Other books are *Constructing Ecoterrorism* (Fernwood, 2016); *Critical Animal Studies: Thinking the Unthinkable* (Canadian Scholars, 2014); *About Canada: Animal Rights* (Fernwood, 2010); *Ape* (Reaktion, 2009); *Culture of Prejudice: Arguments in Critical Social Science* (with Judith C. Blackwell and Murray E. G. Smith; Broadview, 2003); *Ghosts and Shadows: Construction of Identity and Community in an African Diaspora* (with Atsuko Matsuoka; University of Toronto Press, 2001); *Disaster and Development in the Horn of Africa* (Macmillan, 1995); *African Refugees: Development Aid and Repatriation* (co-edited with Howard Adelman; Westview, 1994); and *Imagining Ethiopia: Struggles for History and Identity in the Horn of Africa* (Rutgers University Press, 1993).

Lea Tufford (BA, BEd, MA, PhD) is a full professor in the School of Social Work at Laurentian University where she teaches courses on child abuse and neglect, social work practice with individuals and families, and social work practice with groups. Her research interests include social work education, child abuse and neglect, mindfulness, and eco-social work. She has a particular interest in simulation-based research and learning. Lea has been a clinician for twenty years with individuals, couples, and families and maintains a small private practice.

James Wilkes (BES, MA) is a cultural ecologist and contract faculty member in the Indigenous Environmental Studies and Sciences (IESS) program at Trent University, an instructor in the Indigenous Social Work program at FNTI (First Nations Technical Institute) in Tyendinaga, and a PhD candidate in environmental studies at Queen's University. He works to support the continuation of ecological and cultural diversity through action, teaching, and research.

Kelly Young (BA, BEd, MEd, PhD) is a full professor at Trent University's School of Education and Professional Learning. Her areas of research include language and literacy, curriculum theorizing, leadership in eco-justice environmental education, and arts-informed writing pedagogies. She is the founder of the Learning Garden Alternative program that was developed through a partnership between Trent University and GreenUP/Ecology Park in Peterborough, Ontario. Selected book chapters and journal articles include "Exploring Identities and Place through the Ecological Imagination" and "Eco-literacy Development through a Framework for Indigenous and Environmental Educational Leadership." She co-edited *Contemporary Studies in Environmental and Indigenous Pedagogies: A Curricula of Stories and Place* (Brill/Sense, 2013).

Milton Keynes UK
Ingram Content Group UK Ltd.
UKHW010637290124
436892UK00001B/117